The Civic Culture Transformed
From Allegiant to Assertive Citizens

This book reevaluates Almond, Verba, and Pye's original ideas about the shape of a civic culture that supports democracy. Marshaling a massive amount of cross-national, longitudinal public opinion data from the World Values Survey, the authors demonstrate multiple manifestations of a deep shift in the mass attitudes and behaviors that undergird democracy. The chapters in this book show that in dozens of countries around the world, citizens have turned away from allegiance toward a decidedly "assertive" posture to politics: they have become more distrustful of electoral politics, institutions, and representatives and are more ready to confront elites with demands from below. Most importantly, societies that have advanced the most in the transition from an allegiant to an assertive model of citizenship are better-performing democracies – in terms of both accountable and effective governance.

Russell J. Dalton is a professor of political science and the founding director of the Center for the Study of Democracy at the University of California, Irvine. His recent publications include *Citizen Politics*, sixth edition (2013); *The Apartisan American* (2012); *Political Parties and Democratic Linkage* (2011); and *The Good Citizen* (2009). Dalton has also edited or coedited more than a dozen volumes, including *Citizens, Context and Choice* (2011); *Party Politics in East Asia* (2008); and *Citizens, Democracy and Markets around the Pacific Rim* (2006).

Christian Welzel is a professor of political science and chair of political culture research at the Center for the Study of Democracy, Leuphana University. He is also a foreign consultant for the Laboratory of Comparative Social Research at the Higher School of Economics, St. Petersburg, Russia. He is a former president of the World Values Survey Association. Welzel's recent books include *Freedom Rising: Human Empowerment and the Quest for Emancipation* (Cambridge, 2013, winner of the Alexander L. George Award and the Stein Rokkan Prize); *Democratization* (with Ronald Inglehart, Christian Haerpfer, and Patrick Bernhagen, 2009); and *Modernization, Cultural Change and Democracy* (with Ronald Inglehart, Cambridge, 2005).

Other World Values Survey Books from Cambridge University Press

Christian Welzel, *Freedom Rising: Human Empowerment and the Quest for Emancipation*, 2013 (winner of the Alexander L. George Award and the Stein Rokkan Prize).

Doh Chull Shin, *Confucianism and Democratization in East Asia*, 2012.

Pippa Norris, *Democratic Deficit: Critical Citizens Revisited*, 2011.

Pippa Norris and Ronald Inglehart, *Cosmopolitan Communications: Cultural Diversity in a Globalized World*, 2009.

Ronald Inglehart and Christian Welzel, *Modernization, Cultural Change and Democracy*, 2005.

Pippa Norris and Ronald Inglehart, *Sacred and Secular: Politics and Religion Worldwide*, 2004.

Ronald Inglehart and Pippa Norris, *Rising Tide: Gender Equality and Cultural Change around the World*, 2003.

The Civic Culture Transformed

From Allegiant to Assertive Citizens

Edited by

RUSSELL J. DALTON
University of California, Irvine

CHRISTIAN WELZEL
Leuphana University, Lüneburg

CAMBRIDGE
UNIVERSITY PRESS

CAMBRIDGE
UNIVERSITY PRESS

32 Avenue of the Americas, New York, NY 10013-2473, USA

Cambridge University Press is part of the University of Cambridge.

It furthers the University's mission by disseminating knowledge in the pursuit of
education, learning, and research at the highest international levels of excellence.

www.cambridge.org
Information on this title: www.cambridge.org/9781107682726

© Cambridge University Press 2014

First published 2014

Printed in the United States of America

A catalog record for this publication is available from the British Library.

Library of Congress Cataloging in Publication Data
The civic culture transformed : from allegiant to assertive citizens / edited by Russell J. Dalton,
Christian Welzel.
   pages   cm
Includes bibliographical references and index.
ISBN 978-1-107-03926-1 (hardback) – ISBN 978-1-107-68272-6 (paperback)
1. Political culture.   2. Political participation.   3. Political psychology.   4. Democracy.
5. Government accountability.   I. Dalton, Russell J., editor of compilation.   II. Welzel,
Christian, 1964– editor of compilation.
JA75.7.C59   2014
306.2–dc23   2014018495

ISBN 978-1-107-03926-1 Hardback
ISBN 978-1-107-68272-6 Paperback

To Ronald Inglehart,
for a career of giving voice to citizens and developing
the research infrastructure so others could follow his lead

Contents

List of Figures

List of Tables

Contributors

Paul R. Abramson is professor of political science at Michigan State University. He is the author of *Generational Change in American Politics* (1975), *The Political Socialization of Black Americans* (1977), *Political Attitudes in America* (1983), and *Politics in the Bible* (2012). He is coauthor of *Value Change in Global Perspective* (with Ronald Inglehart, 1995) and coauthor of a series of seventeen books on presidential and congressional elections with John H. Aldrich and David W. Rohde, the most recent of which is *Change and Continuity in the 2012 Elections* (2014). He is also author or coauthor of more than seventy journal articles, including thirteen in the *American Political Science Review*.

Russell J. Dalton is professor of political science at the University of California, Irvine. His research focuses on public opinion, attitudinal change, electoral and political behavior, and party politics in contemporary democracies. He recently authored *Citizen Politics*, sixth edition (2013), *The Apartisan American* (2012), *Political Parties and Democratic Linkage* (2011), *The Good Citizen* (2009), and *Democratic Challenges – Democratic Choices* (2004). Dalton has also edited or coedited more than a dozen volumes, including *Citizens, Context and Choice* (2011); *Party Politics in East Asia* (2008); *The Oxford Handbook of Political Behavior* (2007); *Citizens, Democracy and Markets around the Pacific Rim* (2006); *Democracy Transformed* (2003); and *Parties with Partisans* (2001).

Christian W. Haerpfer is professor of political science and holds the Established First Chair of Politics at the University of Aberdeen, United Kingdom. He is also head of the Department of Politics and International Relations and director of the European Centre for Survey Research at the University of Aberdeen and of the Eurasia Barometer, and President of the World Values Survey Association. His research focuses on democratization, comparative public opinion, and electoral and political behavior in postcommunist Europe and post-Soviet Eurasia. His most recent books include *Living Conditions, Lifestyles and Health in Post-Soviet Eurasia* (with Claire Wallace and Martin McKee, 2013); *Democratization* (with Ronald Inglehart, Chris Welzel, and Patrick Bernhagen, 2009); and *Democracy and Enlargement in Post-Communist Europe* (2002).

Tor Georg Jakobsen is a postdoctoral researcher in political science at the Norwegian University of Science and Technology and an associate professor at Trondheim Business School. His dissertation is "Macro Factors and Public Opinion: An Investigation of Economic Left-Right Attitudes in Advanced Industrialized Democracies." Jakobsen's fields of interest include political behavior, quantitative methods, and conflict and peace studies. Jakobsen has authored and coauthored articles in, among other journals, *European Sociological Review*; *Work, Employment and Society*; and *Social Indicators Research*.

Kseniya Kizilova is a Research Fellow at the European Centre for Survey Research, University of Aberdeen, United Kingdom. She is the manager of the project "ArabTrans: Political and Social Transformations in the Arab World." Kizilova is also vice director of the Eurasia Barometer. Her research interests focus on identities, population health and life quality, political support, and trust. She has more than thirty scientific publications.

Hans-Dieter Klingemann is Professor Emeritus of political science at the Freie Universitaet Berlin, Director Emeritus of the Research Unit "Institutions and Social Change" at the Social Science Research Center Berlin, and Global Professor of Political Science at New York University in Abu Dhabi. His research focuses on the comparative study of political behavior, political parties, and democratic political culture. In 2011, he received the Lifetime Achievement Award of the European Consortium of Political Research. Klingemann's edited and coedited books include *Parties, Policies and Democracy* (1994); *Citizens and the State* (1995); *A New Handbook of Political Science* (1996); *Mapping Policy Preferences* (2001); *Democracy and Political Culture in Eastern Europe* (2006); *Mapping Policy Preferences II* (2006); *The State of Political Science in Western Europe* (2007); *The Oxford Handbook of Political Behavior* (2007); *The Comparative Study of Electoral Behavior* (2009); and *Cultural Diversity, European Identity, and the Legitimacy of the EU* (2011).

Ola Listhaug is professor of political science at the Norwegian University of Science and Technology, Trondheim. His research focuses on public opinion, political trust, and political behavior. Recent books include *Losers' Consent* (with Christopher J. Anderson, André Blais, Shaun Bowler, and Todd Donovan, 2005), *Civic and Uncivic Values – Serbia in the Post-Milosevic Era* (edited with Sabrina Ramet and Dragana Dulic, 2011), *Civic and Uncivic Values in Macedonia* (edited with Sabrina Ramet and Albert Simkus; 2013), and *Bosnia-Herzegovina since Dayton* (edited with Sabrina Ramet, 2013).

Matthew Miles received his PhD from the University of Kansas and now teaches at Brigham Young University in Idaho. His research interests include American politics, comparative politics, and quantitative and experimental research methods. His PhD research examined the interaction between partisanship, policy polarization, and the impact of institutions on electoral campaigns.

Alejandro Moreno Alvarez is professor of political science at the Instituto Tecnológico Autónomo de México and director of the Department of Public Opinion Research at the *Reforma* newspaper, both in Mexico City. He is president (2013–14) of the World Association for Public Opinion Research. He has served as principal investigator in Mexico for the World Values Survey and for the Comparative National Election Project and as managing director for the 2010 and 2011 Latinobarometro surveys. Among his books are *Political Cleavages* (1999), *El votante mexicano* (2003), *Nuestros valores* (2005), *La decisión electoral* (2009), and *Consolidating Mexico's Democracy* (edited with Jorge I. Domínguez and Chappell Lawson, 2009).

Neil Nevitte is professor of political science and public policy and governance at the University of Toronto. He is a coinvestigator of the Canadian Election Study and the principal investigator of the Canadian World Values Survey and has published a number of books, including, most recently, *A Question of Ethics: Canadians Speak Out* (2006), *The Democratic Audit of Canada: Citizens* (2004), *Anatomy of a Liberal Victory* (2002), *Value Change and Governance* (2002), *Unsteady State* (2000), *The Challenge of Direct Democracy* (1996), and *Decline of Deference* (1996). He has contributed to a variety of academic journals. His research interests are in public opinion, voting, value change, and the problems associated with transitional elections.

Pippa Norris is the McGuire Lecturer in Comparative Politics at the John F. Kennedy School of Government, Harvard University, and ARC Laureate Fellow and professor of government and international relations at the University of Sydney. Norris has published more than forty books, including *A Virtuous Circle* (2000), *Digital Divide* (2001), *Democratic Phoenix* (2002), *Rising Tide* (with Ronald Inglehart, 2003), *Electoral Engineering* (2004), *Sacred and Secular* (with Ronald Inglehart, 2004, 2010), *Radical Right* (2005), *Driving Democracy* (2008), *Cosmopolitan Communications* (with Ronald Inglehart, 2009), *Democratic Deficit* (2011), and *Making Democratic Governance Work* (2012).

Mark Peffley is professor of political science at the University of Kentucky. His research focuses on public opinion, political psychology, racial attitudes, and political tolerance. He is director of the Quantitative Initiative for Policy and Social Research and former coeditor of the journal *Political Behavior*. He is coauthor of *Justice in America: The Separate Realities of Blacks and Whites* (with Jon Hurwitz, 2011), the 2011 winner of the Robert E. Lane Award for Best Book in Political Psychology.

Bi Puranen is associate professor in the history of economics at the University of Stockholm. She is also secretary general of the World Values Survey Association and senior research Fellow at the Institute for Future Studies in Sweden. Her research focuses on health, human security, tolerance, and changing values. Puranen coedited *Religion, Democratic Values and Political Conflict* (2009). Her most recent publications include *Willingness to Fight for One's Country and the Importance of Democracy* (2008), *European Values on Security and Defense: An Exploration of the Correlates of Willingness to Fight for One's Country* (2009), *The Transformation of Europe's Armed Forces* (2010), and *How Values Transform Military Culture* (in Swedish, 2012).

Robert Rohrschneider is the Sir Robert Worcester Distinguished Professor in the Department of Political Science at the University of Kansas. His research interests focus on comparative public opinion and parties in advanced industrial democracies. He is the coauthor of *The Strain of Representation* (2012) and authored *Learning Democracy* (1999), which won the 1998 Stein Rokkan Prize for Comparative Social Science Research. His research has also been published in such journals as the *American Journal of Political Science*, *American Political Science Review*, the *European Journal of Political Research*, *Comparative Political Studies*, and the *Journal of Politics*.

Doh Chull Shin is the Jack Peltason Scholar in Residence at the Center for the Study of Democracy at the University of California, Irvine, and Professor Emeritus, Korea Foundation Chair, and Middlebush Chair at the University of Missouri, Columbia. He is the founder of the Korea Democracy Barometer and cofounder of the Asia Barometer. His recent books include *Confucianism and Democratization in East Asia* (2011); *The Quality of Life in Confucian Asia* (2010); *How East Asians View Democracy* (2008); *Citizens, Democracy and Markets around the Pacific Rim* (2006); and *Mass Politics and Culture in Democratizing Korea* (2000).

Christian Welzel is chair in political culture research at the Centre for the Study of Democracy at Leuphana University, Lueneburg, Germany, and foreign consultant at the Laboratory for Comparative Social Research at the Higher School of Economics, St. Petersburg, Russia. He is also past president of the World Values Survey Association. His research focuses on human empowerment, emancipative values, cultural change, and democratization. Author of some hundred scholarly publications, his most recent books include *Freedom Rising: Human Empowerment and the Quest for Emancipation* (2013) – winner of the 2014 Alexander L. George Award and the Stein Rokkan Prize; *Democratization* (with Christian Haerpfer, Ronald Inglehart, and Patrick Bernhagen, 2009); and *Modernization, Cultural Change and Democracy* (with Ronald Inglehart, 2005).

Foreword

Pushing the Envelope – Analyzing the Impact of Values

Marita R. Inglehart

In a sense, this book began when Ronald Inglehart went to Paris in May 1968 to investigate the causes of a student uprising that had just paralyzed France. He mounted a representative national survey of the French public that probed into the motivations underlying the greatest mass uprising since World War II and why the Gaullist government that had opposed it was returned to power by a majority of French voters in subsequent national elections.

When he began to analyze the results, Inglehart was surprised: the data contradicted his expectations. Like most observers – including the strikers and demonstrators themselves – he assumed that the May 1968 uprising was a manifestation of class conflict. Paris was covered with posters attacking capitalist exploitation; French intellectuals interpreted the events in Marxist terms, and the participants used standard Marxist slogans about class struggle. Accordingly, Inglehart initially struggled to make the findings fit Marxist expectations. New elections were held a month after the strikes and demonstrations. His data showed that instead of heightened class polarization, with the proletariat supporting the parties of the Left and the bourgeoisie rallying behind General de Gaulle, a large share of the working-class voters had shifted to support the Gaullist ruling party, contributing to its victory. It was mainly middle-class voters who moved in the opposite direction.

Seeking to understand why this happened, Inglehart analyzed the responses to an open-ended question that asked about the goals of those who had taken part in the strikes and demonstrations. The motivations varied sharply by age and social class. Working-class respondents, especially the older ones, overwhelmingly mentioned higher salaries. Middle-class respondents, especially the younger ones, said they wanted a freer, less impersonal society. Inglehart hypothesized that these age and class differences reflected a process of intergenerational value change linked with the economic miracles of the postwar era.

He reasoned that, throughout history, most people have grown up experiencing economic and physical insecurity. Germany was a particularly striking example that quickly caught Inglehart's attention right after his visits to France. In Germany, the older generations had experienced deprivation and loss of life during World War I, followed by the Great Depression of the 1930s, and then defeat, occupation, and liberation during World War II. The postwar era, by contrast, brought historically unprecedented levels of economic and physical security. During the two decades before 1968, Germany experienced the highest economic growth rates in its history. This economic development, combined with the emergence of the modern welfare state, meant that for the first time in history, a large part of the population had grown up in a society where starvation was virtually unknown. A large part of the postwar generation no longer gave top priority to economic security, instead placing growing emphasis on autonomy and freedom of expression.

A society's basic values, of course, do not change overnight, and older generations continued to emphasize the materialistic goals that had shaped them during their formative years. But the more secure strata of the postwar generation gave higher priority to "postmaterialist" goals, as Inglehart called them.

The student protesters in France, Germany, and elsewhere in the Western world indicated the political emergence of the postwar generation. Although their formative conditions had been present for years, this generation did not become old enough to have an impact on politics until the 1960s, when they were university students. Eventually they would occupy the leading positions in society, but initially they saw themselves as having values that were sharply different from those of their elders. "Don't trust anyone over thirty!" was a widespread slogan. When postmaterialists first emerged as a political force, they tended to express themselves in Marxist slogans, which were then the standard rhetoric of protest in Western Europe. To a large extent, the term "Left" *meant* the Marxist parties, and it was natural for the postmaterialists to assume that they were Marxists. But in fact there were profound differences between the goals of the postmaterialists and those of the Marxist Left, as the postmaterialists gradually discovered.

In 1970, Inglehart tested his postmaterialist value change theory in a six-nation survey of European attitudes with a battery of questions he had explicitly designed to measure materialist versus postmaterialist values. In all six countries (Britain, France, West Germany, Italy, Belgium, and the Netherlands), there were massive differences between the values of young and old respondents. Among those older than sixty-five, materialists outnumbered postmaterialists by a margin of fourteen to one; but among the postwar generation, postmaterialists were more numerous than materialists. Moreover, within each birth cohort, postmaterialists were much more heavily represented among the economically secure strata than among the less-educated and lower-income groups. The article reporting these findings was published in 1971 in the

American Political Science Review, and the concept of postmaterialism entered the vocabulary of modern political science.[1]

Several critics argued that the dramatic value differences between age groups reflected life-cycle effects rather than generational change. Data from a long time series would be needed to answer this question. The four-item materialist-postmaterialist values battery was included in the Eurobarometer surveys beginning in 1973 and was continued for decades. This made it possible to carry out cohort analyses based on data covering a long time series. The results confirmed that a process of intergenerational value change was taking place: given birth cohorts did not become more materialist as they grew older, and as younger cohorts gradually replaced older ones in the adult population, the society as a whole became increasingly postmaterialist. In addition, the wealth of the data in the Eurobarometer studies enabled survey researchers to examine the range of attitudes and behaviors linked to postmaterialist value change, stimulating a growing body of research on this topic.

The research agenda on value change in contemporary societies continued to expand. In 1973, Inglehart developed a broader-based twelve-item battery. With Samuel Barnes, Max Kaase, Warren Miller, Hans-Dieter Klingemann, and Alan Marsh, he helped design the Political Action study, which demonstrated the link between value change and new forms of political action such as protests, petitions, sit-ins, and various other manifestations of contentious action.[2]

The concept of postmaterialist values has become a standard term in social science (in 2014, a Google Scholar search on "postmaterialist values" produced more than 15,000 citations). But in subsequent research, Inglehart found that the value shift he first measured in 1970 was part of a much broader process of intergenerational cultural change linked with modernization.[3] Materialist-postmaterialist values were just one component of a broader dimension of cross-cultural variation, which he called survival–self-expression values. Self-expression values give high priority to environmental protection, tolerance of out-groups, gender equality, and emphasis on participation in decision making in economic and political life. These values reflect mass polarization over gender equality and individual freedoms, which are part of a broader syndrome of tolerance of out-groups, including foreigners and gays and lesbians. The shift

[1] R. Inglehart, "The Silent Revolution in Europe: Intergenerational Change in Post-Industrial Societies," *American Political Science Review* 65 (1971): 991–1017; R. Inglehart, *The Silent Revolution* (Princeton, NJ: Princeton University Press, 1977).

[2] S. H. Barnes, M. Kaase, K. Allerbeck, F. Heunks, R. Inglehart, M. K. Jennings, et al., *Political Action: Mass Participation in Five Western Democracies* (Beverly Hills, CA: Sage, 1979).

[3] R. Inglehart, *Culture Shift* (Princeton, NJ: Princeton University Press, 1990); R. Inglehart, *Modernization and Postmodernization: Cultural, Economic and Political Change in 43 Societies* (Princeton, NJ: Princeton University Press, 1977); P. Abramson and R. Inglehart, *Value Change in Global Perspective* (Ann Arbor: University of Michigan Press, 1995); R. Inglehart and W. Baker, "Modernization, Cultural Change and the Persistence of Traditional Values," *American Sociological Review* 65 (2000): 19–51.

from survival values to self-expression values also includes a shift in child-rearing values, from an emphasis on hard work and conformity to social norms toward emphasis on imagination and tolerance as important values to teach a child. Plus it goes with a rising sense of subjective well-being that is conducive to tolerance, trust, political moderation, and expressive political action – all of which are conducive to democracy.

Building on this revised view of modernization, Inglehart, in collaboration with various colleagues, particularly Christian Welzel and Pippa Norris, developed the *evolutionary modernization theory*. Departing from earlier versions of modernization theory, it abandons simplistic assumptions of linearity.[4] Instead, it emphasizes that modernization is reversible and can change direction. Thus, the transition from agrarian to industrial society was linked with a cultural shift from "traditional" to "secular-rational values," which made the emergence of "electoral democracy" possible, although by no means inevitable. Then, the transition from industrial to postindustrial society brought a shift in a very different direction: from "survival" to "self-expression values," which makes "liberal democracy" increasingly likely. This theory also moves from a narrow focus on changes in objective socioeconomic conditions to examine changes in people's subjective beliefs and the impact of these beliefs on regime institutions and public policies. Finally, this theory recognizes the enduring impact of a society's historic heritage, as is manifest in the robust global cultural zones based on religious and colonial experiences: economic development tends to change a society's culture in roughly predictable ways. But the process is path dependent: the fact that a society was historically Protestant, Catholic, Orthodox, Muslim, or Confucian continues to shape its people's values today.

Nevertheless, it seems clear that rising economic and physical security tends to erode the rigid cultural norms that characterized agrarian societies, leading to norms that allow greater individual autonomy and free choice. Strikingly similar findings have been reported by researchers in other disciplines from anthropology to biology. Thus, Gelfand and colleagues find that nations that encountered severe ecological and historical threats have stronger norms and lower tolerance of deviant behavior than do other nations, arguing that existential pressures determine whether a culture is tolerant of deviance.[5] Similarly, Thornhill and colleagues find that historic vulnerability to infectious disease is linked with collectivist attitudes, xenophobia, and low support for gender equality – all of which hinder the emergence of democracy.[6]

[4] R. Inglehart and P. Norris, *Rising Tide: Gender Equality and Cultural Change around the World* (New York: Cambridge University Press, 2003); P. Norris and R. Inglehart, *Sacred and Secular: Religion and Politics Worldwide*, expanded 2nd ed. (New York: Cambridge University Press, 2011); R. Inglehart and C. Welzel, *Modernization, Cultural Change and Democracy: The Human Development Sequence* (New York: Cambridge University Press, 2005).

[5] M. J. Gelfand, J. L. Raver, L. Nishii, L. M. Leslie, J. Lun, B. C. Lim, et al., "Differences between Tight and Loose Cultures: A 33-Nation Study," *Science* 27 (2011): 1100–4.

[6] R. Thornhill, C. Fincher, and D. R. Murray, "Zoonotic and Non-zoonotic Diseases in Relation to Human Personality and Societal Values," *Evolutionary Psychology* 8 (2010): 151–55.

Inglehart's theory of postmaterialism and the revised theory of modernization that developed from it continue to be the basis of evolving theories. Recent extensions include Welzel's *general theory of emancipation*[7] as well as Dalton and Welzel's *allegiance-assertion theory,* pursued in this volume, which postulates a shift from allegiant to assertive types of citizens. The underlying logic connecting this lineage of theories is that increasing existential security, cognitive mobilization, and other opportunity-widening aspects of modernization tend to make people more self-directed and to shift their emphasis on freedom of choice and equality of opportunities. These values fuel various social movement activities that advocate gender equality, tolerance of gays and lesbians, and participatory democracy throughout societal life.

In 1973, Jacques-René Rabier launched the Eurobarometer surveys and had the foresight to include the materialist-postmaterialist values in a long-term program of monitoring the attitudinal component of social change. This made it possible to test these ideas empirically and to modify and build on them to improve our understanding of how people's beliefs and goals are changing. Rabier is one of the unsung heroes of cross-national survey research. He not only launched the Eurobarometer surveys but also inspired and supported other cross-national survey research programs such as the Latino Barometer, the Afro Barometer, and the East Asia Barometer. He also helped design the European Values Study, launched in 1981 by Jan Kerkhofs and Ruud de Moore, which was carried out by the same survey institutes that did the Eurobarometer and included many of its key indicators, such as materialist-postmaterialist values and unconventional political action measures from the Political Action Surveys. Later, de Moor and Kerkhofs invited Inglehart to help expand the European Values Study (EVS) into a global survey project that in 1990 became the World Values Survey (WVS). In 1995, Inglehart launched a new wave of the WVS on his own, and in 1999, the EVS and WVS were established as two separate groups, which continue to cooperate, sharing key batteries of items to build up an unprecedented time series for the analysis of value change. Kerkhof's and de Moor's work has been carried on with great success by Paul de Graaf, Loek Halman, Jaak Billiet, Jacques Hagenaars, and their colleagues, covering virtually every country in Europe.

The WVS is the most important research project of Inglehart's career. In discussing the WVS, he is clearly expressing his appreciation and gratitude for having been able to work with such colleagues as Miguel Basanez, Russell Dalton, Jaime Díez-Nicolás, Juan Díez-Nicolás, Yilmaz Esmer, Christian Haerpfer, Hans-Dieter Klingemann, Marta Lagos, Shen Mingming, Alejandro Moreno Alvarez, Neil Nevitte, Pippa Norris, Thorleif Pettersson, Bi Puranen, Catalina Romero, Sandeep Shastri, Christian Welzel, Seiko Yamazaki, and many other colleagues in the WVS network. These people, from countries

---

7 C. Welzel, *Freedom Rising: Human Empowerment and the Quest for Emancipation* (New York: Cambridge University Press, 2013).

around the world, have played key roles in carrying out the WVS, analyzing the data, and presenting the findings in publications and conferences around the world. A project of this scope requires people with diverse talents to design, organize, fund, analyze, archive, interpret, and publish findings from this study of social change in more than 100 countries, extending over 30 years. The WVS is diverse not only in talented people but also geographically. The WVS secretariat is based in Stockholm, the archiving is carried out in Madrid, and analysis and interpretation of the data are pursued by thousands of researchers in scores of countries around the world.

In codesigning the WVS, Inglehart emphasized a strategy of diversity, trying to cover the widest possible range of societies. This was a deliberate strategic choice. He was aware that a more cautious approach would have been to limit the data collection to countries with well-developed survey infrastructures, ensuring that fieldwork was carried out by experienced survey institutions. But this would have meant limiting the survey's coverage mainly to prosperous democracies. He was convinced that it was a better overall strategy to push the envelope, maximizing the economic, political, and cultural diversity of the countries covered. This approach greatly increases the analytic leverage that is available for analyzing the role of culture, economic development, and democratic versus authoritarian institutions. But it also tends to increase the possible error in measurement. This is a difficult balancing act, and it is an empirical question whether the gains offset the potential costs.

Extending survey research into developing countries means doing it in places where the infrastructure is less developed and the margin of error is likely to be higher. This raises the question: Is it possible to obtain accurate measures of mass beliefs and values in low-income countries and authoritarian states where survey research is rare? Or is the error margin so large as to render the data useless for comparative analysis? There is no a priori answer to this question; it requires empirical testing. Inglehart and Welzel conducted some relevant tests.[8] They theorized that self-expression values should be strongly correlated with indicators of economic development. Thus, they compared the strength of the correlations obtained from high-income societies with the strength of those obtained from all available societies. Here two effects work against each other: (1) the presumed loss of data quality that comes from including lower-income societies, which would tend to weaken the correlations; and (2) the increased analytical leverage that comes from including the full range of societies, which should strengthen the correlations. Which effect is stronger? They found that among high-income societies, the average correlation between self-expression values and ten widely used economic development indicators was 0.57, whereas across all available societies, the average correlation is 0.77. The data from all available societies explain almost twice as much variance as the data from high-income societies alone.

Their theory also implies that one should find strong linkages between self-expression values, the emergence of civil society, and the flourishing of democratic institutions. As data from scores of countries demonstrate, societal-level self-expression values are indeed closely correlated with a wide range of such indicators, including the "global civil society index" and World Bank indices of "government effectiveness," "rule of law," and "corruption control." They are also strongly correlated with the United Nations Development Programme's "gender empowerment measure" and an "index of effective democracy." Again, the gains obtained by increasing the range of variation more than compensate for any loss of data quality.

Another important reason for covering the whole spectrum of economic and democratic development is that bringing survey research into these societies helps them develop their research capabilities. Survey research can provide valuable feedback for policy makers, and the WVS network is based on the belief that it is the responsibility of social scientists in developed societies to help disseminate survey research techniques. Accordingly, the WVS has produced many publications based on collaboration between social scientists in developing countries and colleagues from countries with a long experience in using survey research. Inglehart was convinced that, over time, the quality of fieldwork in developing countries would be improved, and he considered the effort to do so worth a substantial investment.

For academics, life regenerates itself through students and colleagues. Inglehart takes tremendous pride in the students and colleagues with whom he has worked – some of whom have contributed to this volume. This volume is a tribute to Inglehart's achievements as a modernization theorist and an analyst of sociocultural change and also as a visionary who persistently worked to develop a key data resource, the WVS. I express my deep gratitude to all the authors for producing this volume. It is a testament both to Ronald Inglehart's scholarship and to the continuing importance of studying how changing values are reshaping the societies and political systems in which we live.

Preface and Acknowledgments

Sometime in the 1960–70s, the paradigm of comparative politics began to change in the established democracies. Until this point, one of the field's major concerns was to explain the collapse of democracy in interwar Europe and the rise of fascist governments in their place. The landmark study, *The Civic Culture*, thus looked at postwar Europe and before to assess what type of political culture sustained democracy. Political culture research argued that people's deference and allegiance to democratic institutions, combined with limited, elite-mandating mass involvement, were the foundation of stable democracy.

But societies and their people change. Mass prosperity, education, information, and other forces of social modernization were transforming citizens and the democratic process. New issue demands entered the political agenda, new citizen groups challenged the status quo, and a "participatory revolution" extended popular demands on governments. Usually, scholars and pundits depicted these developments as threats to democracy, often hearkening back to the model of citizenry proposed in the political culture studies of the early postwar era.

One of the first scholars to recognize the erosion of the allegiant model of democratic citizenship was Ronald Inglehart. He has been one of the strongest voices in the political culture field to object to the stereotypical interpretation of "elite-challenging mass action" as antidemocratic. In his landmark work, *The Silent Revolution*, Ronald Inglehart theorized and demonstrated the motivation driving the rise of elite-challenging action – a growing emancipatory spirit visible in increasing postmaterialist values. He further identified the generational increase of existential security and cognitive mobilization as the social forces fueling the rise of these new values. In his revised theory of modernization, Inglehart extended the notion of postmaterialist values into the broader concept of "self-expression values." While a first phase of modernization – the transition from agrarian to industrial society – tends to strengthen "secular-rational values," self-expression values emerge in the second phase of modernization: the transition from industrial to postindustrial society. With this theory, Inglehart enriched the political culture field with a set of ideas and concepts that greatly enhanced our understanding of cultural change.

In addition to his intellectual impact, Inglehart's second crucial contribution was to provide an evidence base for the study of cultural differences and cultural change. At the beginning of his career, the field of comparative political culture research had systematic data for no more than a handful of countries. Inspired by the ambition to improve this situation, Inglehart helped develop the Eurobarometer surveys, contributed to the European Values Study, and founded the World Values Survey – the most encompassing, most widely cited and used, and most widely recognized database for studying political culture and cultural change. Hence Inglehart invented not only some of the most influential concepts but he also created the infrastructure for a major field of comparative politics. The development of these surveys has enabled a generation of scholars to do research in areas where no one had gone before. Both his intellectual and data collection contributions are so exceptional and outstanding that we dedicate this book as a tribute to the lifetime achievements of Ronald Inglehart.

In developing this project, we received essential support from the Alexander von Humboldt Stiftung. The foundation provided a Transcoop grant for collaboration between Welzel and Dalton and their respective universities. In February and March 2011, the Centers for the Study of Democracy at Leuphana University in Germany and at the University of California, Irvine, in the United States held conferences to assemble the contributors to this volume. We appreciate the financial and administrative support from both centers, especially the center directors Ferdinand Muller-Rommel and William Schonfold.

Along the way, many people have assisted in developing this book. Bjoern Buss produced the index. Lewis Bateman, the chief social science editor at Cambridge University Press, and his assistant, Shaun Vigil, provided helpful guidance in getting this book ready for publication. We also appreciate the assistance of Amy Alexander, Natalie Cook, Yilmaz Esmer, Yuliya Tverdova, and Carole Uhlaner in developing this project and the final manuscript. The seed for this project was probably sown in previous collaborations with Almond and Verba that shaped our thinking about political culture, culture change, and the value of individual citizens. We stand on their shoulders, and we hope they would view this positively.

Almond and Verba's *The Civic Culture* gave voice to citizens in five nations and their views of politics and their political role. It created the foundation for political culture research on which we build. One of the major accomplishments of the World Values Survey used in this book is to give voice to people around the world, with surveys spanning nearly half of the nations on the globe, representing roughly 90 percent of the world population. Our argument is that the tenor of this voice has changed in the past half-century, with significant consequences for contemporary politics. We owe a debt to Almond and Verba for launching a research program with the enduring importance that led to the themes we study here.

Russell J. Dalton and Christian Welzel

Political Culture and Value Change

Russell J. Dalton and Christian Welzel

Approximately fifty years ago, Gabriel Almond and Sidney Verba (1963) published *The Civic Culture*, followed soon after by Sidney Verba and Lucian Pye's (1965) *Political Culture and Political Development*. The importance of these two classic studies cannot be overemphasized. They widened the political culture approach into a global framework for the comparative analysis of political change and regime legitimacy in developed as well as developing countries. The guiding question of the Almond-Verba-Pye approach concerned what citizen beliefs make democratic regimes survive and flourish. With the expansion of democracy into new regions of the globe, this civicness question is even more relevant today.

Political Culture and Political Development laid out the analytical tool kit and categories to examine the civicness question empirically. The volume was particularly important on conceptual grounds, yet it lacked systematic cross-national data to support its conclusions because such research was not feasible. Today, this situation has changed dramatically. The World Values Survey (WVS) and other cross-national projects have opened large parts of the developing world to public opinion research. Now there is an abundance of evidence on a wide range of social and political attitudes. This situation creates an excellent opportunity to evaluate contemporary political cultures in terms of the civicness question.

Verba and his colleagues stressed a cluster of orientations that supposedly support a democratic polity: allegiance to the regime, pride in the political system, and modest levels of political participation. This *allegiant model* was most apparent in the United States and Britain, the two mature and stable democracies in their study – and lacking in other democratizing nations. However, the modern wave of comparative research in political culture offers a different answer to the question of what citizen beliefs are congruent with democracy.

Ronald Inglehart and his associates have stressed that the public's values in established democracies have been changing in fundamental ways that conflict with the normative model of *The Civic Culture* (Inglehart 1977, 1990; Abramson and Inglehart 1995; Inglehart and Welzel 2005). This research argued that contemporary publics are developing more *assertive, self-expressive values* that contrast with the allegiant values of the *Civic Culture* model, thus changing the nature of democratic citizenship. Instead of an allegiant and loyal public, established democracies now have a public of critical citizens (Klingemann 1999; Norris 1999; Dalton 2004).[1]

In addition, the expansion of democracy during its third and fourth waves speaks to a democratic potential that was often overlooked in the scholarly community (Huntington 1984). People power movements from the Philippines to communist Eastern Europe to sub-Saharan Africa demonstrate a popular desire for political change that appears inconsistent with the *Civic Culture* model. The *Economist* recognized this development when it described why Egyptians protested for political reform against the various authoritarian regimes they confronted, from the Mubarak regime to the generals controlling the government in late 2013:

[The] worst mistake, however, is to ignore the chief lesson of the Arab Spring. This is that ordinary people yearn for dignity. They hate being bossed around by petty officials and ruled by corrupt autocrats. They reject the apparatus of a police state. Instead they want better lives, decent jobs and some basic freedoms.[2]

These insights produce a far different image of the average person in a developing nation than what was proposed in *Political Culture and Political Development*. Individuals in these societies do not embrace or accept the authoritarian states in which they live, but rather hold unfulfilled aspirations for a better way of life.

Expanding empirical research on developing nations – both democratic and nondemocratic – often finds that citizen values are a poor match to the patterns presented in the early political culture and political development literature (Inglehart and Welzel 2005; Dalton and Shin 2006; Bratton et al. 2004; Moaddel 2007). Many of these publics are politically interested with strong democratic aspirations. In short, some of the stark contrasts the civic culture model posited between developing nations and established democracies seem no longer valid. *The Civic Culture* maintained that allegiant orientations characterize stable democracies and that these orientations need to mature in the developing nations, too, if they ought to become stable democracies as well. Today, however, assertive orientations characterize established democracies, with some evidence that they are also emerging in the developing world.

---

[1] There are, of course, debates on the processes producing value change and the nature of these values. See, for example, Flanagan and Lee (2003), Schwarz (2006), and Abramson (2011).

[2] "The Battle for Egypt," *The Economist*, August 17, 2013, p. 11.

This book is dedicated to a twofold task: analyzing cross-national survey data in light of the initial Almond-Verba-Pye framework and reevaluating the original civic culture model against more recent empirical evidence. To accomplish this task, the contributors to this book use evidence from the WVS. This is an unparalleled resource that allows us to analyze public opinions toward government and democracy, citizen values, and the potential impact of changing values on contemporary societies.

In the parlance of Hollywood filmmaking, we are not sure if this book represents a remake of the early *Civic Culture* study or a sequel to it. However, our intent is to use the basic concepts and ideas of Almond-Verba-Pye as our starting point. Then we reevaluate this theory – and more recent developments in political culture theory – based on the new evidence of the WVS. The results, we believe, shed new light on how global values have been changing and the implications for contemporary political systems.

THE EVOLUTION OF POLITICAL CULTURE RESEARCH

A stable and effective democratic government . . . depends upon the orientations that people have to the political process – upon the political culture. (Almond and Verba 1963, 498)

Gabriel Almond and Sidney Verba's (1963) classic *The Civic Culture* began the systematic effort to identify the citizen beliefs that underlie viable and flourishing democratic institutions. Lucian Pye and Sidney Verba's (1965) *Political Culture and Political Development* put this theme in an even broader cross-national perspective, conceptualizing the role of citizen beliefs in the processes of nation building and democratization.

Although the *Civic Culture* framework is well known, it is worthwhile to summarize the key elements on which we build. Almond and Verba (1963, 15–17) characterized a nation's political culture in terms of two dimensions. First, they used a Parsonian approach to distinguish between *different types of attitudes*: (1) cognitive orientations involve knowledge and beliefs about politics; (2) affective orientations are positive or negative feelings toward political objects; and (3) evaluative orientations involve judgments about political options and processes. Second, they identified four *different classes of political objects* toward which citizen attitudes are directed: (1) the political system in general; (2) input objects, such as political parties, interest groups, or political actors engaged in conveying demands from the citizenry to institutions; (3) output objects, such as government bureaucracies or agents of state authority that implement public policies; and (4) orientations toward the self and others in terms of role models of what the ideal citizen should do.

Combining these two dimensions, Almond and Verba identified three ideal types of political culture. The *parochial culture* exists when individuals are essentially apolitical. People are unaware of the government and its policies and do not see themselves as involved in the political process. The _subject culture_ is one in which individuals are aware of the state and its policy outputs but lack significant orientations toward input objects and toward the individual as an active participant. The subject is aware of politics but only involved as a recipient of orders and an object of mobilization.

In the _participant culture_, people hold orientations toward all four classes of political objects. They are aware of government, the processes of political input, and the outputs of government, and they adopt an activist view of their role as citizens. People know and appreciate that they can express their preferences through interest organizations and political parties, by casting votes for their preferred candidates, or through other political activities.

Almond and Verba portrayed the _civic culture_ that is most conducive to democracy as a mixture of the subject and the participant orientations. In a civic culture, citizens strictly abide the law and respect legitimate political authority. Even as participant citizens, they are aware of their limited role in representative democracies, which focuses on electing representatives within organizations or public office holders. Direct involvement in policy formulations and policy implementations is not part of the ordinary citizen's standard repertoire, not even the participant citizen.

Almond and Verba stressed that the parochial, subject, and participant cultures are ideal-typical models, which do not exist in pure form in any society. But they maintained that elements of the three models exist in significantly different proportions in the world of their time. They postulated that elements of the parochial culture were most widespread in the developing world; elements of the subject culture in the communist world; and elements of the participant culture in the "free world" of the West.

Other scholarship from this period reinforced this basic theoretical framework. For example, Pye and Verba (1965) described the cultural impediments to democracy in Egypt, Ethiopia, and Turkey in terms that evoked the concepts of parochial and subject cultures – and a lack of a participant culture. Daniel Lerner's (1958) *The Passing of Traditional Society* described how socioeconomic development and cognitive mobilization could change the political culture of a nation, bringing a transition from parochial and subject orientations to more participatory orientations. Banfield's (1963) research on a rural Italian village highlighted the conditions producing parochial and subject orientations. Seymour Martin Lipset's (1959, 1994) *social prerequisite* framework considered less-developed nations as lacking the social conditions and public sentiments that favor democracy. Accordingly, democracy required socioeconomic modernization to transform a society and its culture in a democracy-compatible fashion (also see Almond and Coleman 1960; Inkeles 1969, 1983; Inkeles and Smith 1974). This research posited a strong relationship between socioeconomic development and the development of a democratic civic culture.

The political culture literature repeatedly emphasized a central assumption – that a stable political system was more likely when the political culture was congruent with the structures of the political system (Almond and Verba 1963, 23–26; Eckstein 1966; Almond and Powell 1978, Chapter 2). For instance, a parochial political culture should be predominant in traditional peasant societies that have little contact with a national or regional government. A society that is partly traditional and partly modern, typical of many developing nations, presumably has a mixed parochial-subject culture. Most people in such systems are presumably passive subjects, aware of government, complying with the law, but not otherwise involved in public affairs. The parochials – poor and illiterate urban dwellers, peasants, or farm laborers – have limited contact with or awareness of the political system. Only a very small stratum of the public participates in the political process, and even then in highly restricted ways.

At a further stage of social and political modernization, the congruent culture and institutions reflect a different pattern. For instance, in industrialized authoritarian societies, such as fascist states in Western Europe or the former communist nations of Eastern Europe, most citizens are subjects. They are encouraged and even forced to cast a symbolic vote of support in elections and to pay taxes, obey regulations, demonstrate system identification in state-managed public events, and follow the dictates of government. Because of the effectiveness of modern social organization, propaganda, and indoctrination, few people are unaware of the government and its influence on their lives; there are few parochials. At the same time, few people are involved as participants who autonomously express their authentic preferences. It is even questionable if authentic political preferences exist: Participants in the true sense are absent not only because the system would repress them but also because the citizens have not learned the role model of a participant citizen. There is a strong assumption that modern authoritarian-totalitarian systems are successful in using propaganda, indoctrination, and mass organization to infuse public norms that support the system's power structures.

The Civic Culture implied that a modern industrial democracy has a majority of participants (in the limited, allegiant sense), a substantial number of subjects, and a small group of parochials. This distribution presumably provided enough political activists to ensure competition between political parties and sizable voter turnout as well as attentive audiences for debate on public issues by parties, candidates, and pressure groups.

There is an interesting tension in the Almond-Verba framework. On the one hand, their framework is influenced by modernization theory and open to the idea that socioeconomic modernization changes citizen preferences and expectations. For example, they routinely examined educational differences in political attitudes with the implicit argument that social modernization would expand education and thus transform orientations in a pro-democratic direction. The postulated direction of change was to strengthen many aspects of the allegiant model of citizenship, such as various measures of political support. On the other hand, comparative politics scholars largely overlooked the parallel message that social modernization would also increase feelings of efficacy, autonomy, and political tolerance that might lead to new patterns of assertive democratic participants.

In addition, the framework emphasized the indoctrination powers of modern authoritarian systems and their ability to reproduce a culture that is congruent with their authoritarian structures. This was likely a reflection of the Cold War communist experience in Eastern Europe and the Soviet Union as well as the tragic history of Europe in the mid-twentieth century (Almond 1998). The *Civic Culture* framework thus gave less attention to how socioeconomic modernization can give rise to democratic, participatory desires even in nondemocratic systems, accumulating an underground delegitimizing force of authoritarian rule. Rightly or wrongly, many analysts concluded that participant orientations and other democratic orientations can really take root only under existing democratic systems (Rustow 1970; Muller and Seligson 1994; Jackman and Miller 1998; Hadenius and Teorell 2005). This implies a primarily elite-driven model of democratization, if it occurs.

In summary, two broad implications for the democratization process follow from this framework. First, the congruence thesis assumes that regime stability and effective government are more likely if the political culture is congruent with the regime form. Thus, one reason why autocratic governments exist is presumably because they occur in societies where the citizenry tolerates or even expects an autocratic state. Brutally rephrasing Adlai Stevenson, people get the type of government that they deserve. Moreover, if we assume that the political culture is embedded in a network of social relations, traditional norms, and socioeconomic conditions, then cultural change will occur very slowly (Eckstein 1966; Pye 2006). Thus, the congruence thesis implies that autocratic governments endure when there is a parochial and subject culture. Progress toward political modernization is likely to occur slowly and requires profound changes in a nation's political culture that may lag behind institutional change.[3] Cultural-institutional congruence is an important condition for stable regimes.

Second, *The Civic Culture* had a constrained view of the values of the ideal democratic citizen. The specter of hyperparticipation by antidemocratic groups in interwar (and postwar) Europe led them to stress *allegiance* as a core virtue of a stable democracy. Participant orientations are a good thing. However, a civic culture requires that participant orientations be tempered by a strong dose of subject orientations. In their words, "the civic culture is an *allegiant* participant culture. Individuals are not only oriented to political inputs, they are oriented positively to the input structures and the input process" (Almond and Verba 1963, 31; emphasis added).[4] The ideal citizen thus respects political authority

---

[3] Almond and Verba do not say that cultures cannot change or be changed. In fact, the focus on Germany in their study was implicitly to identify how the culture should be changed to produce public values more supportive of postwar German democracy.

[4] Almond and Verba (1963, 31) continue to state that "in the civic culture participant political orientations combine with and do not replace subject and political orientations. Individuals

and accepts the decisions of government; this citizen is a follower rather than a challenger. She supports democracy, is satisfied with the democratic process, has confidence in institutions, and becomes engaged only where institutional mechanisms channel her activities toward orderly outcomes. There is limited room for political dissatisfaction, questioning authority, civil disobedience, or elite-challenging activity in *The Civic Culture*.

A COUNTERVIEW

An initial challenge to the importance of an allegiant citizenry for a flourishing of democracy came from the *Political Action* study (Barnes and Kaase et al. 1979). In reaction to the student protests of the late 1960s, this study examined the expanding use of elite-challenging political action, such as protests, boycotts, wildcat strikes, blockades, occupying buildings, and other contentious actions. The project asked whether the extension of the citizens' repertoire to elite-challenging actions undermined representative democracy, as some critics suspected (Crozier, Huntington, and Watanuki 1975). The Political Action study did not support this suspicion; protesters did not abstain from conventional forms of political participation, and they showed a strong attachment to democratic norms. For sure, protesters were disillusioned about some aspects of the democratic process. However, they did not reject democracy; they were committed to the democratic ideas of citizen participation, freedom of expression, and the elites' obligation to be responsive to public demands. The 1960–70s protesters seemed to anticipate a new model of an assertive democratic citizen that contrasts with the allegiant model of *The Civic Culture*. Ever since, political culture research has seen a latent tension between an allegiant and an assertive model of democratic citizenship.

Recognizing these developments, Almond and Verba (1980) began to explore the dynamics of cultural change in *The Civic Culture Revisited*. They found that the best examples of the civic culture, the United States and Great Britain, had experienced a decline in allegiant, trustful orientations and a rise in challenging political values that was unexpected in the earlier *Civic Culture* volume. Almond (1998, 5–6) wrote retrospectively, "What we learned from the *Civic Culture Revisited* was that political culture is a plastic many dimensioned variable, and that it responds quickly to structural change. It was not that Verba and I failed to appreciate structural variables... But we surely did not appreciate how quickly, and how steep the curves of change were going to be." Thus the research agenda changed from explaining the persistence of

become participants in the political process, but they do not give up their orientation as subjects or parochials... The maintenance of these more traditional attitudes *and their fusion* with the participation orientation lead to a balanced political culture in which political activity, involvement and rationality exist but are balanced by passivity, traditionality, and commitment to parochial values."

political cultures to predicting how they could change, and the consequences of change.

Ronald Inglehart's *The Silent Revolution* (1977) provided a theoretical groundwork for this assertive model of democratic citizenship. Inglehart linked the spread of elite-challenging action to the rise of postmaterialist values, which emphasize self-expression and direct participation in politics. Inspired by modernization theory, he explained the emergence of postmaterialist values as the consequence of the rising existential security and cognitive mobilization that characterized the postwar generations in Western democracies. He held that social modernization would also give rise to postmaterialist values in nondemocratic regimes – which is potentially a powerful delegitimizing force against authoritarianism (Inglehart 1990).

The new type of self-expressive, postmaterialist political protester raised the suspicion of scholars who believed that the functioning of representative democracy requires the dominance of an allegiant citizen model (Crozier et al. 1975). Robert Putnam's (1993) influential study of political culture in Italy also accepted the allegiant model of citizenship – at least implicitly. This is apparent in the way he defined social capital, namely, as "trust, norms, and networks that facilitate cooperation and civic action" (167). Social capital was not only operationalized as trust in fellow citizens but also as trust in institutions, including the institutions of government – which is a key allegiant orientation.

Indeed, further research showed that the processes linked to rising elite-challenging politics and postmaterialist values strained the principle of representative democracy. For one, political and partisan competition added a cultural cleavage focused on lifestyle issues to the long-standing economic cleavage centered on material redistribution. This gave rise to New Left parties that mobilize on environmental and other "New Politics" issues and New Right parties that mobilize on immigration and traditional values (Kitschelt 1989; Norris 2005). Furthermore, electoral participation, party identification, confidence in political institutions, and satisfaction with the democratic process were declining in most postindustrial democracies, while support for democracy as a political system and attachment to basic democratic norms remained stable or increased (Dalton 2004; Norris 2011).

The Civic Culture study and much of the early public opinion research typically focused on established Western democracies. The practical reason was that representative mass surveys could not be conducted in the communist world and large parts of the developing world. This situation changed dramatically when consecutive waves of democratization opened the former communist bloc and large parts of the developing world to survey research. This initiated an unprecedented expansion of cross-national survey programs in addition to the WVS: the International Social Survey Program; the Comparative Study of Electoral Systems; and the democracy barometers in Eastern Europe, Latin America, Asia, Africa, and the Middle East. Much of the work in these programs was inspired by the initial question of the *Civic Culture* study: What types of citizen beliefs are most beneficial to help new democracies survive and flourish and what makes and keeps citizens supportive of the idea of democracy?

These surveys fielded questions on people's regime preferences and their levels of support for democracy, both in its concrete form and as an abstract ideal. The first reports calculated the percentages of democracy supporters in a country or compared the balance of support for democracy against support for alternative regimes (Rose, Mishler, and Haerpfer 1998; Klingemann 1999; Mishler and Rose 2001; Klingemann, Fuchs, and Zielonka 2006). This research yielded the surprising – and consistent – finding that support for democracy as a principle was widespread across established democracies, new democracies, and nondemocracies. In sharp contrast to Almond and Verba, the public in contemporary authoritarian states does not seem to embrace rule by autocrats – at least not when one takes people's overt regime preferences at face value.

Scholars also started to differentiate different types of democratic support, such as *intrinsic* and *instrumental* support (Bratton and Mattes 2001; Inglehart and Welzel 2005), *idealist* and *realist* support (Shin and Wells 2005), or support that is coupled with dissatisfaction with the way democracy works: *dissatisfied democrats* or *critical citizens* (Klingemann 1999; Norris 1999). These classifications qualify democratic regime support for the motives and beliefs that lie behind it (Schedler and Sarsfield 2006). Accordingly, they focus attention on the emergence of a new type of nonallegiant democrat and the implications for the development of democracy.

More recently, researchers have tried to disentangle what people in different parts of the world understand about the term *democracy* (Dalton, Shin, and Jou 2007; Mattes and Bratton 2007; Diamond 2008; Chapter 4). Surprisingly as it may seem from the viewpoint of cultural relativism, there is a core liberal understanding of democracy among ordinary people around the world. What first comes to most people's minds when they think about democracy is the freedom to govern their lives that liberal democracy grants them. Pronounced cultural differences exist, however, in the extent to which the liberal notion of democracy trumps alternative notions of democracy (Welzel 2013, 307–32). Yet, despite these differences in relative importance, freedom seems to have appeal across cultures. Resonating with this broad appeal, freedom is the central theme in Amartya Sen's (1999) interpretation of modernization as "human development." He defines development normatively as the growth of freedom. Clearly this definition of development includes liberal democracy.

Ronald Inglehart and Christian Welzel (2005) further elaborate the idea of human development and integrate it into the political culture field (also Welzel, Inglehart, and Klingemann 2003). In *Freedom Rising*, Welzel (2013) expands this approach to describe the growth of emancipative values among contemporary publics. He equates development with the empowerment of people to exert their freedoms. His theory describes liberal democracy as the "legal component" of empowerment. Its significance from an empowerment perspective is that it grants people the rights that enable them to practice freedoms (both personal and political). However, in the sequence of empowerment, democracy is the third component. For democracy only becomes effective *after* ordinary people have acquired the resources that make them capable to practice freedoms and after they have internalized the values that make them willing to practice freedoms. In this view, participatory resources and values proliferate the material and motivational components of people power. They must be in place before democracy can be effectively practiced. Welzel identifies a set of orientations that are emancipative in their impetus because they merge libertarian and egalitarian orientations. The prevalence of these emancipative values in a society is more closely linked with levels of democracy than any other citizen belief. The most important component of emancipative values in this respect has been found to be liberty aspirations – quite in line with the emphasis that liberal democracy places on freedom (Welzel 2007). In short, the human development model by Inglehart and Welzel and Welzel's emancipatory theory argue for recognition of an assertive model of democratic citizenship.[5]

The revisionist strand of research champions an assertive model of political culture that also can be congruent with democracy, albeit with different political implications. Some of the key contrasts between allegiant and assertive cultures are summarized in Table 1.1. Changing orientations produce a general increase in postmaterialist and emancipative values as well as a shift in basic authority beliefs. These cultural changes manifest themselves in shifting attitudes toward political institutions, the practice of democracy, and even the definition of a good democracy and a good citizen. These political norms carry over to specific policy views that we also examine in this volume. For example, the traditional model of citizen included a strong priority for economic prosperity and little concern for environmental protection. The new pattern of assertive citizenship heightens environmental concerns. Traditional norms gave limited attention on issues of racial and ethnic equality and sexual liberation; these issues receive strong support under the assertive model of citizenship.

In summary, the debates over the role of political culture owe their inspiration to the initial groundwork laid by Almond and Verba in *The Civic Culture* and by Verba and Pye in *Political Culture and Political Development*. Their research focused on an allegiant model of citizenship as essential to stable democracy, whereas the contours of an assertive model of citizenship became clear only recently. The content of a democratic political culture can be more complex than Almond and Verba and Pye initially envisioned, and the spread of democratic orientations differs markedly from earlier expectations of average citizens. The results, we believe, lead to both a reevaluation of the political

---

[5] This same theoretical logic is represented in research on dissatisfied democrats by Klingemann (1999), critical citizens by Norris (1999), and even more clearly the model of engaged citizenship by Dalton (2009).

TABLE 1.1. *Aspects of Allegiant and Assertive Citizenship*

Domain	Allegiant Citizens	Assertive Citizens
Value priorities	Output priorities with an emphasis on order and security limit input priorities that might emphasize voice and participation; materialist/protective values predominate	Input priorities with an emphasis on voice and participation grow stronger at the expense of output priorities with an emphasis on order and security: postmaterialist/emancipative values prevail over materialist/protective values
Authority orientations	Deference to authority in the family, at the workplace, and in politics	Distance to authority in the family, at the workplace, and in politics
Institutional trust	High trust in institutions	Low trust in institutions
Democratic support	Support for both the principles of democracy and its practice (satisfied democrats)	Strong support for the principles of democracy but weak support for its practice (dissatisfied democrats)
Democracy notion	Input-oriented notions of democracy as a means of voice and participation mix with output-oriented notions of democracy as a tool of delivering social goods	Input-oriented notions of democracy as a means of voice and participation become clearly dominant
Political activism	Voting and other conventional forms of legitimacy-granting activity	Strong affinity to nonviolent, elite-challenging activity
Expected systemic consequences	More effective and accountable governance?	

Note: For an operationalization of allegiant and assertive citizens, see Table 12.1 (p. 293).

culture approach and a new sense of the potential for democracy to advance in the world today.

STUDYING VALUES AROUND THE GLOBE

The WVS emerged from the European Values Study (EVS), which in turn has its roots in the Eurobarometer surveys. In contrast to the Eurobarometer and other regional barometers, the WVS/EVS surveys are interested in deep-seated preferences, expectations, and beliefs of the people, not in short-term public opinion topics. The guiding perspective of the value surveys is threefold. One objective is to identify patterns of values that are useful for cross-cultural comparison

TABLE 1.2. *The Five Waves of the World Values Survey*

Regions	Wave 1, 1981–84	Wave 2, 1989–93	Wave 3, 1994–99	Wave 4, 1999–2004	Wave 5, 2005–8
Western democracies	16	18	10	20	15
East Europe/ Post-USSR	1	11	23	21	17
East/South Asia	2	3	6	8	10
Middle East/North Africa	–	1	1	9	6
Sub-Saharan Africa	–	2	2	5	7
Latin America	2	4	10	4	9
Total number of nations	21	39	52	67	62
Total number of respondents	26,511	62,771	77,114	100,052	81,474

and that group societies into distinctive culture zones. Another objective is to determine whether these cultural patterns relate to the institutional forms and the socioeconomic conditions of a society: Is there systematic evidence for a psychological dimension of development and democracy? Another objective focuses on cultural change: Is there evidence for a transformation in human values, and are these changes operating in the same direction under the imprint of similar socioeconomic transformations?

Inspired by these objectives, the WVS/EVS surveys followed three priorities: (1) only ask questions about things that are fundamental to the lives of people in *every* society, whether rich or poor, democratic or autocratic, Western or non-Western; (2) repeat the surveys every five to ten years to build a time series that allows one to trace change in values; and (3) expand the scope of comparison so that it spans all culture zones of the globe to test general theories of mass behavior. The latter point reflects a unique feature of the WVS.

The EVS started with a first round in 1981–83 and included more than a dozen European countries. Additional efforts that then established the WVS added Japan, South Korea, Argentina, Mexico, Australia, the US and Canada. Interestingly, the first round also included two communist samples: a national Hungarian sample and a sample from the Russian oblast "Tambov."

The second round of the WVS was conducted from 1989 to 1991 in some forty societies (see Table 1.2). This round expanded especially into the transforming ex-communist world. In many countries, like the former German Democratic Republic, the survey was done before the political transition was finalized, providing a valuable snapshot of public mood during the transition period. This round of the WVS also expanded to China, India, Chile, Brazil, Nigeria, South Africa, and Turkey.

The third round of the WVS spanned from 1995 to 1997. It included some fifty societies. Thanks to efforts by Hans-Dieter Klingemann, the project had extensive coverage of postcommunist countries in this round. In addition, Columbia, El Salvador, Venezuela, Uruguay, Bangladesh, Pakistan, and Taiwan were surveyed for the first time.

The fourth round, from 1999 to 2001, covered almost sixty societies. The project placed particular emphasis on covering Islamic societies: Algeria, Egypt, Iran, Iraq, Jordan, Morocco, and Saudi Arabia were surveyed for the first time. The WVS also extended the list of surveyed countries in sub-Saharan Africa: Uganda, Zambia, and Zimbabwe. In Asia, the WVS included Indonesia, the Philippines, Singapore, and Vietnam for the first time.

The fifth and most recent round of the WVS was conducted between 2005 and 2008 in some fifty societies. The survey was extended into francophone sub-Saharan Africa, covering Burkina Faso, Cameroon, and Mali, as well as into Ethiopia and Rwanda. In Asia, the WVS included Hong Kong, Malaysia, and Thailand for the first time. The fifth round also revised a considerable portion of the questionnaire: new questions developed by Christian Welzel to measure in-group and out-group trust, meanings of democracy, social identity, citizenship ideals, and media usage were added.[6]

In terms of spatial and temporal scope, the WVS is a unique data source. The survey has included more than ninety societies that represent more than 90 percent of the world population. Counting repeated surveys in the same nations, about 250 country-by-year units are available. About sixty societies have been surveyed at least twice; for about forty-five societies, the WVS provides longitudinal evidence of at least ten years. For another dozen societies, the time series covers the entire period from 1981 to 2006, spanning fully twenty-five years.

The WVS covers topics that are of inherent interest from the civic culture perspective: regime preferences, support for democracy, trust in institutions, social trust, law abidingness, political interest, media usage, voluntary activity, protest participation, authority orientations, liberty aspirations, social tolerance and so on. It is the only international survey that has such basic measures of human values across countries spanning all the regions of the globe.

With this thematic breadth and its spatial and temporal scope, the WVS is clearly the ideal data source to examine the various facets of the civicness question outlined earlier. Hence, the chapters in this book are unified by both their interest in the civicness question and their usage of WVS data as a common source.[7] In that sense, this book is a tribute to the WVS and its founding father, Ronald Inglehart.

---

[6] At the time of this writing, the World Values Survey was about to finish its sixth wave of surveys in more than sixty societies around the globe. The initial release of the sixth wave data was in April 2014: www.worldvaluessurvey.org.

[7] Unless indicated otherwise, the analyses throughout the chapters of this book use WVS data in unweighted form. The experience shows that weighted results usually do not differ significantly. Because the calibration weights provided with past official data releases are not documented equally well for all countries, it seems preferable not to use these weights in the type of large-scale cross-national analyses that the chapters of this volume perform.

PLAN OF THE BOOK

As the WVS has expanded over time, a large number of international scholars have become part of this research project. We have assembled a distinguished subset of these scholars to examine the topics of political culture, global value change, and democratic politics.

The book is organized into three thematic sections. The first section concentrates on the broad process of value change that fuels the transition from allegiant to assertive citizenship. Postmaterialist value change in Western democracies was the foundation for challenging the allegiant model of *The Civic Culture* and led to the broad theory of emancipatory cultural change. Thus, Paul R. Abramson first examines the postmaterialist trend in Western democracies. He tracks the evolution of postmaterialist values across generations spanning forty years of surveys. He also shows how the generational patterns persist across the life cycle of consecutive birth cohorts. The results demonstrate that generational turnover has been a driving force in postmaterialist value change.

Neil Nevitte uses the multiple waves of the WVS to track the decline of deferential orientations in various social domains. The traditional political culture model implies that deference to legitimate authority is a key element of an allegiant culture (Almond and Verba 1963, Chapters 9–12; Eckstein 1966). Thus, the erosion of deference is part of the transition toward a more assertive and elite-challenging citizenry.

Christian Welzel and Alejandro Moreno Alvarez analyze a new set of questions on people's views of democracy. They find that rising emancipative values change the nature of people's desire for democracy in a twofold way: Emancipative values increase (1) the liberalness of people's notion of democracy and (2) the criticalness of their assessment of democracy. Emancipative values make people's democratic desires more liberal and critical in all culture zones and across different social traits and political regimes, which the authors characterize as an "enlightenment" effect.

The second section of this volume identifies some key features that describe the rise of an assertive citizenship. Russell J. Dalton and Doh Chull Shin document the limited applicability of the allegiant model to citizens in established democracies and in developing nations. Support for a democratic regime is widespread across the globe, yet public skepticism of political institutions is also widespread. It is especially striking in many established democracies that were once the bastion of allegiant citizens but now have politically skeptical publics. The authors offer evidence that contemporary democratization stimulates a more critical citizenry.

Hans-Dieter Klingemann then focuses on the new category of dissatisfied democrats in European societies, describing their increase as a consequence of the changing values of contemporary publics. He reflects on the implications of these new assertive citizens for our traditional models of a democratic political culture.

Finally, Christian W. Haerpfer and Kseniya Kizilova describe patterns and change in political support in postcommunist Europe and post-Soviet Eurasia. They find a stronger presence of allegiant orientations in the countries with the largest deficiencies in democracy. By contrast, the countries with the least democratic deficits show a stronger presence of assertive orientations – in line with the theme of this book.

The third section of this book asks how changing values of contemporary publics are affecting more specific political attitudes and behaviors. Robert Rohrschneider, Matt Miles, and Mark Peffley study the relationship between social modernization, values, and environmental attitudes. They find that post-materialist values in developed societies connect current environmental attitudes in these nations to a broader criticism of modes of economic production. The result is a more politicized environmental movement, even when environmental conditions are improving.

Tor Georg Jakobsen and Ola Listhaug analyze the evolution of protest activity from 1981 to 2007. They find that citizens' use of elite-challenging behavior increases with economic development and is especially common among younger generations and postmaterialist citizens.

Pippa Norris studies differences in gender attitudes between Muslim and non-Muslim states. In contrast to those who argue that oil resources entrench the patriarchy of traditional societies, she argues that cultural values leave a deep imprint on the way people see the most appropriate roles for men and women in society – including the contemporary role of women in elected office.

Finally, Bi Puranen examines people's willingness to fight for their country in the case of war, which is a key element of allegiant orientations.[8] She finds that confidence in the armed forces and authoritarian regime preferences – which are in decline in many places – explain people's willingness to fight. This finding suggests that willingness to fight is in decline as well, indicating the erosion of allegiance in one of its core domains.

The conclusion by Welzel and Dalton evaluates the *Civic Culture*'s theoretical framework in light of the findings presented in this book. The previous chapters document the transition from an allegiant to an assertive type of democratic citizen. The conclusion then extends these micro-level analyses to examine the impact of political culture at the aggregate cross-national level. This analysis puts the central assumption of a culture-governance congruence to a direct test. Specifically, the chapter examines the relationship between allegiant and assertive values with governmental capacity and democratic accountability. It finds that allegiant values do not associate with either capacity or accountability, whereas assertive values display strong positive relationships with both. These results suggest that a new style of democratic

---

[8] We, together with Bi Puranen, wish to acknowledge Juan Díez-Nicolás and to thank him for his very valuable contribution to earlier versions of this chapter.

politics is expanding, which should produce a more participatory and more citizen-centered democratic process.

THE *CIVIC CULTURE*'S LEGACY

Almond and Verba's *The Civic Culture* is a major landmark in the study of citizens' relationship with their government. In trying to look back at the failures of democracy in the past, it proscribed a model of citizen values that fit that history. Our book's basic argument is that history has changed and, with it, the values of citizens in contemporary democracies – shaping a new relationship between citizens and their government. The reader will see the evidence in the pages that follow.

At the same time, the legacy of *The Civic Culture* is enduring. As Sidney Verba (2011) has recently written, the lasting impact of the Almond and Verba study is to create a fruitful field of political culture research in which others contribute and continue to expand the research crop. As Verba states, "*The Civic Culture* was fruitful. Its substantive and technical approach was such that it could be improved on, and it has been" (Verba 2011, iv). Thus, we see this book as contributing to the bounty that *The Civic Culture* first sowed more than five decades ago.

PART A

CHANGING VALUES

2

Value Change over a Third of a Century

The Evidence for Generational Replacement[1]

Paul R. Abramson

Four decades ago, Ronald Inglehart (1971) reported that younger Europeans held substantially different values than did their elders. Whereas older Europeans tended to value material security and domestic order, younger Europeans were more likely to value political liberties. Inglehart labeled these priorities as "acquisitive" and "postbourgeois," but he subsequently used the terms "materialist" and "postmaterialist" (Inglehart 1977). This framework of value change subsequently had a major impact in reshaping our understanding of citizenship and political culture in advanced industrial democracies and is a foundation for the transition for allegiant to assertive values that is the primary theme of this book.

Many scholars view Inglehart's prediction as a major insight. On the back of one of his most cited books, *Culture Shift*, Gabriel Almond (1990) argued, "Inglehart's work is one of the few examples of successful prediction in political science."[2] The authors of the five-volume *Beliefs in Government* study found overwhelming evidence of a shift toward postmaterialism, away from religious values, and toward a redefinition of the Left-Right continuum. Elinor Scarbrough (1995, 156), who analyzed materialist-postmaterialist orientations, concluded, "indisputably, across much of Western Europe, value orientations are shifting." General editors Max Kaase and Kenneth Newton (1995, 61) summed up the findings: "We find substantial support for the model which traces social changes to value changes, and value changes into political attitudes and behavior, especially through the process of generational replacement." And Russell Dalton (2014, 89) concluded that in recent decades, researchers have

---

[1] I am grateful to Russell Dalton, Ronald Inglehart, Ellen Mickiewicz, Ani Sarkissian, Brian Silver, and Christian Welzel for their comments and to Inglehart for providing Figure 2.1.
[2] According to Google Scholar, as of May 29, 2014, there were 6,612 citations to Inglehart (1990).

advanced theories to explain how values are changing but argued that Inglehart's research has been the most influential.[3]

Although Inglehart had surveys in Britain, France, West Germany, Italy, the Netherlands, and Belgium only for 1970, he speculated that age-group differences probably resulted from differences in the formative socialization of younger and older Europeans. He acknowledged that they might also result partly from the higher educational levels of the young.[4] In fact, regardless of whether age-group differences resulted from formative socialization, or from educational differences, one would predict a long-term trend toward postmaterialism. Even if economic conditions did not remain rosy after 1971, it seemed highly unlikely that Europeans born after World War II would suffer the deprivations experienced by those who grew up before or during the war or in its immediate aftermath. And there were strong reasons to expect them to have higher levels of education than their prewar counterparts.

If there has been a shift toward postmaterialism, it can have a major impact in transforming the politics and culture of advanced industrial societies. The growth of postmaterialism has eroded the traditional bases of party alignments by contributing to a decline in class voting (Dalton, Flanagan, and Beck 1984; Inglehart 1997; Lipset 1981), a shift away from religious values (Scarborough 1995), and a redefinition of the Left-Right continuum. Dalton (2014, 99–101) argued that the shift toward postmaterialism has five major consequences: It fuels demands for more flexible work environments; it leads to a declining deference toward authority; it leads to less restrictive attitudes toward sex-related issues; it leads to support for new social issues such as environmentalism and gender equality; and it stimulates direct political participation in decision making. I have examined Dalton's claims by studying relationships between using both the four-item and twelve-item measures of postmaterialism in the 2006 World Values Survey and by using the data for the United States, Britain, France, West Germany, and the former East Germany (Abramson 2010). There are substantial cross-sectional relationships to support all five of the relationships Dalton postulated.

---

[3] For Inglehart's most recent discussion of the importance of the shift toward postmaterialism, see Inglehart and Welzel (2005). They view the rise of postmaterialism as "part of a much broader cultural shift that brings increasingly strong demands for democracy (where it does not exist) and for more-responsive democracy (where it does exist)" (104). They also write, "Both the shift toward postmaterialism and the rise of elite-challenging political action are components of a broader shift toward self-expression values that is reshaping orientations toward authority, politics, gender roles, and sexual norms among publics of postindustrial societies" (126). However, whereas we have data about postmaterialist values for thirty-six years, we do not have adequate data to examine the effects of replacement on most of these other value orientations.

[4] The items and procedures used to construct Inglehart's measures have been widely reported, although the procedures used to construct the twelve-item measure have varied over time. For the clearest statement of how these measures are constructed, including the SPSS syntax statements used to create them, see Inglehart (1997, 389).

There has been a great deal of controversy about Inglehart's thesis. Some scholars have questioned the dimensionality of his basic measures, others have questioned their validity, and yet others have questioned whether Inglehart measures the most important dimensions of postwar attitude change. In earlier work, I provide an extensive summary of these controversies (Abramson 2011).

This chapter discusses controversies about the impact of generational replacement and provides additional evidence about its impact. It summarizes some important insights by Dalton on the socialization process and then turns to the evidence published about the impact of replacement between 1970 and 1992. I then discuss W. Phillips Shively's reservations about the meaning of age-group differences and evaluate several critiques by Clarke and his colleagues arguing that the shift observed by Inglehart results from his failure to include fighting unemployment as a goal. I then consider Raymond Duch and Michaell Taylor's argument that cohort differences mainly reflect differences in educational levels among older and younger Europeans. Last, I present new evidence on the impact of replacement, examining value change between 1970 and 2006.

THE AGE OF FORMATIVE SOCIALIZATION

Dalton's (1977) article contributed to our understanding of generational replacement by estimating when formative socialization occurs. He used 1973 survey data from France, Belgium, the Netherlands, Germany, Italy, Denmark, and Great Britain. He showed the relationship between age and values in all seven countries, noting that it is highest in Germany, while it is low in Britain and actually negative in Belgium. Using data on the gross domestic products (GDPs) of these countries beginning in 1913, he modeled the impact of generation, education, life cycle, and income. He concluded that economic conditions at age ten are the most significant.

In my view, Dalton fails to consider that many of these respondents lived through World War I and that most experienced World War II. One basic difference among these countries is that Denmark and the Netherlands were neutral during World War I, and in World War II, Denmark suffered a less draconian occupation than the other West European countries conquered by the Germans. Granted none of these countries suffered as badly as the countries Germany captured in the East, especially Poland and parts of the Soviet Union (Mazower 2008; Snyder 2010), but they had dramatically different experiences, with the Germans brutally treating Italians in German-occupied Italy after Italy surrendered to the Allies. Only Britain avoided occupation. A better analysis would include the effects of war rather than GDP alone. Nonetheless, Dalton performs a clear analysis, and Raymond Duch and Michael Taylor (1993, 758) confirm his finding that the most important socialization experiences occur at about ten years of age.

On one point Dalton was prescient. He correctly argued that the term *revolution* was too strong; furthermore, he argued (Dalton 1977, 470) that support for postmaterialist values would grow at a slower rate than Inglehart predicted. As we see later, in the 2006 World Values Survey, there are virtually no differences in levels of postmaterialism among the four youngest cohorts in our weighted sample of the European public (see Figure 2.1).[5]

GENERATIONAL REPLACEMENT AND VALUE CHANGE, 1970–1992

Between 1970 and 1979, there was little movement toward postmaterialism. According to Inglehart (1981), there was a substantial shift toward postmaterialism in Britain and small shifts in West Germany, France, and the Netherlands. In Italy, there was a substantial shift toward materialist values, and in Belgium, there was no change. Inglehart also presented data from the American National Election Studies surveys conducted in 1972, 1976, and 1980. Overall value scores were identical in 1972 and 1980.[6]

Inglehart argued that the failure of the European public to move toward postmaterialism resulted from period effects caused by adverse economic conditions during the 1970s – global recessions stimulated by oil price increases in 1974 and 1979. In retrospect, the shift toward postmaterialism in Britain was larger than his theory predicts, whereas the small shifts in Germany, France, and the Netherlands were about the order of magnitude that one might predict given the slow rates of generational replacement in modern industrial societies (at least during periods of peace). Inglehart (1981, 890) wrote, "The economic and physical uncertainty of the 1970s produced a significant period effect. The net movement toward Post-Materialism that should have been expected from population replacement slowed to a crawl. By the decade's end, the 15–24 year old group was significantly less Post-Materialist than their counterparts a decade earlier had been."

By 1982, all six countries had clearly moved to postmaterialism. In addition, Denmark, which along with Ireland had been added to the time series in 1973, clearly showed a shift toward postmaterialism. Ireland failed to show any movement toward postmaterialism. In the United States, where postmaterialism was measured by the American National Election Studies (ANES surveys), postmaterialism was markedly higher in 1984 than in 1972.

[5] For similar figures, but without the overall level of postmaterialism superimposed, see Dalton (2014, 98) and Inglehart (2008, 135). Dalton updates his results through 2008 and shows a decline in postmaterialism among all cohorts between 2005 and 2008. In a personal communication (October 28, 2013), Inglehart sent me the cohort results as well as overall PDI scores between 1970 and 2008. Overall levels of postmaterialism changed very little between 2006 and 2008, although there was a slight decline in PDI scores among most cohorts.

[6] As I am using Inglehart's four-item index, my measure is the PDI computed by subtracting the percentage of materialists from the percentage of postmaterialists.

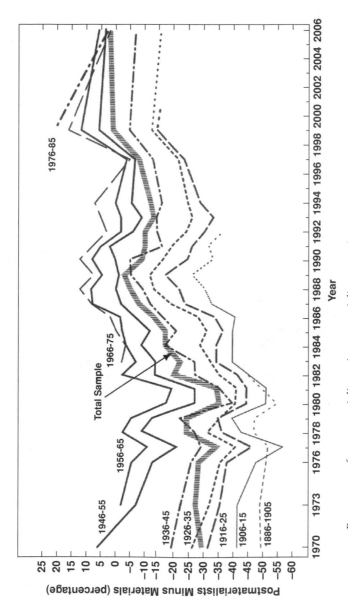

FIGURE 2.1. Percentage of postmaterialists minus materialists over time.
Source: The results from 1970–71 through 1997 are from surveys sponsored by the European Community. Results from 1999 and 2006 are based on the World Values Survey. Figure is based upon a weighted sample of Britain, France, West Germany, Italy, the Netherlands, and Belgium.

At this stage Inglehart and I demonstrated the impact of replacement in contributing to the long-term trend.[7] It was obvious that short-term period effects also affected levels of postmaterialism. However, relying on an algebraic standardization method I developed (Abramson 1983), we compared the observed level of postmaterialism with our estimate of what levels would have been if no new cohorts had entered the adult population and if the cohorts that had died out of the adult population had been immortalized. The problem with this method is that one has to assign an arbitrary value to cohorts that cannot actually be sampled. In my example in *Political Attitudes in America* (Abramson 1983, 56–61), I demonstrated that overall educational levels of the U.S. electorate would have changed very little between 1956 and 1980 if cohorts born after 1935 had been disfranchised and if older cohorts had not diminished through death. But we know that very few Americans raise their level of formal education once they reach adulthood. Making assumptions about political attitudes and values of missing cohorts is problematic.

Even so, Inglehart and I published a series of articles and books using these algebraic standardization procedures (Abramson and Inglehart 1986; Inglehart 1990, 99–100; Abramson and Inglehart 1992; Abramson and Inglehart 1995, 41–73), along with articles and books that projected future levels of replacement based on estimates of future demographic change (Abramson and Inglehart 1987; Inglehart 1990, 101–2; Abramson and Inglehart 1992; Abramson and Inglehart 1995, 89–96).

Abramson and Inglehart (1995, 46–53) presented the Percentage Difference Index (PDI) scores for postmaterialist values among cohorts for West Germany, Britain, the Netherlands, France, Belgium, and Italy between 1970 and 1992 and for Denmark and Ireland between 1973 and 1992. We discussed the possible impact of replacement on value trends, drawing on Abramson (1983). We then estimated the effects of replacement for all eight societies as well as for a combined weighted sample of the six countries sampled between 1970 and 1992. In 1970, only 11 percent of the West European population were postmaterialists, whereas 40 percent were materialists, with a PDI score of −29. In 1992, 16 percent were postmaterialists and only 26 percent were materialists, with a PDI score of −10. During these two decades, there was a nineteen-point shift toward postmaterialism. In the 1992 samples, 42 percent

---

[7] Men have long recognized the possibility that generational replacement could transform society. This is most elegantly argued in Numbers 14. When the Children of Israel accept the ill report of the scouts who warn against invading Canaan, they are told they must spend an additional thirty-eight years in the desert, for a total of forty years. "In this wilderness your corpses will fall... And your little ones, of whom you said they would become booty, I shall bring them and they will know the land that you cast aside" (Numbers 14:28,31). For a discussion, see Abramson (2012, 34–35).

of the respondents were too young to have been sampled in 1970, and some had not even been born.[8]

According to our estimates, if there had been no generational replacement, postmaterialism would have increased only two points between 1970 and 1992. In other words, only about one-tenth of the shift toward postmaterialism would have occurred without replacement. Generational replacement was the major long-term force contributing to postmaterialism. These results also corresponded with multivariate analyses (Abramson and Inglehart 1995, 35–37; Inglehart and Abramson 1994; Abramson, Ellis, and Inglehart 1997) showing that when inflation and unemployment were controlled, PDI scores increased about one point per year, very close to the rate Inglehart's model predicts.

SHIVELY'S CRITIQUE OF THE GENERATIONAL REPLACEMENT THESIS

In his "feature review" of Inglehart (1990), W. Phillips Shively (1991, 235) acknowledged, "This book must be read by anyone interested in advanced industrial societies." But Shively (1991, 236–37) disagreed with Inglehart's discussion of rational choice theory and, more importantly, argued, "The cohort analyses by which he seeks to establish that value change is generational is fundamentally flawed" (237). Inglehart, Shively (1991, 237) noted, acknowledged that one cannot definitively differentiate among generational, life-cycle, and period effects, because when studying a person's age, date of birth, and year of the survey, each of them is a perfect function of the other two. According to Shively, Inglehart (1990, 73) argued that a belief in such an aging effect for differences among cohorts "must depend upon faith alone." Shively (1991, 237) also wrote that Inglehart failed to realize that "assertion of generational effects is similarly a matter of pure faith."

Inglehart and I (Abramson and Inglehart 1995) disagreed with Shively. We acknowledged that Shively "is perfectly correct when he argues that the failure of cohorts to become more Materialist as they age could result from short-term period effects that prevented Materialism from emerging" (55). But, we continued, "Although the life-cycle interpretation cannot be rejected definitively, the life-cycle and generational explanations for age-group differences are not equally plausible. In order to sustain a life-cycle explanation, one would need to specify exactly *what* short-term forces prevented Materialism from emerging."[9]

---

[8] We checked our survey results against demographic data, which showed that 42 percent of European adults in these societies were born before 1956 (see Abramson and Inglehart 1995, 158).

[9] See Glenn (2005) for a summary of developments in cohort analysis.

ECONOMICS AND THE MEASUREMENT OF VALUES

Harold D. Clarke and his colleagues argued that short-term forces contributed to a misleading trend toward postmaterialism. His basic argument, which pervades all his critiques, is that Inglehart's measure of materialism-postmaterialism does not take national unemployment levels into account. One of the four goals in Inglehart's four-choice measure is "fighting rising prices." But Clarke and Nitish Dutt (1991) argue that the respondent faces a dilemma if he or she is concerned about unemployment. As unemployment is not one of the options in the values battery, they argue, respondents are likely to choose the "giving the people more say in important government decisions." They argue that this is likely because, during the 1980s, conservative parties governed many West European societies.

I have always thought that this argument was, as the Marquis of Salisbury said about Disraeli's amendment on Disestablishment (March 30, 1868), "too clever by half." But Clarke and Dutt did not rely on clever arguments alone but on their analysis of data from the European Community Studies and the Eurobarometer studies conducted between 1976 and 1986. Using pooled cross-sectional time series data, they studied change in Belgium, Denmark, France, Ireland, Italy, the Netherlands, and West Germany and provided a more detailed study of Britain. They also conducted a confirmatory factor analysis of data from the Netherlands, West Germany, and the United States. They concluded (Clarke and Dutt 1991, 918) that "the four-item battery regularly included in Euro-Barometer surveys to measure public value priorities does not show a significant trend in the direction of postmaterialist values in a number of Western European nations." Moreover, the measure is very sensitive to short-term economic conditions that alter the public political issue agenda. The nature of this sensitivity is such that sharp increases in unemployment in the early 1980s make it appear, based on the four-item measure, that there was a substantial shift toward postmaterialism. Pooled cross-sectional time series analyses indicate that the failure to include an unemployment statement in the measure does much to account for the apparent postmaterialist trend.

Inglehart and I (Abramson and Inglehart 1994; Abramson and Inglehart 1995) quickly replied. We clearly showed that the long-term trend toward postmaterialism was driven by generational replacement. We showed that there was a trend toward postmaterialism in all eight countries except Belgium. Moreover, there was substantial evidence that the trend resulted from replacement. We presented a figure showing changes in overall scores on the PDI between 1970 and 1992 for a weighted sample for West Germany, France, Britain, Italy, the Netherlands, and Belgium. Except for the oldest cohort (which cannot be tracked over this two-decade period), the cohorts all displayed a modest movement toward postmaterialism. We also superimposed the overall trend line for these societies. The overall trend toward postmaterialism is greater than the increase for any of the cohorts. This is because, during this period, the cohort composition of the European population changed as the result of generational replacement. Older cohorts with heavily materialist values were dying out of the population and were replaced by cohorts who grew up during periods of greater security. We employed least squares regression analysis to demonstrate that, during the two decades between 1970 and 1992, inflation depressed postmaterialism, whereas unemployment had no effect. Moreover, we showed that in 1970, Inglehart asked respondents about "job security" as an overall goal, and in 1973, he asked respondents their occupational goals, one of which included "a safe job." In neither case were these goals related to postmaterialist values.

As in Inglehart and Abramson (1994), we also presented results from forty nations showing that in any society in which there has been substantial economic growth, there is a tendency of the young to have more postmaterialist values than their elders. This relationship tends to be greater in societies with the largest level of growth (see also Abramson and Inglehart 1995, 130–34). The evidence was presented more thoroughly in Inglehart (1997, 131–59), although this evidence is not directly related to the controversy with Clarke and his colleagues.

Clarke, Dutt, and Rapkin (1997a) replied to our response by arguing that there were gaps in our time series between 1970 and 1976 and that the wording of the preamble to the values choices in the surveys conducted before 1976 differed from that used from 1976 onward. Thus, they questioned any time series analyses that merge the 1970 through 1992 period. But they are mainly concerned with the problem of unemployment. They conduct a time series analysis based only on the years between 1976 and 1992 and concluded that respondents shun the "fighting rising prices" option when there are high levels of unemployment. They constructed an economic priority model by subtracting the inflation rate from the unemployment rate and an economic security index, which they note is commonly known as a "misery index," by adding unemployment and inflation rates.[10] They tested both models through pooled regression techniques and concluded that whereas the economic priority measure predicted levels of postmaterialism, the economic security index did not (Clarke, Dutt, and Rapkin 1997a, 30–31). Referring to Paul Sniderman, Richard Brody, and Philip Tetlock (1991) and Sniderman and Thomas Piazza (1993), they stressed the promise of quasi-experimental designs. Interviews are "conversations in context," and one must be aware of the context in which they are held. In the case of Inglehart's measure, when unemployment is high,

---

[10] The illogic of the index is readily apparent. Would the public be more "miserable" if unemployment were at 5 percent and inflation at 5 percent (a "misery index" of 10) than if unemployment were 20 percent and inflation at −10 percent (also a "misery index" of 10). Despite his undergraduate training in economics at Eureka College, Ronald Reagan used this index in 1980 to point out that the misery index was higher in 1980 than in 1976.

respondents are pushed to choose "giving the people more say," because the option of fighting unemployment is unavailable.

As Abramson, Ellis, and Inglehart (1997) pointed out, differences between the Clarke and colleagues results and Inglehart's do not result from the slightly different time series employed or from the different question introduction in 1970 and 1973.[11] Using the same truncated (1976 through 1992) time frame employed by Clarke and his colleagues, they perform estimates for each country using three pooled estimators. They conclude that there is "a significant inverse relationship between inflation and postmaterialism and a significant negative relationship between unemployment and postmaterialism." Abramson and his colleagues also introduce a time trend as a proxy for generational replacement. They show that a trend for time, which Clarke and his colleagues omit, is necessary to properly specify the model because that trend is a proxy for generational replacement. Moreover, while they agreed with Clarke and his colleagues, and with Sniderman, that researchers should consider the questions they do not ask as well as those they do, they reminded readers that a survey is only loosely analogous to a conversation.

Clarke, Dutt, and Rapkin (1997b) argued that more innovative measurement is necessary. Political psychologists do interesting methodological and theoretical work, whereas comparativists pay little attention to this work in political psychology. Major surveys, in particular, face inertia in attempting to innovate. Moreover, they maintain that structural equation models (SEM) could be helpful to test alternative theories about change. However, "the Euro-Barometer values battery with its meager four-choice item and forced-choice format is an unfortunately excellent example of a set of measures that do not lend themselves easily to SEM analysis" (63).

Clarke and his colleagues (1999) continued their critique by conducting a mail survey in Canada in 1995, in-person interviews of West Germans in 1996 and 1997, and East Germans in 1996 and 1997. In both West and East Germany, respondents were asked different versions of the values battery, one of which included "fighting rising prices," whereas the other included "creating more jobs."

In Canada, postmaterialism was higher when measured with the "inflation" question, presumably because Canadians who were not concerned with this goal could not score as materialists. However, the argument that high levels of unemployment produced a demand for giving the "people more say" is dropped from their thesis. Clarke and his colleagues also performed a multinomial logit analysis to argue that values are affected by economic conditions. Likewise, a multinomial logit analysis was conducted for both parts of Germany with the 1997 sample. "These results," they wrote (Clarke et al. 1999, 645), "reinforce

---

[11] As Ostrom (1990) points out, ideally, time series analyses should employ equally spaced intervals: Minor violations of this requirement do not yield biased estimates as long as there is no substantial variability in the variables being employed.

the conclusion that the measured percentages of materialists and postmaterialists, and the net balance of these groups, are powerfully affected by the interaction among the structure and content of the Euro-Barometer values battery, respondents' issue priorities, and the broader economic context that obtains when these batteries are administered."

But as we argued (Inglehart and Abramson 1999, 673), "a basic principle in social science research is that time-series evidence is required in order to demonstrate or refute hypotheses about change." Clarke and his colleagues attempted to make inferences about change in surveys conducted in 1996 in Canada and 1996 and 1997 in Germany. They found that when they changed the values measure, they obtained different results, and they "present this as proof that the original battery is flawed and invalid" (673). We reported that when Inglehart originally developed his measures, he included a question about job security. On the basis of the relationships in his first values survey, he concluded that giving a high priority to reducing unemployment was not a good measure of values. As we wrote (Inglehart and Abramson 1999, 674), "on balance, the unemployment item tends to tap materialist concerns, as one would expect, but it is also something of a catchall that draws support from different groups for different reasons. Therefore, it was an ambivalent measure of values, which is why it was not included when we developed the twelve-item battery."

We also pointed out that the Clarke et al. experiment has another built-in experiment they chose not to discuss. Because it includes a sample of the original Federal Republic of Germany as well as of the newly formed states of the former German Democratic Republic, we can compare values in each. Granted, these countries have had substantially different experiences since the downfall of Hitler, from the trauma of the Russian invasion of the East and the authoritarian rule of a police state. But they have another difference as well. As of April 1997, unemployment in the West was 8.4 percent, whereas the official unemployment rate in East Germany was 19 percent and, for several years, was about twice as high in East Germany as in West Germany.

If unemployment contributed to postmaterialist values, we would expect postmaterialism to be higher in East Germany than in West Germany. The data from Clarke et al. show that, averaged across all three of their surveys, 29 percent were materialists in the West, 55 percent had mixed values, and 16 percent were postmaterialists; in East Germany, 34 percent were materialists, 57 percent were classified as mixed, and only 9 percent were postmaterialists.

Clarke (2000) now maintains that the Inglehart values measure is so flawed that it should be abandoned. But, he acknowledges, this is unlikely, because scientific enterprises have a great deal of inertia. Regardless of the evidence, he writes, "proponents of the 'silent revolution' very likely will continue to proclaim the virtues of the E-B [Eurobarometer] values battery and the wide-ranging explanatory power of materialist to postmaterialist values shift, regardless of what the empirical evidence shows" (492). He concludes, "In this regard, the values shift research program, as currently constituted, risks assuming the characteristics of a religious movement, with acolytes in all corners of the globe working under the auspices of the World Values project to gather data *in support of* an inviolable theory" (492). If Inglehart predeceases me, I will do my best to hurry to his grave site to see what happens on the third day.

THE DEBATE OVER EDUCATION

Duch and Taylor (1993) argue that education is the main factor affecting levels of postmaterialism and that early socialization experiences have little impact. They employ the Eurobarometer surveys conducted in France, Belgium, the Netherlands, Germany, Italy, Denmark, Germany, Italy, and Great Britain between 1973 and 1984. They also include gross national product per capita and urbanization. Their dependent variable is Inglehart's four-item values index.

On the basis of a multivariate analysis, they concluded there is no support for Inglehart's thesis that economic conditions during the respondents' youth have affected their values. Second, they maintained that inflation rates when the survey is conducted greatly affect values. Lastly, they argued (Duch and Taylor 2003, 764) that "education . . . is an overwhelmingly important factor for how respondents rank these four items." They also concluded that as people age, they are less likely to favor postmaterialist items.

Inglehart and I were not persuaded. We pointed out that Duch and Taylor had excluded respondents born before World War II (Abramson and Inglehart 1994). Although they argued this exclusion was necessary because they lacked reliable economic data for earlier periods, this decision drastically truncated variance and excluded the very cohorts that had suffered the greatest deprivation. We maintained that levels of education are best viewed as a proxy for economic security during the respondents' youth. We argued that education does not necessarily contribute to either postmaterialism or to democratic values. We presented the percentage of materialists and postmaterialists for eight European Union countries from 1980 through 1989, showing the results by cohort and level of education. We found a consistent tendency for Europeans with higher levels of education to be less likely to be materialists and more likely to be postmaterialists than those with lower levels of education. In fact, those relationships were even found among the cohorts that were educated in Germany during the Third Reich (the 1916–25 cohort) and educated in Italy under fascism (the 1906–15 and 1916–25 cohorts). Obviously, these relationships did not occur because the German educational system under Hitler or the Italian educational system under Mussolini promoted democratic values. We argued (Abramson and Inglehart 1994, 804), "It seems far more likely that these relationships are found at least partly because Germans and Italians who attained higher educational levels came from more secure social backgrounds." Moreover, we used the 1990–91 World Values Survey to show that, in comparison with West European societies, all six samples from the former Soviet Union had relatively low levels of postmaterialism. Four of the five East European states for which we had data had lower levels of postmaterialism than the richer advanced industrial democracies, with the former East Germany being the only exception (Abramson and Inglehart 1994).

Duch and Taylor (1994) repeated their analyses, adding the older cohorts, and maintained that doing so had little effect on their results. But their basic criticism is that we fail to present multivariate analyses that confirm Inglehart's thesis (Abramson and Inglehart 1994, 823). Abramson and Inglehart (1995) added new evidence. We noted that few surveys provide social background data about respondents when they were growing up and acknowledged that such reports are suspect. But both the five-nation survey (the Netherlands, Britain, the United States, Germany, and Austria) carried out by the European Community Action Survey in 1971 and the *Political Action* survey carried out by Barnes and Kaase and their colleagues in 1974 (Barnes et al. 1979) asked respondents about their fathers' occupation and income when they were growing up. They were also asked standard questions about their own occupation in both surveys. In both surveys, fathers' socioeconomic status (SES) was somewhat more strongly correlated with values than the respondents' own SES.

Regarding the thesis that generational change drives the trend toward postmaterialism, the Duch and Taylor thesis may be consistent with ours. If education does contribute to democratic values, we would still expect postmaterialism to increase if only because educational levels are likely to increase, mainly as a result of replacement.

EVIDENCE ON GENERATIONAL REPLACEMENT FROM 1970 THROUGH 2006

As Inglehart (1971) predicted four decades ago, generational replacement was a major force driving the trend toward postmaterialism. Up to now, I have mainly discussed evidence through 1992. Figure 2.1 shows PDI scores from 1970 to 2006 for a weighted combined sample of Britain, France, West Germany, Italy, the Netherlands, and Belgium. The figure presents the results according to birth cohorts between 1970 and 2006. The thick trend line superimposes the overall level of postmaterialism for the entire population in each year.[12]

---

[12] Dalton (2013, 98) presents a similar figure, without the superimposed trend line, and reports it is based on 400,000 respondents. For the size of each sample between 1970 through 1992, as well as the percentages that allow readers to estimate the size of each cohort, see Abramson and Inglehart (1995, 158–59). Dalton's figure shows a decline in postmaterialism among all cohorts between 2006 and 2008.

A cohort analysis using the more reliable twelve-item measure could be conducted for 1973 and for subsequent World Values Surveys. However, the number of cases would decline dramatically and the number of data points would fall from thirty-three to only six. Moreover, not all six European nations are available in all five World Values Survey waves. Therefore, we rely on the four-item index to provide more robust generational estimates.

The figure reveals five basic findings. First, it demonstrates that replacement occurs. Three cohorts in the first samples cannot be tracked over the entire thirty-six years because there were not enough members surveyed in the later samples. During these three and a half decades, three full cohorts (as well as the partial cohort born between 1986 and 1991) entered the sample. In fact, 45 percent of these younger Europeans had not been born when these surveys began.[13]

Among the respondents sampled in 2006, only 40 percent were old enough to have been surveyed in 1970. And among the cohorts that did survive, the cohort composition was substantially different. As Figure 2.1 shows, the largest cohort differences are between Europeans born between 1936 and 1945 and those born between 1946 and 1955, that is, between cohorts who suffered through World War II and the postwar deprivation and those who came of age when Western Europe began to prosper. Thus, among those old enough to have been sampled in 1970, 86 percent were born before 1946. But by 2006, only 57 percent of the cohorts surveyed in 1970 were born before 1946.

Second, Figure 2.1 demonstrates that there are consistent cohort differences across time among the cohorts born before 1956. Among these cohorts, the young have higher levels of postmaterialism than their elders, and there is rarely a break in monotonicity. However, among the post-1965 cohorts, age-group differences are relatively small. The 1956–65 cohort is significantly more postmaterialist than the 1946–55 cohort, a finding consistent with Inglehart's thesis, because the 1956–65 cohort grew up in far more secure conditions.

Third, there are few differences among the four youngest cohorts. Despite moderate economic growth, rising levels of economic inequality have led to little or no increases in real income for most of the population. Economic security has been reduced by cutbacks in the welfare state and high levels of unemployment, particularly among the young. Indeed, in 2006, the two youngest cohorts seem to be slightly less postmaterialist than the two cohorts born between 1956 and 1965.

Fourth, the figure demonstrates no support for a life-cycle explanation for age-group differences. If a life-cycle interpretation for the postmaterialism of the younger cohorts were valid, we would expect, other things being equal, cohorts to become more materialist as they aged. Clearly they do not. Moreover, the older cohorts gravitate toward postmaterialism. One can always assume that these cohorts would have become more materialist with age, but that period's effects prevented such a move. Neither Inglehart nor I know of any plausible argument supporting such an interpretation. The trend toward postmaterialism does not result from generational replacement alone, for there

---

[13] For the problem of making inferences about nonsurviving cohorts, see Firebaugh (1989).

are clearly short-term fluctuations caused by changing inflation rates (Inglehart and Abramson 1994; Abramson and Inglehart 1995).

Last, the figure strongly suggests that the overall shift toward postmaterialism is at least partly driven by replacement. Because fully 60 percent of the 1970 sample can no longer be sampled in 2006, using the algebraic standardization procedures we applied for the 1970–92 period (Abramson and Inglehart 1995) is problematic. All the same, even an informal examination of this figure demonstrates the importance of replacement. In 1970–71, 40 percent of this combined European sample were materialists, whereas only 11 percent were postmaterialists, yielding a PDI of –29. In 2006, 19 percent were materialists, whereas 21 percent were postmaterialists, yielding a PDI of 2. Overall, there was a 31-point shift toward postmaterialism. Although most cohorts have higher PDI scores in 2006 than they did in 1970, none of these gains is close to this magnitude. Comparing the overall trend line with the trend line for the cohorts makes this clear. The overall rise in the PDI occurs at least partly because over this third of a century, the older, more materialist cohorts were gradually dying and were being replaced by younger, more postmaterialist cohorts.

CONCLUSION

Some of Inglehart's critics would argue that his measure of values is meaningless (see Abramson 2011). So too, they might argue, is the trend described in this chapter.

But there seems to be overwhelming evidence that postmaterialists differ in important ways from the materialists they are replacing. In Western democracies, they are more likely to reject traditional values, especially religious values (Norris and Inglehart 2004). Even though postmaterialists are a minority even in the most postmaterialistic societies, they are a politically active and politically skilled minority (Carena, Ghoshalb, and Ribasa 2011; Dalton 2014). The growth of this active postmaterialist minority is transforming the traditional Left-Right continuum that has defined Western politics since the era of mass enfranchisement (Knutsen 2013; Martin and Pietsch 2013). As one sees in the later chapters of this book, postmaterialism has been a significant influence on the growth of dissatisfied democrats (Chapter 6), the rise of environmentalism (Chapter 8), the growth of contentious political action (Chapter 9), and other changes in democratic politics.

Almond was correct in arguing that there are few examples of successful prediction in political science. Inglehart is among the handful of political scientists to be on target about many important developments. Of course, Inglehart did not predict every development even in the West European societies that he first studied in 1970. There was no way to know that reactions against foreign immigration would become an issue or that there would be periods of economic stagflation in the late twentieth century and a near financial meltdown in the twenty-first. And he could not have predicted the growth of democracy that began in 1984 (Huntington 1991) or the breakup of the Soviet Union.[14] But in the broad outlines of his predictions, first published in 1971, he was far more on target than most of us.

[14] In 1976, Emmanuel Todd predicted the breakdown of Russian dominance over its East European satellites and the non-Russian parts of the Soviet Union. The prediction was based largely on demographic data. He did not specify when this breakdown would occur, but he did write, "Internal pressures are pushing the Soviet system to the breaking point. In ten, twenty, or thirty years, an astonished world will be witness to the dissolution or the collapse of this first of the Communist systems" (3).

3

The Decline of Deference Revisited

Evidence after Twenty-Five Years

Neil Nevitte

The Decline of Deference (Nevitte 1996) aimed to build a theoretical bridge linking authority orientations in "the family," the economy, and politics. That project began with the premise that authority orientations are profoundly political and that they permeate primary relations, the economy, and the polity. The theoretical approach leveraged two lines of theorizing – one coming from political socialization theory and the other primarily from the insights of Eckstein (1966, 1969), Eckstein and Gurr (1975), and Pateman (1970). Combining those two theoretical traditions produced a number of empirical expectations, and those conjectures were empirically tested with data from the first and second waves of the World Values Survey (WVS).

The starting premise of *The Decline of Deference* was that understanding orientations toward authority reveals a great deal about how democracies work. These outlooks are fundamental to legitimacy and to the stability and effectiveness of collective life. Eckstein and Gurr (1975,361) captured the central issue succinctly: "The traits of authority that members of social units think of as most important," they argued, "are those that determine how and whether members comply, cooperate, resist or work for transformation."

Nevitte's (1996) earlier empirical investigation probed several lines of inquiry. First, the study provided empirical support for the contention that authority orientations are connected across different domains. Second, the evidence showed that authority orientations became less deferential in the family, the workplace, and the polity between 1981 and 1990. The trajectories of change operated in the same direction in all twelve advanced industrial states, and in each case, those shifts were systematically related to structural markers, such as levels of education, suggesting that broad processes of social modernization were at work (Inglehart 1990). Third, the study explored whether these shifts were linked to changing patterns of political behavior. Declining levels of deference, it turns out, were systematically associated with lower levels of confidence in such political institutions as legislatures, the civil service, and the police. In addition, declining deference in the family and the workplace was related to rising levels of civil permissiveness and the increasing inclinations of publics to participate in more assertive elite challenging types of political behavior.

This chapter revisits the core concerns of that earlier project. Following a brief summary of the theory driving *The Decline of Deference*, the focus shifts to an empirical examination of three questions. First, do the findings coming from the original project, which was based on the 1981–90 rounds of the WVS, still hold up when the analyses are extended to data across the 1981–2006 time span? The 1981–90 comparison might be considered a relatively short interlude for evaluating value change. The twenty-five-year time span now captured by the WVS presents the opportunity for a far more comprehensive evaluation of the initial study's findings. Moreover, these new data provide a more robust platform for exploring what impacts population replacement and generational turnover might have on these outlooks. Second, the analysis exploits this longer time horizon to explore the question, Do the authority orientations "taught" by adults in the 1980s produce any discernable statistical imprint on "the children" of that earlier cohort? Socialization theory certainly supports that expectation. The third part of the analysis takes advantage of the increasingly broad cross-national scope of the WVS and returns to some of Eckstein's earlier speculations to ask, Do internalized patterns of authority have consequences for institutional performance? That analysis moves beyond the nine advanced industrial states used in the first two sections; it includes data from forty-five countries and links aggregate indicators of political rights and civil liberties to measures of domestic authority patterns: How, if at all, are authority orientations related to the performance of democratic institutions?

SOCIALIZATION, AUTHORITY ORIENTATIONS, AND STRUCTURAL CHANGE IN FAMILY LIFE

Political socialization occupies a central place in theories of political culture (Inglehart 1977, 1990).[1] Cultural predispositions vary from one society to the next, and they reflect processes of what Eckstein calls "culturally determined learning; early learning conditions later learning" that "involves a process of seeking coherence in dispositions" (Eckstein 1988, 792). It is entirely possible that the earliest investigations of political socialization (Greenstein 1960; Hess and Easton 1960; Dawson and Prewitt 1969) might have overstated

---

[1] As Inglehart (1990, 19) puts it, "the political culture approach is distinctive in arguing that (1) people's responses to their situations are shaped by subjective orientations, which vary cross-culturally and within subcultures; *and* (2) these variations in subjective orientations reflect differences in one's socialization experience, with early learning conditioning later learning, making the former more difficult to undo."

somewhat the effects of this process (Cook 1985; Marsh 1971; Niemi and Hepburn 1995). Nonetheless, an impressive body of research plainly demonstrates the importance of preadult socialization in the formation of core political orientations (Galston 2001; Jennings and Stoker 2009; Jennings 2002; Campbell 2006; Miller and Sears 1986). Exactly when these political attitudes are internalized and the precise extent to which values learned during these formative stages are subject to later modification remain matters of some debate. But the consensus is that the formative preadult years are particularly important to understanding the architecture of core political attitudes later in the life cycle.

One of the enduring contributions of the early political socialization research was to demonstrate that the family is a primary site of this process. Scholars justified the focus on the family (and particularly on parents) as a key agent of socialization based on the salience of the family to a child's life, children's prolonged exposure to parents early in the life cycle, and the relatively high degree of stability observed in political cultures (Jennings 2007, 38). Subsequent research underscored the family's centrality to the process of political learning (Miller and Sears 1986; Verba, Schlozman, and Brady 1995).

The conjecture that fundamental political orientations, in this case attitudes toward authority, would have their roots in early family life is intuitively reasonable. As Burns et al. (2001) point out, the family is an institution that is based on "treatment" rather than "selection." The self-selection issue, one that plagues so many studies of institutional socialization, is circumvented in this case. It is reasonable to suppose that the effects that do exist are indeed the result of treatment. Parent-child agreement would represent a plausible causal association as a consequence of one mechanism or some combination of mechanisms. These effects may be rooted in aspects of social learning theory – cue giving and reinforcement processes within the family, the effect of the socioeconomic characteristics of the family (Jennings 2007), or the "social milieu" pathway of parental socialization (Dalton 1982).

A separate line of theorizing emerged in the 1960s and 1970s. It takes as its starting point the centrality of patterns of authority in society and the issue of how those orientations operate across different life domains. The pioneering investigations of Pateman, Eckstein, and Kohn argued for congruence between authority orientations across domains. In some respects those original formulations might be regarded as somewhat fragmentary; they lacked a compelling empirical foundation. Eckstein's (1966, 1969) line of theorizing, for example, focused primarily on the relationship between authority orientations in the family and the polity.[2] That emphasis is entirely consistent with the political socialization claim that social and political orientations are mostly inculcated in that setting. Thus, the expectation is that these authority orientations would be

---

[2] In later work, Eckstein and Gurr (1975) emphasized the importance of viewing all political phenomena through the lens of authority patterns. They advocated this as a paradigm shift within political science.

generalized *from* the family *to* other contexts rather than the other way around. In a parallel fashion, Pateman (1970) theorized that workplace and political orientations are connected. More particularly, she suggested that changes in participation in the workplace are linked to changes in political participation (Pateman 1970). As workplaces became more egalitarian, related attitudinal changes occurred in political arenas more narrowly construed.[3] Kohn (1959) and Kohn and Schooler (1969) made the similar case, namely, that authority orientations in the workplace and in the family are connected. They showed that middle-class people, and in particular those whose occupations allow for a degree of self-direction, are more likely to encourage autonomy in their children than those with occupations that do not make, or do not reward, these kinds of demands.

More recent empirical work on authority orientations has probed these relationships, extending the analysis both within (Flanagan and Lee 2003) and beyond the borders of western states. Dalton and Ong (2006), for example, tested the theory that Confucian value systems, and specifically the presumed connection with patriarchal and deferential authority orientations, might undermine liberal democracy. Using data from the first four rounds of the WVS, they showed that deference to authority, as measured by an index of authority orientations in the workplace, in the family, more generally, does not undermine the development of democratic norms in East Asian counties. That finding holds despite the fact that within Western democracies, orientations toward authority tend to have a negative impact on democratic norms. The speculation in that case was that other countervailing features of Asian culture, such as an emphasis on "community and collective values," balance the effects of relatively high levels of deference (Dalton and Ong 2006, 107).

The first goal of *The Decline of Deference* aimed to build on the insights of those earlier studies by reconceptualizing authority orientations in the family, polity, and workplace in a more unified way – as a triangulated set of relations. Rather than evaluating authority orientations between discrete dyads, such as the workplace and the polity (Pateman 1970), or the family and the polity (Eckstein 1966, 1969), it was suggested that orientations in these three domains can be profitably explored simultaneously in a more unified way. That approach opens up possibilities for more expansive outlooks toward change. The second goal of the earlier project was to investigate what were the empirical bases of those triangulated linkages and to determine whether there was evidence of systematic changes in these orientations. After establishing the direction and scope of those changes, the third task investigated empirically whether these shifts were associated with changes in political behavior.

If authority orientations have their roots in parental socialization, then the expectation is that changes in the structure of the primary family, particularly shifts away from the hierarchy that characterizes this institution, might

---

[3] Pateman (1970) emphasized that the workplace itself constitutes a political arena.

well have political consequences. There is clear evidence that the family has undergone quite striking structural transformations in advanced industrial states during the course of the last twenty-five years. Divorce rates have risen, single-parent families have become increasingly common, marriage rates have declined, and cohabitation has become more common. Women have entered postsecondary education in unprecedented numbers; they now outnumber men in college enrollments in nearly every advanced industrial state. Relatedly, women have increasingly entered the paid workforce and fertility rates have correspondingly plunged. Indeed, fertility rates in some advanced industrial states have fallen below levels required for population replacement (World Bank Data Catalog). Women are not only having fewer children, they are having them later in the life cycle. There are good reasons to suppose that these changes in the structure of the marriage institution and the standing of women in postsecondary education and the workplace would have repercussions on the dynamics of family living. In addition, the broader processes of social change and value change described by Ronald Inglehart (1977, 1990) also suggest a declining deference to authority and hierarchic institutions by Western publics. Together, the collective impact of these changes has been accompanied by a shift away from paternal authority in the family toward a more egalitarian family environment.

All advanced industrial states have experienced these shifts to a greater or lesser extent. One possibility to explore is, Have these structural changes in the family been reflected in the kinds of values that parents aspire to teach their children? What effects might these changes have on general authority orientations and political outlooks? These questions extend beyond the scope of the original analysis in significant ways, and they can be systematically explored by turning to the full scope of the 1981–2006 set of the WVS data.

CONCEPTS, MEASUREMENT, AND DATA

The analyses that follow rely primarily on data from the first, second, fourth, and fifth rounds of the WVS (from 1981 to 2006) for nine advanced industrial states: Canada, France, Germany, Italy, the Netherlands, Spain, Sweden, the United Kingdom, and the United States. Data from the third wave of the WVS (1995) are excluded from this analysis because of incomplete coverage of these nine nations. For comparisons from 1981 to the present, only West German data are used for the sake of cross-time comparability.[4] Missing data are deleted listwise for each component of the analysis.[5] Data are weighted to

---

[4] There were no data from East Germany in 1981. The selection of the nine countries is driven by two practical considerations: the uniformity of the questions asked and participation in the four rounds under consideration.

[5] Multiple imputation of missing data yields similar results.

generate nationally representative samples of equal size in each nation, except in the case of the regression analyses conducted in the second section.

Throughout the investigation, the concept of "general deference" is operationalized by responses to the question: Would "greater respect for authority" in the future be "a good thing, a bad thing, or don't you mind"? The question taps the respondents' level of respect for authority and their willingness to defer decisions to those occupying positions of authority. Arguably, any judgment about whether greater respect for authority is a "good thing" may be contingent on evaluations of how authority operates in the respondent's own immediate context. Asking a person whether more respect for authority in the future is good or bad is an invitation to make a judgment about the status quo as a benchmark for evaluating the desirability of a hypothetical future change. Still, this broad question is particularly useful because it probes people's "general" orientation toward authority; it does not signal how authority is exercised by particular institutions (such as the police) or individuals.

Family authority outlooks are measured with responses to questions that probe which particular values respondents identify as "important to teach children." Here the focus is on responses to two options: "independence" and "obedience."[6] Responses to these questions are related to one another and to other indicators of attitudes toward authority. These are folded into a single two-item Independence-Obedience Index.[7]

Willingness to protest might also be interpreted as reflecting authority orientations in a specific context: the polity. In this case, we rely on the standard Political Action battery of protest items (Barnes, Kaase et al. 1979). Those who either "have" or "would" join in boycotts, sign petitions, and attend demonstrations are considered more assertive, more autonomous, and less deferential in their behavior toward political authority than those who report that they "would never" do one or more of these activities.[8] Similarly, those who express little or no confidence in authoritative institutions such as the police, the army, the civil service, and parliament exhibit less deferential orientations toward political authority than do those who express higher levels of confidence in these institutions. Lastly, willingness to follow instructions at work, regardless of whether one agrees with them, serves as an indicator of authority orientations in the context of the workplace. This question was dropped in the most recent wave of the WVS in all countries in the analysis, except Canada. Thus, 2006

---

[6] Respondents were invited to choose up to five of ten qualities on a list.

[7] A comparison of the 1981 and 1990 data on the child qualities items indicates a change in the response options available to respondents. In 1981, respondents were presented with a list of fifteen qualities from which to choose. In the 1990 WVS, ten of those original options were retained in the battery. It is possible that the reduction in the number of options may have some marginal effect on the results, but the items that were dropped were the least popular selections in the 1981 study.

[8] Note that these "protest potential" responses are inherited from the now classic Political Action study (Barnes, Kaase et al. 1979).

figures involving this item relate only to Canadian data.[9] Orientations toward authority in the workplace, the polity, and the family might be regarded as conceptually distinct. At issue is the question of whether, or how, they are empirically related. With the exception of workplace authority orientations, these variables form the core of the investigation that follows.

The analytic strategy primarily relies on ordinary least squares regression as well as maximum likelihood estimation of a hierarchical linear model. In the latter case, and for methodological reasons, the model uses data from all countries ($n = 7,374$). Significance levels are indicated to the $p = 0.10$ level so that readers can judge for themselves how much uncertainty is associated with the inferences drawn.

GENERAL DEFERENCE AND ITS CONSEQUENCES, 1981–2006

The Unity of Authority Orientations?

Does the interrelationship of authority orientations theorized by Eckstein (1966, 1969) and Pateman (1970), and confirmed by subsequent empirical analyses (Nevitte 1996), still hold up when interrogated with more expansive data? Figure 3.1 stylizes the conceptualization of the triadic relationships between primary relations (the family), the workplace, and the polity and situates general orientations to authority at the center. The coefficients in the figure summarize the relationships between and across these domains for each of the four waves of the WVS.

These results provide evidence, first, of an enduring congruence between orientations toward authority in these familial, economic, and political domains. All of these relationships are in the expected direction, even though the signs of the correlations vary because of how each variable is coded. For example, family authority relations were very strongly related to general deference in the 1981 WVS (−0.49), and this persists in the 2006 survey (−0.45). To be sure, some of these relationships have become slightly weaker over time, whereas others are stable. On balance, the connections between family and general deference are somewhat stronger than are the connections between the other dyads. But the general pattern is a consistent one: Authority orientations are systematically related to each other in predictable ways in multiple settings at multiple time points.

The second noteworthy finding concerns the relationship between the three specific authority domains and the more generalized measure of authority orientations, the general principle that greater respect for authority is a "good thing" (or general deference). Notice that the relationships between authority orientations and the concept of general deference are stronger than the connections between any of the pairs of the specific authority domains. These findings

---

[9] This is the only WVS question measuring authority orientations in the workplace.

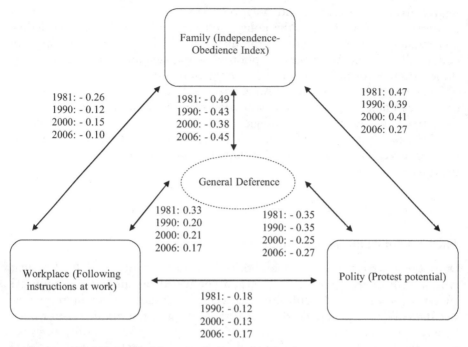

FIGURE 3.1. Stability and change in patterns of authority.
Note: The statistics are tetrachoric rho estimates, based on nine-country aggregated data.
The Independence Index is the percentage of respondents who identify "independence"
(but not "obedience") as an important value to teach children. The workplace authority
question was asked only in Canada in the fifth wave of the WVS.
Source: World Values Survey (1981–2006).

support the conjecture that these patterns exhibit the traits of empirical overlap. The family, the workplace, and the polity may be conceptually discrete
loci for the expression of authority orientations, but general outlooks toward
authority reach into these different domains in similar ways.

Does the Decline Theory Hold Up?

A second question to consider is, Have there been any significant aggregate
changes in levels of deference across the entire twenty-five-year time span of
these data? The evidence needs to be interpreted cautiously (Figure 3.2). On
balance, the data show modest aggregate changes in levels of general deference
among these publics between 1981 and 2006. Not surprisingly, there also is
evidence of some significant cross-national variations. The declines in levels
of deference in Canada, Sweden, Italy, and the United States, for example,
were quite substantial. The drop has been sharpest (some 26 points) and most
consistent in the case of the United States.

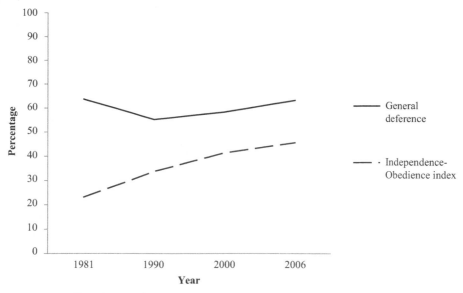

FIGURE 3.2. Trends in authority orientation.
Note: General deference is the percentage of respondents who considered "greater respect for authority" as a "good" thing. The Independence Index is the percentage of respondents who identify "independence" (but not "obedience") as an important value to teach children.
Source: World Values Survey (1981, 1990, 2000, and 2006).

What about the two other two dimensions under consideration? Unlike the indicator of general deference, the independence-obedience indicator explicitly probes authority orientations in the family setting. The percentage of publics identifying independence as an important value to teach children increased in every single country included in the analysis. In all cases, it increased by substantial margins; it is of the order of some 30 percentage points over the twenty-five-year interlude. Once again, there is some cross-national variation in these outlooks (Figure 3.3). The shift was most modest in Spain, which experienced an increase of 7 percent. Sweden, by contrast, experienced a very substantial 60 percent increase in the proportion of the population identifying independence as an important value to teach children. Such a massive shift in the values that parents want to inculcate in their children raises intriguing questions about what impact such a shift might have on the future dynamics of these countries.[10]

The scope of the shift in the Independence-Obedience Index was slightly more than twenty percentage points across the period. The sharpest increase

---

[10] The somewhat more puzzling finding concerns the increase in the proportion of publics identifying obedience as an important value to teach children.

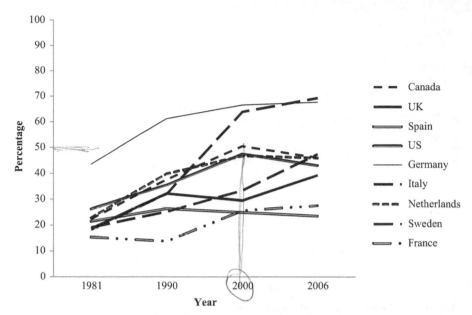

FIGURE 3.3. Cross-national trends in responses to the Independence-Obedience Index. *Note:* Percentage of respondents who identify "independence" (but not "obedience") as an important value to teach children.
Source: World Values Survey (1981, 1990, 2000, and 2006).

in obedience values were in France.[11] The precise reason for that shift is not entirely clear, but it may reflect measurement issues; respondents were offered fewer value choices after 1981. Another possibility is that these changes might signify the increased salience of, and perhaps polarization around, issues relating to authority.[12]

The Political Consequences of General Deference

Given the evidence of both coherent connections across different authority domains and shifts in general orientations toward authority, the next question to ask is, Are these shifts related to other significant political outlooks? If so, how?

---

[11] The 24 percent *increase* in this measure in France is mirrored by a 26 *increase* in support for the notion of general deference.

[12] A closer investigation of the relationship between "independence" and "obedience" indicates that the proportion of respondents identifying one or both of these qualities as "important" to teach children has risen substantially over this interlude (from 47.8 percent in 1981 to 75.8 percent in 2006). This indicates the increased salience of authority orientations. See the WVS sourcebook *Changing Human Values and Beliefs, 1981–2007* for the trends by country.

TABLE 3.1. *The Political Correlates of General Deference*

Country	Confidence in Government	Protest Potential
Canada	0.15	−0.19
France	0.17	−0.14
Germany (West)	0.12	−0.16
Italy	0.28	−0.04
Netherlands	0.09	−0.09
Spain	0.22	−0.09
Sweden	0.04	−0.17
United Kingdom	0.19	−0.09
United States	0.18	−0.10

Note: The above are Pearson's R coefficients, representing the correlations between general deference and confidence in government and protest potential.
Source: World Values Survey (2006).

Protest potential is captured by the respondents' willingness to engage in lawful protest, to sign a petition, and to join in a boycott (Barnes, Kaase et al. 1979). The core finding is that actual protest participation has increased in every country included in the analysis (see Chapter 9). In addition, protest potential, including the willingness to act, has increased on average by a substantial 17 percent. During the same period, confidence in governmental institutions has fallen, albeit more modestly, by an average of 4 percent. These patterns of change, which have been explored in greater detail by others, are systematic.[13] As Table 3.1 shows, general deference is related to both confidence in government and to protest potential. In every country, those who believe that more respect for authority is a "good thing" are significantly more likely to report higher confidence in governmental institutions than those who do not. The inverse holds for protest potential. In every country, those who think that more respect for authority is a "good thing" systematically score lower on the protest potential index than do those who say greater respect for authority is a "bad thing." These relationships are stronger in some countries (Italy, Spain, and France) than in others (Sweden, Canada, and Germany). But more impressive than the cross-national variations is the consistency of the direction of these relationships.

Are the effects the same when the other measures of authority outlooks are considered? The short answer is yes; they seem to operate in the same way. Identifying obedience as an important value to teach children is systematically associated with lower protest potential (data not shown). With the exception of

---

[13] See Chapters 5 and 6.

the United States and Sweden, those who assign obedience a high priority also express a greater level of confidence in governmental institutions. Obversely, those who think that obedience is an important quality express more confidence in governmental institutions.[14]

Is There Evidence of Generational Change?

What factors drive this decline and polarization? One possibility is that these shifts might reflect intergenerational value change (Inglehart 1990, 1977). Another possibility is that these findings are attributable to life-cycle effects, with generational replacement fueling an aggregate trend. Then again, we cannot rule out the possibility that they are attributable to some exogenous historical event. Given the age-period-cohort problem, in which any two of these effects are a perfect linear predictor of the other, it is difficult to conclusively rule out any two of these explanations using only a multivariate analysis with cross-sectional data (Blalock 1966; Glenn 2005). An alternative strategy is to track value change over the life cycle by looking at different birth cohorts. That approach can shed light on the possibility that it is the changing generational composition of Western societies that might account for the observed aggregate value changes in the population.

The evidence suggests that the entry of new cohorts into the population has enhanced the decline in deference, but it did *not* create it. The decline between 1981 and 1990 would have occurred because of society-wide change because all cohorts changed. But this decline was amplified by the entry of new cohorts into (and the exit of older cohorts out of) the population. The essential point is captured by the data summarized in Figure 3.4. Notice that the decline in general deference between 1981 and 1990 was equally steep across all age cohorts. The same applies to the "rebound" that took place between 1990 and 2006. In addition, support for the principle of deference, quite clearly, is stratified by cohort. Those born in earlier time periods are consistently more likely than their younger counterparts to think that greater respect for authority is a good thing. Different cohorts also react to contextual factors in a very similar way. In effect, the most plausible interpretation of these data is that they reflect a combination of both generation and period effects.

The findings concerning the familial authority variable are somewhat different. In this case, there is a consistent, indeed quite dramatic, increase in the priority assigned to independence-obedience over the 1981 to 2006 period. As Figure 3.5 suggests, population turnover played a significant role in this change. Once again, population replacement seems to enhance a trend that affected all cohorts. Put somewhat differently, if there had there been no

---

[14] These relationships between general deference and institutions are stronger for confidence in the army, police, and the civil service than for other political institutions such as parliament and political parties.

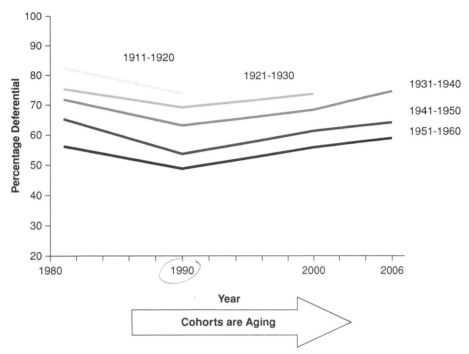

FIGURE 3.4. General deference by cohort, 1981–2006.
Note: The figure plots the percentage of respondents who considered "greater respect for authority" as a "good" thing.
Source: World Values Survey (1981, 1990, 2000, and 2006).

generational replacement during this period, then the increase in the proportion of respondents indicating that the Independence-Obedience Index is an
important value to teach children would have been about 30 percent less steep
than it actually was.[15] As before, the responses to this item seem to be stratified
according to cohort.[16]

The notion that life-cycle effects would be at play seems less plausible here
than with respect to general deference, however. As people move through the
life cycle, they become more likely to occupy positions of authority. From
that vantage point, it is reasonable to suppose that older respondents might
be more inclined to think that greater respect for authority in the future is a
"good thing." It is less plausible to suppose that as people age, they would
increasingly identify "independence" as an important value to teach children.

---

[15] This estimate was derived from the method suggested by Abramson (1983; Abramson and
Inglehart 2007).
[16] Note that in Figures 3.4 and 3.5, the divide between those born before and after 1940 is
wider. The clustering indicates a value divide between members of these cohorts along these
dimensions.

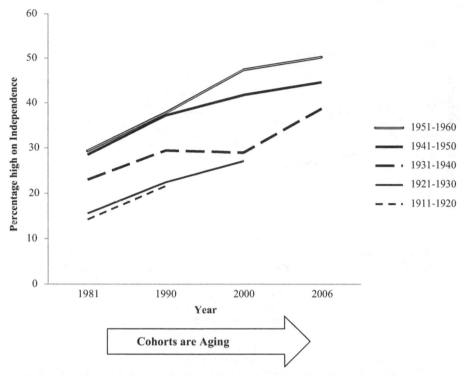

FIGURE 3.5. Changing levels of independence-obedience by cohort, 1981–2006.
Note: The figure plots the percentage of respondents who identify "independence" (but not "obedience") as an important value to teach children.
Source: World Values Survey (1981, 1990, 2000, and 2006).

The implication is that the aging of these cohorts may be capturing period rather than life-cycle effects, and that effect is augmented by intergenerational value change.

FAMILY, SOCIALIZATION, AND ORIENTATIONS TO AUTHORITY

The notion that authority orientations learned in the family setting could have substantial political effects is hardly new. At the turn of the nineteenth century, John Adams speculated that "the source of the revolution" against Britain was "the systematic dissolution of the true family authority" (Wood 1991, 147).[17] Wood more recently makes a strong case that shifting parent-child relations were due to the more consensual relationship that evolved during

---

[17] "There can never be any regular government of a nation," he told one of his sons in 1799, "without a marked subordination of mother and children to the father."

the early modern period between rulers and subjects (Wood 1991, 145–68). Contemporary political socialization scholars provide convincing empirical evidence that family experiences are vital to the development of political attitudes. The relevant implication to explore here concerns whether the values people intended to teach their children in 1981 could have some impact on subsequent orientations toward authority in 2006. Absent panel or experimental data, the WVS data can nonetheless provide what amounts to a plausibility probe.

The 1981 WVS included an item aimed at measuring parental strictness, which provides a way of exploring the plausibility of such an effect. The question put to respondents read, "Some parents are quite strict with their children, telling them clearly what they should do or should not do, what is right and wrong, while others do not think they can or should do so (are less strict). How strict were your parents?" The expectation from socialization theory is that parental strictness should be related to authority orientations learned in the family. The data show that parental strictness does have a substantial and statistically significant effect on general deference, even while controlling for other demographic traits (see Table 3.2). The only exceptions to that pattern are Britain and Sweden. The effects are also consistent with expectations: Those socialized in settings with stricter parents are more likely to think that more respect for authority in the future is a "good thing."

The longer interlude now captured by the WVS presents another opportunity to investigate this question by using a somewhat different inferential approach. In effect, the 2006 WVS data sets include samples of those who, in the statistical sense, could be considered the offspring generation of those who were interviewed in 1981. In that case, the research question of interest is: Did living in a country where adults identified independence or obedience as important to teach children in 1981 have any discernable impact on levels of general deference 2006? That line of reasoning can be probed using a multilevel regression approach. The multilevel model predicts generalized deference to authority in 2006 as a function of individual characteristics of respondents in the 2006 WVS surveys, and the child-rearing values of the nation as of 1981, with additional individual-level and national-level controls.

The results, reported in Table 3.3, should be regarded as suggestive rather than conclusive, but they do indicate that residing in a country in which obedience was emphasized in 1981 turns out to be significantly related to support for general deference in 2006. The effect is statistically significant, and it is substantively quite large, even after other variables in the model are controlled. These findings are entirely consistent with the hypothesis with which we began, namely, that children internalize values, authority values, projected by their parents in the family setting.

A closer inspection of these data yields another intriguing finding. It turns out that these different values are internalized with varying degrees of efficiency.

TABLE 3.2. Determinants of General Deference (Retrospective), 1981

	Canada	France	Germany	Italy	Netherlands	Spain	Sweden	U.K.	U.S.
Family socialization									
Parental strictness	0.14***	0.09*	0.09*	0.08*	0.11**	0.06*	0.06	0.07#	0.05*
	(0.04)	(0.04)	(0.04)	(0.04)	(0.04)	(0.02)	(0.06)	(0.04)	(0.02)
Demographic controls									
Age	0.15***	0.21***	0.38***	0.14***	0.22***	0.13***	0.16**	0.18***	0.05***
	(0.03)	(0.04)	(0.03)	(0.03)	(0.03)	(0.02)	(0.05)	(0.03)	(0.01)
Income	0.03	0.10**	-0.01	-0.07*	0.10**	0.10***	-0.09#	-0.00	0.03#
	(0.03)	(0.04)	(0.04)	(0.03)	(0.03)	(0.02)	(0.05)	(0.03)	(0.02)
Male	0.01	-0.02	-0.00	-0.00	0.01	-0.03*	0.04	0.03	-0.02*
	(0.02)	(0.03)	(0.03)	(0.02)	(0.02)	(0.01)	(0.04)	(0.02)	(0.01)
Education	-0.07**	-0.30***	-0.15***	-0.12***	-0.17***	-0.08***	-0.14***	-0.13***	-0.06***
	(0.02)	(0.04)	(0.03)	(0.03)	(0.03)	(0.02)	(0.04)	(0.04)	(0.01)
N	1007	849	1269	1045	840	1999	838	834	2152
R_2	0.06	0.16	0.13	0.08	0.12	0.05	0.05	0.09	0.03

Note: Method is ordinary least squares regression. Robust standard errors are in parentheses.
#$p < 1.0$. *$p < 0.05$. **$p < 0.01$. ***$p < 0.001$.
Source: World Values Survey (1981).

Parents who want to teach their children the value of independence have less success (−0.07), somewhat ironically, in inculcating that particular value than do those who attempt to teach the value of obedience (1.28). These findings do not seem attributable to composition effects because the model includes controls for respondents' demographic traits.

Postmaterialism also emerges as a statistically significant and substantively important predictor of general deference; materialists are significantly more deferential than postmaterialists. That finding holds across nearly all time points and for all countries under consideration. One possibility is that general deference is just a proxy for postmaterial outlooks. But that interpretation does not hold up under closer scrutiny. The Pearson's *r* correlation between general deference and postmaterialism is quite modest (0.19). Nor, as is clear from Table 3.3, does postmaterialism account for all of the variation in general deference. Each variable, it seems, taps different dimensions of the syndrome of emancipative orientations that others have documented in advanced industrial societies (Inglehart 1977, 1990; Welzel 2013).

What about the effects of other controls? Arguably, people who are more trusting of others might be more likely to defer to authority. To the extent that trust reflects an optimistic orientation toward others (Uslaner 2002), the expectation is that those exhibiting higher levels of trust may also express deference to authority. The effects of interpersonal trust across different countries, however, are less consistent and somewhat weaker. Personal religiosity, though, is a significant predictor. The effects are consistent but weaker than are those for postmaterialism. Ideological self-placement turns out to be somewhat asymmetrical. Left self-placement is a relatively strong predictor that greater respect for authority is a "bad thing." Right self-placement, by contrast, has weak and inconsistent effects. Satisfaction with one's life and finances also predicts deferential outlooks, but these effects are quite weak.

The impacts of education and age are large, consistent, statistically significant, and they operate in the expected direction. Those with higher levels of formal education, and those who are younger, tend to be less deferential toward authority than their counterparts. These findings are only suggestive but provide additional grist to the view that societal changes play a significant role in these transformations.[18]

INSTITUTIONAL PERFORMANCE AND ORIENTATIONS TO AUTHORITY

There is a long and honorable scholarly tradition, reaching at least as far back as Tocqueville (1835) and extending to Almond and Verba (1963) and

---

[18] The relatively modest numbers of countries included in this hierarchical model mean that the MLE estimates are sensitive to biases.

TABLE 3.3. *Detecting Statistical Imprints (Prospective) on
General Deference, 2006*

	Est. (S.E.)
Individual Level	
Postmaterialism	−0.15***
	(0.01)
Interpersonal trust	0.04***
	(0.01)
Personal religiosity	0.07***
	(0.01)
Ideological self-placement	
Left	−0.07***
	(0.01)
Right	0.01
	(0.01)
Satisfaction	
Life satisfaction	0.04***
	(0.01)
Financial satisfaction	0.03**
	(0.01)
Community involvement	0.01
Active associational membership	(0.01)
Demographic controls	
Age	0.04***
	(0.01)
Education	−0.09***
	(0.01)
Income	−0.01
	(0.01)
Male	0.00
	(0.01)
Country Level	
1981 child qualities index scores	
Independence	−0.07
	(0.50)
Obedience	1.28*
	(0.57)
Country-level controls	
GDP	−0.47
	(1.07)
No. of respondents	7374
No. of countries	9
Wald $\chi 2$	702.02***
Log likelihood	−1,640.718

Note: Method is mixed-effects maximum likelihood regression. Outcome
variable is general deference ("greater respect for authority" identified as
"a good thing"). Nine-country aggregated data. GDP data extracted from
OECD databank (February 15, 2011).
#$p < 1.0$. *$p < 0.05$. **$p < 0.01$. ***$p < 0.001$.
Source: World Values Survey (1981 and 2006).

Inglehart (1977, 1990), that is preoccupied with the question of how values are connected to institutions and, more particularly, to institutional performance. Almond and Verba (1963) argued that an allegiant, deferential public was conducive to an effective democratic system (see Chapter 5). Consequently, there are good reasons to investigate whether the particular values explored here might also be related to the performance of democratic institutions.

To investigate this question requires aggregate data at the country level. We turn to the national data on democratic performance generated from the Economist Intelligence Unit's democracy index.[19] The index scores are based on some sixty measures that are clustered into five dimensions of democratic performance: electoral processes, civil liberties, the functioning of government, political participation, and political culture. Higher scores on the index indicate a greater degree of democracy. To what extent are the authority orientations of a nation related to democratic development?

Figure 3.6 plots countries' ranking on this democratic performance index against their scores on general deference for forty-five countries.[20] A negative relationship emerges between democratic performance deference. In other words, the lowest levels of democratic performance are in the most deferential nations. It comes as no surprise to find that there is considerable cross-national variation: The findings do not qualify as a tight linear fit. The significant interpretive point is that the direction of this relationship is quite clear ($r = -0.306$).

An evaluation of the outliers is also instructive. For example, Iraq, Rwanda, and Honduras all score quite low on the democracy index, but they also score quite high on the general deference indicator. As noted before, the question tapping general deference invites respondents to evaluate the present level of deference in their society to inform their evaluations of whether more respect for authority would be a "good thing." It is entirely reasonable to suppose that contemporary levels of violence in a respondents' own society might well drive the country-specific relationships between levels of deference and evaluations of institutional performance in each setting. To that extent, the putatively independent variable in this case, deferential authority orientations, might be more cautiously interpreted as endogenous, as the outcome rather than the cause of a dysfunctional and violent institutional environment.

It is also possible, however, that more participatory publics that actively check government, and that exhibit high interpersonal trust rather than the obverse, nurture more accountable and stable democratic institutions (see Chapters 1 and 12). The data in Figure 3.6 show that authority orientations

[19] These data are more comprehensive than the Freedom House Index. However, substituting the Freedom House statistics yields similar results.

[20] Five countries that were only sampled in 2000 were included in the analysis to increase the sample size at the low end of the index.

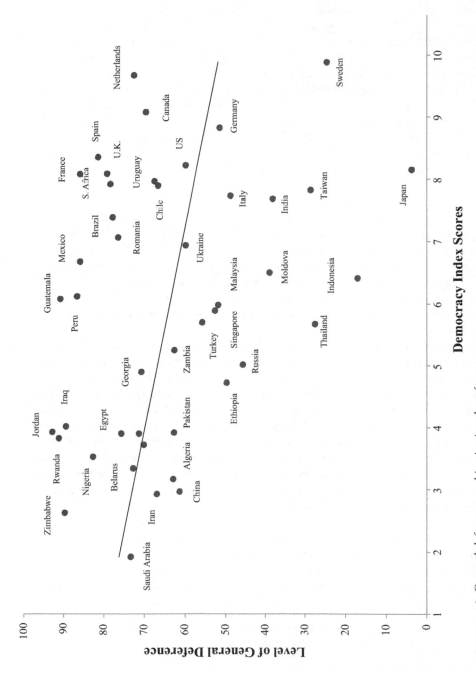

FIGURE 3.6. General deference and institutional performance.
Source: World Values Survey (2000 and 2006) and Economist Intelligence Unit Democracy aggregate index scores (2006).

are indeed related to democratic performance, a finding about which Eckstein speculated but was not in a position to empirically test. The roots of these authority orientations, it seems, lie in the family.

CONCLUDING DISCUSSION

This chapter began with a basic question: Do the findings first reported in *The Decline of Deference* (1996) hold up when the analysis expands to include WVS data covering a twenty-five-year period?

The answer seems to be yes in three respects. First, the more recent evidence confirms the earlier interpretation; authority orientations are indeed coherent, and they operate in systematic ways across different domains. There are theoretical reasons to suppose that authority orientations originate in the family setting and the more comprehensive body of data that support that claim. Second, the patterns of change, more particularly, the shifts in authority orientations, have indeed continued to move along the trajectory that could have been predicted from the trends evident between 1981 and 1990. Third, these shifts are also consistent in another respect; they are associated with public evaluations of confidence in political institutions and with shifts in protest behavior.

The availability of more WVS data from successive rounds of the surveys presented an opportunity to extend the original investigation in new but complementary directions. In one respect, these additional data enhance our ability to examine the impact of population replacement. Once again, the evidence turns out to be consistent with the patterns of societal and value change identified by Inglehart (1990), Abramson and Inglehart (2007), and the other contributors to this volume.

These more expansive data also make it possible to probe important questions concerning the long-run effects of familial socialization and the inculcation of authority orientations. In this respect, the findings lend some support to the conjecture that authority orientations "taught" at one point reverberate in the same populations some twenty-five years later. The evidence does not amount to conclusive proof that these outlooks are transferred in precisely those ways. In the absence of panel data, the best that can be said is that the evidence is consistent with that interpretation.

The process of revisiting these issues has also revealed what looks to be an intriguing puzzle: Why is it that the relationships between "independence" and "obedience" do not operate in entirely symmetrical ways? One possibility is that these uneven results are simply attributable to statistical noise in the data. Another possibility to consider is that there are operational thresholds, or upper and lower limits, that are conditioned by dynamics that are specific to particular moments in particular national contexts. A more definitive interpretation calls for deeper investigation.

It is useful, by way of conclusion, to contemplate how these findings relate to Ron Inglehart's scholarly contributions that have been so influential during the last forty years. One challenging response would be that the thesis advanced here is but another way of describing the same kinds of transformations that Inglehart has so artfully elaborated throughout his career. Certainly there is considerable common ground. Some of that common ground lies in the shared view that structural change must matter and that any persuasive explanation of value change cannot fly free of those structural considerations. Second, there is also a shared view that any persuasive account of value change has to take into account the mechanisms by which the values of one generation are transferred to the next. Inglehart's (1990) own work, and that undertaken in collaboration with others (Abramson and Inglehart 2007), goes a considerable distance in providing a convincing demonstration of both the mechanisms and the effects of population replacement. Third, to move beyond description there must be agency. In addition to structural change, the agency suggested here is political socialization and in particular the role of the family. In short, this investigation falls squarely within the tradition that Inglehart has done so much to pioneer, and it owes several intellectual debts to Inglehart.

The final point to make is that both the earlier project (Nevitte 1996) and this rethinking are entirely consistent with the theory and findings that Inglehart has so productively established over the course of his career. That said, the focal points are not entirely identical. The goal of the earlier project was to dig somewhat deeper into a narrower set of intuitions that have stalked comparative politics for well over five decades. It is only relatively recently that the empirical data have become available to allow us to explore those intuitions more systematically. Inglehart's project has been to bring a sharper and clearer understanding to the large question of how the dynamics of value change work. The scope of this project is more modest: It has been to rehabilitate the importance of authority orientations and to understand better the mechanisms and consequences of shifting orientations toward authority. That project would not have been possible without Inglehart's intellectual guidance driving the WVS. The large debts to Inglehart's contributions, clearly, are not just intellectual; they are also practical. The very existence of the WVS data is a measure of Ron's energy, drive, and foresight. What would the face of cross-national survey research look like if there were no WVS data?

APPENDIX

Variable	Question Wording	Coding
General deference	*"I'm going to read out a list of various changes in our way of life that might take place in the near future. Please tell me for each one, if it were to happen, whether you think it would be a good thing, a bad thing, or don't you mind? Greater respect for authority."*	0 = "bad," 0.5 = "don't mind," 1 = "good"
Workplace obedience	*"People have different ideas about following instructions at work. Some say that one should follow one's superior's instructions even when one does not fully agree with them. Others say that one should follow one's superior's instructions only when one is convinced that they are right. With which of these two opinions do you agree? Follow instructions/must be convinced first/depends."*	0 = not mentioned, 1 = mentioned
Independence-Obedience Index	*"Here is a list of qualities that children can be encouraged to learn at home. Which, if any, do you consider to be especially important? Please choose up to five . . . independence, obedience."*	0 = "independence" not mentioned & "obedience" mentioned, 1 = "independence" mentioned & "obedience" not mentioned
Protest potential	*"I'm going to read out some forms of political action that people can take, and I'd like you to tell me, for each one, whether you have done any of these things, whether you might do it or would never under any circumstances do it . . . joining in boycotts, attending peaceful demonstrations, signing a petition."*	0 = "would never do," 1 = "have done" and "might do"; this index is built as a simple additive scale of these three dummy variables

(*continued*)

(continued)

Variable	Question Wording	Coding
Confidence in government	*"I am going to name a number of organizations. For each one, could you tell me how much confidence you have in them: is it a great deal of confidence, quite a lot of confidence, not very much confidence, or none at all?"*	0 = "none at all" and "not very much," 1 = "quite a lot" and "a great deal"; this index is built as a simple additive scale of these four dummy variables
Personal religiosity	*"For each of the following, indicate how important it is in your life. Would you say it is very important, rather important, not very important, or not at all important?"*	0 = "not very important" and "not at all important," 1 = "rather important" and "very important"
Interpersonal trust	*"Generally speaking, would you say that most people can be trusted or that you can't be too careful in dealing with people?"*	0 = "can't be too careful," 1 = "most people can be trusted"
Age	*"Can you tell me your year of birth please?"*	0 = under 35, 0.5 = 35–64, 1 = 65 and over
Education	*"What is the highest educational level that you have attained?"*	X025r – education recoded 0 = "low," 0.5 = "middle," 1 = "high"
Income	*"Here is a scale of incomes. We would like to know in what group your household is, counting all wages, pensions, and other incomes that come in."*	Steps 1–3 = 0, steps 4–7 = 0.5, steps 8–10 = 1
Life satisfaction)	*"All things considered, how satisfied are you with your life as a whole these days?"*	1–3 = 0, 4–7 = 0.5, 8–10 = 1
Financial satisfaction	*"How satisfied are you with the financial situation of your household"*	1–3 = 0, 4–7 = 0.5, 8–10 = 1
Ideological self-placement	*"In political matters, people often talk of "the left" and "the right." How would you place your views on this scale, generally speaking?"*	1–4 = left, 7–10 = right
Active associational membership	*"Now I am going to read off a list of voluntary associations. For each one, could you tell me whether you are an active member, an inactive member, or don't belong."*	0 = not an active member of any, 1 = an active member of one or more

4

Enlightening People

The Spark of Emancipative Values[1]

Christian Welzel and Alejandro Moreno Alvarez

Based on evidence from fifty societies around the world, this chapter examines the impact of value orientations on three distinct aspects of how people view democracy: the *strength* of their *desires* for democracy, the *liberalness* of their *notions* of democracy, and the *criticalness* of their *assessments* of democracy. We focus on the ways in which "emancipative values" shape people's views of democracy because these are the values that give rise to an assertive political culture – the theme of this book.

We find that emancipative values transform people's desires for democracy profoundly and in a uniform fashion across global cultural zones. This emancipatory transformation can be characterized as an "enlightenment effect" in a double way. For it couples people's democratic desires with (1) a more liberal understanding of what democracy means and (2) a more critical assessment of how democratic their society actually is. The emancipatory transformation originates in the cognitive mobilization of wide population segments. And its enlightenment effect unfolds independent of whether a society has a long, short, or no democratic tradition. Moreover, the emancipatory transformation has far-reaching consequences: Where it does not happen, even widespread desires for democracy coexist easily with deficient or absent democracy. In these cases, people's democratic desires lack the enlightening spark that emancipative values infuse.

These insights need to be seen in the context of the global democratization trend of recent decades. This trend has opened wide areas of the world to comparative survey research. Researchers happily embraced this opportunity and fielded questions to find out how strongly people around the world desire democracy. Time and again, scholars document that great majorities of most societies express strong desires for democracy, even where authoritarian

[1] This chapter largely coincides with Chapter 10 in Welzel's (2013) *Freedom Rising*.

structures persist (Klingemann 1999; Inglehart 2003). This finding seems to confirm Fukuyama's (1992) thesis in *The End of History* that liberal democracy is the only model of society with a universal appeal since the collapse of communism (Diamond 2008).

However, the very universality of democratic desires presents a paradox. Despite the prevalence of these desires, most states around the world today are dominated by deficient democracies, hybrid regimes, or recurrent forms of authoritarianism (Rose 2009; Alexander and Welzel 2011a; Levitsky and Way 2010). Apparently, widespread popular desires for democracy coexist easily with deficient and even absent democracy. Indeed, knowing what percentage of a population expresses a strong desire for democracy very weakly predicts the actual democraticness of a society (Inglehart 2003).

This paradox raises doubts that democratic desires are the best indicator of a population's readiness for democracy. Quite likely, the universality of democratic desires hides profound differences in what people understand under democracy and for what reasons they say they want it (Schedler and Sarsfield 2006). Similar differences might exist with respect to how ready people are to step up for the equal freedoms that define democracy and take action to enforce them (Welzel 2006). Thus, scholars now recognize the need to qualify democratic desires for the kind of understanding and the type of values driving them.

Klingemann and Welzel (2010) provide such a qualification, with strong results. When one reestimates people's desires for democracy on the condition that they are matched by emancipative values, the resulting emancipatory-democratic orientations very accurately predict a society's actual democraticness. In numbers, replacing unqualified with qualified measures of democratic desires enhances the predictive power with respect to systemic democracy by fully fifty percentage points: unqualified measures of democratic mass desires explain some 25 percent of the cross-national variance in systemic democracy, compared to 75 percent for qualified measures. Shin and Qi (2011) report similar findings: The predictive power of democratic mass desires increases massively when these desires involve critical evaluations of a society's institutions. This finding resonates well with results of this chapter, although we will see that emancipative values are the reason why people evaluate institutions critically.

Klingemann and Welzel explain the pro-democratic impact of emancipative values by these values' target. Emancipative values focus on equal freedoms for everyone. Without referring explicitly to democracy, the ideal of free and equal people is the inspirational source of liberal democracy (Dahl 2000; Held 1987). In addition, emancipative values generate an intrinsic drive to take action for their goals (Deutsch, Inglehart, and Welzel 2005; Deutsch and Welzel 2011). Thus, whenever democratic desires are decoupled from emancipative values, people want democracy for other reasons than the equal freedoms that define democracy. Accordingly, people are not ready to take action for precisely these freedoms. In these cases, democratic desires provide no source of democratizing mass pressures. In fact, in these cases, power holders might appeal to people's democratic desires and harness them for goals that are propagated as democratic when in fact they are not.

This proposition informs two hypotheses. First, emancipative values hardly affect the strength of democratic desires because these desires are almost uniformly strong. Second, however, emancipative values profoundly transform the nature of democratic desires, such that these desires become only compatible with liberal democracy. Plausible as these hypotheses are, they have never been tested because the necessary data were not available until recently. The most recent round of the World Values Survey (WVS) has changed this situation. The fifth round of these surveys fielded for the first time a question asking people how they define "democracy."

This chapter demonstrates that emancipative values reshape people's democratic desires in a twofold way. For one, stronger emancipative values lead people to define democracy more exclusively in liberal terms, that is, in terms of the equal freedoms through which democracy empowers the people. Next, people with strong emancipative values have internalized demanding evaluation standards that make them critical in assessing their society's democratic quality. In combination, emancipative values generate a *"critical-liberal"* desire for democracy. As Welzel's (2013, 105–23) *Freedom Rising* shows with ample evidence, this emancipatory transformation of people's democratic desires originates in mass-scale cognitive mobilization but proceeds independent of whether a society has a long, short, or no democratic tradition. Finally, the critical-liberal impulse of emancipative values explains why widespread democratic desires can coexist with deficient or absent democracy: Wherever we find this coexistence, the democratic desires lack the critical-liberal spirit that emancipative values infuse.

To demonstrate these points, the chapter is organized into four sections. Section 1 presents our guiding theoretical perspective: democratic mobilization. This perspective assumes that to affect a society's regime, popular views of democracy must be shaped in ways that make it easier to mobilize people into democratic reform movements. The second section describes new measures of three distinct aspects in people's views of democracy: the notion of what democracy means, the assessment of one's society's democratic quality, and the strength of the desire for democracy. Section 3 formulates the hypotheses of how we think emancipative values reshape these views. The fourth section presents the results. The chapter finishes with a concluding section.

THEORETICAL PERSPECTIVE: DEMOCRATIC MOBILIZATION

Power holders have a vested interest in preserving their power. This creates a natural resistance against democratic reforms because such reforms shift power toward the people. Thus, democratic reforms usually need to be enforced against elite resistance through the mobilization of democracy movements from below (Foweraker and Landman 1997; McAdam, Tarrow, and Tilly 2003; Schock 2005; Uelfelder 2005). This has been shown for both the introduction of democratic standards in undemocratic regimes and the advancement of such standards in democratic regimes (Welzel 2007).

Mass publics can be mobilized for various reforms, democratic or nondemocratic, depending on what beliefs prevail in a population. With respect to the chances of democratic mobilization, we suggest that mass beliefs matter in three aspects.

First, there must be a widespread desire for democracy; otherwise people cannot be mobilized for goals advocated in the name of democracy. Second, people must have a proper notion of democracy; otherwise their democratic desires can be mobilized for any goal propagated in the name of democracy, including nondemocratic ones. Third, people must assess the democratic quality of their society as lower than it actually is; otherwise they lack motivation to engage for improvements of the democratic quality.

To examine these three aspects of people's views of democracy, Welzel designed a new series of questions for wave V of the WVS, addressing (1) notions of democracy, (2) assessments of democracy, and (3) desires for democracy.[2] These questions allow us to qualify democratic desires and to estimate on the basis of these qualifications the potential for democratic mobilization.

MEASURING PEOPLE'S VIEWS OF DEMOCRACY

Notions of Democracy

From the viewpoint of democratic mobilization, knowing how strongly people desire democracy is meaningless unless we also know whether people have a proper understanding of democracy. Only if people understand democracy properly can we be sure that their democratic desires are not mobilized for nondemocratic goals in the name of democracy.

Wave V of the WVS asks respondents to indicate their agreement with ten meanings of democracy. Each meaning is phrased as a short statement and rated on a scale from 1 for the weakest agreement to 10 for the strongest agreement. The wording is documented in the chapter appendix. The ten statements represent four different notions of democracy:

1. a *liberal* notion when respondents support the equal freedoms of the people as the meaning of democracy
2. a *social* notion when respondents support redistributive justice as the meaning of democracy
3. a *populist* notion when people support the delivery of "bread and butter" and "law and order" as the meaning of democracy

---

[2] Wave V of the WVS (World Values Survey Association 2009) was fielded in fifty societies, interviewing roughly fifty-five thousand respondents. A detailed study description, including questionnaires, filed reports, and data, is available from the official homepage of the World Values Survey Association at http://www.worldvaluessurvey.org.

4. an *authoritarian* notion when people support extra powers for military and religious leaders as the meaning of democracy

Of these four notions, only the liberal and social ones are acceptable as "proper" definitions of democracy on the grounds of political theory. The liberal notion is certainly the most consensual one in political theory, championed by prominent theorists such as Rawls (1971), Dahl (1973), Sartori (1984), Huntington (1991), and Sen (1999). Neither in ideological discourses nor in political practice is there a credible alternative to liberal democracy as the lead model of democracy (Diamond 2008).

The social notion of democracy is more contested, depending on whether one prefers a market-liberal or a social-liberal version of democracy (Held 1987). As an ideal type, the market-liberal version grants individuals only personal and political rights but no social rights. This ideal of democracy is based on the belief that personal and political rights are sufficient to create equal opportunities – the basis of a just society in which all advantages emerge from merit, driven solely by differences in individual talent and motivation. The social-liberal version, by contrast, assumes that personal and political rights are not sufficient to eradicate disadvantages inherited by nonmeritocratic group characteristics such as gender, ethnicity, and class. Compensating people for such unjust disadvantage mandates social rights (Marshall 1950). Despite these differences in views of distributional justice, the market-liberal and the social-liberal ideals of democracy are consensual on personal and political rights. In light of this minimal consensus, people's stance on social rights should be counted neither in favor of nor against their liberal understanding of democracy.

Of course, the ubiquitous use of the term democracy in public discourse is not always in accordance with political theory. Many people are probably unfamiliar with political theory. Hence, people might adopt whatever notion of democracy dominates their society's public discourse. Especially in societies where authoritarian rulers and populist politicians misuse the term democracy for their own interests, people might be left with a twisted notion. What is more, precisely because the term democracy is used in different contexts with different meanings, people might feel free to fill it with whatever they value as a desirable outcome of politics. At least, this seems to be a reasonable possibility that deserves an investigation.

To test this possibility, the WVS asks for notions of democracy that are in plain contradiction to political theory but which nevertheless might find people's support, even if mistakenly so. These items include features of politics that many people might value highly and thus might define as features of democracy even though they have nothing to do with democracy in a proper sense. These items also address features of politics that authoritarian and populist rulers may propagate as features of democracy.

As Figure 4.1 shows, the liberal notion is addressed by four items referring to free elections, referenda votes, civil liberties, and equal rights. The social notion

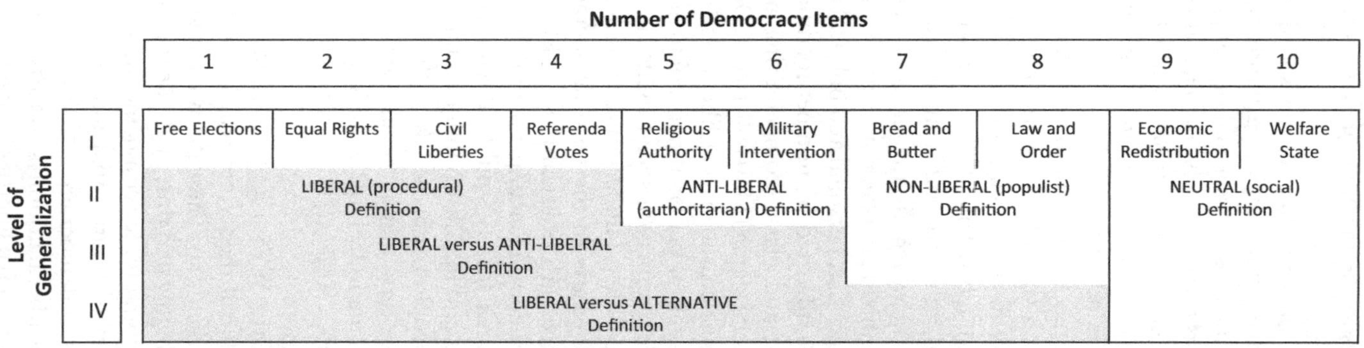

Number of Democracy Items

FIGURE 4.1. A stepwise qualification of people's liberal understanding of democracy.

64

TABLE 4.1. *Empirical Dimensions in Popular Definitions of Democracy*

Items	Dimension 1: Liberal vs. Authoritarian Definition	Dimension 2: Populist Definition	Dimension 3: Social Definition
Free Elections	0.63		
Equal Rights	0.60		
Civil Liberties	0.53		
Referenda Votes	0.50		
Military Intervention	−0.70		
Religious Authority	−0.73		
Bread and Butter		0.76	
Law and Order		0.73	
Economic Redistribution			0.68
Welfare State			0.62
Explained Variance	24%	14%	12%
N	42,376		

Note: Entries are factor loadings. Items are standardized for each respondent's mean rating over all items. Factor analysis specified with varimax rotation under the Kaiser criterion.

Source: Data are the country-pooled individual-level data set of WVS V (2005–8).

is addressed by two items relating to state benefits and income redistribution. The populist notion is included in two questions relating to economic growth as a bread-and-butter issue and fighting crime as a law-and-order issue. The authoritarian notion is covered by two items favoring military intervention and religious authority as definitions of democracy.

The factor analysis in Table 4.1 reproduces these distinct notions of democracy.[3] The liberal notion is manifest on the positive pole of the first dimension; the authoritarian notion appears on the negative pole of this dimension. The populist and social notions each represent a dimension of their own. It is interesting to note that among these three dimensions, the social one is the weakest: It captures the smallest amount of variance in people's understanding of democracy. In other words, redistributive definitions of democracy shape popular understandings of democracy the least. This finding disconfirms a prominent interpretation in political economy according to which the key motivation to desire democracy is the popular interest in redistribution (Boix 2003; Acemoglu and Robinson 2006). Far from it, redistributive understandings of democracy have practically no explanatory power over people's desires for democracy.[4]

---

[3] Note that each respondent's ratings are centered on this respondent's mean rating over all items. This procedure isolates relative item priorities.

[4] If we regress the strength of people's desire for democracy on the four distinct notions of democracy, the social and populist notion together explain *less than 1 percent* of the variance

We do not measure how notions of democracy are organized in people's minds, in the absence of a theoretical norm. This approach would be inappropriate for a concept as inherently normative as democracy. For this reason, we measure people's notions of democracy against the norm of liberal democracy, as defined in political theory. Measured against this norm, the authoritarian notion of democracy is *anti*-liberal: It contradicts the idea of democratic freedoms when one defines the political authority of the military or religious leaders as the core of democracy. The populist notion of democracy is *non*-liberal: Economic growth and crime prevention are aspects of policy performance that have nothing inherently democratic about them; these features might as well characterize authoritarian regimes. Hence, no matter how well democracies perform in economic growth and crime prevention, these performances do not *define* democracy. Therefore, the authoritarian and the populist notions define meanings as democratic that either contradict or rival a liberal notion: These are *alternative* meanings that cannot be incorporated into a liberal definition of democracy. From this follows that one can qualify someone's notion of democracy as truly liberal only if the person emphasizes the liberal meanings of democracy and at the same time rejects the alternative ones. This is what we mean by an *exclusively* liberal notion of democracy.[5]

Consistent with this definition, we calculate each person's average support of the four liberal meanings of democracy and then subtract from this his or her average support of the nonliberal meanings. How exactly the calculations are done is detailed in the appendix. We standardize the resulting difference index into a range from 0 to 1.0. Scores below 0.50 indicate that nonliberal notions dominate over the liberal one; scores above 0.50 indicate the opposite.

Assessments of Democracy

Unless people perceive the democratic quality of their society as lower than it actually is, even a decidedly liberal notion of democracy cannot be mobilized for democratic reforms. Thus, the WVS asks people to assess the democratic quality of their society on a 10-point scale ranging from 1 (not at all democratic)

in people's democratic desires. By contrast, the liberal-versus-authoritarian notion explains 18 percent (results are for 54,024 respondents from 50 societies from each of the world's 10 culture zones). The social notion nowhere dominates people's desires for democracy, not even in highly unequal societies like Brazil and very poor societies like Burkina Faso.

[5] The social notion of democracy is not necessarily part of the liberal notion; yet, it is fully compatible with it. If one endorses both democratic freedoms and redistributive justice as meanings of democracy, one favors a social-liberal notion of democracy (Held 2006). If one endorses democratic freedoms but rejects redistributive justice as meanings of democracy, one favors a market-liberal notion of democracy. Because both of these notions are liberal notions of democracy, one cannot narrow down the latter to any of the two. This leads to a clear conclusion: If one wants to measure the dominance of the liberal over alternative notions, but not over compatible notions of democracy, the social notion of democracy must neither be counted against nor in favor of the liberal notion.

to 10 (fully democratic). The wording of the question is documented in the appendix. Again, we transform the responses into a 0-to-1.0 scale.

We are interested in how critical people assess their society's democratic quality because we believe that people who desire democracy are more easily mobilized for democratic reforms when they assess their society's democratic quality as lower than it actually is. Hence, we estimate the criticalness of people's assessment of democracy relative to a society's actual democratic quality. Information about the actual democratic quality can be taken from any of the various democracy indices used in comparative politics. Among these indices, Welzel (2013, 270–74) identifies the "citizen rights index" as the most valid one; this index summarizes Freedom House's ratings of "civil liberties" and "political rights" together with Cingranelli and Richards's measures of "empowerment rights" and "integrity rights" into an overall index with minimum 0 (lowest democratic quality) and maximum 1.0 (highest democratic quality).[6] We use a five-year average on this index up to the year of the survey in a society as the yardstick to measure how critically a respondent assesses his or her society's democratic quality. The idea is that people's democracy assessment is the less critical the higher they rate their society's democratic quality above its actual quality. By the same token, someone's democracy assessment is the more critical the more it falls below a society's actual democratic quality.

Accordingly, we calculate how much people's assessment of their society's democratic quality exceeds or falls short of the actual quality. The calculation is detailed in the chapter appendix. The midpoint on the resulting index (0.50) indicates that respondents assess their society's democratic quality as equal to the actual quality. A score below 0.50 indicates that respondents evaluate their society's democratic quality as better than the actual quality. A score above 0.50 signifies that they judge their society's democratic quality as worse than the actual quality.[7]

---

[6] Measurement is documented in all detail in the online appendix to Welzel's (2013) *Freedom Rising* at http://www.cambridge.org/welzel at p. 72.

[7] Consider a true example from our data: Against a possible maximum of 1.0, the Chinese rate the democratic quality of their society at about 0.60 points. So do the Dutch. However, this same rating means an enormous overrating of the society's actual democratic quality among the Chinese (China's actual democratic quality scores at 0) and a considerable underrating among the Dutch (the Netherlands's actual democratic quality scores at 0.99). Thus, the question of how critical people's democratic quality ratings are relative to a society's actual democratic quality mandates to treat *similar* ratings *differently* when they relate to different realities. Moreover, people's democratic quality ratings are not automatically more critical simply when the actual democratic quality is better. This would only be true if people's quality ratings were constant across varying actual qualities. This is not the case, however: People tend to rate the quality of democracy higher when the actual quality is higher as well (the two variables correlate at $r = +0.51$ across fifty-one societies). Of course, the actual quality sets certain boundaries as to how critical or uncritical people's quality ratings can be. However, these boundaries do not determine where within their range respondents position themselves. Nor do they determine whether and to what extent this positioning is shaped by emancipative values.

Qualifying Desires for Democracy

A third aspect of people's views of democracy is how strongly they wish to live in a democracy. The WVS addresses this aspect by another 10-point scale from 1 (not at all important to live in a democracy) to 10 (absolutely important). As before, we transform this scale into a range from 0 to 1.0. The wording is documented in the appendix.

Democratic desires are important for the chances of democratic mobilization because, in the absence of them, one cannot mobilize people for goals advocated in the name of democracy. But democratic desires need further qualification. They need to be qualified for the liberalness of people's notion of democracy, so we know these desires can only be mobilized for liberal goals. And they need to be qualified for the criticalness of people's assessment of democracy, so we know the desires are coupled with perceptions of democratic quality lower than the given quality: Only then can democratic desires be mobilized on behalf of further improvements.

Following this logic, we qualify people's democratic desires in two steps. In the first step, we weight the strength of people's democratic desires for the liberalness of their notions of democracy (as detailed in the appendix). The resulting index measures democratic desires in a conditional way, showing not just how strongly people desire democracy but how strongly they desire it on the condition of a truly liberal notion of democracy. The index runs from minimum 0 when someone *either* does not wish to live in a democracy *or* has a nonliberal notion of it, to maximum 1.0 when someone *both* wishes strongly to live in a democracy *and* has a truly liberal notion of it.

In the second step, we qualify liberal democratic desires for the criticalness in people's assessments of democracy, speaking about the desire for democracy in an even more conditional way: the *"critical-liberal* desire for democracy." The "critical-liberal desire" equals 0 if a respondent does not wish to live in a democracy *or* understands democracy in nonliberal terms *or* is uncritical of the society's democratic quality. The index is at its maximum 1.0 if a respondent wishes strongly to live in a democracy *and* understands democracy truly in liberal terms *and* is highly critical of the society's democratic quality. As before, the calculation is detailed in the appendix.

Note that we do *not* assume that people's desires for democracy, their notions of democracy, and their assessments of it reflect interchangeable facets of a single underlying dimension. Hence, critical-liberal desires are not to be mistaken as a latent variable. Instead, they represent a multidimensional construct that weights democratic desires for inherently relevant qualities precisely because these qualities are not automatically incorporated into the desires themselves. This logic provides a conditional measure of democratic desires.[8]

---

[8] As outlined in Welzel's *Freedom Rising* (2013, 259, Box 8.1), a "conditional index" is a multiplicative combination of two or more mutually conditioning properties, measuring each property on the condition of the other's presence. A conditional index requires distinctness of its combined properties, not dimensional identity as in a latent variable.

Emancipative Values

Our main interest is to see how emancipative values vary people's views of democracy. This interest is inspired by recent findings underlining the importance of emancipative values for democracy (Welzel 2006; Klingemann and Welzel 2010). These findings suggest that emancipative values shape people's views of democracy. But this suggestion has not been directly tested, so this is done in the analyses reported here.

Emancipative values emphasize equal freedoms for everyone and are measured by a twelve-item index as described in Welzel's (2013, 58–73) *Freedom Rising*. This multipoint index ranges from minimum 0 to maximum 1.0. The appendix includes an index description. We measure emancipative values at both the individual level and the societal level. In the latter case, we use the population mean as a measure of the prevalence of emancipative values in a society. As is demonstrated by Welzel (2013, 79–86), the population mean validly measures a society's central tendency because in each sample, the distribution on the emancipative values index is mean centered and single peaked.

HYPOTHESES

We expect four hypotheses to be confirmed. These hypotheses describe what we think are the enlightening impulses of emancipative values. The basic assumption is that because emancipative values emphasize equal freedoms for everyone, the features of democracy that address these freedoms become intrinsically appealing under emancipative values. This assumption suggests four hypotheses:

1. Emancipative values anchor people's desires for democracy on exclusively liberal notions of democracy.[9]
2. Emancipative values connect people's desires for democracy with critical assessments of a society's democratic quality.
3. Emancipative values show these effects at both the individual level and the societal level, yet the mechanism of social cross-fertilization applies: Individual-level emancipative values affect democratic orientations the more in the previously described ways the more prevalent these values are at the societal level.
4. The impact of emancipative values on democratic orientations is independent of people's cognitive mobilization as well as their socialization under democracy.

[9] A colleague dismissed this hypothesis as tautological. We agree that there is an obvious plausibility in this hypothesis. Yet, this does not make it tautological but simply logical. There remains a conceptual boundary between what people value in life and how they idealize democracy. For the two to be connected, people have to cross this boundary. As plausible as this crossover might be, it is not self-evident that it happens. Hence, demonstrating it is worthwhile.

The most important control variable at the societal level is democratic traditions. To assume a strong effect of democratic traditions on people's views of democracy is plausible from the viewpoint of institutional learning. Adopting the "proper" views of democracy can be a matter of being socialized into a long collective experience with democratic institutions (Rustow 1970; Rohrschneider 1996). To test this proposition, we use a "democratic traditions index" that measures each society's historically accumulated experience with democracy (Gerring et al. 2005). As outlined by Welzel (2013), the democratic tradition index is also a formidable measure of Western cultural traditions. Thus, when using this index, we do not need an additional measure to depict cultural differences along a Western/non-Western fault line: On the democratic traditions index, this fault line is fully manifest, with Western societies having on average much longer democratic traditions than non-Western societies.

At the individual level, some researchers give people's views of democracy a primarily cognitive reading: People's views reflect what people know about democracy (Shin and Tusalem 2007; Norris 2011). Thus, at the individual level, we test the effect of emancipative values on views of democracy against cognitive variables, including people's level of education, their political interest, and the diversity of their information use. Gender and age are included as routine demographic controls. All these variables are described in the appendix.

As with the dependent variables, all independent variables are measured in a scale range from 0 to 1.0. This gives unstandardized regression coefficients the same meaning for all variables: A coefficient indicates which fraction of an independent variable's score is added to or subtracted from the constant term to obtain the dependent variable's estimated score.

We present our findings in three steps. First, we demonstrate that our qualified measures of people's views of democracy bring differences to the surface that are not visible otherwise. This is done in bar diagrams that show how strongly the different views are held by populations of different culture zones around the world, using the culture zone scheme of Welzel (2013, 25–33). The purpose of this analysis is to demonstrate that people's views of democracy are indeed very different, which underlines the need for explanation. The second step probes into explanation, using line graphs to examine the combined individual- and societal-level effects of emancipative values on people's views of democracy. The third step extends this analysis into a multilevel regression model in which the individual-level effect of emancipative values is controlled for the impact of cognitive mobilization, while the societal-level effect is controlled for democratic traditions.

FINDINGS

Culture Zone Differences

In the first step, we want to see if our qualified measures of democracy bring differences in popular views of democracy to the surface that are otherwise

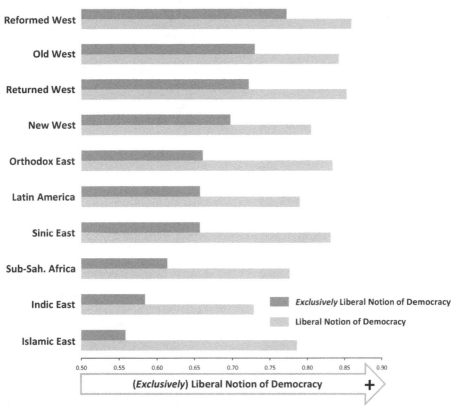

FIGURE 4.2. Definitions of democracy by culture zone before and after qualification. *Note:* Societies are grouped into culture zones as outlined in the online appendix to Welzel's (2013) *Freedom Rising* at http://www.cambridge.org/welzel (p. 28, footer of Appendix Table 2.1). Numbers of respondents and societies per culture zone are given there too. In each culture zone, societies are weighted to equal sample size. *Source:* World Values Survey, fifth wave (World Values Survey Association 2009).

hidden. In other words, "Do qualified views of democracy differ more across different world regions than unqualified ones?"

Figure 4.2 plots for each culture zone how strongly people support the liberal notion of democracy – before and after taking into account *how exclusively* they support this notion. The light gray bars just show how strongly people support the liberal notion, ignoring how exclusively they support this notion. The pattern seems to suggest that the liberal notion has universal support – confirming previous research (Dalton, Shin, and Jou 2007). Indeed, the extent to which people define democracy in liberal terms is above 0.70 scale points in *each* culture zone. People's notions of democracy vary to only 4 percent between culture zones.

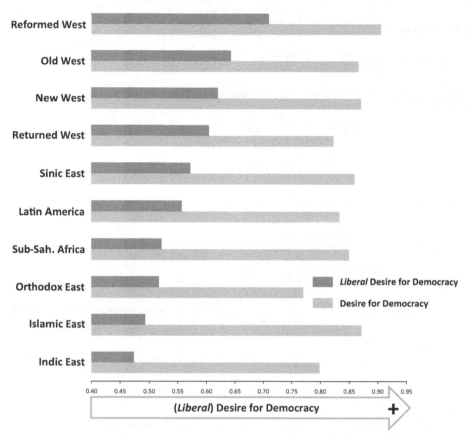

FIGURE 4.3. Desires for democracy by culture zone before and after qualification.
Note: See footer of Figure 4.2.

The picture changes drastically when we take into account how exclusively people support liberal democracy. Support ratings plummet considerably in the dark gray bars in Figure 4.2. Moreover, they plummet to different degrees, making culture zone differences strikingly evident. To be precise, the extent to which people place the liberal over nonliberal notions of democracy varies from a high of more than 0.77 scale points in the Reformed West to a low of 0.56 scale points in the Islamic East. People's notions of democracy vary to about 20 percent between culture zones, if one takes into account how exclusively they support liberal democracy. In the Islamic East, the Indic East, and sub-Saharan Africa, this is the least the case, and a big rift separates these culture zones from the "West."

With desires for democracy, we make a similar observation. Figure 4.3 depicts per culture zone the average strength of people's desire for democracy – *before* and *after* qualification. Before qualification (see light gray bars), it seems

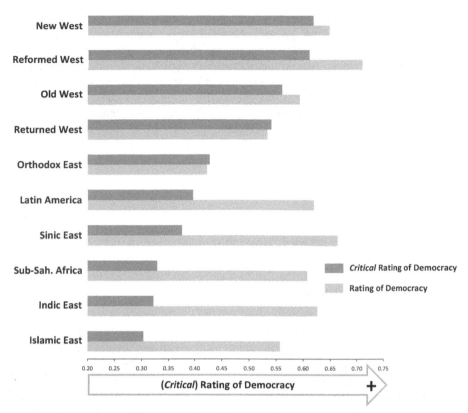

FIGURE 4.4. Ratings of democracy by culture zone before and after qualification. *Note:* See footer of Figure 4.2.

that the desire for democracy is similarly strong across the globe. In all culture zones, the desire for democracy scores at least at 0.77 scale points. Again, people's desire for democracy varies to only 4 percent between culture zones. After qualifying the desire levels for how strongly they are matched by an exclusively liberal notion of democracy, the picture changes drastically once more (see dark gray bars). Desire levels are generally much more modest, and they vary considerably between culture zones. As before, people of the Reformed West show the strongest liberally motivated desire, scoring at about 0.71 scale points. And once more, people in the Islamic and Indic East are at the bottom end, with scores below 0.50. Liberal desires for democracy vary to about 20 percent between culture zones.

Figure 4.4 plots culture zone differences in how people rate their society's democratic quality – again before and after qualification. The pattern is familiar. Before qualification, ratings vary in a very limited range between 0.60 and 0.70 scale points, except for people in the two ex-communist zones – the

Returned West and the Orthodox East – who fall outside this range. Apart from this exception, people around the world rate their society's democratic quality favorably. But the fact that people in sub-Saharan Africa and the Islamic East rate their societies just as democratic as people in the Western culture zones appears odd when one recognizes that most societies' actual democratic quality in sub-Saharan Africa and the Islamic East is very low. Apparently, many people in these culture zones overrate their societies' democratic quality. They rate democracy uncritically.[10] Hence, qualifying people's ratings for how critical they assess democracy relative to the actual democratic quality uncovers a wide chasm between the most critical rating in the New West (0.62) and the least critical rating in the Islamic East (0.30).

These results evidence a pronounced cultural rift between Muslim and Western societies over democratic orientations. At times, this rift has been disputed (Inglehart and Norris 2003). Yet, it is fully visible after we qualify otherwise superficial measures of democratic orientations.

The Effect of Emancipative Values without Controls

What is behind the large culture zone differences in popular views of democracy? Interestingly, it is not culture zones themselves that vary people's views of democracy. It is their difference in emancipative values that does. Indeed, culture zones differ just as much in emancipative values as they differ in people's views of democracy, showing the same Western/non-Western chasm. Thus, if we replace the culture zones with their mean scores in emancipative values, these mean scores account for all the variance in people's views of democracy that seems to be explained by culture zones. Accordingly, it is important to have a closer look at how emancipative values shape people's views of democracy.

Emancipative values can affect people's views of democracy in two ways. First, how strongly a person emphasizes emancipative values can shape her views of democracy, irrespective of how prevalent these values are in the person's society. Second, the prevalence of emancipative values in a person's society can shape her views of democracy, irrespective of how strongly the person herself emphasizes these values. In other words, emancipative values can shape views of democracy through both their individual-level emphasis and their societal-level prevalence.

---

[10] Scholars might suspect that favorable democracy ratings in societies with low democratic qualities reflect the respondents' fear of repression in case of a more critical rating. However, our additional analyses (results available upon request) show that lack of emancipative values is a considerably stronger predictor of uncritical democracy ratings than is the presence of repression.

To visualize the individual-level impact of emancipative values, we group the respondents into ten intervals on the emancipative values index, ordered from weaker to stronger emphasis on these values.[11] To visualize the societal-level impact of emancipative values, we categorize societies according to how prevalent emancipative values are, distinguishing "weakly," "moderately," and "strongly emancipative" societies.[12]

On the basis of these categorizations, Figure 4.5 plots the strength of the respondents' desire for democracy on the vertical axis against the strength of their emancipative values – separately for weakly, moderately, and strongly emancipative societies.

The strength of the desires for democracy is consistently above 0.80 scale points, and whether a society as a whole is weakly, moderately, or strongly emancipative hardly affects the desire strength. As the slopes show, stronger emancipative values strengthen the desire for democracy slightly at best. The weak rootedness of democratic desires in emancipative values already suggests that democratic desires are quite meaningless – unless further qualified.

Looking at notions of democracy, a clearer pattern comes to the surface. Figure 4.6 shows how people's emancipative values vary the liberalness of their notion of democracy. Again, this is shown separately for weakly, moderately, and strongly emancipative societies. In each of the three types of society, there is a pronounced upward slope indicating that individuals with stronger emancipative values define democracy more exclusively liberal, and they do so irrespective of how prevalent emancipative values are in their society. Still, the prevalence of emancipative values matters in two ways. First, irrespective of how strongly the individuals themselves emphasize emancipative values, their liberal notion of democracy is stronger when emancipative values are more prevalent in their society. This is evident from the fact that the line for weakly emancipative societies in Figure 4.6 is below that for moderately emancipative societies, which in turn is below that for strongly emancipative societies. Second, when emancipative values are more prevalent in a society, the individuals' own emphases on emancipative values strengthen their liberal notion of democracy more pronouncedly than in societies in which these values are less prevalent. This is evident from the fact that the slopes of the three lines in Figure 4.6 steepen from weakly to moderately to strongly emancipative societies. The joint individual-level and societal-level impact of emancipative values

---

[11] Respondents are divided into ten ascending brackets on the emancipative value index, each of equal interval size: 0 to 0.10, 0.11 to 0.2, . . . , 0.91 to 1.0. How this is done is documented in the online appendix to Welzel's (2013) *Freedom Rising* at http://www.cambridge.org/welzel (p. 27).

[12] Societies are grouped into the three categories of "weakly," "modestly," and "strongly" emancipative societies using the cutoff points shown in the online appendix to Welzel's (2013) *Freedom Rising* at http://www.cambridge.org/welzel (see p. 61). For the calculation of average scores for these three categories, societies are weighted to equal sample size.

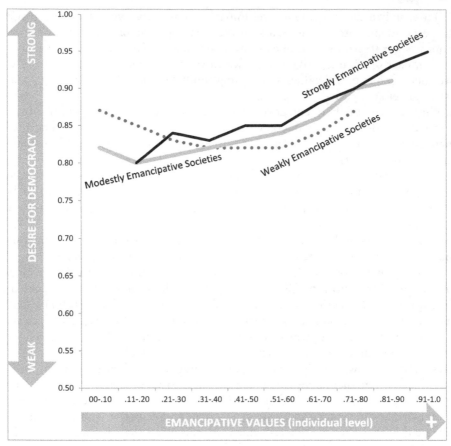

FIGURE 4.5. The combined individual-level and societal-level effect of emancipative values on the strength of people's desires for democracy.

Note: Societies are grouped into the three categories of "weakly," "modestly," and "strongly" emancipative societies as outlined in the online appendix to Welzel's (2013) *Freedom Rising* at http://www.cambridge.org/welzel (p. 62). Numbers of respondents and societies per category are given there too. In each of the three categories, societies are weighted to equal sample size.

Source: World Values Survey, fifth wave (World Values Survey Association 2009).

varies people's liberal notion of democracy by about 0.30 scale points (on a scale whose theoretical range is 1.0).[13]

---

[13] The strong relationship between emancipative values and liberal notions of democracy is *not* due to the fact that one of the four components of emancipative values includes equal opportunities for women while one of the eight components of the liberal notion includes equal gender rights. Although these are the two components that are correlated most strongly between the two concepts, taking these two components out, the two concepts still correlate at $r = 0.38$ ($N = 39,643$), which compares to an $r = 0.26$ correlation for the two most strongly correlated components. Hence, the strong connection between the two concepts cannot be reduced to their small overlap on gender equity issues.

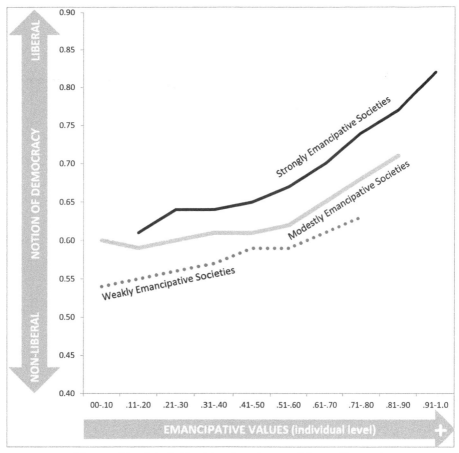

FIGURE 4.6. The combined individual-level and societal-level effects of emancipative values on the liberalness of people's notions of democracy.
Note: See footer of Figure 4.5.

Figure 4.7 illustrates how emancipative values vary the criticalness of people's rating of democracy. Again, strong effects are evident. The combined individual-level and societal-level impact of emancipative values varies the criticalness of people's rating of democracy to about the same extent as it varies the liberalness of their notion of democracy.

There is one pronounced distinction, however: More prevalent emancipative values elevate critical ratings of democracy much more than they elevate liberal notions of democracy. For the latter, individual preferences for emancipative values are more important than they are for critical ratings of democracy. The reason for this pattern is simple: Critical ratings of democracy measure the assessments of individuals against the reference standard of fixed societal-level scores, which evens out individual-level variation to some extent.

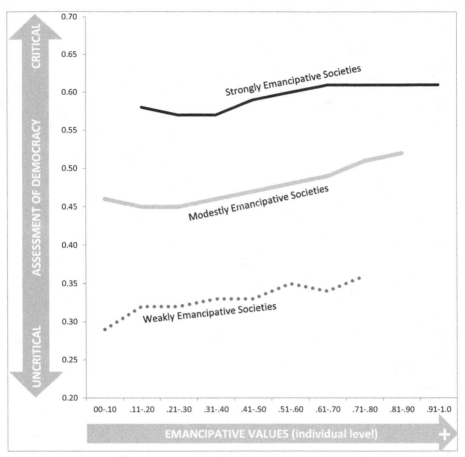

FIGURE 4.7. The combined individual-level and societal-level effects of emancipative values on the criticalness of people's ratings of democracy.
Note: See footer of Figure 4.5.

The liberalness of people's notion of democracy and the criticalness of their assessment of democracy are key qualifications of people's desire for democracy. Because emancipative values vary these qualifications quite strongly, they must also vary the qualified desire for democracy, that is, the "critical-liberal" desire for democracy. Figure 4.8 demonstrates that this is indeed the case. The combined individual- and societal-level impact of emancipative values varies the critical-liberal desire for democracy by 0.38 scale points.

The next question is whether these findings are robust and hold when we control for other plausible influences on people's views of democracy, namely, the length of a society's democratic tradition and the individuals' cognitive mobilization.

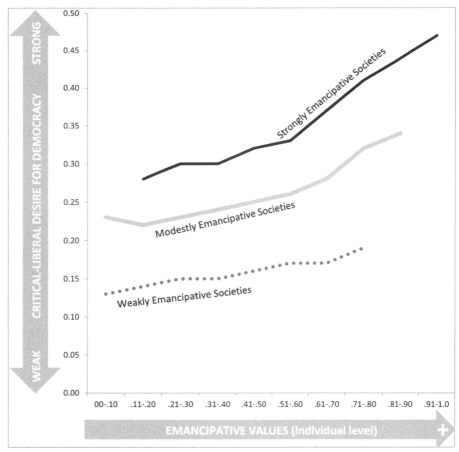

FIGURE 4.8. The combined individual-level and societal-level effects of emancipative values on people's critical-liberal desires for democracy.
Note: See footer of Figure 4.5.

The Effect of Emancipative Values after Controls

The multilevel models in Table 4.2 confirm the previous findings under inclusion of the control variables just mentioned. In the following, we focus on the last model because it explains the most information-rich view of democracy: the critical-liberal desire for democracy. On average, people's critical-liberal desire for democracy scores at 0.27, which is at about one-fourth of the possible maximum.

Individual-level emancipative values add a 0.11-fraction of their given score to the critical-liberal desire. This is by far the strongest individual-level contribution to a critical-liberal desire, stronger than the effects of information diversity, political interest, and formal education. This is remarkable because

TABLE 4.2. *Testing Individual-Level and Societal-Level Effects of Emancipative Values on Popular Views of Democracy: MLMs*

	Dependent Variables				
Predictors	Strength of Desire for Democracy	Liberalness in Notion of Democracy	Criticalness in Rating of Democracy	Liberal Desire for Democracy	Critical Liberal Desire for Democracy
Intercept	0.58 (81.7)***	0.67 (119.6)***	0.45 (40.8)***	0.58 (81.7)***	0.27 (37.4)***
Societal-level effects (SL):					
Democratic tradition	N. S.	N. S.	0.12 (2.4)**	N. S.	0.07 (2.1)*
Emancipative values	0.58 (5.4)***	0.55 (6.6)***	0.70 (5.9)***	0.58 (5.4)***	0.68 (8.3)***
Individual-level effects (IL):					
Female sex	−0.01 (−3.3)***	−0.01 (−4.6)***	−0.01 (−2.4)**	−0.01 (−3.3)**	−0.01 (−5.5)***
Biological age	0.10 (6.0)***	0.05 (6.9)***	N. S.	0.10 (6.0)***	0.05 (6.3)***
*Cross-level Interactions (SL * IL):*					
Formal education (IL)	0.07 (9.7)***	0.05 (9.3)***	N. S.	0.07 (9.7)***	0.03 (8.0)***
* Democratic tradition (SL)	N. S.	N. S.	N. S.	N. S.	N. S.
* Emancipative values (SL)	N. S.	N. S.	N. S.	N. S.	N. S.
Political interest (IL)	0.06 (7.2)***	0.01 (2.3)*	−0.04 (−7.6)***	0.06 (7.2)***	0.01 (2.3)**
* Democratic tradition (SL)	N. S.	N. S.	N. S.	N. S.	N. S.
* Emancipative values (SL)	N. S.	N. S.	N. S.	N. S.	N. S.
Information diversity (IL)	0.06 (6.6)***	0.02 (3.6)***	N. S.	0.06 (6.6)***	0.02 (4.2)***
* Democratic tradition (SL)	N. S.	N. S.	N. S.	N. S.	N. S.
* Emancipative values (SL)	N. S.	N. S.	N. S.	N. S.	N. S.
Emancipative values (IL)	0.15 (9.5)***	0.12 (10.4)***	0.04 (4.0)***	0.15 (9.5)***	0.11 (11.5)***
* Democratic tradition (SL)	N. S.	0.10 (1.8)*	0.11 (2.1)*	N. S.	0.08 (1.9)*
* Emancipative values (SL)	0.77 (3.7)***	0.32 (2.1)**	−0.31 (−2.2)*	0.77 (3.7)***	0.30 (2.6)**
Reduction of error:					
Within-societal variation of DV	05.3%	09.2%	03.2%	10.1%	09.1%
Between-societal variation of DV	08.9%	70.5%	69.3%	66.6%	80.9%
Variation in effect of values	27.9%	45.9%	07.7%	45.1%	48.5%
N (number of observations)	44,201 respondents in 45 societies				

Note: Models estimated with HLM 6.01. Entries are unstandardized regression coefficients with T-ratios in parentheses. Individual-level variables are group-mean-centered; societal-level variables are grand-mean-centered.

the latter three are important indicators of cognitive mobilization. From each of these indicators one would assume that it creates greater awareness of democracy's defining features and – because of this greater awareness – makes people more critical. As the positive coefficients of all three variables show, this is the case. Yet, emancipative values trump the effects of the cognitive variables clearly. Even combined, information diversity, political interest, and formal education contribute less to a critical-liberal desire for democracy than emancipative values alone do. Thus, orientations toward democracy are more an evaluative matter than a cognitive matter: People's responses to democracy questions indicate less what people know about democracy than what they wish democracy to be.

Of course, this does not mean that cognitive mobilization is unimportant. Quite the contrary, as Welzel (2013, 108–20) shows with ample evidence in *Freedom Rising*, the cognitive mobilization of wide population segments is a major driver of rising emancipative values. Together with the findings here, this means that the effect of cognitive mobilization on people's democratic desires is mostly indirect: It operates via this process's tendency to strengthen emancipative values.

Let us look at the societal-level determination of the critical-liberal desire for democracy. As the coefficients tell, the prevalence of emancipative values in a society adds a 0.68 fraction of its score to people's critical-liberal desire for democracy. This is by far a stronger and more significant contribution than that of a society's democratic tradition. The latter adds only a 0.07 fraction of its score to the critical-liberal desire. Hence, critical-liberal desires for democracy can grow on all levels of democratic tradition, and even in the absence of it, provided that emancipative values become more widespread.

The model also shows that the prevalence of emancipative values in a society amplifies the effect of an individual's preference for emancipative values on the critical-liberal desire. This is obvious from the positive coefficient for the interaction term between societal-level and individual-level emancipative values. The interaction illustrates the mechanism of "social cross-fertilization" (Welzel 2013, 110–12, Box 3.1): When an individual-level attribute has an inherent tendency, this tendency unfolds more freely when the attribute in question is more prevalent in a society. The reason is that more individuals who carry the attribute meet each other then, which creates a sense of confirmation that lets the individuals follow more freely their tendency. In our case, the tendency of emancipative values toward a critical-liberal desire unfolds more freely when these values are more prevalent in a society.

As the other models in Table 4.2 show, similar findings apply to the constituents of the critical-liberal desire for democracy. Only the unqualified desire for democracy (see the first model in Table 4.2) sticks out, showing a much weaker determination pattern. Bare of the critical-liberal fundament, the strength of the desire for democracy is a quite meaningless phenomenon, however. In the analysis of Table 4.2, this is echoed by a weak determination pattern. In any case, the four hypotheses outlined in Section 2 are by and large confirmed.

CONCLUSION

With unqualified measures of popular desires for democracy, we are confronted with the coexistence paradox: Strong desires for democracy coexist easily with the lack of democracy. With qualified measures, the paradox dissolves: Wherever democracy is absent or deficient, people's desire for democracy lacks the enlightened views that emancipative values infuse. Figure 4.9 demonstrates this point.[14] The horizontal axis measures the extent to which people's democratic desires are detached from a liberal notion of democracy. The vertical axis measures the mismatch between a society's actual democratic quality and people's desires for democracy. As one can see, the size of this mismatch is explained to 61 percent by the extent to which people's democratic desires lack a liberal notion. In short, what matters for a regime's actual democratic quality is not the strength of people's desire for democracy but the spirit by which it is infused.

These results resonate with recent findings. Shin and Qi (2011) show that the predictive power of democratic desires with respect to a society's actual level of democracy increases considerably if these desires go together with a critical assessment of institutions. However, these authors do not place this result into a wider theoretical context because they make no effort to highlight the sources of the citizens' criticality. To the contrary, they pitch the impact of critical assessments against that of emancipative values, ignoring the fact that these values do not operate against critical assessments but actually nurture them – as we have seen. Critical citizens are enlightened by emancipative values.

Another related finding is provided by Norris (2011), who shows that Inglehart and Welzel's (2005) "self-expression values" do not strengthen people's desire for democracy. We have seen that the same holds true for emancipative values, which is not surprising because these values are an improved measurement of self-expression values. Norris reads her finding as disproving Inglehart and Welzel's theory, which she thinks posits that stronger emancipative values make people's desire for democracy stronger.

However, Inglehart and Welzel (2005, 178–85) have themselves demonstrated a weak effect of emancipative values on the desire for democracy. As they point out, the role of emancipative values is not to strengthen the democratic desire but to enlighten this desire and to make it consequential by coupling it with an urge to take action in the pursuit of it. Bare of a solid grounding in emancipative values, a strong desire for democracy is an inconsequential phenomenon that is not worth much bothering.

---

[14] A detailed description of the variables used in Figure 4.9 can be found in the online appendix to Welzel's *Freedom Rising* at http://www.cambridge.org/welzel (p. 102–3).

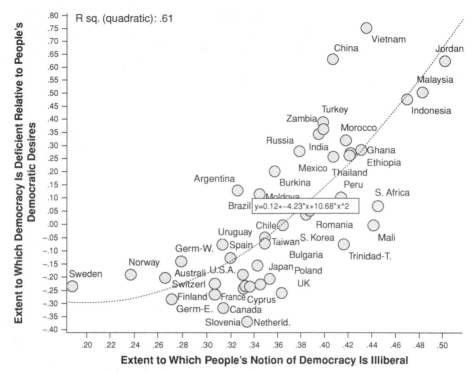

FIGURE 4.9. Dissolving the coexistence paradox.
Note: World Values Survey, fifth wave (World Values Survey Association 2009). Increasing scores on the horizontal axis show the extent to which national populations lack an unequivocally liberal understanding of democracy (calculating the inverse of unequivocally liberal understandings for democracy for each respondent and then calculating the national population averages on this deficit index). Increasingly positive scores on the vertical axis show the extent to which a regime's actual level of democracy falls short of what people's unqualified desires seem to suggest. Interpretation: With an increasing detachment of people's democratic desires from liberal notions of democracy, the regimes' actual levels of democracy fall increasingly short of what people's desires seem to suggest. In other words, where desires for democracy coexist with the absence of democracy, these desires lack a liberal notion of democracy.

The findings of this chapter highlight how emancipative values improve the conditions for democratic mobilization. Consider the evidence that emancipative values focus people's desire for democracy ever more sharply on democracy's liberal qualities: Because of this, people's desire for democracy can only be mobilized for the sake of universal freedoms, not against them. Or consider the evidence that emancipative values couple people's desire for democracy with a more critical rating of their society's actual democratic quality: Because of this, it is easier to mobilize this desire for pressures to improve the democratic quality of this society.

In conclusion, emancipative values shape the conditions of democratic mobilization: Where emancipative values are strong, these conditions are favorable, and pressures to make governance more accountable and responsive tend to be strong; where emancipative values are weak, the conditions are unfavorable, and such pressures tend to be weak or inexistent.

APPENDIX

Below follows the wording of the questions used to measure emancipative values. After that we document the wording of the democracy-related questions.

Measuring Emancipative Values

The measurement of emancipative values is based on twelve theme-grouped items, with four groups of three items that each create a separate subindex. Thus, there is a subindex for autonomy, equality, voice, and choice. Subindexes are the score average across the included items, after recoding all items into the same polarity and same scale range from minimum 0 (least emancipative) to 1.0 (most emancipative), with fractions such as 0.25, 0.33, 0.50, 0.66, and 0.75 for positions in between. Then the four subindex scores are averaged into the overall emancipative values index. A more detailed documentation of the measurement (including syntax and treatment of missing values) as well as extensive validity and reliability tests are available in the online appendix to Welzel's (2013) *Freedom Rising* at http://www.cambridge.org/welzel (pp. 20–28).

Subindex "Autonomy"
Here is a list of qualities that children can be encouraged to learn at home. Which, if any, do you consider to be especially important? Please choose up to five! (*Code five mentions at the maximum*)

		Mentioned	Not Mentioned
V12.	Independence	1	2
V13.	Hard work	1	2
V14.	Feeling of responsibility	1	2
V15.	Imagination	1	2
V16.	Tolerance and respect for other people	1	2
V17.	Thrift, saving money and things	1	2
V18.	Determination, perseverance	1	2
V19.	Religious faith	1	2
V20.	Unselfishness	1	2
V21.	Obedience	1	2

Mentioning of independence is coded 1 and nonmentioning 0. The same applies to imagination. Obedience, however, is coded 1 for nonmentioning and 0 for mentioning. Then the scores for the three items are averaged.

Subindex "Equality"
For each of the following statements I read out, can you tell me how strongly you agree or disagree with each. Do you strongly agree, agree, disagree, or strongly disagree? (*Read out and code one answer for each statement*)

		Strongly Agree	Agree	Disagree	Strongly Disagree
V60.	Being a housewife is just as fulfilling as working for pay.	1	2	3	4
V61.	On the whole, men make better political leaders than women do.	1	2	3	4
V62.	A university education is more important for a boy than for a girl.	1	2	3	4
V63.	On the whole, men make better business executives than women do.	1	2	3	4

Do you agree, disagree, or neither agree nor disagree with the following statements?

		Agree	Neither	Disagree
V44.	When jobs are scarce, men should have more right to a job than women.	1	2	3

Scores in V44 are recoded in ascending order into 0, 0.50, and 1.0. Scores in V61 and V62 are recoded in ascending order into 0, 0.33, 0.66, 1.0. Then the average over the three scores is calculated.

Subindex "Voice"
V69. People sometimes talk about what the aims of this country should be for the next ten years. On this card are listed some of the goals which different people would give top priority. Would you please say which one of these you, yourself, consider the most important? (*Code one answer only under "first choice"*)

V70. And which would be the next most important? (*Code one answer only under "second choice"*)

	V69 First Choice	V70 Second Choice
A high level of economic growth	1	1
Making sure this country has strong defense forces	2	2
Seeing that people have more say about how things are done at their jobs and in their communities	3	3
Trying to make our cities and countryside more beautiful	4	4

V71. If you had to choose, which one of the things on this card would you say is most important? (*Code one answer only under "first choice"*)

V72. And which would be the next most important? (*Code one answer only under "second choice"*)

	V71 First Choice	V72 Second Choice
Maintaining order in the nation	1	1
Giving people more say in important government decisions	2	2
Fighting rising prices	3	3
Protecting freedom of speech	4	4

No priority for each of the gray-shaded items is coded 0, second priority 0.50, and first priority 1.0. Then the three-item average is calculated.

Subindex "Choice"

Please tell me for each of the following actions whether you think it can always be justified, never be justified, or something in between, using this card. (*Read out and code one answer for each statement*)

		Never Justifiable					Always Justifiable				
V198.	Claiming government benefits to which you are not entitled	1	2	3	4	5	6	7	8	9	10
V199.	Avoiding a fare on public transport	1	2	3	4	5	6	7	8	9	10
V200.	Cheating on taxes if you have a chance	1	2	3	4	5	6	7	8	9	10
V201.	Someone accepting a bribe in the course of their duties	1	2	3	4	5	6	7	8	9	10
V202.	Homosexuality	1	2	3	4	5	6	7	8	9	10
V203.	Prostitution	1	2	3	4	5	6	7	8	9	10
V204.	Abortion	1	2	3	4	5	6	7	8	9	10
V205.	Divorce	1	2	3	4	5	6	7	8	9	10
V206.	Euthanasia – ending of the life of the incurable sick	1	2	3	4	5	6	7	8	9	10
V207.	Suicide	1	2	3	4	5	6	7	8	9	10
V208.	For a man to beat his wife	1	2	3	4	5	6	7	8	9	10

Scores for V202, V204, and V205 are recoded in ascending order from 0 to 1.0. Then the three-item average is calculated. The encompassing index of emancipative values is the average over the four subindex scores.

Questions Used to Measure Popular Views of Democracy

Notions of Democracy

Many things may be desirable, but not all of them are essential characteristics of democracy. Please tell me for each of the following things how essential you think it is as a characteristic of democracy. Use this scale where 1 means "not at all an essential characteristic of democracy" and 10 means it definitely is "an essential characteristic of democracy." (*Read out and code one answer for each*)

		Not an Essential Characteristic of Democracy								An Essential Characteristic of Democracy
V152.	Governments tax the rich and subsidize the poor.	1	2	3	4	5	6	7	8	9	10
V153.	Religious authorities interpret the laws.	1	2	3	4	5	6	7	8	9	10
V154.	People choose their leaders in free elections.	1	2	3	4	5	6	7	8	9	10
V155.	People receive state aid for unemployment.	1	2	3	4	5	6	7	8	9	10
V156.	The army takes over when government is incompetent.	1	2	3	4	5	6	7	8	9	10
V157.	Civil rights protect people's liberty against oppression.	1	2	3	4	5	6	7	8	9	10
V158.	The economy is prospering.	1	2	3	4	5	6	7	8	9	10
V159.	Criminals are severely punished.	1	2	3	4	5	6	7	8	9	10
V160.	People can change the laws in referendums.	1	2	3	4	5	6	7	8	9	10
V161.	Women have the same rights as men.	1	2	3	4	5	6	7	8	9	10

Scores are recoded into a scale range from minimum 0 to maximum 1.0. On this basis, the liberal notion of democracy (without further qualification) is the average over the items V154, V157, V160, and V161. The unequivocally liberal notion is calculated as the average over the same four items and the inverse of items V153, V156, V158, and V159. Scores below 0.50 indicate that people define democracy more in nonliberal than liberal terms; scores above 0.50 indicate the opposite.

Desires for Democracy

V162. How important is it for you to live in a country that is governed democratically? On this scale, where 1 means it is "not at all important" and 10 means "absolutely important," what position would you choose? (*Code one number*)

Not at all Important									Absolutely Important
1	2	3	4	5	6	7	8	9	10

Scores are recoded into a scale range from minimum 0 to maximum 1.0. This measures the desire for democracy, without further qualification. The liberal desire for democracy is the desire for democracy weighted for how unequivocally liberal people define democracy. The critical-liberal desire for democracy is further weighted for how critical people rate democracy (see later).

Ratings of Democracy

V163. And how democratically is this country being governed today? Again using a scale from 1 to 10, where 1 means that it is "not at all democratic" and 10 means that it is "completely democratic," what position would you choose? (*Code one number*)

Not at all Democratic									Completely Democratic
1	2	3	4	5	6	7	8	9	10

Scores are recoded into a scale range from minimum 0 to maximum 1.0. To calculate the critical rating of democracy, scores are subtracted from Welzel's (2013) citizen rights index, averaged over the five years preceding a survey. Effective democracy measures the actual level of democracy also on a scale range from 0 to 1.0. The resulting difference index is again standardized into a scale range from 0 to 1.0. Scores below 0.50 indicate that people rate their country's democracy better than it is; scores above 0.50 indicate the opposite.

PART B

CHANGING IMAGES OF GOVERNMENT

5

Reassessing the *Civic Culture* Model

Russell J. Dalton and Doh Chull Shin

Gabriel Almond and Sidney Verba's (1963) seminal *The Civic Culture* described the characteristics of a political culture that presumably enables nations to develop stable democratic processes. The civic culture was a mix of many traits, but several features were prominent in their descriptions of democracy in the United States and Britain. A democratic political culture is based on an aware, participatory public, although participation is often a potential rather than a reality. Similarly, a democratic culture requires a supportive public that identifies with the political community and trusts the institutions of government. They highlighted this pattern with the allegiant citizen described in the following example (Almond and Verba 1963, 443–44):

Miss E. is well informed on the uses of tax funds and is on the whole satisfied with the way in which tax money is being used. She has had some routine official contacts at the local Social Security office for instance, and she found the officials "in every way as nice as could be." She remembers her father's writing to the government about a state problem and receiving a pleasant and courteous reply. She feels that she would always be treated with friendliness and consideration by any government officials.

To many readers this description of the "good" democratic citizen must seem like an image of a different political era.

In addition, the early political culture studies described the political cultures of many Third World nations that supposedly lacked these civic traits (Pye and Verba 1965; Almond and Coleman 1960; Lerner 1958). These scholars maintained that many people in these nations were unaware of and uninvolved in politics. The everyday needs of life and limited social skills and experiences created parochial citizens. Furthermore, even among the politically aware, social norms and history had socialized acceptance of tradition, hierarchy, and an autocratic form of government. In contrast to the participatory citizens in established democracies, these cultures were often characterized by a mix of parochial and subject political orientations.

This chapter argues that the reality of contemporary political cultures – for established democracies and developing nations – is much different today than in the 1950s and early 1960s. Citizens in established democracies now appear less allegiant and more willing to pursue contentious courses of political action. In addition, democracy has spread across the globe, even in nations where the civic culture theory might not expect democratization. Systematic empirical evidence on political attitudes in developing nations is now quite extensive, which alters our understanding of the political culture in these societies. These changes are reshaping our images of the cultural foundations of democracy or at least how well contemporary publics fit long-standing theoretical models.

This chapter reviews several of the basic premises of the *Civic Culture* model based on analyses of the World Values Survey (WVS). First, we consider the levels of political attentiveness and awareness across nations, testing the contrast between parochial and participatory cultures as a condition for political development. Second, we examine attitudes toward the institutions of government to evaluate the assumption that democracy requires a supportive public. Third, we examine how contemporary publics view alternative regime choices spanning democracy and autocracy – and how support for government and support for democracy are interrelated in contemporary societies. We conclude with a revisionist view of the role of these attitudes in the democratic politics.

POLITICAL CULTURE AND DEMOCRACY

Modern political culture research was born from the experience of Europe in the first half of the twentieth century. The communist assault on democracy eroded support for the democratic ideal among some Europeans on the Left; then the fascist assault eroded support for democracy by extremists on the Right (Bermeo 2003; Linz and Stepan 1978). Limited support for governments in many nations seemed to create a fundamental threat for democracies that depend on popular support as a basis of legitimacy. The political turmoil of interwar Europe and the collapse of Weimar democracy were major stimuli for *The Civic Culture* and subsequent research on political culture.

As a first point, the *Civic Culture* framework assumed that citizens in established democracies are broadly aware of the political process and the institutions of government. Although democratic publics can vary in their opinions, the researchers believed that *cognition of government* and its institutions is an initial step in developing a civic culture. They also maintained that *positive affect toward the institutions of representative government* is essential for a well-functioning democracy. In Almond and Verba's words, "in the first place, the civic culture is an allegiant participant culture. Individuals are not only oriented to political inputs, they are oriented *positively* to the input structures and input processes" (31; emphasis added). Legitimacy in a democracy seemingly rests on the public's positive opinions of representative government and its institutions. Theoretical studies similarly stressed the importance of diffuse support for government as a prerequisite for a stable democratic system (Eckstein 1992; Easton 1965).

The Civic Culture did not explicitly measure *support for the democratic regime* and its principles, but the expectations were clear. A stable, successful democracy required that the public (and elites) hold democratic values and support democratic processes. An oft-cited example is Weimar Germany, which succumbed to an authoritarian challenge because it apparently lacked sufficient popular support for the principles of democratic government. Indeed, even postwar public opinion surveys demonstrated substantial support for authoritarian figures and nondemocratic government among the West German public (Merritt and Merritt 1970). In contrast, Almond and Verba maintained that the United States and Britain persisted as democracies in the face of these same interwar challenges because of the reservoir of popular support among their citizens. Trust in government is vital in democratic systems because legitimacy derives from the social contract between citizens and their representatives.

Much of the initial scholarship on political culture and political development similarly maintained that less developed nations lacked this civic, allegiant, democratic political culture. Almond and Verba (1963) discussed how a limited political cognition created a "parochial culture" in these nations, with many individuals divorced from politics in either physical or psychological terms. This theme of the parochial peasant or rural villager was common in research on less developed nations during this period (Banfield 1963; Lerner 1958; Binder 1965).

People in less developed nations also supposedly lacked positive affect toward government. For instance, Lucian Pye and Sidney Verba (1965) stated that limited trust in government impeded democratic development in Italy, Mexico, Ethiopia, and Egypt. Pye's (1985) description of Asian political cultures stressed the limitations of democracy in societies that emphasized hierarchic authority patterns and deference to authority. In short, the political culture in less developed nations supposedly lacked both support for the institutions of a democratic regime and more generalized support for democratic principles.[1]

The *Civic Culture* framework has shaped our thinking about the role of political culture in the democratization process. Thus, studies of the democratic transitions in postwar Western Europe stressed the need to develop the elements of the civic culture as essential to these political transformations (McDonough et al. 1998; Baker, Dalton, and Hildebrandt 1981). Robert Putnam's (1993)

---

[1] Even if people trusted government in autocratic societies, legitimacy would be based on non-democratic principles, such as hereditary succession, religious authority, ideology, or tradition, or would be mobilized by the agents of an authoritarian state. There was a general presumption that autocratic governments persisted because the public tolerated or even endorsed their autocratic structure.

study of Italian regional government emphasized the open, trusting norms of Northern Italy (and its better functioning regional governments) in comparison to the politically alienated culture of the Mezzogiorno. Much of the initial literature on the 1990s democratic transitions in Eastern Europe focused on the development of a supportive political culture among the citizenry (Klingemann, Fuchs, and Zielonka 2006; Rose, Haerpfer, and Mishler 1998), as did studies of democratization in East Asia and Africa (Dalton and Shin 2006; Chu et al. 2008; Bratton et al. 2004).

However, recent scholarship challenges the basic premises of the *Civic Culture* framework on at least two fronts. One set of findings involves the decline of political trust in postindustrial democracies. So central was *The Civic Culture*'s framework of the allegiant democratic citizen that the first signs of decreasing political trust in established democracies during the 1970s generated widespread academic and political concern. Almond and Verba (1980) recognized this trend in *The Civic Culture Revisited* and remained cautious about its implications. Across the trilateral democracies, Michel Crozier and his colleagues (Crozier, Huntington, and Watanuki 1975) viewed the public's increasing skepticism of government and the rise of protest politics as a "crisis of democracy." If trust in government were essential to an efficient and effective democracy, then the erosion of trust was a cause for serious concern.

The second new development is the expansion of systematic public opinion research to less developed nations. Instead of relying on the insights of national experts, researchers could directly assess the citizenry's opinions and values. There is now considerable cross-national variation in public opinion, and much of this new empirical evidence appears inconsistent with the imagery of the *Civic Culture* model. For instance, few contemporary societies can be characterized as disproportionately comprising parochials. Recent research repeatedly describes levels of political awareness in less developed and undemocratic states that belie the imagery of a parochial public (Bratton et al. 2004; Chu et al. 2008; Shin 2012). Many of these publics are less politically engaged than those in established democracies, but it is a matter of degree rather than a qualitative difference.

Even more striking are the cross-national patterns in regime preferences. Ronald Inglehart (2003) used data from the WVS to show that expressed support for a democratic regime is widespread around the globe – even in many authoritarian regimes (also see Gallup-International 2005; Pew Center 2002). Similarly, the initial surveys of postcommunist publics in Eastern Europe found broad support for democracy, which was in marked contrast to the evidence from democratic transitions in Germany, Italy, and the Iberian Peninsula decades earlier (Rose et al. 1998; Klingemann et al. 2006). Modern survey research documents widespread democratic aspirations in East Asia (Dalton and Shin 2006; Chu et al. 2008; Shin 2012) and in Africa (Bratton et al. 2004). Studies of Muslim states uncovered a surprising endorsement for democracy in these nations (Moaddel 2007; Norris and Inglehart 2003). Even when there is residual support for autocratic forms of government in non-democracies, this typically falls far short of support for a democratic form of government.

Although we cannot fully examine the processes that may have produced such changes from the *Civic Culture* model, it seems likely that the twin forces of social modernization and globalization have transformed contemporary political cultures. Inglehart (1977, 1990) was one of the first to describe how affluence and social modernization have created a new type of democratic citizen in postindustrial democracies: citizens who are less deferential to political elites and more willing to use elite-challenging forms of political participation (also Inglehart and Welzel 2005). Christian Welzel (2013) has expanded this into a general model of human development in which value change plays a prominent role. Typically, citizens in established democracies are politically engaged and critical of government and the institutions of representative democracy, while strongly endorsing democratic values.

In addition, social modernization and globalization have the potential to transform the political culture of developing nations. The political culture literature argued that the course to a democratic civic culture came through social modernization that produced an expansion of education, access to the mass media, an occupation that integrated workers into a national economy, and a broadening (and more tolerant) world view (Banfield 1963; Lerner 1958; Binder 1965). The process of social modernization would increase political awareness among the citizenry at large, then develop values that are more consistent with a democratic system. Even if this logic is still accepted to some degree, the range of social experiences has changed dramatically since the 1950s. Even poor nations now often have extensive cell phone networks and satellite television (Inglehart and Norris 2009). Although too many people still struggle to develop a modest standard of living, there are now few places that experts can describe as the isolated parochial societies presented in the early political culture and development literature. The development of a globalized economic system has also transformed employment and life conditions in many still developing nations. In addition, globalization has produced a diffusion of information and international norms, which appear to be socializing more cosmopolitan values even in less developed nations (Sandholtz and Stiles 2009). The world today is much smaller than that studied by Almond, Verba, and their colleagues.

This chapter examines the potential change in the political cultures of contemporary societies. Our analyses are possible only because of the unparalleled resources of the WVS.[2] The five waves of the WVS provide for longitudinal comparisons in several nations. Even more valuable, the WVS is exceptional for

[2] The data for this paper were downloaded from the World Values Survey website (http://www.worldvaluessurvey.org). The website also has the questionnaires for each survey and additional information on survey sampling and methodology.

the diverse range of nations it surveys. Most advanced industrial democracies participated in at least one wave of the WVS. In addition, an exceptional number of democratizing nations and autocratic states are included in the project. This enables us to examine political culture across nearly the full range of social and political conditions existing today.

POLITICAL INTEREST AND ATTENTIVENESS

Almond and Verba maintained that a democratic political culture requires that a substantial proportion of the public follows national politics. Without being informed about the national political system, people are likely to remain apathetic to the system. The classic *Civic Culture* imagery portrayed many individuals in developing nations as lacking this awareness; most people were supposedly parochials who were unaware of or disinterested in politics. Even in established democracies, there is a significant core of apathetic and apolitical citizens.

However, the world is much smaller today. Technological change has brought satellite television, radio, and cell phones to most of the globe (Inglehart and Norris 2009). The expansion of a globalized economy and social system touches even rural areas that once might have fit *The Civic Culture*'s description of a parochial society. For example, one can pass through the urban slums in India and see families with few possessions except a television set. Bruce Gilley (2009, 78) cites a similar example from a Ugandan government official:

With a radio deep in a rural village, a person is abreast with a bomb blast in Bombay, and can follow a political crisis in Moscow . . . People will take sides on issues far beyond their national borders. Whether the wife of dictator Ferdinand Marcos should be prosecuted or should be pardoned; whether the genocide in Rwanda could have been averted are issues which are enlivening beer-drinking discussions on a scale unprecedented in African history . . . This knowledge revolution is making it difficult for African leaders to keep people ignorant of what they are entitled to or to stop them from demanding change and working for it. Hence there are shivers of change all over the continent.

In such an environment, it seems less likely that a nation's political culture could still be predominately composed of people who are unaware of the national government and its activities.

To examine citizen awareness and engagement in politics, we asked whether general interest in politics varies systematically by the economic development of a nation.[3] In other words, are people in less developed nations disengaged from politics? As previous research has shown, public interest in politics is moderate; just less than half of the WVS respondents express interest in politics. However, a nation's level of socio-economic development (measured by the

---

[3] See the appendix for question wording.

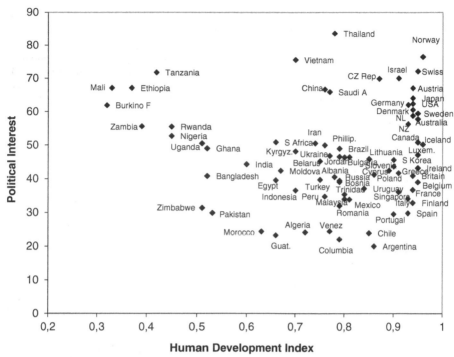

FIGURE 5.1. Human development and political interest.
Note: The figure plots national scores on these two dimensions: UN Human Development Index 2003 and percentage who are very or somewhat interested in politics.
Source: World Values Survey IV and V (*N* = 78).

United Nations Human Development Index) is essentially unrelated to levels of political interest (Figure 5.1). Among the affluent, developed societies, overall political interest ranges from about one-third of the public to well over three-quarters. However, in the half dozen least developed nations, about three-fifths of the public say that they are interested in politics. Table 5.1 shows that politics can attract the public's interest regardless of the nation's level of economic or political development.[4]

The Civic Culture even more strongly argued that many people in less developed nations lacked an awareness of national politics. It is possible, for instance, that expressions of interest are referring to local politics and that there is little

---

[4] Socio-economic development is measured by the United Nations Human Development Index for 2003; for political development, we use the World Bank's Voice and Accountability Index for 2006 (http://info.worldbank.org/governance/wgi/index.asp). This measures the extent to which a country's citizens are able to participate in selecting their government as well as freedom of expression, freedom of association, and a free media. When a nation was included in both the fourth and fifth waves of the WVS, we combined the surveys to produce a single data point for each nation.

TABLE 5.1. *The Correlates of Cultural Traits*

	Socioeconomic Development–UN Human Development Index	Political Development– WB Voice and Accountability
Interest/attentiveness		
Political interest	−0.06	0.05
Have opinions about government	0.26*	0.35*
Trust in government		
Confidence in government	−0.36*	−0.37*
Confidence in parliament	−0.32*	−0.25*
Confidence index	−0.36*	−0.34*
Regime support		
Support democracy	0.21	−0.07
Support autocracy	−0.41*	−0.55*
Democracy-autocracy index	0.25*	0.47*

Note: Table entries are the Pearson correlations between economic and political development indicators and various aspects of the political culture. The number of countries for each correlation typically ranges from sixty-three to eighty-six. Coefficients significant at the 0.05 level are denoted by an asterisk.

Source: National aggregates from nations included in World Values Survey IV or V.

awareness of national government – this was the core of the parochial hypothesis. To tap such cognitive awareness, we relied on three questions asking about confidence in national political institutions (see the appendix). We assess opinion holding by counting the "don't know" responses in evaluating the national government, and parliament.

Only a small minority of the overall WVS sample (approximately 5 percent) give even one "don't know" response to any one of these three questions. As we might expect, the percentages lacking an opinion are generally higher in less developed nations. For example, the six nations with the largest percentage of "don't know" responses on any of the three questions were India (25 percent), the Ukraine (23 percent), Jordan (14 percent), China (15 percent), Russia (13 percent), and Burkina Faso (13 percent). Yet, if this is an indication of the parochial, unaware sector of the public, the overall pattern suggests more citizen awareness than might be expected. Among less developed African and Middle Eastern nations, for example, fewer than one-tenth express one or more "don't know" opinions, which is barely more than the 5 percent average for established Western democracies. Table 5.1 shows that this measure of opinion holding is significantly related to a nation's level of socioeconomic or political development, but the correlations are modest.

In the modern world, which includes satellite television, cell phone networks, and Internet cafes even in developing nations, few individuals are unaware of government – or at least unwilling to share an opinion. Interest in politics similarly seems to transcend the economic or political circumstances of a nation. Thus, these results speak against the civic culture framework that emphasized the political engagement of established democracies and the parochial and somewhat apolitical nature of people in developing nations.

SUPPORT FOR GOVERNMENT

Another important element of the political culture is the public's evaluation of government and its institutions. The *Civic Culture* model implies that democracy relies on a public that positively supports its government. This is the heart of the allegiant model of citizenship, as seen in the description of Miss E. at the start of this chapter. Virtually all of the political culture research in the postwar era echoed this refrain.

The WVS measures public confidence in government and parliament, which we combined into a single index of confidence in government.[5] Figure 5.2 displays the confidence in government by national scores on the Human Development Index. In contrast to expectations derived from the *Civic Culture* model, several nondemocratic states display great support for both governmental institutions: Vietnam, China, Jordan, and Malaysia. Rather than being bastions of allegiant, supportive citizens, most of the established democracies are located in the middle of this cross-national distribution. The greatest public skepticism exists in a set of developing nations that are often struggling with poor performance in political terms, economic terms, or both, such as Argentina, Serbia, Moldova, and the Ukraine.[6] Confidence in government is *negatively* related to the socioeconomic and political development of a nation (Table 5.1), although this relationship is modest, as it is with the Voice and Accountability Index.

Would early political culture researchers have expected the Vietnamese public to express more confidence in their governmental institutions than Americans, Britons, or Norwegians? We think not. This presents a puzzle about the nature of trust in government and its relationship to political development.

One explanation for the pattern in this figure is that the basis of legitimacy may vary across nations (Almond and Powell 1984). Whereas people in established Western democracies may judge their confidence in government on democratic criteria such as the representation of public preferences and acceptance of the rule of law, other nations may employ more instrumental criteria. Cultural norms may also come into play. People in Middle Eastern states presumably use different criteria than Western publics in judging their

---

[5] See the appendix for question wording. We constructed a simple additive index that combines scores on both items and divides by 2 so that the resulting index runs from 1 (no confidence) to 4 (very great confidence).

[6] People generally express more confidence in a nonpolitical institution – the courts – than they do in government and the parliament. This might suggest that attitudes toward the institutions of administration come before support for governing institutions, except that all of the established democracies also follow this pattern.

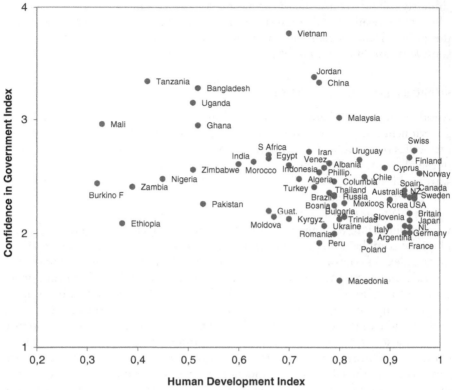

FIGURE 5.2. Human development and confidence in government.
Note: The figure plots national scores on these two dimensions: UN Human Development Index 2003 and an index combining confidence in government and parliament ranging from 1 (no confidence) to 4 (very great confidence).
Source: World Values Survey IV and V ($N = 63$).

governments. The high institutional confidence among people in autocratic states also may reflect political norms that encourage them to believe in (or publicly say they believe in) the legitimacy of their countries' institutions. If this were so, confidence ratings can be meaningfully interpreted only in the context of people's basic value orientations and the type of regime in which they take place.

Patterns of government performance may also explain cross-national variation in confidence in governing institutions. For instance, the dramatic economic progress of the Chinese and Vietnamese economies in recent years might stimulate confidence in government for different reasons (Gilley 2009). But systematically evaluating this topic is complicated if the standards of performance evaluations differ as a function of social modernization and political development. No single measure can define the outputs of government in all their variation. As a partial test of this performance hypothesis, we correlated confidence in government with the World Bank's index of government effectiveness, which is designed to measure how well government functions.[7] Instead of government effectiveness positively correlating with citizen confidence in government, we actually found a weak *negative* relationship between both measures ($r = -0.10$). As more democratic nations tend to score higher in government effectiveness, this suggests that rising expectations rather than performance are producing this *negative* relationship.

We believe the explanation of these cross-national patterns is complex. Established, successful democracies were once characterized by a more trusting public. However, the evolution of political values in advanced industrial democracies has created a new assertive form of citizenship (Inglehart 1990; Dalton 2009). Citizens' expectations for government and their willingness to challenge political elites have increased, even while the public remains committed to democratic values. These new assertive citizens are more likely to express criticism of government. Russell Dalton (2004, Chapter 2), for instance, used long-term national survey series to show that trust in parliament has generally declined in twelve of the fifteen established democracies for which long-term time series are available (also see Norris 2010).

This same pattern of declining trust occurs for the established democracies in the WVS. Figure 5.3 compares trust in parliament for the democracies that were surveyed in the first wave of the WVS and then again in either the fourth or fifth wave. Confidence in parliament has decreased in most nations over the roughly two-decade span of these surveys. The notable exceptions are the Scandinavian democracies, but longer time series suggest that trust in parliament and government trended downward even in Scandinavia (see Dalton 2004). Indeed, given the specific events that might influence the pair of surveys in these comparisons and the shortness of some trends, the evidence of general decline across a diverse set of nations is even more impressive.[8] This presents us with the contrarian finding that trust in government is decreasing in those nations where democracy is most consolidated.

In contrast, one might expect political trust to grow in new democracies. After all, the essence of the *Civic Culture* model holds that people need to develop support for political institutions and democratic values if democracy is to endure. The Third Wave brought democratization to many of the nations in the WVS. However, if we extend the logic of assertive citizenship, it suggests

---

[7] This index combines measures of the quality of public service provision, the quality of the bureaucracy, the competence of civil servants, the independence of the civil service from political pressures, and the credibility of the government's commitment to policies (http://info.worldbank .org/governance/wgi).

[8] For instance, some surveys may have coincided with a short-term political crisis or a dramatic event and thus created short-term perturbations from the longer trends we are trying to observe. This is why more extensive trend data from nation surveys are important in verifying these downward trends. See Dalton (2004, Chapter 2).

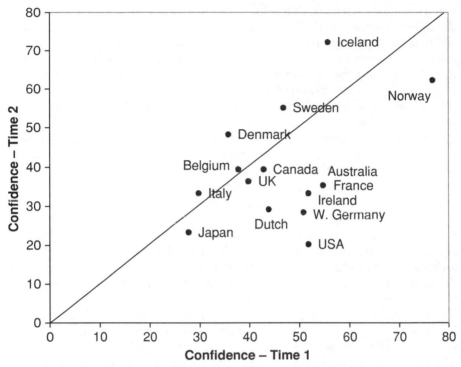

FIGURE 5.3. Confidence in parliament over time in advanced industrial democracies. *Note:* Figure presents the percentage confident in parliament from the first available WVS time point to the last available time point.
Source: World Values Survey, various years.

that contemporary democratization may actually stimulate a more critical public because dissent and debate are tolerated and encouraged in a democracy. In contrast, an autocratic state suppresses dissent and controls the flow of information to support the government's positions, regardless of how specious. Ironically, modern democracy may teach citizens to be critical of their government.

One could do a thought experiment to explore this claim. If one had access to a public opinion survey in the German Democratic Republic in the mid-1980s (or another communist state), most survey respondents presumably would have expressed confidence in their government. In part this would be a sign of the government's successful propaganda efforts and extensive socialization campaigns. In part it might reflect an individual's hesitancy to be critical in a system where the Stasi monitored individual behavior and enforced allegiance to the regime. If one surveyed the same individuals today, they might be more critical about how the current democratic government is addressing their needs, how political parties have overlooked the East, and how democratic institutions struggle to fulfill their democratic ideals.⁹ This could occur even though their life conditions and political freedoms have dramatically improved because of the democratic transition.

Unfortunately, systematic comparisons of public opinion before and after a democratic transition are quite rare. However, the WVS includes four nations surveyed through a democratic transition: Hungary (surveyed from 1982 until 1999), South Korea (from 1982 until 2005), Poland (from 1989 until 2005), and Mexico (from 1990 until 2005).¹⁰ Hungary and Korea are the two clearest cases of closed autocratic governments giving way to democracies during the span of the surveys (Korea in 1987 and Hungary in 1990). The first Polish surveys were conducted as political change was sweeping through Eastern Europe and spanned the historic 1989 parliamentary elections. Mexico also made a democratic transition in 2000, but its initial situation and its relationship to the United States make this a less sharp transition.

Figure 5.4 tracks confidence in parliament for these four nations across the WVS surveys. In Hungary, for example, 92 percent of the public expressed confidence in the communist parliament in 1982; this is a level of political support that would make virtually any democracy jealous. However, the 1991 survey after the democratic transition shows a marked decline in confidence that continues over time.¹¹ The 1989 Polish survey found 89 percent of the public were confident in the parliament, which was perhaps shaped by the euphoria of the 1989–90 transition; by 2005, this was 12 percent. South Korea follows the same pattern: from 68 percent confident in 1982, when an autocratic government was in control, to only 25 percent confident about their democratic government in 2005. The trend in Mexico is less marked but also tracks a downward course.¹²

We cannot be certain, but we expect this pattern may apply to some of the autocratic governments that have high levels of political confidence in

⁹ In fact, the first WVS survey in East Germany was conducted in fall 1990, and 41 percent expressed confidence in the Bundestag; this dropped to 16 percent in the 2006 survey. Nationally representative surveys before the Berlin Wall fell are not available.

¹⁰ According to Freedom House's combined ratings of political rights and civil liberties, Hungary transitioned from a score of 11 (not free) in 1982 to a score of 3 (free) in 1999; Poland went from a score of 7 in 1989 (4 in 1990) to 2 in 2005; South Korea changed from a score of 11 in 1982 to a score of 3 in 2005; Mexico changed from a score of 8 in 1990 to a score of 4 in 2005.

¹¹ With more frequent and finer measurements, one might expect an increase in political support immediately after a popular democratic transition as individuals embrace the new regime. But as politics normalizes, the skepticism we describe might emerge. A similar pattern appeared for voting turnout, which often surged in the first democratic election and then dropped to a lower level in subsequent elections.

¹² South Africa is another possible comparison. The first WVS came after Nelson Mandela's release in 1990 but before the end of apartheid in 1992. Trust in parliament drops from 66 percent in 1990 to 60 percent in 2001, before rising to 65 percent in 2006. There are, however, much different trends between whites and minorities because of the overlap of political regimes and apartheid.

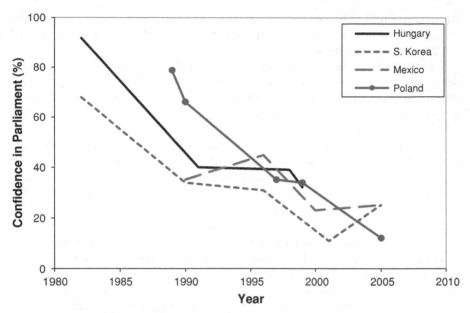

FIGURE 5.4. Confidence in parliament before and after democratic transition.
Source: World Values Survey, various years.

Figure 5.2. High levels of support in some nations may represent the closed nature of a political system that restricts public expressions of dissatisfaction. Such a high level of support might benefit a nation that is struggling with the challenges of economic and social development, at least in the short term. Ironically, success in economic and political development might erode this support by changing to a more open political regime.

The other broad longitudinal trends captured by the WVS involve the publics of Eastern Europe (also see Chapter 7). The 1989–91 wave of the survey included several of the newly postcommunist states that were resurveyed in subsequent waves of the WVS. Certainly these nations experienced a difficult transition in social and economic terms, but politically, they gained new rights and freedoms. By the end of our time series, most of these nations – with the exception of Russia and several other post-Soviet states – were members of the European Union, with higher living standards and more personal freedoms than in the communist era.

The *Civic Culture* model predicts that support for the democratic institutions should increase over time as nations consolidate their democratic gains. However, in most cases, confidence in parliament has decreased since the first posttransition survey (Figure 5.5). In addition to the dropoffs we previously noted for Hungary and Poland, the WVS also tracks declines in Bulgaria (−27 percent), the Czech Republic (−25 percent), Romania (−4 percent), and Slovenia (−20 percent). Slovenia is a significant case because it probably was the most successful in making the economic and political transitions to a market

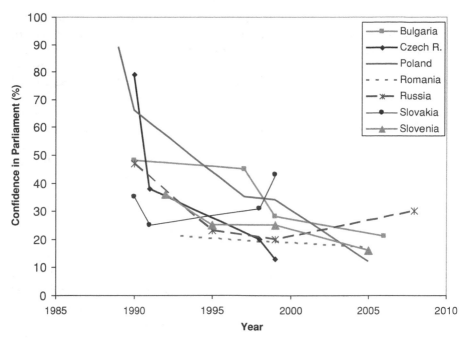

FIGURE 5.5. Confidence in parliament in postcommunist nations.
Source: World Values Survey, various years.

economy and democracy – and thereby improving the living conditions of its citizens. Yet, Slovenians' confidence in parliament notably decreases over time.

The clearest anomaly is Russia, which partially validates the general process we are describing. Russians' confidence in parliament decreased from 1990 until 1999, but the reassertion of strong state authority under Putin coincided with increased confidence in the 2008 survey. From another angle, this seems to confirm the pattern that higher confidence rates are often expressed in more authoritarian settings. Accordingly, high confidence ratings in more authoritarian settings do not mean that people have *internalized* autocratic norms; it may be that *social pressures* make them hesitant to express feelings of distrust (also see Chapter 7).

Taken alone, these trends might imply that Eastern Europeans are disenchanted by their democratic experience or that they are retreating from the political enthusiasm that initially greeted the democratic transition. However, this pattern mirrors the pre- and posttransition comparisons in Figure 5.5. Consequently, we think the postcommunist trends reflect the irony of modern democracy: Dramatic gains in democratic development go hand in hand with a more skeptical and assertive public – even when social and economic conditions are improving.

In summary, in contrast to the expectation of growing affective support for the institutions of government as democracy consolidates, our findings suggest that confidence in government is decreasing in contemporary democracies. Citizens in the advanced industrial democracies are becoming less likely to express confidence in parliament. Confidence may also decline after a transition from a functioning authoritarian state to an open democracy. Even in the democratizing nations of Eastern Europe, confidence in parliament has eroded since the democratic transition. However, these findings also raise doubts that confidence ratings have the same meaning in different regime contexts. Apparently, high confidence rates in authoritarian regimes do not necessarily indicate regime support, and low confidence rates in democracies do not necessarily mean weak legitimacy of the democratic regime. In most highly consolidated democracies, confidence in central democratic institutions has been falling in recent decades. Political criticism is the spirit of the contemporary age.

ORIENTATIONS TO DEMOCRACY AND ITS ALTERNATIVES

The research and policy literature maintains that democratization is incomplete until a majority of the public embraces democracy as the only legitimate form of government (Linz and Stepan 1996; Diamond 1999). The *Civic Culture* model suggests that public acceptance of democracy requires that the political culture undergo a long, slow process of attitudinal adjustment and value change. For this process to succeed, people must both support the principles of the newly installed democratic system and reject those of the old authoritarian system. In essence, people must shift their value system from a pro-authoritarian political culture to an anti-authoritarian and pro-democratic political culture.

To examine this question, we assess citizens' preference for democratic and authoritarian regime forms. We measure sentiments toward a democratic regime by a direct question about approval of "a democratic political system" (see the appendix). The WVS also asked respondents to rate the two most common authoritarian alternatives – civilian dictatorship and military rule – on the same 4-point scale.[13] We compared each respondent's ratings of civilian dictatorship and military regime *and chose the higher of these two* as the person's affinity for a nondemocratic regime. Most previous research looked only at support for democracy or simply averaged all autocratic regime types together. We think it is important to compare democracy to its alternatives and to measure authoritarian orientations as the choice of the most liked autocratic regime (rather than the average of both options). This is because the alternatives to democracy can systematically vary across cultural zones and historical experiences. For instance, in Latin American and African nations, the major alternative has been military regimes, but states in other regions have experienced autocratic civilian or monarchical regimes.[14]

---

[13] See the appendix for question wording.
[14] For evidence on East Asia, see Dalton and Shin (forthcoming). In other nations, theocracy may be the major rival to democracy. However, this option was not systematically included in the WVS comparisons of regime alternatives. This question was included in the 2006 Iraq survey:

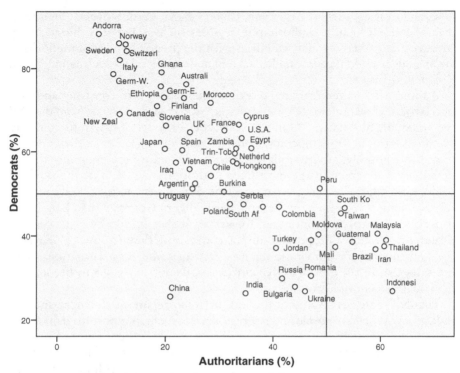

FIGURE 5.6. The distribution of authoritarians and democrats.
Note: The figure plots the percentage preferring democracy and the percentage prefer-
ring autocracy in each nation.
Source: World Values Survey V (*N* = 54).

To summarize contemporary regime orientations, we compared preferences
for democracy versus autocracy across nations (Figure 5.6).[15] Of the fifty-
four countries, a majority express approval of democracy in thirty-three countries and a plurality in six countries. A majority approve of an authoritarian
regime in nine countries and a plurality in six countries (authoritarians combine
those preferring an authoritarian alternative and those evaluating democracy
and authoritarian regimes equally). The countries with the preponderance of
democrats include all the established democracies in the West and several

46 percent were positive toward an Islamic government where religious leaders have absolute
power. Only 21 percent were positive toward a civilian autocracy; 18 percent were positive
toward a military government. A full 88 percent were positive toward democracy.
[15] We constructed this index as the simple difference between support for democracy and its
primary autocratic alternative on the 4-point good/bad scale. This variable is heavily skewed,
with 61 percent favoring the democratic alternative, 28 percent equal ranking, and 11 percent an
autocratic regime. We dichotomized this variable including the latter two categories into support
for autocracy on the presumption that democracy requires an affirmative public preference and
not neutrality. However, in no country does the percentage favoring an autocratic regime
(excluding neutrals) exceed the percentage favoring democracy.

new democracies, such as Argentina, Chile, Ghana, Peru, Slovenia, and Zambia. They even include authoritarian regimes such as Egypt, Ethiopia, Iraq, Morocco, and Vietnam. The countries with the preponderance of authoritarians include Iran, Malaysia, and Russia and new democracies such as Indonesia, Korea, and Taiwan.

Another way to summarize the regime preferences is to construct an index of relative regime preference by subtracting ratings of democracy from those of the autocratic alternative.[16] On this scale, the entire set of fifty-four countries averaged +1.0, a pro-democracy score substantially higher than the midpoint of 0. More notably, all fifty-four countries scored above the midpoint, that is, preferring democracy to the most-liked authoritarian rule. Yet, the levels of democratic regime preference vary a great deal across nations. For instance, relative support for democracy is ten times higher in Germany than in Bulgaria (+2.00 vs. +0.20) and more than four times higher in non-English-speaking protestant Western Europe than in postcommunist Eastern Europe. There is residual support for autocratic regimes even in some Western nations. This indicates that in the eyes of global citizenries, democracy is yet to become the final achievement of history.

Finally, Table 5.1 examines the link between regime preferences and our indicators of socioeconomic and political development. Support for democracy taken alone is nearly ubiquitous across different national conditions for social development and regime form, producing statistically insignificant relationships in the table. However, there are significant declines in support for an autocratic regime with economic and political development. Similarly, there are significant correlations for the democracy-autocracy index that compare the two regime forms. In other words, it is not that support for democracy increases with development but that support for autocratic alternatives decreases.

MERGING GOVERNMENT AND REGIME ORIENTATIONS

Contrary to what the civic culture model implies, we have found that citizen allegiance to their government is declining in many democracies, whereas support for democracy is widespread in many new and established democracies and even in autocratic states. Researchers have variously described this new pattern of citizenship as a "dissatisfied democrat" (Klingemann 1999; Chapter 6), "critical citizen" (Norris 1999), "emancipative citizen" (Welzel 2007, 2013) or "engaged citizen" (Dalton 2009). Contemporary democracies are increasingly characterized by a public that is critical of politicians and political institutions – while embracing democratic norms and holding higher expectations for

---

[16] The resulting index ranges from a low of −3 to a high of +3. Positive scores on this 7-point index are considered indicative of preference for democracy, whereas neutral and negative scores are considered indicative of an authoritarian regime. The higher the positive and negative scores are, the greater the preference for democratic and authoritarian regimes is, respectively.

TABLE 5.2. *A Typology of Political Orientations*

	Favor Democracy	Favor Autocracy	Totals
Confident in parliament	Allegiant democrat 24%	Allegiant autocrat 14%	38%
Not confident in parliament	Dissatisfied democrat 37%	Dissatisfied autocrat 25%	62%
Totals	61%	39%	100%

Note: See the text on the construction of these two dimensions.
Source: World Values Survey IV and V.

government. This gives rise to a new style of citizenship that has the potential to transform the democratic process. Most of this research has focused on these patterns in advanced industrial democracies; we now extend this research to the global scale of the WVS.

This conceptual framework leads to a simple two-by-two typology of government and regime orientations (Table 5.2). One dimension taps relative support for democracy or an autocratic regime, as in Figure 5.6. The other dimension taps confidence in parliament collapsed into "confident" and "not confident" responses.

Across all the nations in the WVS's fourth and fifth waves, a plurality of respondents is *dissatisfied democrats*; they favor a democratic regime but are critical of their national legislature. By comparison, *allegiant democrats*, who formed the core of the *Civic Culture* framework – confident in parliament and favoring a democratic regime – compose barely one-quarter of the WVS respondents. Only a modest number fit what might be described as a subject political culture – people who favor an autocratic regime and are satisfied with the current government. The final category is *dissatisfied autocrats*, who compose about one-quarter of the WVS sample.

Of course, the significance of these political orientations partially depends on their congruence with the social and political structure of the nation. Chapter 6 in this volume examines this group of dissatisfied democrats among European states. Almond and Verba posited that allegiant democrats are an essential component of a democratic civic culture: They endorse the values of the regime and have confidence in the political institutions. Dissatisfied democrats, in contrast, lack this confidence in the existing political institutions. They may be supporters of the opposition parties who are displaying their disagreement with government policies, or they may harbor deeper desires to reform the structure of representative democracy. In the United States, for example, this category might include Common Cause reformers, Libertarians, Tea Party members, Occupy Wall Street protestors, and critics of the imperfections in representative democracy. In short, dissatisfied democrats are often agents for political reform and further political development in a democratic setting.

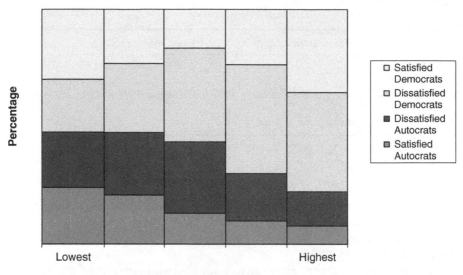

FIGURE 5.7. Democratic development and citizenship orientations.
Note: The figure plots the percentage of each category by the World Bank's Voice and Accountability Index. See Table 5.2 on the construction of these categories.
Source: World Values Survey, various years.

In contrast, in autocratic settings, those who endorse democracy are opposing the norms of the current regime. In this setting, dissatisfied democrats may be the primary supporters of regime change because they endorse democracy and lack confidence in the current autocratic government. Allegiant democrats are a contradiction in autocratic states. They have democratic regime preferences that run counter to the existing political system as generally understood, yet they also express confidence in the present autocratic government. One expects that the advocates for democratization in China, for example, are disproportionately assertive democrats.

Conversely, autocratic preferences hold different implications depending on the political regime. In democracies, these individuals are supporting political norms that run counter to those of the democratic state. Fascists in democratic Spain or unreformed communists in democratic Eastern Europe exemplify this group. In autocracies like Vietnam and China, they support the existing regime's principles, even if some lack confidence in the current government.

The congruence between citizenship norms and regime forms is displayed in Figure 5.7. We grouped nations according to their ratings on the World Bank's Voice and Accountability Index as a measure of democratization. The figure shows that the majority of the public prefers democracy to its autocratic alternatives regardless of the nature of the political system in which they live. This alone is striking evidence of how the world is different than *The Civic*

Culture presumed. Even in the nations ranked as least democratic by the World Bank index, 53 percent of the public favor democracy (satisfied and dissatisfied democrats combined). Support for a democratic regime systematically increases with democratic development to 78 percent in the nations highest on voice and accountability. Equally important, as the level of democratic development increases, this does not produce more *satisfied democrats*, as suggested by the classic civic culture literature. Instead, the proportion of *dissatisfied democrats* nearly doubles across the range of the voice-accountability scale, becoming the plurality (42 percent) among the most democratic nations.

Support for democracy is higher in nations with a higher voice-accountability score, and public support for an autocratic regime naturally is lower. In the least democratic regimes, nearly one-half of the public favors an autocratic regime, and one-third prefers democracy but simultaneously expresses confidence in their nondemocratic government. This latter group is a bit oxymoronic; for example, 68 percent of the Vietnamese claim to prefer democracy to either autocratic alternative, yet they simultaneously express confidence in the autocratic and unrepresentative National Assembly.

By comparison, barely one-fifth of the public in the least democratic nations favors democracy and is unsupportive of their current autocratic parliament. To an extent, this group of *dissatisfied democrats* should constitute the real popular basis for political change in autocratic states. These people are likely to endorse reforms of the existing political system to move closer to a democratic regime and take action in pursuit of this goal. In our Vietnamese example, *dissatisfied democrats* are barely a trace element among the Vietnamese public (1 percent), which suggests a limited base for popular action challenging the current regime. Then, at higher levels of voice and accountability, the proportions of satisfied and dissatisfied autocrats are lower. However, a significant minority still endorse a nondemocratic regime form even in the most democratic nations. Democracy is preferred, but it is not the only alternative for the citizens of contemporary democracies.

CONCLUSION

Nearly five decades have passed since Gabriel Almond and Sidney Verba proposed the civic culture model of democratic development on the basis of their public opinion surveys in four Western democracies and Mexico. As they aptly characterized it, their research represented the first systematic endeavor to develop "a scientific theory of democracy" (Almond and Verba 1963, 10). Unlike their predecessors, who sought to infer cultural norms and values from citizen behavior and institutional performance, these two political scientists specified the properties of democratic culture and directly assessed the political attitudes held by the citizenry in these states. Furthermore, they empirically explored the impact of culture on democratic political stability and effectiveness by examining whether the dominant pattern of citizen attitudes in each country was congruent with the structure of its political system. For these reasons alone, their study constitutes a pathbreaking investigation of democracy from a cultural perspective.

Since Almond and Verba's investigation of political cultures, powerful waves of socioeconomic and political transformation have swept every corner of the globe. The forces of modernization and globalization have liberated countless numbers of people from poverty and illiteracy and exposed them to foreign cultures, ideas, and products. The forces of political democratization and economic liberalization have expanded the spectrum of the political rights and civil liberties that people can enjoy. These structural and institutional changes have undoubtedly transformed contemporary cultures by shaping and reshaping not only the way ordinary people live and interact with others but also the way they think about and get involved in politics. Such shifts in mass political attitudes and behavior make it *necessary* to reassess whether the civic culture model proposed five decades ago still "fits" the real world of democratic politics.

The Third and Fourth waves of global democratization, moreover, have brought about a great deal of expansion in the comparative study of political cultures through public opinion surveys. A new generation of social scientists regularly conducts public opinion surveys in non-Western democracies that were not included in earlier empirical studies of political culture. In these new surveys, researchers have asked old and new questions to monitor citizen reactions to democracy and explore the impact of those reactions on the process of institutional democratization. The WVS is the exceptional example of this new research, spanning both a broad range of nations and tracking opinions over five waves of the survey. The accumulation of new surveys makes it possible to reassess the civic culture model that Almond and Verba proposed as that basis for stable and effective democracy.

We first note that the civic culture model was essentially based on the surveys in the United States and Great Britain, two stable first-wave democracies of the West. In these two nations, stability and effective performance were considered the overriding concerns of their democratic rule. Two of the other three nations – Germany and Italy – were drawn from modern Western nations. Only Mexico provided a glimpse of the political culture in a developing nation. As a result, the civic culture model was limited in assessing the democratization processes of transforming less developed authoritarian regimes into democracies. *Substantively*, therefore, this model was limited in studying two of the three key phases of democratization, that is, democratic transition and democratic consolidation.

Conceptually, the civic culture model was based on the age-old notion that democracy is government by the consent of the people and thus it cannot endure or thrive for an extended period of time unless people generally remain supportive of its process and institutions. The participation of ordinary citizens and their allegiance to democratic institutions were specified as the two key components of the model of stable democracy. Even in principle, therefore, this model did not allow citizens to do much politically besides expressing allegiance to or support for political institutions and their policies. These views were undoubtedly influenced by the recent turmoil in interwar European politics, especially the collapse of the Weimar Republic. However, this framework leaves little room for political competition and opposition among citizens with conflicting interests and preferences.

Moreover, the same model implies that positive orientations to democratic structures and processes contribute to all the phases of democratization, including those of transforming limited democracies into fully democracies and transforming ineffectively functioning democracies into effective democracies (Almond and Verba 1963, 30). Undoubtedly, positive orientations can be conducive to maintaining the stability of the existing democratic regimes regardless of the level of their democratic development. Such positive orientations, however, should not be considered the only type of political attitude conducive to democratization. The literature on civic activism argues that critical or negative orientations often drive people to demand reforms of ineffectively performing structures and processes (Burnel and Calvert 2004; Karatnycki and Ackerman 2005).

Thus, the evidence culled from the recent waves of the WVS makes it clear that people in all global regions tend to view democracy as a multilayered phenomenon, and they often react differently to the various layers of the same phenomenon. Specifically, a majority of contemporary publics is positively oriented to democracy as a political system and its fundamental values. And yet these supporters of a democratic regime are simultaneously more critical toward its institutions and processes (Chu et al. 2008; Shin and Wells 2005). Even in the most democratically developed countries, dissatisfied democrats, not allegiant democrats, constitute a plurality of their electorates.

More notably, citizen allegiance to governmental institutions is typically greatest at the lowest level of democratic development. This indicates that many countries have authoritarian systems when citizens are less critical of institutions or less willing or able to express criticism. Thus, countries that are more democratic (or less authoritarian) have citizens who are more critical of governmental institutions while embracing democratic ideals. This finding runs counter to the *Civic Culture* model, which holds that democracies become stable and effective with allegiant democrats, not with critical democrats. Obviously, the *Civic Culture* model of allegiant democrats is at odds with respect to democratization in the world today.

In addition, a dichotomized contrast between democracy and authoritarian regimes can overlook the sizeable percentage of people who express an affinity (or ambiguity) toward both regime forms. In overall terms, more than one-quarter of the respondents in the WVS fall into this category.[17] This produces a hybrid pattern in which many people, especially in newly democratizing

[17] See note 16.

and authoritarian countries, simultaneously give approval of democracy and autocratic regimes. In their minds, democracy is a political system that is not fundamentally different in kind from its authoritarian alternatives; they think in terms of a mixed or hybrid system that includes both authoritarian and democratic politics (Shin and Wells 2005).

Theoretically, the *Civic Culture* model holds that all political systems including democracies become stable and effective when their respective structures and cultures are congruent with each other (Almond and Verba 1963, 366; Eckstein 1992). When they are incongruent, the political system supposedly becomes unstable, and regime change becomes more likely (Almond and Verba 1963, 20). In the real world of contemporary nondemocratic countries, socioeconomic modernization and globalization have spawned a growing number of citizens who embrace democracy as their preferred regime. As a result of growing citizen preference, the incongruence between democratic culture and authoritarian politics is widening much more than was previously expected.

More notably, the *Civic Culture* model did not fully consider that democracies also experience the incongruence between culture and structure. Democracies experience the incongruence between the level of democracy supplied by institutions and that demanded by the citizenry (Welzel 2013; Inglehart and Welzel 2005; Mattes and Bratton 2007). This form of incongruence is not likely to cause the breakdown of democratic rule. Instead, it is likely to contribute to the further democratization of the political system through institutional reform. When democratic demand and supply are in congruence or in equilibrium at their low levels, moreover, democracy is known to remain "broken-back" (Rose and Shin 2001). In the world of newly emerging democracies, therefore, democratic progress may be more likely to take place when structure and culture are more incongruent than congruent. The failure of the civic culture model to consider the potentially positive role of such incongruence is a limitation in applying it as a cultural theory of democratic development.

The *Civic Culture* model as a theory of democratization at least partially implies that a political culture is exogenous to democratic development. In contrast, a number of newly democratized countries display a significant decline in institutional trust in the wake of a democratic regime change. Citizens of South Korea, Mexico, and most of the former communist countries became less confident in their parliaments as they democratized. This finding attests to the existence of an endogenous relationship between culture and democracy. Failing to consider such a reciprocal relationship offers an incomplete account of democratization that is currently taking place around the globe (Shin 2012).

Why is it that the *Civic Culture* model of allegiant and compliant democrats no longer fits today's democratic world, in which critical and defiant democrats prevail over their allegiant and allegiant counterparts? Why is it that this model is not fully capable of accounting for the dynamics of democratization? The first question deals with the specific components of the model; it involves the various changes occurring in societies over the past five decades and the liberalizing effects of those changes on citizens' mind-sets (Inglehart and Welzel 2005; Welzel 2013). Structural and institutional changes have enabled many people to accumulate a variety of socioeconomic and psychological resources, which enable them to become more assertive and critical rather than acquiescent and allegiant in the political process.

The second question concerning the *Civic Culture* model as a theory of democracy has to do with the overgeneralization of the findings from a small set of nations. In addition, it involves the way the model was specified. The exclusive concern with the stability of the democratic polity makes it impossible to understand democratic political development from a dynamic perspective and the positive role that the incongruent relationship between democratic culture and infrastructure plays in the process. All in all, our reassessments of the *Civic Culture* model indicate that the particular type of political culture that is most suitable for democratic development varies in kind across national political histories, and it also varies from one wave of democratization to another.

APPENDIX

Concept	Question	Codes
Political interest	"How interested would you say you are in politics? Are you:" (1) Very interested; (2) Somewhat interested; (3) Not very interested; (4) Not at all interested	Recoded so (4) Very interested and (1) Not at all interested
Confidence in institutions	"I am going to name a number of organizations. For each one, could you tell me how much confidence you have in them: is it a great deal of confidence, quite a lot of confidence, not very much confidence or none at all?" Parliament; government	Recoded so (4) Great deal of confidence and (1) No confidence at all
Regime preferences	"I'm going to describe various types of political systems and ask what you think about each as a way of governing this country. For each one, would you say it is a very good, fairly good, fairly bad or very bad way of governing this country?" Having a strong leader who does not have to bother with parliament and elections; Having the army rule; Having a democratic political system	Inverted the coding to range from 0 (very bad) to 3 (very good)

6

Dissatisfied Democrats

Democratic Maturation in Old and New Democracies[1]

Hans-Dieter Klingemann

From the beginning, political culture research has argued that, to persist, democracies need a supportive public (Almond and Verba 1963, Chapter 12). Recent evidence, however, indicates a change in the nature of democratic political culture. While support for democracy as a principle is widespread, many citizens have become less satisfied with the way democracy performs (Klingemann 1999; Dalton 2004). Norris (1999, 2010) characterizes this discrepancy as the rise of the "critical citizen." This term implies a positive message: Critical citizens improve the quality of the democratic process.[2] This chapter shows whether this optimistic perspective is empirically justified in Europe.

The possible combination of principled support for democracy with dissatisfaction about its performance has been anticipated by Easton (1965; 1975), who called for an analytical distinction between support for a political regime and support for its specific institutions and the authorities running them. Cross-national evidence shows that contemporary citizens do indeed make this distinction (Klingemann 1999; Dalton 1999). People who support democracy as a form of government can either be satisfied or dissatisfied with the design of political institutions and the performance of the political actors of their country. This finding may surprise skeptics who are cynical about the political sophistication of citizens, yet it speaks to the increasing cognitive mobilization

[1] I owe many thanks for critical reading and suggestions to Catherine Corrigall-Brown, Russell Dalton, John Keane, David Laycock, Steven Weldon, Christian Welzel, and Bernhard Wessels. It was a privilege to discuss earlier versions of this chapter with participants of a seminar of the School of Politics and International Relations, the Australian National University, organized by Ian McAllister and John Ravenhill, and with participants of a joint seminar hosted by the Department of Government and Social Relations and the Sydney Democracy Initiative, University of Sydney, organized by John Keane and Paul Fawcett.
[2] Klingemann (1999) classifies the same species as "dissatisfied democrats," which reflects the wording of the measurement instrument.

and rising levels of expectation among modern mass publics (Inglehart 1970; 1990; Inkeles 1975; Gouldner 1979; Klingemann and Fuchs 1995; Inglehart and Welzel 2005; Welzel 2013).

In most countries surveyed today, declared supporters of democracy constitute a clear majority. Thus, an analysis of political culture by country-level differences in the distribution of democrats and nondemocrats has limited importance. Divisions within the group of democrats become more important. Schedler and Sarsfield (2007) argue convincingly that "democrats with adjectives" deserve more attention. Among these "democrats with adjectives," "dissatisfied democrats" are a particularly interesting species. They are interesting because their proportion varies greatly between countries and because different theoretical approaches come to divergent conclusions as to whether large proportions of dissatisfied democrats are a bless or a bliss for democracy (Norris 1999, 2011).

Dalton and Welzel distinguish two models of a democratic political culture, contrasting the classic *allegiant model* and a newly emerging *assertive model* (for an operationalization and measurement, see Chapter 12). They use the term *allegiant participant culture* to describe Almond and Verba's vision of a civic culture. Support of representative institutions and their elected personnel, combined a commitment to democratic values are regarded as its major characteristics. This allegiant model leaves only limited room for political dissatisfaction, critical distance to authorities, or elite-challenging activity. Inspired by Inglehart's (1977) theory of postmaterialism and Welzel's (2013) general theory of emancipation, Dalton and Welzel propose a new model of an "assertive democratic political culture." This model tries to incorporate the types of attitudes and behaviors that contradict important assumptions of the allegiant model. Evaluated from the allegiance perspective of the civic culture model, dissatisfied democrats and their claims are a problem because they constitute a potential source of trouble, turbulence, and delegitimization (Crozier, Huntington, and Watanuki 1975; O'Donnell, Schmitter, and Whitehead 1986; Nye, Zelikow, and King 1997). By contrast, evaluated from the assertive perspective, dissatisfied democrats are a source of healthy pressures on office holders to improve on meeting democratic standards in daily political practice.

In light of these contradictory views, this chapter aims to illuminate the "true" nature of dissatisfied democrats by providing an updated and in-depth profile of their political attitudes. I suggest a fourfold typology that distinguishes (1) between citizens who support democracy as a form of government or an ideal ("democrats") and those who don't ("nondemocrats") as well as (2) between citizens who are "satisfied" and those who are "dissatisfied" with their countries' political performance.

The analysis focuses on Europe because I am interested in the contrast between old and new democracies. The evidence to answer this question is uniquely rich in Europe, where both types of democracy are represented by an exceptionally large number of countries. In addition, I take a longitudinal perspective to find out whether dissatisfied democrats are on the rise or in decline. Data are available for two points in time. For pragmatic reasons, the distinctions between old and new democracies, on one hand, and Western and Eastern Europe, on the other hand, are used interchangeably throughout this chapter.

STUDY OUTLINE

I start with an operationalization of democrats and nondemocrats and describe the proportion of democrats in Western and Eastern European countries for two time points. The first time point (T_1) covers the period around 1999, the second one (T_2) includes the period around 2008. The time comparison shows whether the proportion of democrats has changed in the forty-three countries under study. Second, I examine the citizens' evaluation of the performance of their countries' regimes. Third, the combination of the two dimensions – regime support and performance satisfaction – allows me to define "dissatisfied" and "satisfied" democrats and nondemocrats. Because I am mainly interested in the dissatisfied democrats (and nondemocrats usually represent a minority), the major focus is, fourth, on contrasting satisfied and dissatisfied democrats. I expect that democrats, satisfied and dissatisfied alike, will not differ on a key set of civic attitudes. They may, however, differ on basic value orientations, in particular, postmaterialism. Indeed, I suggest that dissatisfied democrats are inspired by postmaterialism. Thus, their dissatisfaction partially reflects a critical distance to authorities and a critical evaluation of political performance that derives in good part from postmaterialist values.

On the basis of this evidence, and assuming that the impact of postmaterialism has increased over time, it is reasonable to expect that dissatisfied democrats will become an important political grouping that puts pressure on political actors and institutions to improve on democratic standards in the practice of power.

The analysis is divided into three major sections. I begin with a description of the data. After that, I introduce the variables. In the third section, I report the findings. In concluding, I discuss the relevance of the results for a democratic political culture and the future of democracy.

DATA RESOURCES

This study requires representative survey data from at least two time points for all the variables of interest and for as many European countries as possible. The European Values Study (EVS) and the World Values Survey (WVS) provide a database that meets these criteria.[3] I operate with a broad definition of

---

[3] The European Values Study and the World Values Survey are both large-scale, cross-national, and longitudinal survey research projects. Detailed information is available at http://www.europeanvaluesstudy.eu and http://www.worldvaluessurvey.org.

Europe, including all countries that are accepted members of the Council of Europe (CoE) plus Belarus, whose membership is currently suspended. The EVS/WVS provide data for forty-three countries, surveyed in or around both 1999 and 2008. I rely on 86 surveys and a total of 117,890 interviews. There are twenty Western European and twenty-three Eastern European countries. Table 6.A1 in the appendix provides a detailed documentation.

I am pragmatic in assigning countries to Western or Eastern Europe, the two groups we want to compare. Some may question the assignments of Turkey and Malta to Western Europe or of Armenia, Azerbaijan, and Georgia to Eastern Europe. However, all Eastern European countries in this study share a postcommunist past; insofar as they are democratic, they constitute the "new" democracies. By contrast, the Western European countries have been democracies for a longer period of time. Disregarding the variance in this group, they constitute the "old" democracies. Pragmatism is also needed to define the two time points. Most of the surveys were conducted around 1999 and around 2008, with some differences in the timing of the fieldwork (Table 6.A1). To avoid clumsy detailed description, I refer to the two time points as T_1 (fieldwork around 1999) and T_2 (fieldwork around 2008).

VARIABLES

There are good reasons to expect that regime attitudes are affected by the actual regime type (Fails and Pierce 2010). To relate regime type and regime support, I classify the countries for each time point by the combined Freedom House/Polity IV scores, as suggested by Hadenius and Teorell (2005).[4] To even out erratic fluctuations, I average the scores over a three-year period preceding the fieldwork in all countries.

I assume that citizens support democracy when they prefer democracy over autocracy as a form of government. These preferences are measured by the following two questions (also see Table 6.A2 in the appendix):

1. I am going to read off some things that people sometimes say about a democratic political system. Could you please tell me if you agree strongly, agree, disagree, or disagree strongly, after I read each of them? Democracy may have problems but it's better than any other form of government.

2. I am going to describe various types of political systems and ask what you think about each as a way of governing this country. For each one,

---

[4] These authors have shown that an average index, composed of Freedom House scores (transformed to a 0–10 scale) and Polity2 scores (transformed to a 0–10 scale), performs better both in terms of validity and reliability than its constituent parts (Hadenius and Teorell 2005). The data are taken from the Quality of Government Project (Teorell et al. 2011); T_1 scores for Yugoslavia and T_2 scores for Serbia and Montenegro are our own calculations. For a classification of countries based on Freedom House data, compare LeDuc, Niemi, and Norris (1996, 2010).

would you say it is a very good, fairly good, fairly bad, or very bad way of governing this country? Having a democratic system.

Obviously, this way of measuring support of democracy leaves open how individual respondents define democracy. Unfortunately, our database does not include further information for all countries and both time points to establish the precise subjective meaning of democracy that citizens associate with the concept. However, evidence from open-ended survey questions shows that citizens across the world seem to agree that democracy, above all, means freedom, political rights, and free elections (Dalton, Shin, and Jou 2007). Evidence from the recent wave of the WVS underscores this finding. Welzel and Moreno (Chapter 4) report that a primarily liberal understanding of democracy prevails around the globe.

In contrast to democratic orientations, an autocratic orientation is measured by the following two items:

3. I am going to describe various types of political systems and ask what you think about each as a way of governing this country. For each one, would you say it is a very good, fairly good, fairly bad, or very bad way of governing this country? Having a strong leader who does not have to bother with parliament and elections.
4. Having the army rule the country.

Country-by-country factor analyses of all four items indicate that they have strong loadings on the first principal component with opposite signs in the expected direction (factor analysis results available from the author). This justifies the construction of a democracy-autocracy preference index by (1) adding the scores of the two democracy items, (2) doing the same for the two autocracy items, and then (3) subtracting the latter from the former.

The democracy-autocracy preference index runs from −6 (autocrats) to +6 (democrats). The index measures different levels of intensity at which democracy or autocracy are supported. For the analysis, I define democrats as citizens who prefer democracy over autocracy (scoring +1 to +6 on the democracy-autocracy preference index). I calculate the proportion of democrats based on the total number of respondents in a country. This provides a conservative estimate because all nonrespondents are counted as nondemocrats.

Satisfaction with a regime's performance is analytically distinct from regime orientation. Following standard practice, I measure (dis)satisfaction with democracy using a question that asks respondents to indicate how satisfied they are with "the way democracy develops in their country" (see Table 6.A2 in the appendix for the precise wording).[5] It makes perfect sense to ask this question

---

[5] At T_1 this question had not been asked in five countries: Norway, Switzerland, Azerbaijan, Armenia, and Georgia. However, the following question was available: "How satisfied are you with the way the people now in national office are handling the country's affairs? Would you say

irrespective of whether a country is a democracy: If a country is *not* a democracy, a democrat should be dissatisfied about its democratic performance; if the respondent is a nondemocrat, he or she should be satisfied. By the same token, a nondemocrat in a functioning democracy should be dissatisfied precisely because the regime performs too well on democratic standards. On the basis of previous experience with this question, we have to take into consideration that respondents do not necessarily express (dis)satisfaction with their country's *democratic* performance but often express (dis)satisfaction with their country's *policy* performance in general, including its economic performance. Yet, this property of the response pattern speaks even more for this question as a measure of generalized performance satisfaction. It is, thus, well suited to distinguish between citizens who are politically satisfied or dissatisfied. As with the democrats, we base the proportion of dissatisfied citizens on the total number of respondents.

Besides regime preferences and performance evaluations, we look at a third set of politically relevant orientations: civic attitudes. Civic attitudes do not necessarily refer to a political object in the narrow sense; they indicate more broadly how citizens relate to their community and how they define their own political roles and those of their fellow citizens. Even though civic attitudes do not directly indicate an orientation toward democracy, they provide the psychological predispositions that shape a belief system supportive of democratic values (Lasswell 1951; Almond and Verba 1963; Putnam 1993).

Klingemann et al. (2006) specify "interpersonal trust," "acceptance of deviant behavior," "rejection of violence," "political motivation," and nonviolent "protest behavior" as important predispositions of support for democracy. Welzel and Klingemann (2011) propose a similar set of attitudes: "civic power," "participation in civic actions," "tolerance of nonconformity," "civic efficacy," and "civic trust." From the surveys available, I am able to construct eight indicators of civic attitudes. Indicators composed of more than one variable have been checked for dimensionality. To ease comparison, I rescale all indicators to range from a minimum of 1 to a maximum of 10. Table 6.A2 provides more detailed documentation.

Three of the eight civic attitudes are related to social norms: law abidance, ethical tolerance, and interpersonal trust. The *law abidance* index is composed of two questions asking whether it is always or never justified to claim government benefits to which one is not entitled or to cheat on taxes. *Ethical tolerance* is operationalized as the toleration of "divorce" and "abortion" as justifiable acts. *Interpersonal trust* is measured by the standard trust question asking if

that you are very satisfied, fairly satisfied, fairly dissatisfied or very dissatisfied?" This substitute question is probably a more valid operationalization of the concept in the historical context of December 1996 to February 1997 for the three postcommunist countries. We have, however, similarly included Switzerland (June 1996) and Norway (October 1996), well knowing that this decision can be disputed.

people think that others can generally be trusted or that one cannot be too careful in dealing with other people.

Another set of civic attitudes relates to specific objects of state organization: confidence in the parliament, the police, and the army. Factor analyses show that confidence in these three objects represents a single underlying dimension, but for theoretical reasons, we keep *confidence in parliament* separate from confidence in the police and the army. The latter two items are combined in an index labeled *confidence in order institutions*. Further analyses reported later justify this theoretically motivated distinction.

The last manifestations of civic attitudes relate to political involvement. The *political motivation* index summarizes responses to two questions. The first question asks the respondent to evaluate the importance of politics in her or his own life; the second question asks how often one discusses politics with friends. A second indicator measures *vote intention* (data on actual voting are not available). Finally, we use an index of *protest potential*, combining responses to a question asking whether one has already signed or would sign a petition and whether one has already or would attend a peaceful demonstration (for precise question wordings, compare Table 6.A2). As a summary measure of civic attitudes, we use an additive index across all eight component measures.

Besides civic attitudes, a more deeply layered value orientation is expected to be characteristic of democrats in general and of dissatisfied democrats in particular. Among the various potential value orientations, the one most tried and tested for its political relevance is postmaterialism (Inglehart 1977; 1990; 1997; 2008). In fact, some scholars have used postmaterialism as a shorthand for democratic values (Opp 1990). We measure the extent to which a respondent prioritizes freedom of speech and the people's voice over economic and physical security with the standard four-item materialism-postmaterialism index.

For analytical reasons, the following discussion keeps civic attitudes and value orientations apart. While we test the proposition that all democrats should support the eight civic attitudes described earlier – as suggested in the literature – we do not want to argue that only postmaterialists are inclined to support democracy. Instead, their value orientations become relevant for the distinction between political satisfaction and dissatisfaction among those citizens who are democrats. Specifically, I assume postmaterialism to provide the value basis that feeds the dissatisfied democrats' critical attitudes.

FINDINGS

Support for Democracy

The numbers in the top panel of Table 6.1 are based on the pooled, unweighted national samples of the forty-three countries. As a consequence, small countries, such as Luxembourg, count as much as big ones, such as Russia. By comparison, the bottom panel of Table 6.1 presents the averages of the separate country

TABLE 6.1. *Democrats as Defined by the Democracy-Autocracy Index*

	Europe (43 Countries)		Western Europe (20 Countries)		Eastern Europe (23 Countries)	
	T_2 (2008)	T_1 (1999)	T_2 (2008)	T_1 (1999)	T_2 (2008)	T_1 (1999)
% Democrats[a]	67.8	70.9	77.5	81.2	59.7	62.2
Undecided	6.9	4.3	4.3	3.2	9.0	5.2
Autocrats	5.0	4.3	4.3	2.5	7.0	5.9
Not classified because of missing data	20.3	20.5	15.7	13.1	24.2	26.8
Total	100%	100%	100%	100%	100%	100%
N	63,895	54,495	29,131	25,065	34,764	29,430
% Democrats[b]	68.5	71.5	78.6	81.3	59.7	63.0
SD	15.3	15.2	13.2	10.7	11.0	13.6

[a] Proportions based on unweighted, pooled individual respondents.
[b] Mean of country-level proportions.
Source: 1999 EVS/WVS and 2008 EVS/WVS; adult population aged 18 years and older.

estimates. The averages of the country means are largely the same as the means based on the pooled national samples because sample sizes for each country are roughly the same. For all practical purposes, the slight deviation of the two estimates can be neglected.

On average, the countries of Europe show a level of support for democracy of roughly 70 percent at both periods of time. The proportion of democrats in a country correlates fairly strongly with the country's level of democracy as measured by the combined Freedom House/Polity IV index (T_1: $r = 0.73$; T_2: $r = 0.58$). The causal interpretation of this relationship is an open question, but assuming causality makes sense in both directions of impact: Countries might have a high level of democracy because support for democracy is widespread since long. Alternatively, support for democracy might have become an integral part of a country's political culture because it is democratic since long. Either way, the linkage testifies to the existence of a culture-regime nexus.

Figure 6.1 shows that support levels are substantially higher among Western European (about 80 percent) than among Eastern European countries (around 60 percent). Denmark, Norway, Greece, and Iceland show more than 90 percent democrats at both time periods. At T_1 and T_2, Moldova, the Ukraine, Russia, and Bulgaria do not reach the 50 percent mark. Only slight changes can be observed for the two regions over the roughly decennial period of observation. On average, there is a decline of three percent points. Luxembourg shows the greatest increase in the proportion of democrats (+14.8) among Western European countries, and Ireland (−23.9) suffers the greatest decline. Russia and Croatia mark the end points among the Eastern European countries, with the democrats gaining 10.7 percent points in Russia and losing

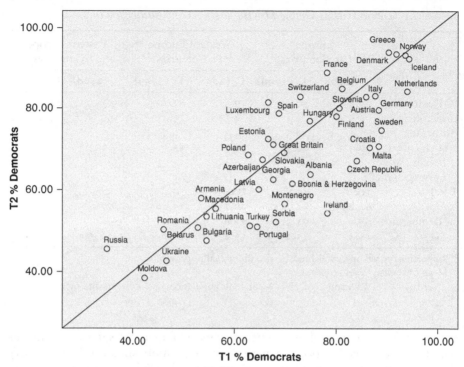

FIGURE 6.1. Proportion of democrats over time.
Note: $R = 0.83$; $y = 8.957 + .833x$; significance $p < 0.000$; $N = 43$.
Source: 1999 EVS/WVS and 2008 EVS/WVS.

17.5 percent points in Croatia (Figure 6.1; Table 6.A3). In summary, despite a few exceptions, citizens in most European countries express high and relatively stable levels of support for democracy: The correlation over time is substantial ($r = 0.83$).

Performance Evaluation

Performance evaluations are analytically distinct from regime preferences. The average percentage of citizens who are dissatisfied with their regime's performance is rather stable across Europe as a whole: around 50 percent at both periods of time (Figure 6.2). Yet, there is a gap between the Western and Eastern European countries. At T_1, some 35 percent of Western European citizens are dissatisfied with their regime's performance, while the same is true for roughly 68 percent of Eastern European citizens. But this situation is different at T_2. The percentage of dissatisfied citizens increased by 6.9 percent points in the West, whereas it decreased by 8.4 percent points in the East (Table 6.2). Even though the West continues to show a lower proportion of dissatisfied citizens

TABLE 6.2. *Citizens with a Negative Performance Evaluation of Democracy*

	Europe (43 Countries)		Western Europe (20 Countries)		Eastern Europe (23 Countries)	
	T_2 (2008)	T_1 (1999)	T_2 (2008)	T_1 (1999)	T_2 (2008)	T_2 (1999)
% Negative performance evaluation	50.8	52.5	41.1	35.2	59.2	67.6
SD	17.4	20.9	13.9	15.2	15.8	11.1

Note: Table entries are mean of country-level proportions.
Source: 1999 EVS/WVS and 2008 EVS/WVS.

at T_2, over time, the East-West gap has narrowed from 32.4 to 18.1 percent points.

The proportion of dissatisfied citizens is less stable over time than the proportion of democrats: The correlation between the country-level proportions of democrats over time is $r = 0.83$, compared to $r = 0.48$ for the proportions

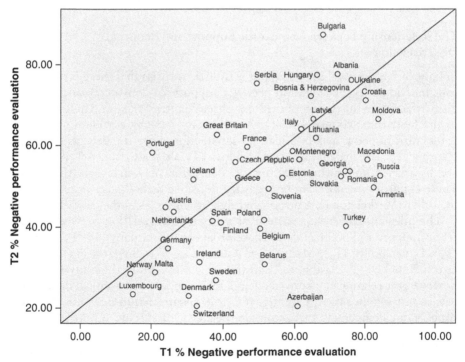

FIGURE 6.2. Negative performance evaluations over time.
Note: $R = 0.58$; $y = 25.395 + .483x$; significance $p < 0.000$; $N = 43$.
Source: 1999 EVS/WVS and 2008 EVS/WVS.

of dissatisfied citizens. This could have been expected because, in an imagined hierarchy of political orientations, regime preferences represent a more basic and thus stable orientation than performance evaluations, which should be more affected by short-term performance fluctuations. In Eastern Europe, the proportion of dissatisfied citizens declined the most in Azerbaijan (-40.2 percent points). In Western Europe, the decline is most pronounced in Turkey (-34.4 percent points).[6]

It is tempting to speculate about the reasons for the enormous decrease in the number of dissatisfied citizens in countries like Azerbaijan or Turkey. It is obvious that the evaluation is not an evaluation of *democratic* performance alone. Instead, it seems to be a generalized performance evaluation that in particular takes into account the economic performance of the regime – no matter how democratic. In Azerbaijan, the real gross domestic product per capita in constant 1990 U.S. dollar prices increased by 252 percent from T_1 to T_2 (Teorell et al. 2011). More generally, we observe a negative relation between GDP per capita and dissatisfied citizens at the country level (T_1: $r = -0.78$; T_2: $r = -0.57$). These findings corroborate our interpretation of the performance evaluation as a measure of general *political* (dis)satisfaction rather than specific *democratic* (dis)satisfaction.

The Relationship between Democratic Support and Political Dissatisfaction

In light of the previous conclusion, it is of little surprise that there is no significant individual-level correlation between support for democracy and political dissatisfaction in thirty-four of the forty-three countries at T_1 and in thirty-eight of the forty-three countries at T_2. A significant *positive* correlation between democratic support and political *dis*-satisfaction exists in Belarus (T_1, T_2), Georgia (T_2), Azerbaijan (T_1), and Moldova (T_1). In these countries, democrats are dissatisfied, and the fact that they are democrats may, in fact, be the reason: These countries' regimes can be regarded defective democracies in one way or the other (Merkel 2004), if not outrightly autocratic, as in the case of Belarus.

The allegiant-citizenship pattern of a *negative* correlation between democratic support and political dissatisfaction exists in Germany (T_1, T_2), Austria (T_1), Luxembourg (T_1), Malta (T_1), Poland (T_1, T_2), Bulgaria (T_1), and the Czech Republic (T_1) (Table 6.A5 in the appendix). More than anything else, however, the relationship between democratic support and political dissatisfaction is not significant. Apparently, political dissatisfaction does not diminish support for democracy. In Easton's terms, lack of specific support does not necessarily translate into lack of diffuse support.

The relative independence between democratic support and political dissatisfaction means that no objections can be raised to combine the two measures

---

[6] Table 6.A2 provides detailed documentation.

TABLE 6.3. *Dissatisfied Democrats*

	Europe (43 Countries)		Western Europe (20 Countries)		Eastern Europe (23 Countries)	
	T_2 (2008)	T_1 (1999)	T_2 (2008)	T_1 (1999)	T_2 (2008)	T_1 (1999)
% dissatisfied democrats	33.7	35.7	32.1	28.0	35.0	42.5
SD	11.6	12.8	12.5	11.5	10.8	9.7

Note: Mean of country-level proportions.
Source: 1999 EVS/WVS and 2008 EVS/WVS.

to generate a typology. Our typology defines dissatisfied democrats as citizens who support democracy and who are dissatisfied with the performance of their regime. Likewise, satisfied democrats are citizens who support democracy and who are satisfied with the performance of their country's political performance. In this analysis, we mainly focus on the group of dissatisfied democrats.[7]

Table 6.3 presents the proportions of dissatisfied democrats. The overall proportion of dissatisfied democrats in Europe hovers around 36 percent at T_1 and 34 percent at T_2, indicating a slight decrease between the two time points. Again, however, the overall average hides differences between the two parts of Europe. At T_1, the proportion of dissatisfied democrats amounts to roughly 44 percent in Eastern Europe, compared to only 28 percent in Western Europe. After nine years, this gap has almost vanished, diminishing from some 15 percent points at T_1 to roughly 3 percent points at T_2. The pattern underscores opposite dynamics that have led to a convergence of the two regions: In the mature democracies of Western Europe, the proportion of dissatisfied democrats has significantly increased; in the young and partly fledgling democracies of Eastern Europe, it has decreased (Figure 6.3).[8]

Why is such a sizeable portion of European democrats dissatisfied? And why does its proportion go up in the old democracies, whereas it is going down in the new democracies? As we have seen, the proportion of dissatisfied citizens correlates with the development of the economy. A similar mechanism seems to be at work when it comes to the dissatisfaction of the democrats. Satisfied democrats tend to live in countries with higher levels of GDP (T_1: $r = 0.79$; T_2: $r = 0.75$), whereas lower levels of GDP characterize countries where we find higher proportions of dissatisfied democrats (T_1: $r = -0.57$; T_2: $r = -0.18$). However, the situation is more complex; economic determinism alone does not explain the difference between satisfied and dissatisfied democrats. In fact, the impact of economic prosperity on the proportion of dissatisfied democrats has declined over time. This might indicate that citizens have learned to focus

---

[7] There are missing values regarding the performance question. We add the few respondents with missing values to the group of satisfied democrats (the "rest").

[8] Table 6.A4 provides detailed documentation.

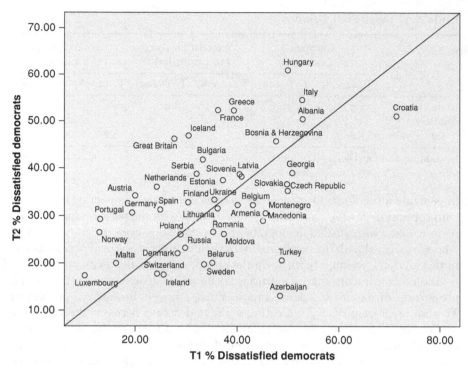

FIGURE 6.3. Dissatisfied democrats over time.
Note: $R = 0.47$; $y = 18.487 + .425x$; significance $p < 0.002$; $N = 43$.
Source: 1999 EVS/WVS and 2008 EVS/WVS.

their performance evaluations more narrowly on the democratic performance in particular. Such a possible change in evaluative orientations refers to the role of civic attitudes and value orientations.

CIVIC ATTITUDES AND THE (DIS)SATISFACTION OF DEMOCRATS

A large number of characteristics may differentiate satisfied and dissatisfied democrats, ranging from demographic to psychological characteristics. For reasons of parsimony, I will not attempt a comprehensive analysis taking into account all possibilities. To make the task more feasible, I select a set of civic attitudes that have been suggested as important psychological prerequisites of democratic support in the studies cited earlier. Because both the satisfied and the dissatisfied democrats are *democrats* in the end, I suggest that the two groups should *not* differ on the psychological prerequisites of democratic orientations.

At both points in time, overall and in the two regions, we find stable levels of civic attitudes (Table 6.4). Measured on a ten-point scale, law abidance shows the highest levels (T_1 8.5; T_2 8.7), followed by vote intention (T_1 6.9; T_2 7.6)

TABLE 6.4. *Rank Order of Levels of Civic Attitudes*

Indicators	Europe (43 Countries)		Western Europe (20 Countries)		Eastern Europe (23 Countries)	
	T_2 (2008)	T_1 (1999)	T_2 (2008)	T_1 (1999)	T_2 (2008)	T_1 (1999)
Law abidance	8.7	8.5	8.9	8.7	8.6	8.4
Vote intention	7.6	6.9	8.1	7.0	7.1	6.8
Confidence in order institutions	6.1	5.8	6.5	6.1	5.7	5.4
Political motivation	4.9	4.9	5.2	4.9	4.7	5.0
Protest potential	4.9	5.3	6.0	6.2	4.0	4.5
Ethical tolerance	4.9	4.9	5.5	5.3	4.3	4.6
Confidence in parliament	4.7	4.6	5.2	5.1	4.3	4.2
Interpersonal trust	3.8	3.5	4.6	4.2	3.1	2.9

Note: Scale values run from 1 (low level) to 10 (high level).
Source: 1999 EVS/WVS and 2008 EVS/WVS.

and confidence in order institutions (T_1 5.8; T_2 6.1). Confidence in parliament and interpersonal trust are trailing behind, leaving ethical tolerance, political motivation, and protest potential with mean levels in between. An additive index representing the average level of these eight civic attitudes by country reflects this high degree of stability over time (T_1 5.6; T_2 5.7, $r = 0.83$; see Table 6.A7 in the appendix).

The results presented in Figure 6.4 indicate a clear East-West divide in levels of civic attitudes. Of the nineteen countries above the mean at T_2, seventeen are Western; twenty-one of the twenty-four countries below the mean are Eastern. From T_1 to T_2, the East-West divide has even slightly increased.[9] This result is in line with core assumptions of socialization research showing that it takes generations to change civic attitudes.[10]

The closeness of the correlation between civic attitudes and support for democracy reflects the degree to which democratic support is rooted in a broader democratic culture. We examine the number of significant positive correlations across the forty-three countries. Thus, each civic attitude can

---

[9] Table 6.A5 provides detailed documentation.
[10] M. Kent Jennings (2007) provides a comprehensive overview. More recent empirical evidence in support of the early socialization effects model is presented in Jennings, Stoker, and Bowers (2009). Mishler and Rose (2007) argue a lifetime learning model emphasizing the adaptability by adults to changing circumstances. See also Converse (1969).

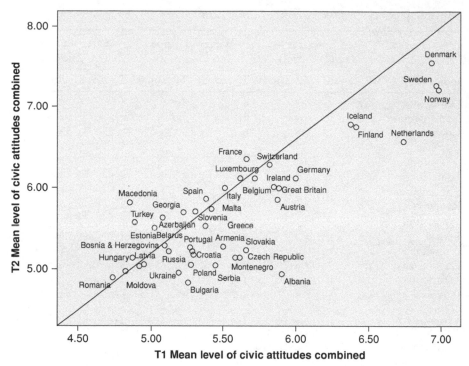

FIGURE 6.4. Civic attitudes over time.
Note: Scale of civic attitudes combined: 1–10. $R = 0.83$; $y = 0.289 + .974x$; significance $p < 0.000$; $N = 43$.
Source: 1999 EVS/WVS and 2008 EVS/WVS.

potentially reach a maximum of forty-three positive correlations (twenty West, twenty-three East) at each point in time. To ease comparison between East and West, I present the number of positive correlations (Table 6.5, Figure 6.5) as a proportion of the total number of possible correlations (Table 6.A8 in the appendix).

Across Europe as a whole, ethical tolerance shows the largest proportion of significant positive correlations with support for democracy (79 percent at T_2), followed by protest potential (74 percent), law abidance (67 percent), political motivation (54 percent), and interpersonal trust (51 percent). In contrast, vote intention (44 percent), confidence in parliament (30 percent), and confidence in order institutions (7 percent) show a much lower proportion of positive correlations with support for democracy. Overall, the evidence indicates that support for democracy is firmly rooted in a basic set of important civic attitudes, except for institutional confidence and interpersonal trust. These two orientations provide a considerably less firm basis of democratic support, much in contrast to what the burgeoning trust literature assumes almost axiomatically. I address this problem subsequently.

TABLE 6.5. *Association of Levels of Civic Attitudes and the Democracy-Autocracy Index*

Europe T$_2$	Europe T$_1$	Western Europe T$_2$	Western Europe T$_1$	Eastern Europe T$_2$	Eastern Europe T$_1$
79% (34) Ethical tolerance*	79% (34) Protest potential	90% (18) Protest potential	85% (17) Protest potential	78% (18) Ethic tolerance	74% (17) Protest potential
74% (32) Protest potential	56% (24) Ethic tolerance	80% (16) Ethic tolerance	80% (16) Ethic tolerance	61% (14) Protest Potential	35% (8) Ethic tolerance
67% (29) Law abidance	51% (22) Political motivation	80% (16) Political Motivation	75% (15) Political motivation	57% (13) Law abidance	30% (7) Law abidance
54% (23) Political motivation	40% (17) Law abidance	80% (16) Interpersonal trust	55% (11) Interpersonal trust	30% (7) Political Motivation	30% (7) Political Motivation
51% (22) Interpersonal trust	35% (15) Interpersonal trust	80% (16) Law abidance	50% (10) Law abidance	26% (6) Interpersonal trust	17% (4) Interpersonal trust
44% (19) Vote intention	23% (10) Confidence in parliament	65% (13) Vote intention	45% (9) Confidence in parliament	26% (6) Vote intention	13% (3) Vote intention
30% (13) Confidence in Parliament	22% (5) Vote intention	55% (11) Confidence in Parliament	10% (2) Vote intention	9% (2) Confidence in Parliament	4% (1) Confidence in Parliament
7% (3) Confidence in order institutions	2% (1) Confidence in order institutions	5% (1) Confidence in order institutions	0% (−) Confidence in order institutions	9% (2) Confidence in order institutions	4% (1) Confidence in order institutions
N = 43	N = 43	N = 20	N = 20	N = 23	N = 23

Note: Cell entries are civic attitudes and express the number of significant positive correlations of the civic attitude and the democracy-autocracy index as a proportion of the total number of possible significant positive correlations (forty-three for Europe, twenty for Western Europe, and twenty-three for Eastern Europe). Absolute numbers of significant positive correlations in parentheses.

Source: 1999 EVS/WVS and 2008 EVS/WVS.

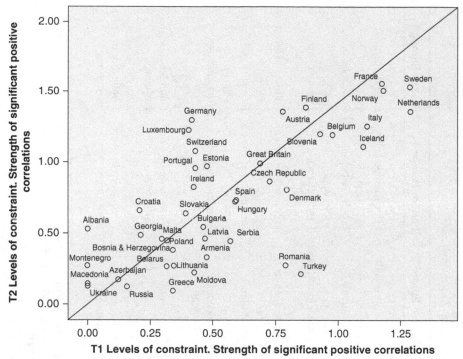

FIGURE 6.5. Levels of constraint over time.
Note: Scores of the scale levels of constraint range between 0 and 8. $R = 0.74$; $y = 0.215 + 0.941x$; significance $p < 0.000$; $N = 43$.
Source: 1999 EVS/WVS and 2008 EVS/WVS.

We observe a clear East-West divide in the proportion of significant correlations between support for democracy and civic attitudes. With the exception
of confidence in order institutions (significantly correlated with support for
democracy in just one Western European country), all civic attitudes are significantly correlated with democratic support in more than half of the Western
European countries at T_2. Compared to T_1, two more civic attitudes have
passed the halfway point in the old democracies: vote intention (from 10 to 65
percent) and confidence in parliament (from 45 to 55 percent). Confidence in
order institutions (0 to 5 percent) is trailing far behind. Overall, however, in
Western Europe, support for democracy can be regarded as firmly embedded
in a broad set of civic orientations.

In Eastern Europe, just one civic attitude, protest potential, correlates significantly and positively with support for democracy in seventeen countries
(74 percent) at T_1. Thus, even ten years after the revolutions, "protest" was
the only civic attitude associated with a preference for democracy. However,
this situation has changed. At T_2, a higher number of civic attitudes correlates
with support for democracy. In addition to protest potential, ethical tolerance
(from 35 to 78 percent) and law abidance (from 30 to 57 percent) are added

to the group of civic attitudes with a large proportion of positive correlations (greater than 50 percent). Furthermore, in all other instances, the number of significant positive correlations has increased over time, too. This means that Eastern Europe catches up as far as the embedding of democratic support in a broad set of civic orientations is concerned. Democratic support becomes more based on civic attitudes.

To sum up, the findings show the following: (1) To a significant extent, support for democracy is an expression of civic mindedness and part of a more comprehensive democratic belief system, and (2) this pattern is more characteristic of Western than Eastern Europe; (3) however, over time, the East-West gap is closing as democratic preferences in the East become more grounded on civic attitudes.

Civic Attitudes Discriminating between Satisfied and Dissatisfied Democrats

At the outset, I hypothesized that satisfied and dissatisfied democrats should not differ over basic civic attitudes. The reason is that civic attitudes should feed democratic support, no matter how politically dissatisfied the respective supporters are. However, the evidence just discussed suggests a qualification of this assumption: The hypothesized irrelevance of civic attitudes to distinguish between satisfied and dissatisfied democrats may not apply to all civic attitudes. Civic attitudes that show a strong association with democratic support could be more likely to discriminate between satisfied and dissatisfied democrats as compared to civic attitudes with a weak linkage to democratic support. The suspects in this regard are interpersonal trust and confidence in institutions in particular, which – contrary to my initial expectation – show a very weak link to democratic support.

The weak link of institutional confidence and democratic support justifies a reinterpretation of the civic quality of institutional confidence. Initially, I followed the mainstream in interpreting institutional confidence as an inherently civic attitude that reflects the citizens' recognition of the indispensability of particular institutions for the functioning of the political process. From this followed the assumption that, if democratic support is a civically based orientation, it should be strongly linked to institutional confidence. However, this assumption is not supported by the empirical evidence. Thus confidence in institutions might not reflect a recognition of the institutions' principled legitimacy. Instead, the confidence measures may express an evaluation of the institutions' actual performance and of the authorities running them. In this case, satisfied and dissatisfied democrats are very likely to differ over confidence in institutions: Dissatisfied democrats should report lower confidence in institutions than satisfied democrats.

I examine this possibility by a logistic regression, analyzing whether a democrat is more likely to be satisfied (coded 1) than to be dissatisfied (coded 0) depending on his or her level of confidence in institutions. Focusing on the

TABLE 6.6. *Predicting Satisfied and Dissatisfied Democrats*

Indicators	T_2 (circa 2008)			T_1 (circa 1999)		
	Coefficients	Robust SE	Prob.	Coefficients	Robust SE	Prob.
Constant	−2.279	0.240	0.000	−3.075	0.263	0.000
Law abidance	−0.024	0.021	0.247	0.027	0.019	0.162
Ethical tolerance	0.007	0.015	0.638	0.021	0.018	0.237
Interpersonal trust	0.042	0.005	0.000	0.037	0.007	0.000
Confidence in parliament	0.267	0.021	0.000	0.195	0.026	0.000
Confidence in order institutions	0.111	0.017	0.000	0.118	0.019	0.000
Political motivation	−0.007	0.008	0.367	−0.004	0.012	0.719
Vote intention	0.025	0.009	0.005	0.030	0.006	0.000
Protest potential	−0.013	0.013	0.320	0.003	0.015	0.857
Western versus Eastern Europe	0.362	0.167	0.031	1.194	0.224	0.000
Pseudo R^2 0.123	0.123			0.147		
N of cases	36,593			32,181		

Note: Coefficients are from a logistic analysis. Dependent variable scored 0 = dissatisfied democrats, 1 = satisfied democrats. Eastern versus Western Europe scored 0 = Eastern Europe, 1 = Western Europe. All other variables scored 1 (low) to 10 (high).
Source: 1999 EVS/WVS and 2008 EVS/WVS.

democrats means that all nondemocrats are excluded from this analysis.[11] Next to institutional confidence, the other civic orientations are also included as predictor variables in the regression. Models are run over the country-pooled individual-level data, with national samples weighted equally.

Because I am interested in the comparison between Western and Eastern Europe across time, I estimate the models separately for Western and Eastern Europe and separately for both time periods (Table 6.6).[12]

For both regions and at both time points, results show four statistically *in*-significant predictors: law abidance, ethical tolerance, political motivation, and protest potential. This result meets the initial expectation that satisfied and dissatisfied democrats do not differ over civic attitudes. Logically, this applies in particular to those civic attitudes for which the analysis in the previous section found an especially strong link to democratic support.

---

[11] Logistic regressions for T_1 and T_2 show that all eight civic attitudes are significantly related to the democrat versus nondemocrat division at the 0.000 level. However, confidence in order institutions has the "wrong" sign, indicating that nondemocrats have a higher preference for law abidance.

[12] Tables 6.A7a–6.A7d in the appendix provide detailed documentation.

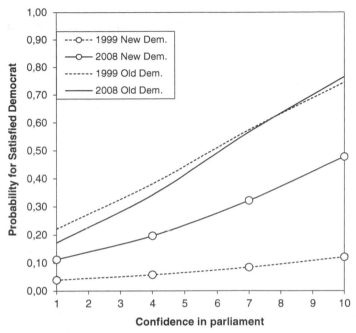

FIGURE 6.6. Confidence in parliament and the probability of being a satisfied democrat.
Note: Relationships estimated from separate regional logistic models.
Source: 1999 EVS/WVS and 2008 EVS/WVS.

However, interpersonal trust flatly contradicts the no-difference expectation: the lower the level of interpersonal trust, the higher the probability of being a dissatisfied democrat. There is no directly testable explanation for this result, but one can try an informed guess: Because dissatisfied democrats are disillusioned about ill-performing institutions, they might perceive their fellow citizens as less trustworthy because they sense that malfunctioning institutions nurture asocial behavior among citizens.

This interpretation is supported by the fact that confidence in parliament and confidence in order institutions increase the probability of being a satisfied democrat. Put differently, dissatisfied democrats are indeed dissatisfied because they are disillusioned about the institutions' performance. Both confidence in institutions and interpersonal trust can be regarded as investments in the future based on the expectation that the institutions or the trusted other will behave properly. From this perspective, confidence in institutions is driven by performance evaluations, and so is trust in fellow citizens.

Patterns of change have implications for a convergence or divergence of a democratic culture in Europe. Figure 6.6 shows the marginal effect of confidence in parliament on the probability of democrats being satisfied, estimated from identical models in Western and Eastern Europe for the two points in time. In Western Europe, democrats are increasingly more likely to be satisfied with higher levels of confidence in parliaments, and there is almost no difference between the two points in time. In Eastern Europe, in contrast, the effect of confidence in parliament becomes much stronger over time: The likelihood of democrats to be satisfied alongside higher confidence levels in parliament has increased. The picture is the same for confidence in order institutions and interpersonal trust, although the effects are weaker. This indicates that the gap between Western and Eastern Europe is slowly closing. Vice versa, it is obvious from these results that the increase of dissatisfied democrats in Western Europe coincides with dropping confidence levels in institutions.

Is the probability of becoming a satisfied democrat caused by changing levels in the evaluation of parliaments, or is it caused by a growing degree of association between the evaluation of parliaments and political satisfaction? We suggest an answer to this question by breaking down the total effect predicting satisfied democrats into a component that reflects an effect due to a change in the level of parliamentary performance evaluations from T_1 to T_2, and a "learning effect" that is manifest in a stronger relationship between confidence in institutions and support of democracy.[13] Results show that the increasing association between civic attitudes and support for democracy in Eastern Europe drives the process of convergence in the proportions of satisfied democrats between East and West.

I believe that this finding is an essential contribution to a better understanding of the process of democratic consolidation in the Eastern European countries. In addition to the implementation of democratic institutions, and the emergence of a system of interest representation, our result highlights the importance of a more comprehensive democratic political culture. Independent of the *level* of civic attitudes, the *relation* between democratic support and civic attitudes has become stronger over time. Eastern European citizens' preference for democracy has become increasingly grounded in a broader set of civic attitudes that provide the standards to critically judge democratic politics.

Dissatisfied Democrats and Their Values

Civic attitudes provide no exhaustive explanation of the difference between satisfied and dissatisfied democrats. This invites speculation about how else the belief systems of the two groups might differ. An even more deeply layered psychological characteristic than civic attitudes is value orientations. Postmaterialism, in particular, is a value orientation long associated with democratic inclinations (Inglehart 1971; 1977; 1990; 2008). In contrast to materialists, who give top priority to economic and security issues, postmaterialists tend to push policies protecting self-expression ("protecting freedom of speech") and

---

[13] It is gratefully acknowledged that the method for separating level effects and learning effects (constraint) has been suggested by Bernhard Wessels.

TABLE 6.7. *Dissatisfied Democrats and Postmaterialist Value Orientations*

	Europe (43 Countries)		Western Europe (20 Countries)		Eastern Europe (23 Countries)	
Over- and underrepresentation of postmaterialist orientation[a]	T_2 (2008)	T_1 (1999)	T_2 (2008)	T_1 (1999)	T_2 (2008)	T_1 (1999)
Dissatisfied democrats	113	115	111	115	114	114
Satisfied democrats	101	102	101	101	102	103

[a] Means of country distributions, standardized on the margins. Percentage postmaterialist orientation = 100. T_1 missing data for Great Britain.
Source: 1999 EVS/WVS and 2008 EVS/WVS; nondemocrats not included in the table.

people power ("giving people more say in important government decisions"). To explore the relation between dissatisfied democrats and postmaterialism, we consider (1) the representation of postmaterialists among dissatisfied and satisfied democrats and (2) the correlation pattern of dissatisfied and satisfied democrats and the materialism-postmaterialism index. The overall results are presented in Table 6.7 and Figure 6.7.

Figure 6.7 shows that postmaterialists are represented in significantly larger proportions among dissatisfied than among satisfied democrats. Differences between Eastern and Western Europe are small. However, there is no under-representation of postmaterialists among satisfied democrats; they tend to

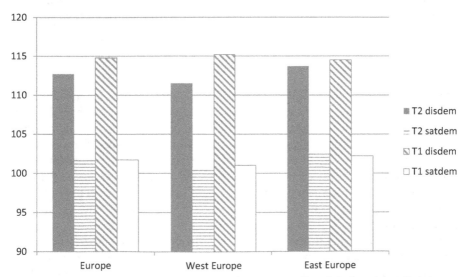

FIGURE 6.7. Representation of postmaterialists among dissatisfied and satisfied democrats.
Note: Figure entries are average of country distributions that are standardized at the margins. Percentage postmaterialists = 100.
Source: 1999 EVS/WVS and 2008 EVS/WVS.

TABLE 6.8. *Correlations between Dissatisfied Democrats and the Materialism-Postmaterialism Index*

	Europe (43 Countries)		Western Europe (20 Countries)		Eastern Europe (23 Countries)	
No. significant positive	19 (44%)	12 (29%)	10 (50%)	8 (42%)	9 (39%)	4 (17%
No. significant negative	3 (7%)	5 (12%)	0 (–)	0 (–)	3 (13%)	5 (22%)
No. insignificant positive	9 (21%)	16 (38%)	4 (20%)	8 (42%)	5 (22%)	8 (35%)
No. insignificant negative	12 (28%)	9 (21%)	6 (30%)	3 (16%)	6 (26%)	6 (26%)
N	43	42	20	19	23	23

Note: Level of significance is $p < 0.05$. Satisfied democrats: 0, dissatisfied democrats: 1. Materialist-postmaterialist index: 1 (low) to 10 (high).
Source: 1999 EVS/WVS and 2008 EVS/WVS.

be postmaterialists too, but to a smaller extent than their dissatisfied counterparts.[14] Where postmaterialists are truly underrepresented is in the group of nondemocrats (not shown here). This finding highlights the democratic impetus of postmaterialism: Postmaterialist values contribute to the separation of both democrats from nondemocrats and of dissatisfied from satisfied democrats.

This picture is corroborated by a correlation analysis. The correlation between dissatisfied democrats and postmaterialism at T_2 is significant and positive in twenty-nine out of forty-three countries; twenty-one of the non-significant coefficients have a positive sign. Whereas the number of significant positive relations has increased over time, the general pattern of relationships stays the same (Table 6.8).[15]

CONCLUSION

This analysis has focused on dissatisfied democrats in Europe. I have both examined their distribution across twenty Western and twenty-three Eastern European countries and explored the association of a preference for democracy and civic attitudes. Differences between satisfied and dissatisfied democrats are explained by differences in performance evaluations. A postmaterialist value orientation is overrepresented among dissatisfied democrats. This leads to the suggestion that the dissatisfied democrats might mobilize political pressures for democratic innovation and reform by addressing new issues and opening up the political process (Dalton 2006, 262–67).

Are the citizens of Europe supportive of democracy as a form of government? The evidence shows that they are. On average, more than two-thirds of Europeans prefer democracy over autocracy around the year 2008. This proportion has not changed much when compared with 1999. I find a decline

[14] Table 6.A8 provides detailed documentation.
[15] Table 6.A9 provides detailed documentation.

of just three percentage points overall. How do the citizens of Europe evaluate the functioning of democracy in their own countries? On average, about half of the forty-three countries' adult populations come up with a negative performance evaluation in 2008, again, with little overall change – a two percentage point decline – as compared to 1999. On average about one-third of the citizenry values democracy as an ideal but expresses dissatisfaction with how the democratic regime performs in reality at both points in time. I have labeled this group of citizens "dissatisfied democrats."

The broad picture differs for the Western and Eastern European countries in two respects. First, in the old democracies, we find a higher proportion of democrats and a lower level of negative performance evaluation at both points in time as compared to the new democracies. Second, although the rate of change is similar for the proportion of democrats in the two groups of countries, it differs significantly with respect to performance evaluation: Negative performance evaluation rises by six percentage points in the West and declines by nine percentage points in the East. This means that the proportion of dissatisfied democrats falls by eight percentage points in the new democracies (43 to 35 percent), whereas it rises by fourteen percentage points in the West (28 to 42 percent).

What does this picture mean for the future of democracy in Europe? The widespread preference for democracy over autocracy seems to indicate that the values of an overwhelming part of European citizens are congruent with democratic principles. The question is, however, how well this preference for democracy is rooted in a broader set of civic attitudes that give meaning to the concept. The critical evaluation of the way democracy is functioning in one's own country raises the question of the particular nature of this criticism. Given the support of democratic principles, it does not seem to signal a desire for autocratic government. However, does it apply to input processes, to output processes, or both? Does it imply institutional change within the general framework of representative democracy, or does it go beyond?

To determine the rootedness of a preference for democracy in a broader democratic belief system, I considered a set of eight civic attitudes. I looked at the levels of law abidance, ethical tolerance, interpersonal trust, confidence in parliament, confidence in order institutions, political motivation, vote intention, and protest potential. Change over time is small, as are level differences between East and West. To conclude from this result that the preference for democracy is, indeed, well rooted in a more general democratic culture would be premature. If we require, as we should, that people relate the concept of democracy and civic attitudes in their minds, we find a surprisingly large difference between specific civic attitudes and between the old and the new democracies. While ethical tolerance and protest potential strongly associate with democratic support, confidence in order institutions is barely associated with democratic support at all. More important, however, is the development over time. In both Western and Eastern European countries, the link between democratic support and our broad set of civic attitudes becomes closer over time. The effect is particularly pronounced in the new democracies. Thus, a process of maturation that anchors democratic support more and more firmly in civic orientations writ large is well on its way. The criteria that European democrats apply in their evaluation of the democratic process become more adequate over time.

In an earlier analysis, I have postulated that, with the disappearance of the confrontation between the communist regimes in the East and the democratic regimes in the West, citizens will more likely concentrate their attention on the functioning of democracy in their own countries rather than on the general principles of democracy. Thus, Western democracies in particular should become increasingly dependent on political performance for securing their legitimacy. "This claim relates to both the capacity of democratic systems to solve certain societal problems and to attain certain democratic standards. Thus, the legitimation of democracy by its citizens becomes conditional in two ways. The source of support for a democratic system is therefore likely to shift away from 'ideal normative agreement' toward 'instrumental acceptance'" (Held 1987, 238). "If, over and beyond this conditional support, the critical competence of citizens is taken into account, then we can expect a more skeptical attitude on the part of the citizens towards the reality of democracy" (Fuchs and Klingemann 1995, 440–41).

This seems, indeed, what has happened. In an effort to explore differences between dissatisfied and satisfied democrats, I have estimated the likelihood to be a satisfied democrat using the set of eight civic attitudes as the independent variables. All of these attitudes have been associated with a democratic belief system in the literature. Thus, I expected that they should not explain the difference between these two types of democrats. However, this is not what the results show. The two types of democrats do, indeed, share four of the eight civic attitudes: law abidance, ethical tolerance, political motivation, and protest potential. Dissatisfied democrats differ from satisfied democrats, however, by a lower confidence in institutions, lower levels of interpersonal trust, and a weaker vote intention. Lower confidence in order institutions and the parliament are the two characteristics generating the most important differences by far.

The indicators are not specific enough to decide whether critical citizens aim to replace key parts of the institutional setup of representative democracy. One could well argue that they probably demand more direct channels of citizen input because they have low confidence in parliament. It would be more difficult to construct a similar argument for low confidence in order institutions. Alerted by particularly high levels of institutional confidence in countries such as Azerbaijan, I have suggested a performance interpretation of confidence in institutions. This perspective would interpret low confidence in parliament as well as low confidence in order institutions as dissatisfaction with the policy performance that the citizens associate with these institutions. Parliament does not enact their preferred policies, and the order institutions could do much more in the battle against crime and corruption.

The performance interpretation of confidence in institutions suggests the continuing persistence of democratic regimes because democratic government regulates policy conflict through competitive elections at the level of the authorities. In this case, the probability is low that dissatisfaction affects democratic structures at a higher level of the political system. However, better indicators are needed to empirically support and validate this perspective.

I interpret the emergence of democratic values and civic attitudes in the context of modernization theory. From this perspective, political change is regarded as caused by processes of societal and individual modernization. At the individual level, this framework predicts an increase in personal skills and a rise of more emancipatory value orientations. The last part of our analysis consisted of a short exploration of the relation of the two types of democrats and a key manifestation of emancipatory values orientations: postmaterialism. I expected that the critical attitudes of dissatisfied democrats might be part of the syndrome of emancipatory orientations that is characteristic of postmaterialists. Indeed, I find that postmaterialists are overrepresented among both satisfied democrats and dissatisfied democrats when compared to the nondemocrats. However, postmaterialists are even more heavily overrepresented among the dissatisfied democrats in particular. This is true for both points in time and for the citizens in old and new democracies. More analysis is needed to systematically look at the consequences of this finding.

I speculate that the postmaterialist value orientation might color the dissatisfied democrats' type of policy demands. Their inclination to political participation might also increase the pressure on political elites in old and new democracies to keep improving on democratic standards and policy performance. In that respect, dissatisfied democrats strengthen the participatory elements of a democratic political culture as it shifts into an assertive direction. Viewed in that context, the "dissatisfied democrats" might as well deserve the label of "critical citizens," in line with Norris's positive vision mentioned at the beginning of this analysis. This vision gets even more support by the most important empirical result of my analysis. In all European countries, East and West, we observe that a preference for democracy is increasingly firmly embedded in a broad set of civic attitudes that speak of an appropriate understanding of the democratic process. The dynamics of this learning process is stronger in the East than in the West. If this process continues, it has the potential to bridge the gap in the development of a democratic political culture in the two parts of Europe.

APPENDIX

TABLE 6.A1. *The European Values Surveys/World Values Surveys of Europe*

Country	Beginning of Fieldwork T_1	N Cases T_1	Beginning of Fieldwork T_2	N Cases T_2	Months $T_1 - T_2$	Freedom House – Polity2 T_1	Freedom House – Polity2 T_2
Turkey	09 2001	1,206	11 2008	2,325	81	6.33	7.58
Portugal	10 1999	1,000	05 2008	1,553	103	10.00	10.00
Ireland	10 1999	986	04 2008	980	104	10.00	10.00
Finland	09 2000	1,015	07 2009	1,134	106	10.00	10.00
Luxembourg	07 1999	1,161	05 2008	1,609	106	10.00	10.00
Sweden	11 1999	1,015	09 2008	1,174	106	10.00	10.00
Austria	08 1999	1,522	07 2008	1,510	107	10.00	10.00
Germany	10 1999	2,034	09 2008	2,051	107	9.58	10.00
Denmark	04 1999	1,023	04 2008	1,507	108	10.00	10.00
France	03 1999	1,615	05 2008	1,501	110	9.33	9.75
Netherlands	03 1999	1,002	05 2008	1,551	110	10.00	10.00
Spain	03 1999	1,200	05 2008	1,497	110	9.58	9.58
Greece	06 1999	1,111	09 2008	1,498	111	9.17	9.58
Malta	03 1999	1,000	06 2008	1,497	111	10.00	10.00
Great Britain	10 1999	969	08 2009	1,547	118	9.58	10.00
Belgium	03 1999	1,899	04 2009	1,509	121	9.58	9.50
Iceland	06 1999	968	07 2009	808	121	10.00	10.00
Italy	03 1999	2,000	10 2009	1,519	127	9.58	9.79
Norway	10 1996	1,127	04 2008	1,090	138	10.00	10.00
Switzerland	06 1996	1,212	05 2008	1,271	143	10.00	10.00
Western Europe	1996–2001	25,065	2008–2009	29,131			
Mean		1,253		1,457	108	9.64	9.81
SD		358		338	13.3	0.82	0.55

Albania	02 2002	1,000	07 2008	1,534	77	6.11	8.08
Moldova	01 2002	1,008	07 2008	1,550	78	7.67	7.28
Bosnia-H.	12 2001	1,200	07 2008	1,512	79	4.13	6.34
Macedonia	11 2001	1,055	07 2008	1,493	80	6.92	8.08
Serbia	10 2001	1,200	07 2008	1,512	81	6.05	7.27
Montenegro	10 2001	1,060	11 2008	1,516	85	6.05	7.07
Belarus	03 2000	1,000	06 2008	1,500	99	1.58	1.17
Ukraine	12 1999	1,195	07 2008	1,507	103	7.17	8.00
Lithuania	11 1999	1,018	07 2008	1,499	104	9.58	10.00
Estonia	10 1999	1,005	07 2008	1,518	105	8.67	9.75
Romania	07 1999	1,146	04 2008	1,489	105	8.67	8.92
Bulgaria	06 1999	999	04 2008	1,500	106	8.25	9.33
Hungary	11 1999	998	11 2008	1,513	109	9.58	10.00
Croatia	03 1999	1,003	04 2008	1,498	109	3.75	8.92
Slovakia	06 1999	1,331	07 2008	1,509	109	8.61	10.00
Czech R.	03 1999	1,901	05 2008	1,793	110	9.58	9.50
Russia	04 1999	2,500	06 2008	1,490	110	6.03	4.92
Latvia	03 1999	1,013	06 2008	1,506	111	8.94	9.22
Poland	02 1999	1,095	06 2008	1,479	112	9.33	10.00
Armenia	02 1997	1,831	06 2008	1,477	136	2.22	2.00
Azerbaijan	02 1997	1,944	07 2008	1,505	137	5.33	5.69
Georgia	12 1996	1,924	08 2008	1,498	140	5.75	6.86
Eastern Europe	1996–2002	29,430	2008–2009	34,764			
Mean		1,280		1,511	104	6.94	7.76
SD		425		70	18.2	2.38	2.45
Europe	1996–2002	54,495	2008–2009	63,895			
Mean		1,267		1,496	108	8.19	8.71
SD		390		285	16.4	2.27	2.09

TABLE 6.A2. *Concepts and Measures of Civic Attitudes*

Concept	Measurement	Codes
Value (Cultural) Level		
Law abidance (additive index)	Please tell me for each of the following statements whether you think it can always be justified, never be justified, or something in between, using this card.	Index values: 1 (low law abidingness) to 10 (high law abidingness)
	(1) Claiming state (1999)/government (2008) benefits which you are not entitled to; (2) Cheating on taxes	
Ethical tolerance (additive index)	Please tell me for each of the following statements whether you think it can always be justified, never be justified, or something in between, using this card. (1) Abortion, (2) Divorce	Index values: 1 (low ethic tolerance) to 10 (high ethic tolerance)
Interpersonal trust	Generally speaking, would you say that most people can be trusted or that you can't be too careful in dealing with people?	1 (Can't be too careful with people [plus dk and na]) to 10 (Most people can be trusted)
Structural Level		
Confidence in Parliament	Please look at this card and tell me, for each item listed, how much confidence you have in them, is it a great deal, quite a lot, not very much or none at all? Parliament	1 (low confidence) to 10 (high confidence)
Confidence in order institutions (additive index)	Please look at this card and tell me, for each item listed, how much confidence you have in them, is it a great deal, quite a lot, not very much or none at all? (1) the police; (2) the armed forces	1 (low confidence) to 10 (high confidence)
Process Level		
Political motivation (additive index)	(1) When you get together with your friends, would you say you discuss political matters frequently, occasionally, or never?	Index values: 1 (low political motivation) to 10 (high political motivation)
	(2) Please say, for each of the following, how important it is in your life? "politics"; very important, quite important, not important, not at all important	

Vote intention	1999: If there was a general election tomorrow, which party would you vote for? 2008: If there were a general election tomorrow, for which party on this list would you vote?	1 (no vote intention) to 10 (vote intention)
Protest potential (additive scale)	Now I'd like you to look at this card. I'm going to read out some different forms of political action that people can take, and I'd like you to tell me, for each one, whether you have actually done any of these things, whether you might do it or would never, under any circumstances, do it? (1) signing a petition; (2) attending lawful demonstrations	Index values: 1 (no protest behavior) to 10 (high protest behavior)
Political satisfaction	On the whole are you very satisfied, rather satisfied, not very satisfied or not at all satisfied with the way democracy is developing in our country.	Index values: 1 (not at all satisfied) to 10 (very satisfied)
Support for democratic regime	(1) I am going to read off some things that people sometimes say about a democratic political system. Could you please tell me if you agree strongly, agree, disagree or disagree strongly, after I read each of them? Democracy may have problems but it's better than any other form of government. (2) I am going to describe various types of political systems and ask what you think about each as a way of governing this country. For each one, would you say it is a very good, fairly good, fairly bad or very bad way of governing this country: Having a democratic system?	
Support for autocratic regime	I am going to describe various types of political systems and ask what you think about each as a way of governing this country. For each one, would you say it is a very good, fairly good, fairly bad or very bad way of governing this country? (1) Having a strong leader who does not have to bother with parliament and elections. (2) Having the army rule the country.	

[a] All scores are rescaled to a 1–10 scale.

TABLE 6.A3. *Democrats as a Proportion of the Adult Population by Country*

Country	T$_2$ (ca. 2008), %	N	T$_1$ (ca. 1999), %	N	T$_2$ − T$_1$, % points
Albania	63.9	1,534	74.9	1,000	− 11.0
Armenia	58.1	1,477	53.5	1,831	+4.6
Austria	79.7	1,510	88.4	1,522	− 8.7
Azerbaijan	67.5	1,505	65.5	1,944	+2.0
Belarus	50.9	1,500	52.8	1,000	− 1.9
Belgium	84.9	1,509	81.1	1,899	+3.8
Bosnia-Herzegovina	61.6	1,512	71.4	1,200	− 9.8
Bulgaria	47.7	1,500	54.5	999	− 6.8
Croatia	70.8	1,498	88.3	1,003	− 17.5
Czech Republic	67.2	1,793	84.0	1,901	− 16.8
Denmark	93.9	1,507	90.6	1,023	+3.3
Estonia	72.6	1,518	66.6	1,005	+6.0
Finland	78.1	1,134	80.0	1,015	− 1.9
France	88.9	1,501	78.2	1,615	+10.7
Georgia	62.6	1,498	67.6	1,924	− 5.0
Germany	83.1	2,051	87.6	2,034	− 4.5
Greece	93.5	1,498	92.1	1,111	+1.4
Hungary	76.9	1,513	74.8	998	+2.1
Iceland	92.3	808	94.4	968	− 2.1
Ireland	54.4	980	78.3	986	− 23.9
Italy	82.9	1,519	85.9	2,000	− 3.0
Latvia	60.2	1,506	64.8	1,013	− 4.6
Lithuania	53.6	1,499	54.2	1,018	− 0.6
Luxembourg	81.4	1,609	66.6	1,161	+14.8
Macedonia	55.5	1,493	56.4	1,055	− 0.9
Malta	70.4	1,497	86.5	1,000	− 16.1
Moldova	38.6	1,550	42.3	1,008	− 3.7
Montenegro	56.6	1,516	69.8	1,060	− 13.2
Netherlands	84.2	1,551	94.0	1,002	− 9.8
Norway	93.3	1,090	93.6	1,127	− 0.3
Poland	68.6	1,479	62.7	1,095	+5.9
Portugal	51.1	1,553	64.4	1,000	− 13.3
Romania	50.4	1,489	46.1	1,146	+4.3
Russia	45.6	1,490	34.9	2,500	+10.7
Serbia	52.2	1,512	68.1	1,200	− 15.9
Slovakia	69.2	1,509	69.7	1,331	− 0.5
Slovenia	80.2	1,366	80.5	1,004	− 0.3
Spain	78.8	1,497	68.6	1,200	+10.2
Sweden	74.7	1,174	88.8	1,015	− 14.1
Switzerland	83.0	1,271	72.9	1,212	+10.1
Turkey	51.3	2,325	63.0	1,206	− 11.7
Great Britain	71.2	1,547	67.6	969	+3.6
Ukraine	42.8	1507	46.6	1,195	− 3.8
Europe					
Mean	68.5	43	71.5	43	− 3.0
SD	15.3		15.2		8.9
Western Europe					
Mean	78.6	20	81.3	20	− 2.6
SD	13.2		10.7		10.3
Eastern Europe					
Mean	59.7	23	63.0	23	− 3.3
SD	11.0		13.6		7.8

Source: 1999 EVS/WVS and 2008 EVS/WVS (adult population aged 18 years and older).

TABLE 6.A4. *Citizens with a Negative Evaluation of the Performance of Democracy*

Country	T₂ (ca. 2008), %	N	T₁ (ca. 1999), %	N	T₂ − T₁, % points
Albania	77.8	1,534	72.1	1,000	+5.7
Armenia	49.7	1,477	82.5	1,831	−32.8
Austria	44.8	1,510	24.0	1,522	+20.8
Azerbaijan	20.5	1,505	60.7	1,944	−40.2
Belarus	30.8	1,500	51.6	1,000	−20.8
Belgium	39.6	1,509	50.2	1,899	−10.6
Bosnia-Herzegovina	72.3	1,512	64.4	1,200	+7.9
Bulgaria	87.6	1,500	67.9	999	+19.7
Croatia	71.3	1,498	80.2	1,003	−8.9
Czech Republic	56.6	1,793	61.1	1,901	−4.5
Denmark	23.1	1,507	30.6	1,023	−7.5
Estonia	52.2	1,518	56.5	1,005	−4.3
Finland	41.1	1,134	39.4	1,015	+1.7
France	59.7	1,501	46.4	1,615	+13.0
Georgia	53.7	1,498	75.5	1,924	−21.8
Germany	34.7	2,051	24.6	2,034	+10.1
Greece	56.0	1,498	43.4	1,111	+12.6
Hungary	77.6	1,513	66.2	998	+11.4
Iceland	51.7	808	31.9	968	+19.8
Ireland	31.4	980	33.6	986	−2.2
Italy	64.1	1,519	61.8	2,000	+2.3
Latvia	66.6	1,506	65.2	1,013	+1.4
Lithuania	61.9	1,499	65.8	1,018	−3.9
Luxembourg	23.4	1,609	14.8	1,161	+8.6
Macedonia	56.5	1,493	80.7	1,055	−24.2
Malta	28.9	1,497	21.0	1,000	+7.9
Moldova	66.6	1,550	83.8	1,008	−17.2
Montenegro	58.6	1,516	59.4	1,060	−0.8
Netherlands	43.7	1,551	26.3	1,002	+17.4
Norway	28.5	1,090	14.1	1,127	+14.5
Poland	41.6	1,479	51.4	1,095	−9.8
Portugal	58.3	1,553	20.3	1,000	+38.0
Romania	53.7	1,489	74.2	1,146	−20.5
Russia	52.6	1,490	84.3	2,500	−31.7
Serbia	75.5	1,512	26.1	1,200	+26.1
Slovakia	52.5	1,509	73.2	1,331	−20.7
Slovenia	49.4	1,366	52.7	1,004	−3.3
Spain	41.5	1,497	37.1	1,200	+4.4
Sweden	27.0	1,174	38.0	1,015	−11.0
Switzerland	20.7	1,271	32.9	1,212	−12.1
Turkey	40.2	2,325	74.6	1,206	−34.4
Great Britain	62.7	1,547	38.3	969	+24.4
Ukraine	76.3	1,507	76.1	1,195	+0.2
Europe					
Mean	50.8	43	52.5	43	−1.8
SD	17.4		20.9		17.8
Western Europe					
Mean	41.1	20	35.2	20	+5.9
SD	13.9		15.2		16.1
Eastern Europe					
Mean	59.2	23	67.6	23	−8.4
SD	15.8		11.1		16.9

Source: 1999 EVS/WVS and 2008 EVS/WVS.

TABLE 6.A5. *Association of Proportion of Democrats and Negative Evaluation of the Performance of Democracy in Their Own Country by Country*

Country	T$_2$ (ca. 2008), %	N	T$_1$ (ca. 1999), %	N
Albania	0.041 (0.107)	1,534	−0.057 (0.073)	1,000
Armenia	0.006 (0.824)	1,477	0.055 (0.018)	1,831
Austria	−0.071 (0.006)	1,510	−0.088 (0.001)	1,522
Azerbaijan	−0.040 (0.121)	1,505	0.375 (0.000)	1,944
Belarus	0.191 (0.000)	1,500	0.319 (0.000)	1,000
Belgium	−0.078 (0.002)	1,509	−0.033 (0.154)	1,899
Bosnia-Herzegovina	0.061 (0.018)	1,512	0.080 (0.006)	1,200
Bulgaria	0.011 (0.677)	1,500	−0.161 (0.000)	999
Croatia	0.032 (0.216)	1,498	0.038 (0.226)	1,003
Czech Republic	−0.058 (0.015)	1,793	−0.087 (0.000)	1,901
Denmark	0.040 (0.123)	1,507	0.039 (0.212)	1,023
Estonia	−0.018 (0.493)	1,518	−0.016 (0.621)	1,005
Finland	0.039 (0.193)	1,134	−0.055 (0.077)	1,015
France	−0.048 (0.061)	1,501	−0.009 (0.720)	1,615
Georgia	0.224 (0.000)	1,498	−0.005 (0.814)	1,924
Germany	−0.121 (0.000)	2,051	−0.142 (0.000)	2,034
Greece	−0.012 (0.645)	1,498	−0.039 (0.192)	1,111
Hungary	0.071 (0.006)	1,513	0.021 (0.513)	998
Iceland	−0.055 (0.117)	808	0.031 (0.331)	968
Ireland	0.020 (0.536)	980	−0.037 (0.242)	986
Italy	0.079 (0.002)	1,519	−0.014 (0.520)	2,000
Latvia	−0.055 (0.033)	1,506	−0.071 (0.024)	1,013
Lithuania	−0.065 (0.011)	1,499	0.024 (0.450)	1,018
Luxembourg	−0.098 (0.000)	1,609	0.015 (0.599)	1,161
Macedonia	−0.037 (0.152)	1,493	0.010 (0.747)	1,055
Malta	−0.017 (0.519)	1,497	−0.134 (0.000)	1,000
Moldova	0.021 (0.409)	1,550	0.111 (0.000)	1,008
Montenegro	−0.037 (0.154)	1,516	0.076 (0.013)	1,060
Netherlands	−0.037 (0.140)	1,551	−0.041 (0.199)	1,002
Norway	−0.012 (0.694)	1,090	−0.018 (0.539)	1,127
Poland	−0.107 (0.000)	1,479	−0.135 (0.000)	1,095
Portugal	−0.020 (0.433)	1,553	0.007 (0.835)	1,000
Romania	−0.020 (0.436)	1,489	0.052 (0.080)	1,146
Russia	−0.028 (0.285)	1,490	0.022 (0.262)	2,500
Serbia	−0.027 (0.299)	1,512	−0.067 (0.020)	1,200
Slovakia	−0.047 (0.066)	1,509	−0.052 (0.058)	1,331
Slovenia	−0.068 (0.012)	1,366	−0.074 (0.019)	1,004
Spain	−0.068 (0.008)	1,497	−0.026 (0.376)	1,200
Sweden	−0.021 (0.468)	1,174	−0.011 (0.736)	1,015
Switzerland	0.035 (0.207)	1,271	0.012 (0.682)	1,212
Turkey	0.001 (0.977)	2,325	0.089 (0.002)	1,206
Great Britain	0.072 (0.005)	1,547	0.078 (0.015)	969
Ukraine	0.038 (0.141)	1,507	0.003 (0.909)	1,195
Europe				
Sign. correlations	5 (11.6%)	43	9 (20.9%)	43
Sign	pos. 2, neg. 3		pos. 3, neg. 6	
Western Europe				
Sign. correlations	2 (10.0%)	20	3 (15.0%)	20
Sign	pos. 0, neg. 2		pos. 0, neg. 3	
Eastern Europe				
Sign. correlations	3 (13.0%)	23	6 (26.1%)	23
Sign	pos. 2, neg. 1		pos. 3, neg. 3	

Note: Nondemocrats 0, democrats 1; positive performance evaluation 0, negative 1.

Source: 1999 EVS/WVS and 2008 EVS/WVS.

TABLE 6.A6. *Dissatisfied Democrats as a Proportion of the Adult Population (18 Years and Older) by Country*

Country	T$_2$ (ca. 2008), %	N	T$_1$ (ca. 1999), %	N	T$_2$ − T$_1$, % points
Albania	50.5	1,534	52.9	1,000	2.4
Armenia	29.0	1,477	45.1	1,831	− 16.1
Austria	34.3	1,510	20.0	1,522	+14.3
Azerbaijan	13.1	1,505	48.5	1,944	− 35.4
Belarus	20.1	1,500	35.2	1,000	− 15.1
Belgium	32.3	1,509	40.1	1,899	− 7.8
Bosnia-Herzegovina	45.8	1,512	47.7	1,200	− 1.9
Bulgaria	41.9	1,500	33.3	999	+8.6
Croatia	51.2	1,498	71.4	1,003	− 20.2
Czech Republic	36.7	1,793	49.9	1,901	− 13.2
Denmark	22.1	1,507	28.3	1,023	− 6.2
Estonia	37.5	1,518	37.3	1,005	+0.2
Finland	32.9	1,134	30.4	1,015	+2.5
France	52.4	1,501	36.3	1,615	+16.1
Georgia	39.1	1,498	50.9	1,924	− 11.8
Germany	30.6	2,051	19.4	2,034	+11.2
Greece	52.3	1,498	39.4	1,111	+12.9
Hungary	60.9	1,513	50.0	998	+10.9
Iceland	47.0	808	30.5	968	+16.5
Ireland	17.6	980	25.6	986	− 8.0
Italy	54.6	1,519	52.8	2,000	+1.8
Latvia	38.8	1,506	40.6	1,013	− 1.8
Lithuania	31.6	1,499	36.2	1,018	− 4.6
Luxembourg	17.4	1,609	10.1	1,161	+7.3
Macedonia	30.5	1,493	45.7	1,055	− 15.2
Malta	20.0	1,497	16.3	1,000	+3.7
Moldova	26.2	1,550	37.4	1,008	− 11.2
Montenegro	32.3	1,516	23.4	1,060	− 10.9
Netherlands	36.1	1,551	24.3	1,002	+11.8
Norway	26.5	1,090	13.0	1,127	+13.5
Poland	26.1	1,479	28.9	1,095	− 2.8
Portugal	29.3	1,553	13.2	1,000	+16.1
Romania	26.6	1,489	35.3	1,146	− 8.7
Russia	23.3	1,490	29.8	2,500	− 6.5
Serbia	38.9	1,512	32.1	1,200	+6.8
Slovakia	35.3	1,509	50.0	1,331	− 14.7
Slovenia	38.3	1,366	40.9	1,004	− 2.6
Spain	31.3	1,497	24.9	1,200	+6.4
Sweden	19.8	1,174	33.6	1,015	− 13.8
Switzerland	17.8	1,271	24.3	1,212	− 6.5
Turkey	20.6	2,325	48.8	1,206	− 28.2
Great Britain	46.3	1,547	27.7	969	+18.6
Ukraine	33.5	1,507	35.6	1,195	− 2.1
Europe					
Mean	33.7	43	35.7	43	− 2.0
SD	11.6		12.8		12.6
Western Europe					
Mean	32.1	20	28.0	20	+4.1
SD	12.5		11.5		12.4
Eastern Europe					
Mean	35.0	23	42.5	23	−7.4
SD	10.8		9.7		10.2

Source: 1999 EVS/WVS and 2008 EVS/WVS.

TABLE 6.A7. *Combined Levels of Eight Civic Attitudes by Country*

Country	T_2 (ca. 2008) Mean	T_1 (ca. 1999) Mean	$T_2 - T_1$ Difference	Rank 2008	Rank 1999
Albania	4.95	5.91	−0.96	41	8
Armenia	5.28	5.50	−0.22	26	20
Austria	5.86	5.88	−.002	16	9/10
Azerbaijan	5.64	5.08	+0.56	21	35
Belarus	5.51	5.02	+0.49	24	36
Belgium	6.12	5.62	+0.50	09/10/11	16/17
Bosnia-Herzegovina	5.22	5.29	−0.07	29/30	26/27
Bulgaria	4.84	5.26	−0.42	43	30
Croatia	5.18	5.29	−0.12	31	26/27
Czech Republic	5.15	5.62	−0.47	32/33	16/17
Denmark	7.55	6.94	+0.62	1	3
Estonia	5.30	5.09	+0.20	25	34
Finland	6.76	6.41	+0.34	5	5
France	6.36	5.66	+0.69	7	14/15
Georgia	5.70	5.23	+0.48	20	31
Germany	6.12	6.00	+0.12	09/10/11	7
Greece	5.53	5.38	+0.16	23	23/24
Hungary	5.14	4.87	+0.27	34	40
Iceland	6.79	6.38	+0.41	4	6
Ireland	6.00	5.88	+0.12	13	9/10
Italy	5.99	5.51	+0.48	14	19
Latvia	5.04	4.92	+0.12	38	38
Lithuania	5.06	4.95	+0.11	35/36	37
Luxembourg	6.12	5.72	+0.40	09/10/11	13
Macedonia	5.82	4.85	+0.97	17	41
Malta	5.74	5.42	+0.32	18	22
Moldova	4.98	4.82	+0.15	39	42
Montenegro	5.15	5.59	−0.44	32/33	18
Netherlands	6.57	6.74	−0.17	6	4
Norway	7.21	6.99	+022	3	1
Poland	5.06	5.28	−0.22	35/36	28
Portugal	5.27	5.27	−0.01	27	29
Romania	4.90	4.74	+016	42	43
Russia	5.22	5.12	+0.10	29/30	33
Serbia	5.05	5.45	−0.40	37	21
Slovakia	5.24	5.66	−0.42	28	14/15
Slovenia	5.71	5.31	+0.41	19	25
Spain	5.87	5.38	+0.49	15	23/24
Sweden	7.27	6.97	+0.30	2	2
Switzerland	6.28	5.82	+0.46	8	12
Turkey	5.58	4.89	+0.69	22	39
Great Britain	6.02	5.85	+0.17	12	11
Ukraine	4.96	5.19	−0.24	40	32
Mean	5.70	5.55	+0.15		
SD	.69	.59	.39		
West					
Mean	6.25	5.94	+0.32		
SD	.37	.37	.06		
East					
Mean	5.22	5.22	+0.00		
SD	.28	.30	.43		

Source: 1999 EVS/WVS and 2008 EVS/WVS.

TABLE 6.A8. *Strength of the Association between Civic Attitudes and Democratic Support at T₁ and T₂ by Country*

Country	T_2 (ca. 2008) Number of significant positive correlations	T_2 (ca. 2008) Sum of strength of significant positive correlations[a]	T_1 (ca. 1999) Number of significant positive correlations[a]	T_1 (ca. 1999) Sum of strength of significant positive correlations[a]	$T_2 - T_1$ Difference of sums of strength of significant positive correlations
Albania	4	0.531	0	0.000	+0.531
Armenia	2	0.334	3	0.476	−0.142
Austria	6	1.360	5	0.779	+0.581
Azerbaijan	1	0.177	1	0.121	+0.056
Belarus	2	0.268	2	0.316	−0.048
Belgium	5	1.196	5	0.975	+0.221
Bosnia-Herzegovina	2	0.451	2	0.316	+0.135
Bulgaria	3	0.546	3	0.462	+0.084
Croatia	5	0.661	1	0.206	+0.455
Czech Republic	5	0.868	5	0.727	+0.141
Denmark	5	0.807	4	0.795	+0.012
Estonia	7	0.972	2	0.478	+0.494
Finland	7	1.389	5	0.869	+0.520
France	7	1.561	7	1.174	+0.387
Georgia	3	0.489	1	0.211	+0.278
Germany	8	1.299	2	0.416	+0.883
Greece	1	0.097	2	0.342	−0.245
Hungary	5	0.724	4	0.589	+0.135
Iceland	6	1.113	5	1.100	+0.013
Ireland	5	0.825	2	0.424	+0.401
Italy	6	1.257	6	1.115	+0.142
Latvia	3	0.463	2	0.470	−0.007
Lithuania	2	0.274	2	0.344	−0.070
Luxembourg	7	1.229	3	0.403	+0.826
Macedonia	1	0.149	0	0.000	+0.149

(continued)

TABLE 6.A8 (continued)

Country	T₂ (ca. 2008) Number of significant positive correlations	T₂ (ca. 2008) Sum of strength of significant positive correlations[a]	T₁ (ca. 1999) Number of significant positive correlations	T₁ (ca. 1999) Sum of strength of significant positive correlations[a]	T₂ − T₁ Difference of sums of strength of significant positive correlations
Malta	2	0.462	2	0.296	+0.166
Moldova	2	0.224	2	0.426	− 0.202
Montenegro	2	0.274	0	0.000	+0.274
Netherlands	6	1.362	6	1.289	+0.073
Norway	7	1.511	6	1.180	+0.331
Poland	2	0.384	2	0.340	+0.044
Portugal	5	0.961	2	0.430	+0.531
Romania	2	0.276	4	0.789	−0.513
Russia	1	0.127	1	0.157	−0.030
Serbia	3	0.448	3	0.569	−0.121
Slovakia	4	0.640	3	0.392	+0.248
Slovenia	6	1.202	5	0.926	+0.276
Spain	5	0.735	2	0.593	+0.142
Sweden	6	1.537	6	1.288	+0.249
Switzerland	6	1.080	3	0.429	+0.651
Turkey	2	0.216	3	0.850	−0.634
Great Britain	5	0.996	4	0.688	+0.308
Ukraine	1	0.131	0	0.000	+0.131
Europe	175	Mean 0.735 SD 0.458	128	Mean 0.552 SD 0.361	Mean +.183 SD 0.308
Western Europe	105	Mean 1.049 SD 0.420	80	Mean 0.772 SD 0.341	Mean +0.278 SD 0.355
Eastern Europe	70	Mean .461 SD 0.282	48	Mean 0.362 SD 0.257	Mean +0.100 SD 0.238

Note: The table presents the number of significant positive correlations and sum of the strength of significant positive correlations of eight civic attitudes and the democracy-autocracy index by country.

[a] Scores running from 0 (minimum) to 8 (maximum).

TABLE 6.A9A. *Predicting Satisfied and Dissatisfied Democrats in Twenty Western European Countries at* T_2

Indicators	Coefficients	Robust SE	Prob.
Constant	−1.881	0.354	0.000
Law abidance	0.010	0.031	0.747
Ethical tolerance	0.011	0.019	0.564
Interpersonal trust	0.040	0.006	0.000
Confidence in parliament	0.306	0.029	0.000
Confidence in order institutions	0.061	0.024	0.010
Political motivation	−0.026	0.011	0.019
Vote intention	0.018	0.014	0.217
Protest potential	−0.025	0.019	0.190

Note: Dependent variable scored 0 − dissatisfied democrats, 1 = satisfied democrats. All other variables scored 1 (low) to 10 (high). Number of observations: 19.684; pseudo R^2 0.104.
Source: 2008 EVS/WVS.

TABLE 6.A9B. *Predicting Satisfied and Dissatisfied Democrats in Twenty Western European Countries at* T_1

Indicators	Coefficients	Robust SE	Prob.
Constant	−1.522	0.275	0.000
Law abidance	−0.002	0.026	0.950
Interpersonal trust	0.037	0.010	0.000
Ethical tolerance	0.001	0.022	0.951
Confidence in parliament	0.259	0.023	0.000
Confidence in order institutions	0.097	0.029	0.001
Political motivation	−0.005	0.019	0.809
Vote intention	0.032	0.008	0.000
Protest potential	−0.027	0.018	0.126

Note: Dependent variable scored 0 = dissatisfied democrats, 1 = satisfied democrats. All other variables scored 1 (low) to 10 (high). Number of observations: 17.705; pseudo R^2 0.090.
Source: 1999 EVS/WVS.

TABLE 6.A9C. *Predicting Satisfied and Dissatisfied Democrats in Twenty-Three Eastern European Countries at T_2*

Indicators	Coefficients	Robust SE	Prob.
Constant	− 2.290	0.293	0.000
Law abidance	− 0.057	0.022	0.010
Ethical tolerance	0.003	0.024	0.899
Interpersonal trust	0.043	0.007	0.000
Political motivation	0.008	0.011	0.478
Vote intention	0.033	0.010	0.001
Protest potential	− 0.001	0.018	0.939
Confidence in parliament	0.220	0.027	0.000
Confidence in order institutions	0.169	0.016	0.000

Note: Dependent variable scored 0 = dissatisfied democrats, 1 = satisfied democrats. All other variables scored 1 (low) to 10 (high). Number of observations: 16.909; pseudo R^2 0.110.

TABLE 6.A9D. *Predicting Satisfied and Dissatisfied Democrats in Twenty-Three Eastern European Countries at T_1*

Indicators	Coefficients	Robust SE	Prob.
Constant	−3.343	0.341	0.000
Law abidance	0.046	0.022	0.035
Ethical tolerance	0.046	0.022	0.035
Interpersonal trust	0.040	0.006	0.000
Confidence in parliament	0.135	0.037	0.000
Confidence in order institutions	0.142	0.020	0.000
Political motivation	− 0.003	0.016	0.824
Vote intention	0.027	0.009	0.003
Protest potential	0.028	0.018	0.113

Note: Dependent variable scored 0 = dissatisfied democrats, 1 = satisfied democrats. All other variables scored 1 (low) to 10 (high). Number of observations: 14,476; pseudo R^2 0.057.

TABLE 6.A10. *Above Average and Below Average Presence of Postmaterialists (Average = 100) among Satisfied and Dissatisfied Democrats at T_1 and T_2 by Country*

Country	Dissatisfied Democrats T_2	Satisfied Democrats T_2	Difference T_2	Dissatisfied Democrats T_1	Satisfied Democrats T_1	Difference T_1
Albania	106	100	+6	113	85	+28
Armenia	115	103	+12	127	114	+13
Austria	107	107	+1	124	98	+26
Azerbaijan	88	104	−16	115	72	+43
Belarus	158	84	+74	145	74	+71
Belgium	101	106	−5	116	97	+19
Bosnia-H.	120	79	+41	96	90	+6
Bulgaria	117	124	−7	127	118	+9
Croatia	110	102	+8	110	67	+43
Czech R.	102	117	−15	100	113	−13
Denmark	127	95	+32	105	103	+2
Estonia	122	93	+29	102	108	−6
Finland	125	91	+34	113	96	+17
France	111	103	+8	103	112	−9
Georgia	133	99	+34	116	72	+44
Germany	112	101	+11	115	99	+16
Greece	109	89	+20	108	97	+11
Hungary	112	82	+30	113	95	+18
Iceland	97	107	−10	132	87	+45
Ireland	109	119	+10	109	100	+9
Italy	117	80	+37	108	101	+7
Latvia	114	91	+23	126	105	+21
Lithuania	109	130	−21	116	106	+10
Luxembourg	126	99	+27	138	100	+38
Macedonia	106	98	+8	113	44	+69
Malta	77	115	−38	98	101	−3

(continued)

TABLE 6.A10 (continued)

Country	Dissatisfied Democrats T₂	Satisfied Democrats T₂	Difference T₂	Dissatisfied Democrats T₁	Satisfied Democrats T₁	Difference T₁
Moldova	132	77	+55	127	95	+32
Montenegro	129	80	+49	91	113	−22
Netherlands	107	104	+3	104	102	+2
Norway	104	100	+4	125	100	+25
Poland	106	110	−4	108	117	−9
Portugal	102	124	−22	130	112	+18
Romania	109	96	+13	131	171	−40
Russia	99	119	−20	126	120	+6
Serbia	103	119	−16	121	117	+4
Slovakia	101	126	−25	105	124	−19
Slovenia	108	101	+7	98	108	−10
Spain	110	99	+11	116	106	+10
Sweden	119	108	+11	114	95	+19
Switzerland	124	100	+24	116	107	+9
Turkey	125	84	+41	114	106	+8
Great Britain	111	93	+18	MD	MD	MD
Ukraine	116	119	−3	108	141	−33
Europe	113	101	+12	115	102	+13
SD	13.5	13.3	23.5	11.8	20.1	23.5
Western Europe	111	101	+10	115	101	+14
SD	12.2	10.3	19.9	10.6	5.9	13.2
Eastern Europe	114	102	+12	114	103	+11
SD	14.4	16.0	26.7	12.9	26.8	29.5

Note: Cell entries are means of country distributions, standardized on the margins. Percentage postmaterialist orientation = 100. Figures for nondemocrats not shown.

Source: 1999 EVS/WVS and 2008 EVS/WVS.

TABLE 6.AII. *Association of Postmaterialism with Satisfied versus Dissatisfied Democrats at T_1 and T_2 by Country*

Country	T_2 1 satdem vs. 0 disdem[a]	T_1 1 satdem vs. 0 disdem[a]
Albania	−0.017	−0.026
Armenia	−0.080*	−0.069*
Austria	0.009	−0.105*
Azerbaijan	0.059	−0.016
Belarus	−0.254*	−0.178*
Belgium	0.006	−0.099*
Bosnia-H.	−0.097*	0.015
Bulgaria	0.013	0.036
Croatia	−0.018	−0.203*
Czech R.	0.095*	0.069*
Denmark	−0.127*	−0.011
Estonia	−0.074*	0.086*
Finland	−0.144*	−0.065
France	−0.060*	0.036
Georgia	−0.116*	−0.057*
Germany	−0.029	−0.054*
Greece	−0.078*	−0.088*
Hungary	−0.068*	−0.004
Iceland	0.062	−0.150*
Ireland	−0.080	−0.034
Italy	−0.208*	−0.024
Latvia	−0.099*	−0.009
Lithuania	0.105*	0.011
Luxembourg	−0.057*	−0.145*
Macedonia	−0.059	−0.076
Malta	0.041	0.040
Moldova	−0.146*	−0.035
Montenegro	−0.208*	0.103*
Netherlands	−0.018	0.010
Norway	0.005	−0.038
Poland	0.019	0.048
Portugal	0.069	−0.067
Romania	−0.022	0.105*
Russia	0.024	−0.013
Serbia	0.049	−0.043
Slovakia	0.069*	0.097*
Slovenia	−0.033	0.026
Spain	−0.051	−0.074*
Sweden	−0.101*	−0.108*
Switzerland	−0.091*	−0.054
Turkey	−0.136*	−0.068
Great Britain	−0.066*	MD
Ukraine	0.035	0.055
Europe	sign. neg. 19; sign. pos. 2	sign. neg. 12; sign. pos. 5
Western Europe	sign. neg. 10; sign. pos. 0	sign. neg. 8; sign. pos. 0
Eastern Europe	sign. neg. 9; sign. pos. 2	sign. neg. 4; sign. pos. 5

Note: Table entries are association of materialist-postmaterialist orientations ranging from 1 (materialist) to 10 (postmaterialist) and dissatisfied/satisfied democrats.

[a] Based on total N of democrats.

* Significant at the 0.05 level.

Source: 1999 EVS/WVS and 2008 EVS/WVS.

7

Support for Democracy in Postcommunist Europe and Post-Soviet Eurasia

Christian W. Haerpfer and Kseniya Kizilova

The transformation of Central and Eastern European (CEE) political systems since the double "big bang" of November 1989 in communist Europe and December 1991 in the Soviet Union represents one of the most profound institutional changes in modern political history. This chapter analyses the political cultures in postcommunist Europe and post-Soviet Eurasia in roughly the two decades following these transitions. We compare countries along a continuum from authoritarian to democratic regimes in the years since the big bang. Resonating with the theme of this book, we demonstrate that the course toward democracy has been more successful where the political configuration approaches the features of an "assertive culture," combining strong support for the principles of democracy with weak support for concrete political institutions. This pattern is more pronounced in the western portions of the postcommunist world and contrasts with an eastern pattern of largely failed attempts at democratization. The eastern nations often display a political culture in which the "allegiant" elements are more pronounced, especially where this tends to be counterproductive to democratic improvements: the concrete political institutions.

The postcommunist world's eruptive transformation produced a massive and compact "fourth wave" of democratization (McFaul 2002). During the Cold War, the region was regarded as the Second World: the camp of one-party states with a dictatorial communist political system and a centrally planned economy. This Second World of communist nations took its final shape with the erection of the Iron Curtain in 1948. The First World of liberal democracies developed a culture that Western scholars described in such terms as "participant liberalism." They also contrasted it with a culture of "authoritarian statism" in the Second World, which supposedly persisted for more than seventy years in the Soviet Union and for more than forty years in its satellite states in CEE.

Between 1989 and 1999, there was a rapid triple transformation of the political, economic, and social systems in some thirty communist countries. One might quickly conclude that the general direction of the transition is predestined: It is moving from a totalitarian regime to a pluralistic democracy; from a planned economy toward a free market; and from a commanded society forced into machine-like organizations to a civil society of voluntary associations. Yet, the more eastward we look, the more thwarted – and in parts even reverted – these transitions appear to be. And as we will see, the juxtaposition of allegiant and assertive cultures has its particular manifestations in the ex-communist world. Where the allegiant elements of political culture are weaker and the assertive ones stronger, transitions have been moving more smoothly into a liberal democratic direction.

The transitions did not produce similar outcomes in all countries but they confront the same severe challenges: The postcommunist societies suffered considerable economic hardship, loss of security and social benefits, and a collapse of order and institutions around them. Indeed, the whole process has been more problematic than many had at first assumed. Furthermore, political democratization may not develop in tandem with economic marketization while civil society is far from being well developed in many of these countries.

Nevertheless, there are also indications of success that defy a view of the transition countries as being mired in an inevitable and insurmountable backwardness (Longworth 1992; Chirot 1989). Europe had no experience in transforming a planned economy into a market economy. Hence, the economic transformation after 1989 in CEE was even more difficult and cumbersome than the political transformation from authoritarian regimes toward a pluralistic democracy in Spain, Portugal, and Greece.[1] The development of civil society may take the longest time of all but may also be the element that ensures the long-term stability of the other two processes of transition in a stable and expanded Europe (Dahrendorf 1991).

Thus, one should see these transformations as open-ended processes. They involve developments that can be better illuminated through comparative study between nations and comparisons over time. This would also enable us to judge which reforms and which conditions are most effective for the peaceful transition to an open, democratic, and market-oriented society. Against this backdrop, Figure 7.1 conceptualizes the transition process in its entirety; simultaneous processes of *democratization, marketization,* and the *development of civil society.* The figure illustrates the multidimensionality of the transition in CEE, which makes this a herculean challenge. This has to be kept in mind when evaluating how the citizens adapt and how their attitudes develop in this challenging process.

---

[1] Although there is a substantial literature on economic reform by economists, there is less systematic or comparative material about public attitudes to market reform and the behavior of market actors (Vecernik 1996; Piirainen 1997).

Field of Transformation	Government	Economy	Society
Process of Transformation	Democratization	Marketization	Development of civil society
Level of Transformation	Political System	Economic system	Civic system
a. Macro-level	Political institutions and parties	Economic institutions and factors (GDP, productive output, unemployment, etc.)	Civic institutions (media, trade unions, churches)
b. Meso-level	Political activities	Economic activities, companies, firms	Forms of public participation, NGOs
c. Micro-level	Citizens and voters	Economic actors and households	Families and social networks

FIGURE 7.1. Three processes of transformation on three levels.
Source: Developed by the authors.

This chapter relies on the *historical comparative model* developed by Haerpfer (2002) and Rose, Mishler, and Haerpfer (1998). This model contends that the legitimacy of the democratic regime is shaped largely by the extent to which its economic and political performance is valued *relative* to that of its authoritarian predecessor. The more negatively or less positively people perceive the performance of the present democratic regime with that of the past communist regime, the less they are likely to embrace democracy as their preferred regime. Nostalgia for the authoritarian past is regarded as a crucial deterrent to the legitimation of democracy-in-the-making.

Our analyses are based on twenty-two transition countries from the former communist regions of CEE for which survey data are available from the World Values Survey (WVS) and European Values Study (EVS). We build on the previous chapter by Klingemann, focusing more specifically on the cultural transformation of the postcommunist world. We arrange the postcommunist nations into five groups based on their political histories and geographic locations:

- **Northern Europe:** the three post-Soviet Baltic states – Estonia, Latvia and Lithuania
- **Central Europe:** the four Visegrad countries – Poland, Czech Republic, Slovakia, and Hungary
- **Southeastern Europe:** the nine Balkan countries – Bulgaria, Romania, Moldova, Croatia, Slovenia, Bosnia-Herzegovina, Serbia, Montenegro, and Albania
- **Eastern Europe:** Ukraine, Belarus, and the Russian Federation
- **The Caucasus:** Georgia, Armenia, and Azerbaijan

Out of these five groups, the Baltic countries, the Visegrad countries, and Croatia and Slovenia form what Inglehart and Welzel (2005) call the "ex-communist West." All the other countries form the "ex-communist East." The dividing line is that the countries of the western group share a legacy of Western (i.e., Catholic or Protestant) Christianity and have been more exposed to emancipatory Western traditions, from the Enlightenment to market liberalism and representative democracy. Accordingly, people in the western group perceived the collapse of communism more clearly as the liberation from a historically imposed yoke and embraced it more openly as an opportunity to reapproach Western liberal ideals. People in the eastern group, by contrast, have non-Western historic identities based on Christian-Orthodox, Islamic, pan-Slavic, and Turkic traditions that resist an easy adoption of liberal Western ideals. For these reasons, we assume that the emergence of the liberal-democratic culture is significantly more advanced in countries of the western group than in the eastern group.

We assemble evidence from the WVS and EVS in these nations. The WVS examined public opinions in many postcommunist nations around 1995, soon after the beginning of the democratic transition, and then again in 2005. In addition, the EVS interviewed respondents in many of these countries in 2000 and 2008, using the same questions on political support. These four waves provide unique evidence to describe the evolution of the political culture in this region – and thus their cultural transition toward democracy or renewed authoritarianism (see also Chapter 6).

Our theoretical framework is based on the concept of political support by Easton (1975) and its further development by Norris (1999, 2011), Klingemann (1999), and Dalton (2004). This conceptual lineage overlaps with the distinction between "realist" and "idealist" forms of political support by Rose et al. (1998) as well as the distinction between "intrinsic" and "instrumental" support by Bratton and Mattes (2001) and Inglehart and Welzel (2005).

The organization of the chapter follows the Eastonian framework of three levels of political support. These levels are organized hierarchically from more encompassing at the base to more specific objects of support at higher levels. Thus, the first section of the chapter tracks support for the political community from 1995 to 2008, as represented by feelings of national pride. The second level of political support taps public commitment to the principles of democracy – democratic values and norms combined with the rejection of autocratic alternatives to autocracy. The third level involves support for specific political institutions, including the national government, parliament, and parties – whether they are democratic or not.

The concepts of "allegiant" and "assertive" political cultures underlying this book involve different expectations as concerns the levels in the support that are most important for a flourishing democratic culture. Following the allegiance concept, it is important that support builds from the broadest level – community support – to more specific levels, possibly excepting incumbent support as most specific. From the viewpoint of allegiance, skepticism of incumbents is the only level where lack of support is tolerable, allowing for shifting votes in elections and, hence, replacement of incumbents in power when citizens become dissatisfied with their performance. Disenchantment is not supposed to involve broader objects of support if the democratic culture is to remain stable.

From the viewpoint of assertive political culture, this looks different. It is acceptable if dissatisfaction broadens from incumbents to images of political institutions. The true firewall of a viable democratic culture is support for the regime principles of democracy. In fact, the assertive concept implies a healthy tension between normative commitment to the principles of democracy and dissatisfaction with the actual democratic performance of institutions and incumbents. Such a tension is seen as the driver of popular pressures on those in power to improve on democratic standards (Shin and Qi 2011; Welzel 2013; Chapters 4, 5, and 12).

This chapter first describes the emergence of a new political culture in post-communist states. Under communism, we could speak of the political culture of authoritarian statism. With the collapse of communism, that specific political culture lost its ideological frame, leaving a vacuum for the emerging postcommunist regimes that needs to be filled by a new political culture. This new political culture has been in development since 1989 and 1992 – we are still in the middle of an open-ended transition.

The second goal is to describe the idea of a "pyramid of political support," which is assuming that diffuse support for the national community is at the broad base of this pyramid. The level of support in this pyramid gets smaller as we analyze more and more specific and less diffuse support for the democratic regime and then the political institutions in postcommunist states.

SUPPORT FOR THE NATIONAL COMMUNITY

The most encompassing and basic level of political support according to Easton's framework is support for the national community. Easton (1965, 1975) noted that national identity is essential for the endurance of a nation-state and could provide a reservoir of diffuse support in time of political stress. Similarly, Almond and Verba (1963) emphasized the importance of national pride as part of the civic culture, especially as it involves pride in the political accomplishments of the nation. They contrasted the relatively high levels of national pride in the United States and Britain to the low levels of pride in Germany and Italy as evidence of this linkage.

The existence of national pride in postcommunist states could be considered highly uncertain. On one hand, the rhetoric of communist allegiance to the Soviet Union and a socialist brotherhood should have undercut feelings of nationalism in many communist states. This was a conscious goal of Moscow both in the USSR and in CEE states. Moreover, several of these states were incorporated in the formal institutional structure of the USSR. In the wake of democratization, some of the previous Eastern European states fragmented, especially in the case of Yugoslavia and Czechoslovakia. On the other hand, even in this context, national identities often endured, sometimes as a shield of resistance against communist indoctrination. The Baltic states retained distinct identities as a mental escape from being a formal part of the USSR. Several CEE nations – such as Poland and Hungary – emphasized their long historical traditions and autonomy even while existing as part of the Communist Bloc. In fact, in countries that would not have joined the communist empire in the absence of Soviet troops on their territory, it is doubtful whether communism ever had majority support. In these cases, preserving national identity retained a psychological shield against the Soviet doctrine.

The difficult task for the postcommunist states is to create a new political community in consolidating the process of nation building. In some countries, it was possible to revive historically rooted identities, for example, in Poland or Hungary. In other countries, like in Belarus or Moldova, the process of nation building had to start from scratch. This process of nation building included the rewriting of a national history by postcommunist historians, the creation of national symbols, and new narratives. The process of nation building was easier in those countries, where it was possible to reconnect with a previous nation that existed before the communist take-over in that specific country.

The WVS/EVS measures diffuse support for the national community by asking respondents whether they are very proud, fairly proud, not so proud, or not proud at all of their nation (see the appendix for question wording). Table 7.1 shows that popular support for the nation is relatively stable across time and across postcommunist countries. A full 77 percent of all postcommunist citizens express pride in their nation in 1995 – a time point six years after the first political transition in November 1989 (and three years after the December 1991 transition in the USSR). Across all these nations combined, feelings of national pride remained stable through 2008 (78 percent for all nations). Underneath this aggregate stability, there has been a considerable variety in regional longitudinal patterns.

The greatest increase of national pride – from 68 percent in 1995 to 79 percent in 2008 – occurred in the eastern region, which includes Russia, Ukraine, and Belarus. The rise of national pride was particularly strong in the Russian Federation (+18 percent points), about average in Ukraine (+9 percent points), and less than average in Belarus (+6 percent points). In terms of international law, the Russian Federation is the successor state of the Soviet Union, which caused the end of Soviet identity and the complicated rebirth of a Russian national identity. Russia as the successor of the USSR was also the biggest loser of the postcommunist revolution, which caused a tremendous turmoil regarding support of the new political community in Russia. The transition from a "homo Sovieticus" to a post-Soviet Russian citizen was full of uncertainty and sociopsychological stress, which caused – among other public health factors – a dramatic decline of life expectancy, especially among Russian men,

TABLE 7.1. *Support for the Political Community*

Country	1995	2000	2005	2008	Change
Northern Europe	57	55	*	63	+6
Estonia	53	52	*	65	+12
Latvia	52	59	*	62	+10
Lithuania	66	54	*	63	−3
Central Europe	88	84		84	−4
Poland	95	95	96	88	−7
Czech Republic	83	79	*	79	−4
Slovakia	84	75	*	86	+2
Hungary	90	87	*	84	−6
Southeastern Europe	82	77	77	78	−4
Slovenia	86	89	87	91	+5
Bulgaria	77	67	74	77	0
Romania	82	85	82	81	−1
Moldova	74	62	66	76	+2
Bosnia-Herzegovina	85	65	*	57	−28
Serbia	*	*	75	79	+4
Montenegro	*	*	*	77	*
Albania	85	92	*	83	−2
Eastern Europe	68	64	74	79	+11
Ukraine	61	57	67	70	+9
Belarus	74	66	*	80	+6
Russia	69	68	81	87	+18
Caucasus	89	*	*	86	−3
Georgia	93	*	97	94	+1
Armenia	80	*	*	87	+7
Azerbaijan	94	*	*	76	−18
Postcommunist Europe	77	76	*	78	+1

Note: Table entries are the percentage feeling "very proud" and "proud" of their nation.
Source: World Values Surveys 1995, 2005; European Values Survey 2000, 2008.

between 1992 and 2000. Marketization produced widespread suffering among the public at large. At the beginning of the transition, during the turbulent era of President Yeltsin, only 69 percent of Russians were proud of the new Russia, which means one-third of all Russians had limited identification with their nation three years after the beginning of the transformation. In 2008, after eight years of Putin's presidency, a strong majority of Russians were proud of the new Russian state.

However, the Russian experience illustrates that national pride itself is a rather doubtful indicator of a healthy democratic culture, unless the feelings of pride ally with democratic regime preferences. National pride can reflect the popular legitimacy of the nation-state, independent of support for a specific regime form. It enhances the stability of the state rather than the content of the regime. By restoring order to a country that seemed to be falling apart and strengthening the economy, Putin increased national pride, but these feelings allied with ideals of strong leadership that allowed Putin to reverse Russia's democratic progress without much resistance from the population. Since 2003, the Freedom House has rated Russia as an "unfree" country.

Within Eastern Europe, the lowest level of support of the new nation-state is in Ukraine. Owing to peculiarities of its historical and cultural development, the Ukrainian society is deeply divided into the western part with Ukrainian language, Ukrainian national identity, and pro-Western orientation, and the eastern part, with Russian as the main language and a Russian identity and orientation. As a consequence of these deep cultural divisions, only 61 percent expressed pride in the new Ukrainian state in 1995. The support for the new Ukraine increased slowly to 70 percent in 2008, but one-third of the public still does not support the political community; psychologically, they have not yet embraced the new independent Ukraine as their political home.

National identity in Belarus after the end of the Soviet Union was quite modest in 1995, three years after gaining national independence in January 1992. The long-lasting electoral autocracy of President Lukashenka resulted in an increase of Belarusian national pride to 80 percent in 2008. Again, this underlines the inherently ambiguous status of national pride with respect to a democratic culture.

A significant increase in national pride also occurred in the Baltic States, increasing from 57 percent in 1995 to 63 percent in 2008. This is not surprising because the end of the Soviet Union in 1991 constituted the chance for national independence by the Baltic states and the beginning of statehood. Also, national independence in the Baltics was a triumph of people power movements, which should quite naturally increase national pride. The rise of national pride was particularly strong in Estonia and in Latvia. It needs to be emphasized, however, that support for the national community differs considerably between the Latvian, Estonian, and Lithuanian majorities in the three Baltic states and the sizable Russian-Byelorussian minorities.[2] Generally, support is significantly lower among the Russian-Byelorussian minorities, whose members do not feel to be part of the new national communities; significant shares of them remain to be preoccupied with Soviet nostalgia.

The general level of support for the national community is quite high in the Central European states, which were historically reestablished after the fall of the Iron Curtain in 1989. Five years after the annus mirabilis 1989, 88 percent of all Central European citizens were proud of their nation. This support

---

[2] At the time of this writing, the Russian-Byelorussian minorities consist of about 31 percent of the population in Latvia, 27 percent in Estonia, and 7 percent in Lithuania. The percentage of residents with a strong or fair amount of national pride is 76 percent among the Latvian majority in Latvia and 57 among the Russian-Byelorussian minority. In Estonia, the figures are 63 percent for the Estonian majority and 42 percent for the Russian-Byelorussian minority.

of the nation-state remained at a high level through 2008 among Central European citizens. National pride is highest in Slovenia, followed by Poland and Slovakia.

In those countries of Southeastern Europe that started the transition at a relatively high level of support for the political community (82 percent on average), the level of national pride remained stable or changed only a little. This reflects the historical peculiarities of these countries, the timing of their nation-building process, and the absent role of a supranational "soviet identity." The creation of most states in Southeastern Europe – except Albania – was the historical result of the violent breakup of the Republic of Yugoslavia. The civil wars during the collapse of Yugoslavia, the wars between the new political units, and the high ethnic heterogeneity in many of these new states caused low levels of national identity and pride. Hence barely half of the population of Bosnia-Herzegovina is proud of their new country. Support for the national community is higher in Kosovo, Montenegro, and Serbia. The high ethnic homogeneity of the population in Albania may explain the even greater support for their state, which has a long political history.

National pride has been stable over time in Bulgaria and Romania. Both countries had national independence within the Soviet Bloc; hence there was no opportunity for national renaissance as in the Baltic or Eastern European states. The general level of support for the national community was rather weak in Moldova. The society in this country is split into a pro-Western Moldovan part, which speaks the Romanian language and feels close to Romania and Western Europe, versus a pro-Russian part, which speaks Russian and identifies itself with Russia.[3]

The breakup of the Soviet Union created a unique opportunity in the South Caucasus to transform Georgia, Armenia, and Azerbaijan into new and independent states. This constitutes a major difference in historical opportunities to the North Caucasus, whose territorial units – including Chechnya, Ossetia, Ingushetia, and Dagestan – remained subnational units within the Russian Federation. The local conflicts and regional wars during the last fifteen years in the North Caucasus, most notably in Chechnya, have been an expression of these unequal historical opportunities for national liberation between North and South Caucasus.

By far the highest level of national pride exists in Georgia, which can be explained by the surge of political sentiment after Georgia was "reborn" as an independent state in 1992. Support for the nation-state went even higher in 2008 during the conflict with the Russian Federation. The new state of Armenia also found wide support, probably linked to wars and conflicts with neighboring states, especially with Azerbaijan about the territory of Nagorno-Karabakh. Similarly, nearly all Azerbaijanis supported their new nation-state in response

[3] In addition, Trans-Nistria is a rogue territorial unit within the territory of the Republic of Moldova, outside the control of the Moldovan government.

to military attacks from Russia at the end of the Soviet Union and the beginning of the independent existence of Azerbaijan.

In summary, we find a mixed pattern of national pride across the post-communist and post-Soviet states. National identity is usually weaker in eth-nolinguistically and religiously divided societies where various parts of the population want to pull the country into different directions – the decisive conflict mostly focusing on a pro-Western versus pro-Russian course. This conflict reflects a deep-seated historic cleavage, dividing a camp of "Westerners" whose supporters favor the association of Central and Eastern Europe with the West (partly as an escape from Russian dominance) and a camp of "Slavophiles" whose supporters idealize some sort of pan-Slavic federation under Russian leadership. The salience of this cleavage confirms the theory that ethnic and religious diversity is an impediment for developing a national community in new states. In contrast, national pride tends to be higher in countries where national independence represents successful resistance against Russian dominance.

If low national identification can be problematic to develop a viable democratic culture, the reverse does not hold true: Higher national pride and identification is not necessarily an indicator of a flourishing democratic culture. It depends on whether the national identification allies with a belief in democratic principles. Reflecting historic proximities to the West, the latter seems to be much more the case in postcommunist Europe than in post-Soviet Eurasia – as the next section shows.

SUPPORT FOR DEMOCRATIC VALUES AND PRINCIPLES

The next level of political support is concerned with democracy as a political regime as well as democratic principles and values. The collapse of the communist one-party states bereaved the communist culture of its official ideological and institutional frame. But the communist value system did not disappear overnight and is uneven across social groups. Instead, the orientations survived in the form of an emerging nostalgia for communism, especially among the older population and within the communist parties, for example, in the Communist parties in the Russian Federation or Ukraine.

With varying success, new political forces tried to establish democratic principles and socialize democratic values after the collapse of communism. Among the various elements of a democratic culture, the idea that democracy is preferable to any of its authoritarian regime alternatives is considered fundamental to a stable democratic system (Rose et al. 1998; Diamond 1999, 2008; Linz and Stepan 1996). This is because commitment to democracy as the preferred form of government implies rejection of antidemocratic movements whose proponents aim to undermine or overthrow a newly emerging democratic regime. Democracy is more deeply rooted when the citizenry embraces it as "the only game in town" (Diamond 1999, 2008; Linz and Stepan 1996). From the

TABLE 7.2. *Support for the Democratic System*

Country	1995	2000	2005	2008	Change
Northern Europe	78	71	*	69	−9
Estonia	81	71	*	74	−7
Latvia	79	76	*	69	−10
Lithuania	74	67	*	65	−9
Central Europe	86	79	*	75	−11
Poland	*	72	74	76	+4
Czech Republic	86	89	*	72	−14
Slovakia	88	75	*	74	−14
Hungary	83	79	*	78	−5
Southeastern Europe	82	77	77	75	−7
Slovenia	80	83	78	83	+3
Bulgaria	69	71	72	65	−4
Romania	80	75	83	73	−7
Moldova	78	59	83	68	−10
Bosnia-Herzegovina	91	83	*	77	−14
Serbia	*	*	70	78	+8
Montenegro	*	*	*	76	*
Albania	94	92	*	82	−12
Eastern Europe	55	59	67	64	+9
Ukraine	55	64	66	56	+1
Belarus	66	67	*	73	+7
Russia	45	46	67	62	+17
Caucasus	81	*	*	76	−5
Georgia	85	*	92	82	−3
Armenia	76	*	*	84	+8
Azerbaijan	82	*	*	62	−20
Postcommunist Europe	75	75	*	73	−2

Note: Table entries are the percentage saying that having a democratic system is "very good" and "fairly good."
Source: World Values Surveys 1995, 2005; European Values Survey 2000, 2008.

perspective of an assertive democratic culture, this domain of support is the key battleground on which the viability of a democratic culture is decided.

We measure support for democratic values and principles with a question on approval of democracy as a political system (see the appendix). There are alternative measures of democratic values (see Chapters 4 and 5), but this item has the advantage of being included in multiple waves of the WVS/EVS.

In the set of all postcommunist nations, support for democracy as a political system is rather constant with 75 percent support in 1995 and 73 percent in 2008 (Table 7.2). Again, this aggregate pattern glosses over significant differences between different regions. As Klingemann has shown in a snapshot of two surveys in the previous chapter, this overall stability involves a mix of nations with increasing and decreasing support over time. Thus, if we consider regional patterns, Eastern Europe (Russia, Ukraine, and Belarus) is the only group of countries that is characterized by increasing support for democracy. All other groups of countries experienced a small or modest decrease in democratic support during the period from 1995 to 2008.

The strongest support for democracy as a political system is found in the new democracies of Central Europe. Countries with a democratic past like Hungary, Poland, Bulgaria, or the Czech Republic could revive the memory of this past, proving helpful in building a democratic culture. There was a collective memory of democratic institutions – like competitive elections, multiparty parliaments, critical media, and free associations – and democratic principles, such as human rights, rule of law, and political opposition. In these countries, a new cohort of democratic historians and political scientists who have been educated in the United States or Western Europe guided the revival of a democratic culture. An alternative recruitment reservoir consisted of regime dissidents and social movement activists of an emerging civil society under communism whose proponents confronted the one-party states with claims for civil rights and democratic principles. This liberal-democratic underground was specific to the "ex-communist west," visible in such persons as Lech Walesa, Vaclav Havel, and Joachim Gauck.

Support for democracy as a political system is also rather high in the countries of Southeastern Europe from the beginning of the transition in 1995 until the last observation in 2008. Thus, nearly four-fifths of the population support democracy as a political system in the successor states of Yugoslavia (Kosovo, Serbia, Bosnia-Herzegovina, and Montenegro) and Albania. The share of "democrats" in other countries of this group – like Bulgaria or Moldova – persists at a proportion of some two-thirds of the population over time. This implies that even in new European Union member states, like Romania and Bulgaria, substantial shares of the population do not support democracy as a political system.

We find a short-lived euphoria for democracy in the Baltic region immediately after the end of the Soviet Union, which partially faded away later. In 1995, for example, 79 percent of Latvians supported democracy as a political system, which dropped to 69 percent in 2008. Similar but smaller declines were registered in Estonia and Lithuania.[4]

Apart from the Baltics, the weakest support for democracy as a political system exists in the other post-Soviet countries of Eastern Europe. This finding is consistent over the entire observation period. The longitudinal pattern in Belarus, which some scholars describe as the "last dictatorship" in Europe,

---

[4] With respect to the national community, the Russian-Byelorussian minorities in the Baltic countries show significantly lower support than the majorities in these countries. This pattern is much less pronounced with respect to support for democracy as a political system. The biggest difference exists in Estonia where the Russian-Byelorussian minority's support is six percentage points lower than that of the national majority.

is rather interesting. The Byelorussians' support for democracy as a political system increased over time. This suggests that the autocratic president of Belarus, Alexander Lukashenka, is ruling a society that favors a more democratic system. Apparently, then, Belarus is a case of increasing popular demand for democracy, suggesting a decreasing popularity of its autocratic government. From the viewpoint of congruence theory, this indicates an increasing mismatch between supply of and demand for democracy in Belarus. Alternatively, more people may believe the government's propaganda and think that their country is fairly democratic. The future will show which of these two interpretations holds true.

Support for democracy in Russia was constantly weak during the political transformations since 1992, when Russia was formed as a new state. During the 1990s, less than half of the Russians supported democracy as a system of government: only 45 percent during the first term of Yeltsin as president. This changed a little after his resignation in 1999. Support for democracy rose to 62 percent in 2008, after two terms of office of President Putin. Still, a solid third of all Russians in 2008 think that it is *not good* to have a democratic system.

Ukraine displays the weakest support for democracy as a system of government; only 55 percent of Ukrainians supported democracy in 1995. Support for democracy then increased and culminated during the "Orange Revolution" in 2005 under President Yuschtschenko and Prime Minister Timoshenko: At this point in time, 66 percent of the Ukrainians responded that they support democracy as a system of government. The failure of the Orange Revolution and the subsequent authoritarian change under President Yanukovitch resulted in a significant drop in support for democracy.

In the Southern Caucasus states, public support for democracy was very strong in 1995 and remained so until 2008. It found its political expression in the Rose Revolution in Georgia, followed by active political debates, high levels of political participation, and exceptionally successful fights against corruption. Azerbaijan is another interesting case: Movement toward a more autocratic political regime over time correlates with decreasing support for democracy. Support for a democratic system decreased by 20 percentage points from 82 to only 62 percent in 2008. With the notable exception of Georgia, trends in most post-Soviet societies indicate a reviving popularity of authoritarian government. Amid chaotic transformations, democracy came to be associated with disorder. Hence, the idea of a ruler who governs with an iron fist to restore order, the economy, and national strength regained popularity.

In conclusion, even using the longer time series of WVS/EVS surveys in these postcommunist nations compared to Chapter 6, there is little evidence of a systematic increase in support for democracy as a system of government in the more than two decades since the first surveys in 1995. In fact, support for democracy is often decreasing in nations where the democratic system seems to be functioning reasonably well – the Baltic states and Central Europe.

By contrast, increases in support for democracy as a system of government happened in East European/post-Soviet states where democracy has actually been under assault. Despite these increases, solid proportions of the population still do not support democracy as a system of government.

TRUST IN POLITICAL INSTITUTIONS

Trust in the political institutions that exist in democratic and other types of regime is a more specific level of political support than preferences for different regime types. This section examines trust in the national government, the parliament, and political parties. Trust in these institutions is an essential element of a flourishing political culture from an allegiant point of view, as Almond and Verba (1963) stressed the need for citizens to support their governments. However, this is not the case from an assertive point of view (see Chapter 1), where skepticism of institutions and their performance is paired with strong democratic values. One should also be cautious not to misread the following trust figures as measuring the believed necessity of these institutions. More plausibly, the statistics measure an evaluation of the respective institutions' current performance (see Chapter 6). Thus, they are more indicative of the respondents' expectations than the institutions' objective performance.

National Government

The broadest measure of institutional support is confidence in the national government as an entity (see the appendix for question wording). Across all postcommunist states, Table 7.3 finds that nearly half of the public had confidence in the national government at the beginning of the time series. This rather strong support for the early postcommunist governments was likely part of the postrevolutionary euphoria that spread across the Eastern Bloc. Many people initially hoped that things would quickly improve in approaching the world of prosperous democracies. This initial optimism evaporated rapidly and gave way to increasing skepticism in almost all postcommunist societies. The result was decreasing trust in national government: In 2008, only about one-third of all Eastern European citizens expressed confidence in their national governments. The few exceptions from this trend are the countries with successful transitions, especially Slovenia and the Czech Republic.

Trust in the national government is quite high in the post-Soviet countries of Eastern Europe, mainly because Belarus and Russia have very high levels of support for their autocratic governments. The Russian government in the Yeltsin era was only supported by 25 percent of the population; this grew to 43 percent at the end of Putin's first term and to 58 percent in the last year of his second term. This is a sign of consolidating authoritarian institutions in the new Russia between 1995 and 2008. A similar pattern exists in Belarus during the era of President Lukashenka. At the beginning of institution building in

TABLE 7.3. *Confidence in National Government*

Country	1995	2000	2005	2008	Change
North Europe	40	*	*	26	−14
Estonia	49	*	*	35	−14
Latvia	37	*	*	21	−16
Lithuania	33	*	*	23	−10
Central Europe	38	*	*	27	−11
Poland	36	*	17	21	−15
Czech Republic	30	*	*	20	−10
Slovakia	42	*	*	49	+7
Hungary	43	*	*	16	−27
Southeast Europe	47	41	28	26	−21
Slovenia	39	*	23	39	0
Bulgaria	56	*	34	13	−43
Romania	20	*	25	24	+4
Moldova	57	36	32	33	−24
Bosnia-Herzegovina	69	29	*	20	−49
Serbia	*	*	25	14	−11
Montenegro	*	*	*	36	*
Albania	38	57	*	25	−13
Eastern Europe	38	*	34	46	+8
Ukraine	41	*	24	23	−18
Belarus	48	*	*	58	+10
Russia	25	*	43	58	+33
Caucasus	59	*	*	52	−7
Georgia	50	*	31	45	−5
Armenia	41	*	*	52	+11
Azerbaijan	86	*	*	59	−27
Postcommunist Europe	46	*	*	35	−11

Note: Table entries are the percentage "very confident" and "fairly confident" in the national government.

Source: World Values Survey 1995, 2005; European Values Survey 2000, 2008.

Belarus in 1995, 48 percent of all Byelorussians showed confidence in the new national government, which increased to 58 percent in 2008.

The previous analyses of support for democracy in these two countries have to be interpreted in this context: When support for democracy allies with trust in a basically autocratic government, it is highly doubtful that we are really measuring support for democracy (Shin and Qi 2011). Lukashenka, Putin, and other autocrats get their way because they meet no powerful resistance in a culture whose enthusiasm for true democratic principles is modest at best.

The chronic political crisis in Ukraine is clearly visible at this level of political support. Almost two-fifths of Ukrainians expressed trust in the national government in 1995 after becoming an independent state, but this decreased by nearly half in 2008.

Different trends could be observed in other post-Soviet countries composing the Caucasus region. Confidence in national government in Georgia reflects the recent political history of this state. Thus, owing to the population's high expectations and euphoria, it was quite high at the beginning of the transition period in 1995, decreased essentially by the middle of 2000 during the turmoil of the Rose Revolution, and increased almost to the initial level in 2008. Armenia is characterized by a slow and steady increase in trust in government from 1995 to 2008, while the situation in Azerbaijan during the last twenty years caused some decrease of confidence in the government.

The general low level of support for the national governments in the countries of Southeastern Europe, like Bulgaria and Romania, is likely linked with extensive corruption and the lack of control of organized crime, especially in Bulgaria. Moldovans also became more skeptical regarding their national government; this is likely caused by a long stalemate between the pro-Russian governments of the Communist Party and the pro-European coalition governments of the anticommunist parties.

Postcommunist Central Europe shows high diversity in the longitudinal patterns. In Slovakia, trust in government increased slightly over time, which is very much against the general trend. In Slovenia, trust in the national government is stable over time. In contrast, Polish and Czech confidence in their respective national governments decreased across these surveys. In 2008, only one-fifth of the Polish and Czech people trusted their own government; confidence in government collapsed even more precipitously in Hungary. The erosion of trust in the Hungarian government may reflect the attempt by successive Hungarian governments to hide the true extent of public debt and the state deficit, which triggered widespread and violent demonstrations in Budapest and other major cities over the last years. Similar trends could be observed in countries of Northern Europe, where the initially modest level of trust in national government (40 percent in 1995) has considerably dropped (to 20 to 30 percent in 2008).

Trust in Parliament and Political Parties

Although trust in the national government might tap specific support for those in power and their policies, trust in parliaments and political parties should reflect a more diffuse form of support for institutions that are the key symbols of representation. From the perspective of an allegiant democratic culture, the ideal situation is when legitimate dissatisfaction with an incumbent government does not generate a more general dissatisfaction with parliaments and parties as the institutions of representation. Thus, distrust in government should preferably not translate into distrust in parliaments and parties.

Trust in parliaments and trust in political parties follow similar patterns over time (Tables 7.4 and 7.5). Both show slight overall declines from the beginning to the end of the survey period. The parallel development of trust

TABLE 7.4. *Confidence in National Parliament*

Country	1995	2000	2005	2008	Change
North Europe	30	20	*	21	−9
Estonia	42	25	*	28	−14
Latvia	24	26	*	20	−4
Lithuania	24	10	*	14	−10
Central Europe	29	29	*	26	−3
Poland	31	31	12	18	−13
Czech Republic	20	13	*	16	−4
Slovakia	29	39	*	47	+18
Hungary	37	31	*	21	−16
Southeast Europe	39	28	20	27	−12
Slovenia	24	24	15	44	+20
Bulgaria	42	26	20	11	−31
Romania	18	18	16	23	+5
Moldova	40	33	28	35	−5
Bosnia-Herzegovina	55	20	*	26	−29
Serbia	*	*	20	12	−8
Montenegro	*		*	35	*
Albania	56	44	*	31	−25
Eastern Europe	27	25	23	35	+8
Ukraine	34	25	17	14	−20
Belarus	26	33	*	52	+26
Russia	21	18	28	39	+18
Caucasus	45	*	*	48	3
Georgia	39	*	23	33	−6
Armenia	29	*	*	39	+10
Azerbaijan	67	*	*	71	+4
Postcommunist Europe	38	27	*	31	−7

Note: Table entries are the percentage "very confident" and "fairly confident" in the national parliament.
Source: World Values Survey 1995, 2005; European Values Survey 2000, 2008.

in parliaments and parties is not surprising because parliaments consist of parties.

The following discussion focuses on political parties because this institution highlights the particular difficulties of trust building in the institutional vacuum left behind by the collapse of the previous order. One of the major problems of postcommunist political systems was and still is the creation of an open, pluralistic, and competitive party system to replace the one-party system of the communist regime. In a few postcommunist countries, the founding and early elections were dominated by personalities who were known as courageous opponents of the communist regimes and were widely popular because of that. The most prominent examples include the writer and later Czech president Vaclav Havel and the trade union leader and later Polish president Lech Walesa.

TABLE 7.5. *Confidence in Political Parties*

Country	1995	2000	2005	2008	Change
North Europe	15	*	*	11	−4
Estonia	22	*	*	12	−10
Latvia	10	*	*	14	+4
Lithuania	12	*	*	8	−4
Central Europe	16	*	*	15	−1
Poland	11	*	7	11	0
Czech Republic	14	*	*	15	+1
Slovakia	21	*	*	24	+3
Hungary	19	*	*	10	−9
Southeast Europe	23	22	14	15	−8
Slovenia	13	*	8	22	+9
Bulgaria	27	*	17	9	−18
Romania	13	*	12	17	+4
Moldova	17	23	21	18	+1
Bosnia-Herzegovina	46	14	*	12	−34
Serbia	*	*	13	6	−7
Montenegro	*	*	*	15	*
Albania	22	29	*	21	−1
Eastern Europe	16	*	18	22	+6
Ukraine	17	*	15	16	−1
Belarus	14	*	*	26	+12
Russia	18	*	21	24	+6
Caucasus	31	*	*	39	8
Georgia	33	*	16	21	−12
Armenia	15	*	*	30	+15
Azerbaijan	46	*	*	66	+20
Postcommunist Europe	23	*	*	20	−3

Note: Table entries are the percentage "very confident" and "fairly confident" in political parties.
Source: World Values Survey 1995, 2005; European Values Survey 2000, 2008.

In the absence as much as in the presence of such charismatic personalities, building a functioning multiparty system proved difficult in all postcommunist countries.

Few people even in established democracies have much confidence in parties as political institutions. Across all the postcommunist nations combined, about one-quarter of all citizens trusted the new political parties in 1995 (Table 7.5). This figure remained more or less the same in 2008. The highest level of support for political parties was found in the Southern Caucasus, largely because of Azerbaijan. Even in 1995, Azerbaijanis were likely to trust parties, so this seems particular to this nation.

The low level of support for political parties in the post-Soviet countries is relatively constant. The Russian party system, which is under almost complete control of the central power structure in Moscow rather than being a pluralist system, is supported by only one-quarter of the population. Such low levels of support for key institutions of the democratic electoral process suggest a limited belief in electoral politics, which is also reflected in the other nations of this region like Ukraine and Belarus.

Support for political parties in Central Europe is even lower, however. There is above average support in Slovakia but markedly low confidence in the Czech Republic, Poland, and Hungary. The patterns are quite similar in Southeastern Europe and the Baltic states. As others have found out, even in established democracies, political parties generate little confidence among the people. This general rule holds true in the postcommunist states as well (Dalton 2004; Chapters 5 and 6). As Table 7.4 shows, the same conclusion holds for confidence in parliaments.

Taking the perspective of an allegiant model of a democratic culture, one might conclude that high trust ratings in political institutions, such as governments, parliaments, and parties, are a sign that things are going well. However, from the viewpoint of an assertive model, a different interpretation seems more accurate. In this perspective, trust ratings should be interpreted in connection with people's support for democratic principles. Thus, high trust ratings in political institutions are not automatically good and low ratings are not automatically bad. High trust in political institutions can be an inverse indicator of a viable democratic culture if these ratings are paired with low support for democratic principles (Shin and Qi 2011; see Chapter 6). Conversely, low confidence in political institutions may be a sign of a viable democratic culture if these ratings ally with strong support for democratic principles (Welzel 2013).

Supporting evidence of this point from the postcommunist world is shown in Figure 7.2. On the horizontal axis, the graph plots the fraction of respondents in each nation who give their national government a negative trust rating but at the same time prefer democracy over its authoritarian alternatives.[5] This is an operationalization of Klingemann's dissatisfied democrats from the previous chapter and a measure of assertive democratic citizens. The vertical axis represents a country's level of civil and political rights taken from Freedom House for 2006, which is approximately the time of our last wave of survey data.[6]

Indeed, among the roughly twenty countries with available data, the fraction of distrustful democrats in the population is positively related to the regime's performance in guaranteeing civil and political rights. This one variable

---

[5] This score is calculated as the percentage of those who lack confidence in the national government among those who also express approval of democracy.

[6] Freedom House's "civil liberties" and "political rights" ratings are averaged, then inverted so that larger numbers indicate more liberties and rights, and finally standardized into a scale from minimum 0 to maximum 1.0.

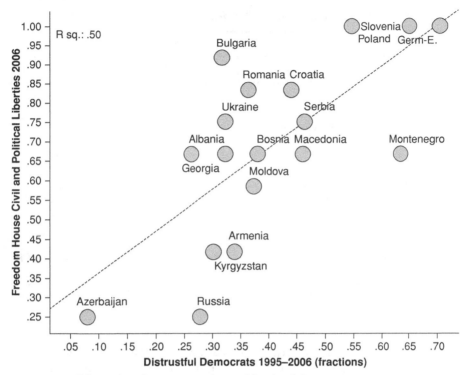

FIGURE 7.2. Distrusting democrats and actual levels of democracy.
Source: dissatisfied democrats measure from WVS/EVS; Civil and Political Liberties from Freedom House (http://www.freedomhouse.org).

explains roughly 50 percent of the variance in civil and political rights. For example, Poland, East Germany, and Slovenia have the highest scores on the Freedom House measure as well as a high proportion of dissatisfied democrats. Conversely, Azerbaijan and Russia have the lowest Freedom House scores and also relatively small proportions of dissatisfied democrats. In short, even in the postcommunist nations of Europe and Asia, allegiant orientations to political institutions are not as clearly linked to democratic politics as are assertive orientations. This pattern does not only apply to mature postindustrial democracies.

MULTIVARIATE ANALYSES

Our presentation has stressed the differential meaning and the differential levels of political support in the postcommunist world. The last step in our analysis is to consider the varied social and political bases of these three levels of political support. We use multivariate regressions to examine the most common correlates of the three different levels of political support in the postcommunist

TABLE 7.6. *Correlates of Support for Political Institutions*

Rank	Item	B	SE	β
1	Satisfaction with democracy	0.87	0.01	0.28
2	Positive rating of system of government	0.22	0.01	0.21
3	Rejection of military regime	0.28	0.01	0.09
4	Politics important for personal life	0.24	0.01	0.09
5	Democracies are efficient	0.21	0.01	0.07
6	High interest in politics	0.15	0.01	0.06
7	Greater respect for authority is good	0.15	0.01	0.05
8	Unfair society	0.04	0.01	0.05
9	Informal social capital	0.04	0.01	0.04
10	Follow politics in media	0.06	0.01	0.03
11	Democracy good for economy	0.01	0.01	0.03
12	Generalized trust	0.17	0.02	0.03
	Constant	9.775	0.114	
	Model 1	R	R^2	Adjusted R^2
		0.51	0.26	0.26

Note: OLS regression analysis; beta coefficients given for variables significant at the 0.001 level.
Source: European Values Study 2008.

world, such as interpersonal trust, political interest, satisfaction with democracy, and a notion that one's society is fair. Explorative factor analysis[7] demonstrates that the three levels of support we distinguished conceptually also exist empirically: support for political institutions, for democracy as a system of government, and for the national community are three separate things.

We begin by examining the correlates of support for political institutions in Table 7.6. Controlling for other civic culture attributes, satisfaction with

---

[7] The analysis is conducted with the country-pooled, unweighted individual-level data, using the latest survey from each country. We employ the Kaiser criterion and request a varimax-rotated extraction of factors.

	Support for Political Institutions	Support for Democracy		Communality
Trust in political parties	0.84	0.09	0.01	0.71
Trust in parliament	0.83	0.07	0.07	0.70
Trust in government	0.85	0.07	0.10	0.74
Good having a democratic system	0.08	0.88	0.05	0.78
Churchill thesis democracy	0.09	0.88	0.04	0.78
National pride	0.10	0.07	0.99	**0.99**
% Variance explained	35.7	26.1	16.7	

TABLE 7.7. *Correlates of Support for Democracy as a System of Government*

Rank	Items	B	SE	β
1	High interest in politics	0.19	0.01	0.08
2	Democracy is efficient	0.15	0.01	0.05
3	Has signed a petition	0.14	0.01	0.05
4	Higher household income	0.06	0.01	0.04
5	Higher education	0.07	0.01	0.04
6	Younger age	0.00	0.00	0.04
7	Follow politics in media	0.06	0.01	0.03
8	Satisfaction with democracy	0.09	0.01	0.03
9	Against military regime	0.09	0.01	0.03
10	Male	0.14	0.01	0.03
11	Against strong leader	0.06	0.01	0.03
12	General life satisfaction	0.01	0.00	0.02
	Constant	1.463	1.308	
	Model 2	R	R^2	Adjusted R^2
		0.38	0.14	0.14

Note: OLS regression analysis; beta coefficients given for variables significant at the 0.001 level.
Source: European Values Study 2008.

how democracy works shows the strongest positive linkage with support for political institutions. The next most important correlate is a positive rating of one's society's system of government. Thus, support for political institutions closely reflects other positive performance evaluations related to one's country's politics. In addition, several variables indicate that the politically engaged tend to be more supportive of political institutions.

Our second model examines the correlates of support for democracy as a system of governance (Table 7.7). The regression analysis shows that political engagement – interest in politics and participation in such activities as petitions – as well as the disposal of politically relevant resources such as income, education, and media access correlate most positively with support for democracy. This pattern resonates with Verba, Schlozman, and Brady's (1995) "civic voluntarism" model because it shows that support for democracy is a civic maturation product of greater participatory resources and stronger participatory motivations. In contrast, many of the performance variables that are important for support of political institutions did not emerge as relevant for democratic support. This contrast appears to underscore the diffuse nature of democratic norms versus the specific nature of support for political institutions.

Finally, considering the correlates of support for the national community in Table 7.8, this model explains much less variance than the previous two models. In general, the civic characteristics of individuals – be it resources or motivations – generally play a much less important role in structuring these opinions. Only satisfaction with democracy generates a substantial coefficient,

TABLE 7.8. *Correlates of Support for the National Community*

Rank	Items	B	SE	β
1	Satisfaction with democracy	0.16	0.01	0.11
2	High importance of politics	0.07	0.01	0.06
3	Positive rating of government	0.02	0.00	0.06
4	Personal happiness	0.09	0.01	0.05
5	Greater respect for authority in future is good	0.07	0.01	0.05
6	Follow politics in media	0.04	0.01	0.05
7	General life satisfaction	0.01	0.00	0.04
8	Frequent political discussions with friends	0.06	0.01	0.04
9	Higher household income	0.02	0.01	0.03
10	Support of current society	0.09	0.01	0.03
11	Bigger role of the state	0.01	0.00	0.03
12	In full employment	0.01	0.01	0.02
	Constant	3.875	0.066	
	Model 3	R	R^2	Adjusted R^2
		0.24	0.06	0.06

Note: OLS regression analysis; beta coefficients given for variables significant at the 0.001 level.
Source: European Values Study 2008.

and we have previously noted the mixed meaning of democratic evaluations across postcommunist states. These results seem to indicate that identification with one's national community is the result of historic configurations and identities that play out at the national level much more than at the individual level.

CONCLUSIONS

The postcommunist nations of Europe were the major contributors to the fourth wave of democratization, and their political and economic transformations reshaped the map of Europe and the world. From the outset, however, there has been widespread concern about whether the transforming political culture of these nations would generate genuine support for democracy (Rose et al. 1998; Diamond 1999, 2008; Linz and Stepan 1996; Rohrschneider 1999). Generations of socialization under authoritarian regimes must be overcome for a culture supporting democracy to take root.

This chapter has described the political culture of these nations and how the elements of the culture have changed in the period between the mid-1990s and the mid-2000s based on the WVS (1995 and 2005) and the EVS (2000 and 2008).

Figures 7.3 provides a general overview of our findings on political support across all postcommunist nations by ordering them in a pyramid from

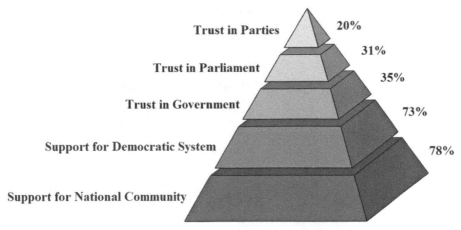

FIGURE 7.3. The pyramid of political support in postcommunist countries.
Source: World Values Surveys of postcommunist nations combined.

community support to specific support for political institutions. The broadest base of support is pride in the nation, with 78 percent of postcommunist citizens expressing national pride. A slightly smaller percentage says they approve the democratic regime – albeit with different intentions, as we have noted earlier. Slightly fewer postcommunist citizens have confidence in parliaments, and the least confidence is expressed for political parties.

However, the average support ratings across all postcommunist states mask important East-West differences. The difference is most pronounced when we juxtapose the support pyramids of Central and Eastern Europe. Figure 7.4 shows that in Central European nations, the support pyramid is stronger where it matters most for a flourishing democratic culture: the democratic system. By contrast, the Eastern European support pyramid is relatively stronger in terms of trust in the government and other specific institutions.

Accordingly, one of our main findings is that the transformation from communist one-party states to multiparty democracies is not a linear transition with identical longitudinal patterns in all countries. Between a more successful course toward democracy in Central Europe and failed democratization attempts in Eastern Europe, we find a wide variety of different forms and sequences of political transformations in these countries, all starting from communist regimes but ending in sometimes very different political regimes. Consequently, the public's images of democracy and political institutions are also quite varied across nations and across time.

This study shows that in terms of support for democracy, the Czech Republic and Slovakia in Central Europe, followed by Slovenia and Croatia in Southeastern Europe, achieved a full and successful transformation from a communist

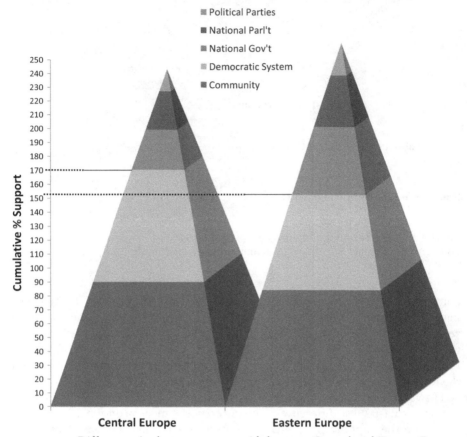

system to multiparty democracies that are fully integrated within the European Union and the euroregion. The evolution of the political culture parallels these developments: These are nations with high proportions of dissatisfied democrats – a healthy feature from the viewpoint of the assertive model of democratic culture.

A second group of postcommunist countries are multiparty democracies that have deficits in both democratic culture formation and democratic institution building. Countries within that group include Estonia, Latvia, Lithuania, Poland, Hungary, Bulgaria, and Romania. The majority of the population expresses approval of democracy, but there are signs of tentativeness in the solidity of this approval.

The third group of postcommunist systems are electoral democracies in a more limited sense: Bosnia-Herzegovina, Serbia, Montenegro, Albania,

Moldova, Georgia, and Armenia. These are countries with a minimum set of conditions in terms of support for democracy, such as modest approval of democracy or acceptance of nondemocratic institutions.

The fourth type of postcommunist system displays a process of failed democratization. This includes electoral autocracies in Ukraine, Russia, and Azerbaijan and an outright autocracy in Belarus. In these countries, the contemporary political culture exhibits modest support for democracy but high levels of national pride. At the same time, citizens in these semi-authoritarian states show rather strong confidence in their political institutions. This pattern of an allegiant culture actually operates against democracy when it appears in a semi-authoritarian setting.

This juxtaposition of democratic and nondemocratic developments largely confirms the hypothesized East-West division in the postcommunist world: The first two groups belong (with the exception of Bulgaria and Romania) to the western camp of the ex-communist world. They are, accordingly, more advanced on their way to developing a democratic culture. Democratization and cultural change have gone hand in hand. The last two groups form the eastern camp and have not followed a trajectory to a democratic culture. Rather, it seems that they retain or revive elements of an authoritarian culture. The prospects for democracy are uncertain here.

None of the ex-communist countries, whether in the eastern or western camp, meets the conditions for an allegiant political culture supportive of democracy as described in the original Almond-Verba model. One main reason is that support for political institutions is nowhere strong. But from the perspective of an assertive political culture, this weak support for specific institutions is not necessarily detrimental to democracy – provided it is support paired with solid support for democracy in principle. Such an assertive political culture seems to take shape in most of the western camp of the ex-communist world – very much in line with patterns known from Western Europe and the United States.

APPENDIX A: CONCEPTS, MEASUREMENT, AND CODES

Concept	Measurement	Codes
Political Community		
National pride	How proud are you to be [nationality]?	National pride
Democratic Regime		
Support for democracy	I'm going to describe various types of political systems and ask what you think about each as a way of governing this country. For each one, would you say it is a very good, fairly good, fairly bad, or very bad way of governing this country? Having a democratic political system.	1 Very good 2 Fairly good 3 Fairly bad 4 Very bad
Trust in Government		
Confidence in national government	Please look at this card and tell me, for each item listed, how much confidence you have in them, is it a great deal, quite a lot, not very much, or none at all? The government (in your nation's capital).	1 A great deal 2 Quite a lot 3 Not very much 4 None at all
Trust in Political Institutions		
Confidence in parliament	Please look at this card and tell me, for each item listed, how much confidence you have in them, is it a great deal, quite a lot, not very much, or none at all? Parliament.	1 A great deal 2 Quite a lot 3 Not very much 4 None at all
Confidence in political parties	Please look at this card and tell me, for each item listed, how much confidence you have in them, is it a great deal, quite a lot, not very much, or none at all? Political parties.	1 A great deal 2 Quite a lot 3 Not very much 4 None at all

APPENDIX B: DESCRIPTION OF VARIABLES USED IN THE
REGRESSION MODEL

Item	Measurement	Codes
Satisfaction with democracy	On the whole are you very satisfied, rather satisfied, not very satisfied, or not at all satisfied with the way democracy is developing in our country?	1 Very satisfied 2 Rather satisfied 3 Not very satisfied 4 Not at all satisfied
Positive rating of system of government	People have different views about the system for governing this country. Here is a scale for rating how well things are going: 1 means very bad; 10 means very good.	1 Very bad 2 3 4 5 6 7 8 9 10 Very good
Rejection of military regime	I'm going to describe various types of political systems and ask what you think about each as a way of governing this country. For each one, would you say it is a very good, fairly good, fairly bad, or very bad. Way of governing this country? Having the army rule the country?	1 Very good 2 Fairly good 3 Fairly bad 4 Very bad
Politics important for personal life	Please say, for each of the following, how important it is in your life. Politics.	1 Very important 2 Quite important 3 Not important 4 Not important at all
Democracy is efficient	I'm going to read off some things that people sometimes say about a democratic political system. Could you please tell me if you agree strongly, agree, disagree, or disagree strongly, after I read each of them?	1 Agree strongly 2 Agree 3 Disagree 4 Disagree strongly
High interest in politics	How interested would you say you are in politics?	1 Very interested 2 Somewhat interested 3 Not very interested 4 Not at all interested

(continued)

(continued)

Item	Measurement	Codes
Greater respect for authority is good	Here are two changes in our way of life that might take place in the near future. Please tell me for each one, if it were to happen, whether you think it would be a good thing, a bad thing, or don't you mind? Greater respect for authority.	1 Good 2 Bad 3 Don't mind
Unfair society	Using this card, do you think that most people would try to take advantage of you if they got the chance, or would they try to be fair? How would you place your view on this scale?	1 Most people would try to take advantage of me 2 3 4 5 6 7 8 9 10 Most people would try to be fair
Informal social capital	Would you say that most of the time people try to be helpful or that they are mostly looking out for themselves?	1 People mostly look out for themselves 2 3 4 5 6 7 8 9 10 People mostly try to be helpful
Follow politics in media	How often do you follow politics in the news on television or on the radio or in the daily papers?	1 Every day 2 Several times a week 3 Once or twice a week 4 Less often 5 Never
Democracy good for economy	I'm going to read off some things that people sometimes say about a democratic political system. Could you please tell me if you agree strongly, agree, disagree, or disagree strongly, after I read each of them? Democracies are indecisive and have too much squabbling.	1 Agree strongly 2 Agree 3 Disagree 4 Disagree strongly

Item	Measurement	Codes
Generalized trust	Generally speaking, would you say that most people can be trusted or that you can't be too careful in dealing with people?	1 Most people can be trusted 2 Can't be too careful
Has signed a petition	I'm going to read out some different forms of political action that people can take, and I'd like you to tell me, for each one, whether you have actually done any of these things, whether you might do it or would never, under any circumstances, do it. Signing a petition.	1 Have done 2 Might do 3 Would never do
Household income	Here is a list of incomes, and we would like to know in what group your household is, counting all wages, salaries, pensions, and other incomes that come in. Just give the letter of the group your household falls into, after taxes and other deductions.	1 Less than €150 2 €150 to under €300 3 €300 to under €500 4 €500 to under €1,000 5 €1,000 to under €1,500 6 €1,500 to under €2,000 7 €2,000 to under €2,500 8 €2,500 to under €3,000 9 €3,000 to under €5,000 10 €5,000 to under €7,500 11 €7,500 to under €10,000 12 €10,000 or more
Education	What is the highest level you have completed in your education?	0: Preprimary education or none education 1: Primary education or first stage of basic education 2: Lower secondary or second stage of basic education 3: (Upper) secondary education 4: Postsecondary nontertiary education 5: First stage of tertiary education 6: Second stage of tertiary education

(continued)

(continued)

Item	Measurement	Codes
Age	Can you tell me your year of birth, please	19...
Gender	Sex of respondent	1 Male 2 Female
Against strong leader	I'm going to describe various types of political systems and ask what you think about each as a way of governing this country. For each one, would you say it is a very good, fairly good, fairly bad, or very bad way of governing this country? Having a strong leader who does not have to bother with parliament and elections.	1 Very good 2 Fairly good 3 Fairly bad 4 Very bad
General life satisfaction	All things considered, how satisfied are you with your life as a whole these days?	1 Dissatisfied 2 3 4 5 6 7 8 9 10 Satisfied
Personal happiness	Taking all things together, would you say you are:	1 Very happy 2 Quite happy 3 Not very happy 4 Not at all happy
Frequent political discussions with friends	When you get together with your friends, would you say you discuss political matters frequently, occasionally, or never?	1 Frequently 2 Occasionally 3 Never
Support of current society	On this card are three basic kinds of attitudes vis-à-vis the society we live in. Please choose the one which best describes your own opinion.	1 The entire way our society is organized must be radically changed by revolutionary action 2 Our society must be gradually changed by reforms 3 Our present society must be valiantly defended against all changes

Item	Measurement	Codes
Bigger role of the state	On this card you see a number of opposite views on various issues. How would you place your views on this scale?	1 Individuals should take more responsibility for providing for themselves 2 3 4 5 6 7 8 9 10 The state should take more responsibility to ensure that everyone is provided for
In full employment	Are you yourself gainfully employed at the moment or not? Please select from the card the employment status that applies to you.	Paid employment 01 30 hours a week or more 02 Less than 30 hours a week 03 Self-employed No paid employment 04 Military service 05 Retired/pensioned 06 Housewife not otherwise employed 07 Student 08 Unemployed 09 Disabled

PART C

THE IMPACT OF CULTURAL CHANGE

8

The Structure and Sources of Global Environmental Attitudes

Robert Rohrschneider, Matthew Miles, and Mark Peffley

Across the world, environmental concerns deepen. Citizens across a broad swath of nations – from affluent Germany and the Netherlands to publics in lesser affluent countries like Ghana and Vietnam – express unease about pollution problems. What explains this global concern with environmental issues?

We hope to contribute an answer to this question by examining the structure and sources of environmental concerns. First, we compare the attitudinal structure across the globe. Here we address the question of whether environmental attitudes occupy a comparable position in the minds of publics across diverse countries. Is environmentalism connected to economic views outside Western countries, as one might speculate on the basis of the prior literature? Or do environmental and economic views constitute separate dimensions everywhere? The theoretical relevance and the political implications of environmentalism partly depend on an answer to this question. For example, if environmental views are independent from economic orientations, it would make environmental demands more difficult to satisfy by policy changes limited to the economic realm. It would also increase the stability of these orientations and provide fertile ground for entrepreneurial activists to found groups and parties to translate these orientations into political action.

Then, in a second step, we model the attitudinal and contextual sources of environmental concerns. Here we step into a debate in the literature about the relationship between postmaterialism and environmentalism as a possible example of the cultural changes described in this book. Environmentalism is often cited as one of the clearest consequences of postmaterialist value change. A debate has been taking place for at least two decades: To what extent can Inglehart's theory of postmaterialism explain the rise of global environmental attitudes not only in the affluent West but also in other parts of the world? By and large, the environmentalism literature assumes that postmaterialist explanations must be limited to the affluent Western world given its precepts. According to this widely shared perspective – including by Inglehart (see later) – we must search for other explanations such as pollution perceptions to model the rise of environmental orientations. We argue, however, that although postmaterialism is an important predictor of environmental views in advanced democracies, it is *nowadays* also relevant outside the West, as levels of affluence are transforming previously poor countries on an unprecedented scale. Moreover, we show that pollution perceptions are not limited to polluted areas of the world but are widespread everywhere and linked to a greater willingness to support environmental remedies globally.

To make headway in our goals, this chapter first outlines the central tenets of postmaterialism and shows how the environmentalism literature has partly gone awry in modeling environmental concerns. The chapter then examines the structure of environmental attitudes and explains their development on the basis of individual-level and contextual factors. The conclusions will highlight the central implications of this research.

POSTMATERIALISM AND POLICY PRIORITIES AMONG MASS PUBLICS

Ronald Inglehart's widely cited theory of postmaterialism is based on three central premises initially developed to explain the rise of middle-class activism in advanced industrial democracies during the 1960–1970s: scarcity, political socialization, and national conditions (Inglehart 1971, 1977; also see Chapter 2). At the micro-level, individuals presumably fulfill their goals in hierarchical fashion by first focusing on material goals (food, safety, shelter) before moving onto higher, postmaterialist goals (aesthetics, ecology, self-fulfillment). Rooted in Maslow's hierarchy of psychological needs, Inglehart's theory has clear equivalents in the political sphere. When scarcity prevails, material value priorities lead people to desire policies of economic growth, law and order, and national security, but once material needs can be taken for granted, postmaterialist value priorities will lead to policies that promote, for example, environmental protection, gender equality, and individual freedom of expression.

Although Inglehart sought to explain individual-level shifts in value priorities and policies in Western societies over time, his theory explicitly accounts for how national conditions stimulate an increase in the proportion of postmaterialists. In short, shifts in priorities at the individual level occur in significant numbers only if countries provide a context that secures the provision of economic and safety goods to most (if not all) citizens. It is, in other words, not enough that a single individual feels materially secure to turn him or her into a postmaterialist; it is the collective experience of material security that increases the odds of a shift in priorities toward postmaterialism. Advanced industrial democracies after the Second World War provided the primary examples for this reality, as when Western Europe experienced unprecedented prosperity and security. The development of the welfare state also secured a level of material safety that mass publics had not experienced on this scale (Inglehart 2008). Changing societal conditions thus helped explain the shift away from materialist values and policies (e.g., keeping inflation and unemployment rates low) to postmaterialist value priorities. This explains why the 1960s and 1970s spawned a series of protest movements, including the peace, environmental, and antinuclear energy movements, which challenged the economic policy priorities of governments and most interest groups in affluent democracies.

While the first two components of the theory – scarcity and national conditions – provide a dynamic for changing value priorities and politics, political socialization regulates the rates of change in value priorities among different age cohorts. The value priorities of youth change more dramatically in response to national contexts. After individuals reach adulthood, their value priorities are more resistant to change. This helps to explain why younger citizens are especially likely to participate in protest movements. Surely, dramatic upheavals – witness the fall of the Iron Curtain in 1990 – can alter the policy priorities of even the oldest and most ardent proponent of specific policies. For example, the economic strain associated with Germany's unification after 1990 made environmentalism less important for all West Germans, including younger ones. But this is also in keeping with the scarcity component of Inglehart's theory. The saying that green parties in Europe are increasingly supported by gray (i.e., older) voters reflects the possibility that priorities can alternate between material and postmaterial value priorities across times and generations.

All in all, the theory of postmaterialist value change assumes that the societal conditions in affluent and stable democracies can lead to a far-reaching shift in value priorities of especially younger citizens. From this perspective, the rise of social movements in the Western world, the changing patterns of citizens' political participation, and the rise of green parties evolved because the basic priorities of Western publics demanded a content and style of politics consistent with their altered policy priorities.

THE RISE OF A GLOBAL ENVIRONMENTAL MOVEMENT

Against this backdrop, the literature on environmental attitudes has led to a debate over the theoretical reach of the theory. Analyses in the 1970s up to the early 1990s focused on explaining the reasons why younger generations supported the environmental movement in Western democracies (Inglehart 1990; Milbrath 1984; Rohrschneider 1990), the conditions under which environmental groups emerge (Cotgrove 1982; Lowe and Goyder 1983; Dalton 1994), and how political parties respond electorally to the presence of newly founded green parties (Mueller-Rommel 1985; Rohrschneider 1993). Most of these studies used the postmaterialism framework to explain why citizens sympathize with the environmental movement and why green parties formed in

Western Europe. To be sure, numerous critics have launched a range of challenges to the postmaterialism theory even as it is applied to affluent democracies (see Chapter 2). However, hardly any analyst questioned whether values in advanced democracies have changed at a massive scale.

Another innovation by Inglehart, however, offered critics the opportunity to test postmaterialism theory more globally outside the realm of affluent democracies. Thanks to Inglehart's pioneering efforts in getting the World Values Survey (WVS) off the ground, it is now possible to study environmental attitudes in affluent *and* less wealthy countries. Starting with the 1990 survey, the WVS provides an invaluable database of survey information from an increasingly representative sample of the global population, including a range of indicators of various environmental attitudes (pollution perceptions, economic and environmental priorities, membership in environmental organizations), which allows analysts to compare the attitudinal roots of environmental movements in the affluent West with less affluent countries from the 1990s onward (Inglehart 1995; Adeola 1998; Mertig and Dunlap 2001).

Generally, these studies arrived at two basic conclusions. On one hand, environmental concerns exist across the globe. Citizens in the Netherlands are as concerned as individuals in Mexico with pollution problems – albeit different problems. On the other hand, public concern about the environment in many less developed nations was seen as challenging the postmaterialism thesis. How can the theory be correct, these critics asked, if publics in less wealthy nations support environmental attitudes, even though these nations do not meet the conditions of the postmaterialism thesis (Dunlop and Mertig 1997; Freymeyer and Johnson 2010)? Inglehart's (1995) preemptory response to this challenge was to point to the multifaced origins of environmental concerns: In the West, citizens often support the environment because they hold postmaterialist values; in non-Western nations, they often do so because they observe firsthand the severity of environmental problems. Consistent with this interpretation is the general pattern that Western publics are more likely to support environmental protection even when it is costly (either personally or as a nation), whereas publics in non-Western countries may perceive more pollution problems but may also balk at more costly measures to remedy the situation (Freymeyer and Johnson 2010; Welzel 2013, 376–92).

PROBLEMS IN THE RESEARCH LITERATURE

Such findings are typical of studies of global environmental attitudes, as a recent review makes plain (Dunlap and Yolk 2008). There are, however, at least three fundamental problems with prior studies that need to be surmounted before progress can be made in this area. First, there is no systematic examination of the structure of environmental attitudes (though see Dunlap and Yolk 2008). While analysts assume that perceptions of pollution, concerns about the environment, and economic orientations are distinct dimensions, we know very little about how such attitudes cohere in the minds of publics. This is a serious problem because, as will become clear, knowledge about attitude structure must guide decisions about model specification in analyses of environmental attitudes.

Second, virtually all studies assume that the influence of country variables, such as affluence, on environmental attitudes is simple, additive, and direct. For example, analysts typically assess the influence of nations' human dimension ratings on perceptions of pollution or other ecological attitudes. But the theoretical arguments in the literature often emphasize the *mediating* influence of national context, not just its direct influence. To take just one example, the controversy over the power of postmaterialist values to adequately predict pollution perceptions largely hinges on whether postmaterialist values are more powerful antecedents in more affluent countries than in the less affluent nations (Dunlap and Yolk 2008). As far as we can determine, however, apart from Welzel (2013, 376–92), not a single study in this area examines how national context *moderates* the influence of individual-level predictors of environmental attitudes.

Third, this literature suffers from a host of methodological problems. The most serious problem is the failure to account for the multilevel nature of the data where citizens are nested within countries. As numerous recent studies make plain, failure to account for the fundamental nature of multilevel data leads to serious errors in estimating and interpreting the impact of national contexts (e.g., Gelman and Hill 2007). Moreover, this is not an arcane methodological issue for those who study comparative politics but a well-established method for anyone who uses comparative public opinion data.

THE MODEL

Given the state of the literature, we first examine the dimensionality of various environmental and economic attitudes (see the following discussion). This analysis documents that environmental attitudes are structured similarly in more and less affluent countries. We then turn to an examination of the antecedents of environmental attitudes using the model depicted in Figure 8.1.

The primary dependent variable in our analysis is the willingness of citizens to pay for cleaning up the environment (which we also refer to as environmental concern). This is measured by individuals' agreement (on 4-point scales) with two Likert statements indicating a willingness to contribute one's personal income and support a tax increase to protect the environment (see the appendix for complete wording):

I would give part of my income if I were certain that the money would be used to prevent environmental pollution.

I would agree to an increase in taxes if the extra money were used to prevent environmental pollution.

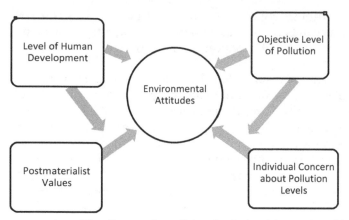

FIGURE 8.1. The direct and conditional relationships explored in this study.

This focus is warranted, we maintain, for at least two reasons. First, much of prior research regularly found such attitudes to be more widespread in affluent democracies than elsewhere (Inglehart 1995; Dunlap and Yolk 2008). This has become an axiom in the research literature that mainly more affluent publics are willing to contribute scarce resources to protect the environment.

This, however, is no longer true, as is revealed in the scatterplot of countries in Figure 8.2, where the average willingness of citizens to devote personal income and tax dollars to prevent environmental pollution is captured on the vertical axis and the nation's position on the Human Development Index (HDI) is arrayed on the horizontal axis. This figure shows, albeit crudely, that by the year 2000, people in affluent countries were *not* more likely than publics in poorer nations to contribute resources to protect the environment.

There are various possible explanations for this unexpected pattern. Pollution problems may be so severe in less affluent countries that publics are willing to devote resources to protecting the environment even if they are less well-off relative to publics in more affluent countries. Alternatively, by 2000, many non-Western nations now enjoy a level of affluence that was enjoyed by only a handful of privileged nations in the immediate post–World War II years.[1] Therefore, our analysis uses citizens' commitment to protecting the environment as our primary dependent variable not only because such attitudes reflect one's dedication to environmental goals versus myriad other policy goals but also because the existing pattern in Figure 8.2 calls for an explanation of why the prevailing consensus of stark differences in such attitudes across more and less affluent countries no longer appears to hold.

---

[1] An impressive illustration of this development can be found in Hans Rosling's presentation of quality of life data covering the last two hundred years: http://www.youtube.com/watch?v=jbkSRLYSojo.

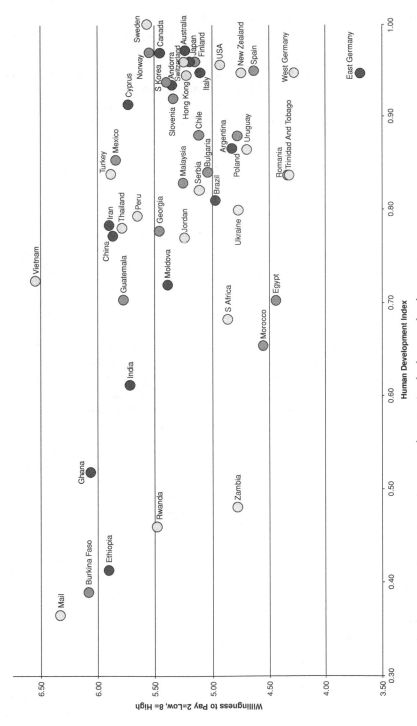

FIGURE 8.2. Average commitment to environmental protection by human development. *Source:* World Values Survey 2008.

THE STRUCTURE OF ENVIRONMENTAL ATTITUDES

We begin by examining whether the structure of environmental attitudes varies across more and less affluent countries. For example, if left-right economic attitudes are closely connected to ecological attitudes (Kitschelt 1989), it would be difficult to focus on the sources of environmentalism without accounting for the economic sphere. If, however, the two constitute separate dimensions in the minds of publics, we would be less concerned with the way that economic and environmentalism affect each other. For the same reason, we do not know whether citizens inside and outside of affluent nations hold differently structured attitudes as the research literature tends to imply and, consequently, we do not know whether we can use the same model to advance our understanding of the origins and policy consequences of environmental concerns across the globe. The lack of systematic dimensional analyses thus raises a host of difficult issues that can only be laid to rest with a clear dimensional analysis (to follow).

Critics of the environmentalism measures in the WVS have questioned whether they form one dimension or whether they conflate environmental and economic concerns (Dunlap and Yolk 2008). Therefore, we begin by estimating a measurement model of environmentalism to ensure that standard WVS indicators form a coherent attitudinal dimension that is distinct from economic attitudes.

We use the two items about individuals' willingness to pay for environmental protection to measure environmental concerns. Views about economic equality are measured with two questions intended to reflect preferences for economic equality and the role of government in providing social welfare programs (see the appendix for complete wording). These issues divide the left from the right on economic issues in a variety of national contexts (Jost et al. 2003):

Incomes should be made more equal.	vs	We need larger income differences as incentives for individual effort.
The government should take more responsibility to ensure that everyone is provided for.	vs	People should take more responsibility to provide for themselves.

Table 8.1 presents the results of a confirmatory factor analysis estimating a measurement model that specifies two latent factors: *commitment to environmentalism* and *economic equality*. The appropriate fit indices, the RMSEA and the Comparative Fit Index (CFI), indicate an excellent fit between the model and the data. In fact, the CFI for both OECD and non-OECD countries indicates a near-perfect fit.[2] In addition, all of the factor loadings are significant

---

[2] Statistically, because the chi-square test is known to be biased for large sample sizes (Cheung and Rensvold 2002; Meade, Johnson, and Brady 2008), we also present the statistical significance of the RMSEA (Steiger 1990) and test of model fit and the CFI (Bentler 1990). It should be noted that the fit indices for a one-factor model making no distinction between environmental and economic attitudes indicate a comparatively poor fit.

TABLE 8.1. *A Two-Factor Model of Environmentalism and Economic Ideology*

		Advanced Democracies	All Other Countries
Factor Loadings			
Income	Environmentalism	1.000 (0.756)	1.000 (0.844)
Tax increase	Environmentalism	1.275 (0.964)	1.007 (0.850)
Income equality	Economic ideol.	1.000 (0.449)	1.000 (0.343)
Gov. responsibility	Economic ideol.	1.328 (0.588)	1.529 (0.529)
Factor Covariance			
Environmentalism *with* Economic Ideol.		−0.086 (−0.095)	−0.193 (−0.224)
Model fit indices			
RMSEA		0.027	0.052
(90% confidence interval)		(0.017 0.040)	(0.045 0.060)
CFI		1.000	0.999
Chi-square model fit		15.830	137.346
Degrees of freedom		1	1
N (individuals)		19,934	50,300
N (countries)		16	34

Note: Main entries are unstandardized maximum likelihood coefficients. The numbers in parentheses are standardized coefficients. Confirmatory factor analysis conducted in Mplus version 6.1.
Source: World Values Survey 2008.

($p < 0.05$) and load strongly on the appropriate factors. Most important for assessing the criticism of the WVS environmental measures, the correlation between the environmentalism and economic factors is quite low, even after correcting for random measurement error. In OECD countries, the correlation is only −0.095 and in non-OECD countries it is −0.224, indicating a slight tendency for economic leftists to be less committed to protecting the environment. Overall, then, our results clearly indicate that economic and environmental attitudes are distinct for both OECD and non-OECD nations (cf. Dunlap and Yolk 2008).

We want to push the analyses a step further, however. Many analysts note that a commitment to environmentalism (such as a willingness to pay) constitutes a different set of attitudes than pollution perceptions. In addition, pollution perceptions and postmaterialism are often treated as causally prior to environmentalism. What is more, there exists a presumption that perceptions of pollution are more prevalent outside the OECD because the objective state of the environment is worse in less affluent countries. By contrast, in more affluent democracies, postmaterialism presumably dominates the formation of environmentalism (Inglehart 1995; Freymeyer and Johnson 2010). If this portrayal is correct, pollution perceptions may be more closely related to environmental concerns in lesser affluent countries than within the OECD, to the point where environmentalism and pollution perceptions form a single, undifferentiated factor.

TABLE 8.2. *A Three-Factor Model of Environmentalism and Local and Global Pollution Perceptions*

		Advanced Democracies	All Other Countries
Factor Loadings			
Income	Environmentalism	1.000 (0.897)	1.000 (0.974)
Tax increase	Environmentalism	0.907 (0.813)	0.757 (0.737)
Water quality	Local pollution	1.000 (0.851)	1.000 (0.804)
Air quality	Local pollution	0.998 (0.882)	1.151 (0.893)
Poor sanitation	Local pollution	0.993 (0.850)	1.044 (0.851)
Global warming	Global pollution	1.000 (0.646)	1.000 (0.744)
Loss biodiversity	Global pollution	1.266 (0.806)	1.072 (0.780)
Water pollution	Global pollution	0.979 (0.745)	1.044 (0.814)
Factor Covariance			
Environmentalism *with* Local Pollution		0.063 (0.071)	0.080 (0.076)
Local Pollution *with* Global Pollution		0.108 (0.248)	0.218 (0.463)
Environmentalism *with* Global Pollution		0.119 (0.307)	0.061 (0.144)
Model fit indices			
RMSEA		0.022	0.045
(90% confidence interval)		(0.019, 0.024)	(0.044, 0.047)
CFI		0.996	0.980
Chi-square model fit		173.503	1783.455
Degrees of freedom		17	17
N (individuals)		19,901	50,415
N (countries		16	34

Note: The entries are unstandardized maximum likelihood coefficients. The numbers in parentheses are standardized coefficients. Confirmatory factor analysis conducted in Mplus version 6.1.
Source: World Values Survey 2008.

To test this assumption, we conduct another confirmatory factor analysis that includes commitment to environmentalism and two sets of concerns about pollution: *local pollution perceptions*, measured by asking citizens to rate the seriousness of poor water quality, air quality, and sewage in their community, and *global pollution perceptions*, measured by rating the seriousness of global warming, endangered species, and the pollution of waterways "in the world as a whole" (see the appendix).

The results are surprisingly clear in light of the ambiguities in the research literature. Contrary to the claims of others (Kidd and Lee 1997), the confirmatory factor analysis in Table 8.2 shows that local and global pollution perceptions are distinct views in the public mind. What is more, this is true for citizens of both advanced democracies and less affluent democracies. To be sure, people who view local pollution problems as more serious tend to rate global pollution as serious, and this is more true in non-OECD countries (correlation = 0.46) than in OECD countries (correlation = 0.25). Evidence of covariation, however, does not alter the conclusion that the two types of pollution perceptions are distinct from each other and from environmentalism. All the goodness of fit measures indicate that a three-factor model fits the data quite well, meaning that the three environmental attitudes are distinct. Environmentalism is essentially unrelated to local pollution perceptions in OECD and non-OECD nations. There is only a modest association between environmentalism and perceptions of global pollution in advanced democracies ($r = 0.30$) but not outside the OECD ($r = 0.14$).

These results highlight some of the empirical patterns found in the literature, but they also tell a partially different story. Familiar is the linkage between global and local pollution perceptions outside the OECD. This is consistent with arguments that point to the severity of objective pollution problems as a base for the linkage between perceptions of the local and global environment – a relationship that is a bit more tenuous in less polluted countries. What is new, however, is the conclusion that the three sets of environmental attitudes constitute separate factors and that the same model of attitude structure emerges from inside and outside the OECD.[3]

THE SOURCES OF ENVIRONMENTAL ATTITUDES

The similar structure that underlies environmental attitudes in more and less affluent countries greatly simplifies our analysis. We can estimate a single multilevel model predicting commitment to environmentalism for individuals in these forty-six countries. At the national level, we include a measure of a nation's actual level of environmental quality using the Environmental Performance Index (EPI), which combines twenty-five indicators about the degree to which countries reduce environmental stresses to human life and protect ecosystems and natural resources.[4] The index is coded so that higher values indicate better environmental conditions. Another country-level indicator is the United Nations Human Development Index (HDI), which combines health, education, and living standards measures to indicate the overall living conditions of a country. In our sample, as expected, more affluent countries, as indicated by HDI, tend to enjoy better environmental conditions ($r = 0.77$).

At the individual level, we include Inglehart's twelve-item postmaterialism index to measure individual value priorities. We enter predictors of local and global pollution perceptions (based on the additive indices of the indicators

---

[3] We conducted a multilevel CFA model for each of the forty-six countries in the analysis. This confirmed that the three-factor solution was not only appropriate for the OECD/non-OECD country dichotomy but is, by and large, appropriate for each of the countries as well.

[4] More information is available at http://epi.yale.edu/.

presented in Table 8.2) and economic ideology (by adding the responses to the indicators presented in Table 8.1). We include a second measure of economic attitudes tapping how individuals view the connection between competition and hard work, labeled Competition, which is a more generic measure of how people evaluate the nature of market-based economies than is the economic equality index (Milbrath 1984).[5] Finally, we added respondents' age and education in our model because these demographics are often correlated with environmentalism.

In general, we expect each of these variables to influence environmentalism. As the model in Figure 8.1 suggests, however, the impact of some individual-level predictors should vary across national context. For example, consistent with prior research (Inglehart 1995), the impact of postmaterialism on commitment to environmentalism should be stronger in more affluent countries. In the context of a multilevel model, this amounts to allowing the slope of an individual-level predictor to vary across countries.[6] In our study, we expect the level of human development in a country to mediate the relationship between postmaterialist values and environmentalism, so we include an interaction between HDI and postmaterialism to model this hypothesized conditional effect. This is precisely the sort of conditional influence implied in prior research (i.e., postmaterialism has a greater effect on environmentalism in more affluent countries) that is usually not directly tested. In addition, because prior studies suggest that pollution perceptions have a greater impact on environmentalism in more polluted countries, we include an interaction between actual level of environmental quality (measured by the EPI index) and local and global pollution perceptions.

Our analysis begins by estimating a baseline model that specifies additive impacts of all the predictors before proceeding to more complex models that allow some of the coefficients for key attitudinal measures to vary interactively across national contexts. The results for the baseline model are displayed in the first column of coefficients in Table 8.3 (model 1). All predictors have the expected sign, and all are statistically significant, which is hardly surprising considering that we have more than fifty thousand respondents. The results for model 1 reflect the basic findings in the literature – postmaterialist values, along with global and local pollution perceptions, increase citizens' commitment to protect the environment, as does younger age and higher education.

---

[5] This indicator did not load on the equality index, probably because it measures a basic trait of market-based economies, whereas responses to the equality indicators reflect an orientation to the more specific conception of Western-style welfare regimes.

[6] If the variance component of the slope for postmaterialism on environmentalism is statistically significant, we can surmise that, ceteris paribus, the influence of postmaterialism varies across nations. Once we have determined that individual-level predictors vary across national contexts, it is important to include measures of theoretically relevant national conditions in the model to identify the precise conditions over which micro-factors vary.

TABLE 8.3. *Models Predicting Commitment to Environmental Protection*

Variables	(1)	(2)	(3)	(4)
National-Level Variables				
EPI (environmental	−0.011	−0.0030	−0.026	−0.017
conditions)	(0.011)	(0.014)	(0.017)	(0.012)
HDI (societal development)	−1.31$^+$	−1.60	−2.62*	−1.71*
	(0.70)	(0.93)	(1.10)	(0.79)
Individual-Level Fixed				
Postmaterialist values	0.12**	0.12**	0.12**	−0.13*
	(0.0059)	(0.0059)	(0.0058)	(0.063)
Local pollution perceptions	0.012**	0.043	0.014**	0.012**
	(0.0027)	(0.040)	(0.0027)	(0.0027)
Global pollution	0.11**	0.11**	−0.057	0.11**
perceptions	(0.0040)	(0.0041)	(0.052)	(0.0040)
Economic equality	0.013**	0.013**	0.014**	0.014**
	(0.0015)	(0.0015)	(0.0015)	(0.0015)
Competition (reverse coded)	−0.013**	−0.013**	−0.014**	−0.013**
	(0.0016)	(0.0016)	(0.0016)	(0.0016)
Age	−0.0013**	−0.0013**	−0.0015**	−0.0015**
	(0.00044)	(0.00044)	(0.00044)	(0.00044)
Education	0.053**	0.053**	0.054**	0.053**
	(0.0031)	(0.0031)	(0.0031)	(0.0031)
Variance Component				
Local pollution		0.043**		
		(0.0056)		
Global pollution			0.054**	
			(0.0073)	
Postmaterialist values				0.078**
				(0.0105)
Cross-Level Interactions				
EPI * Local Pollution		−0.00049		
		(0.00064)		
EPI * Global Pollution			0.0030**	
			(0.00083)	
HDI * Postmaterialist				0.31**
Values				(0.078)
Constant	7.83**	7.55**	9.83**	8.81**
	(0.97)	(1.03)	(1.10)	(1.00)
Observations	50,238	50,238	50,238	50,238
Number of groups	46	46	46	46

Note: Standard errors in parentheses. $^{**}p < 0.01$; $^*p < 0.05$. $^+p < 0.10$.
Source: World Values Survey 2008.

Note, however, that the two country-level variables are insignificant at the conventional significance level ($p < 0.05$) – neither affluence (HDI) nor objective environmental conditions (EPI) appear to influence commitment to environmentalism, though we note that the HDI indicator just misses statistical significance ($p = 0.062$). The poor showing of the two national-level measures, however, is doubtless due to their considerable overlap ($r = 0.77$) with forty-six countries in the analysis. When we include the national affluence indicator or the EPI indicator alone in the model (not shown), both are highly significant, suggesting publics in more affluent countries or in countries with less pollution are more committed to protecting the environment. However, given their overlap, it would be inappropriate in our view to conclude that both matter to the same degree. Our interpretation, tentative as it must be, is that the HDI indicator is the more relevant predictor, given its significance at the $p < 0.10$ level. In contrast, the objective state of the environment (EPI) has little independent influence on environmental concerns.[7]

Model 2 shows that the significant variance component of local pollution indicates that perceived local pollution has a varied effect across countries. We therefore added an interaction term between perceived local pollution and the objective state of the environment (EPI), hypothesizing that citizens who perceive serious pollution in their community will be more committed to environmentalism in countries with higher levels of pollution. The cross-level interaction between EPI and local pollution perceptions in model 2 is not significant, however, so the interactive hypothesis is rejected in this case.

Model 3 in Table 8.3 considers whether the impact of concerns about *global* pollution on environmentalism varies across countries. Again, this question is answered in the affirmative, as the random (variance) component for global pollution is statistically significant. In addition, consistent with Inglehart (1995), we hypothesize that this relationship is conditioned by objective environmental conditions (EPI) in a country. Indeed, the cross-level interaction term is statistically significant which means that the effect of global pollution perceptions depends on country's pollution levels (we further explore this relationship subsequently).

Finally, model 4 in Table 8.3 explores whether the influence of postmaterialist values on environmentalism is conditioned by the level of societal development (HDI) in a country. As can be seen at the bottom of the table, the coefficient for the cross-level interaction between postmaterialism and HDI is statistically significant, which means that postmaterialism is more important in increasing a commitment to environmentalism in more affluent countries.

---

[7] One might argue that the objective environment influences environmental concerns through pollution perceptions. Our preliminary analyses, however, suggest that the relationship between objective conditions and pollution perceptions (both local and global) is weak. The impact of the EPI index on both perceptions is statistically insignificant even it is the only predictor considered in the model.

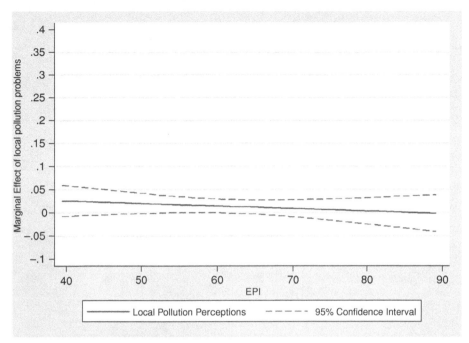

FIGURE 8.3A. Concerns about local pollution on environmentalism conditioned by actual pollution levels (EPI).
Note: Marginal effect based on model 2 in Table 8.3.
Source: World Values Survey 2008.

To gain a better understanding of the substantive impact of the coefficients, we display the marginal effects of each individual-level predictor (i.e., concerns about local and global pollution and postmaterialism), which represent the influence of a predictor on environmental concerns across different levels of the mediating variable. For example, Figure 8.3 displays the influence of concerns about local and global pollution on environmentalism for different levels of pollution (EPI) across countries. The solid line displays the predicted relationship and the dotted lines denote the 95 percent confidence interval. If the confidence interval overlaps with the zero-line on the vertical axis, the relationship is not statistically significant at that level of pollution.

Figure 8.3a shows that local pollution perceptions have no significant effect on environmentalism at any level of pollution: Not only is the solid line essentially flat, the zero-line extended from the y-axis is always included in the confidence interval, illustrating the nonsignificant coefficient for the cross-level interaction in model 2 of Table 8.3.

Figure 8.3b, however, reveals a very different pattern for perceptions of global pollution, where pollution levels make a clear difference in the degree to which global concerns influence environmentalism. Viewing the graph from

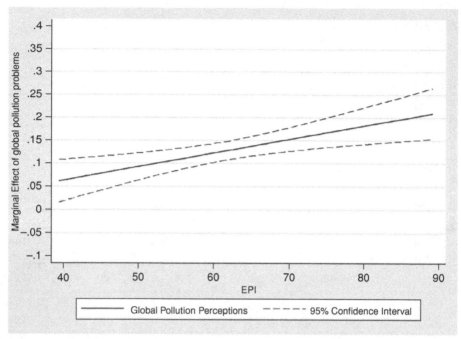

FIGURE 8.3B. Concerns about global pollution on environmentalism conditioned by actual levels of pollution (EPI).
Note: Marginal effect based on model 3 in Table 8.4.
Source: World Values Survey 2008.

left to right, as a country's pollution level declines, the relationship between global pollution perceptions and pro-environmental attitudes *increases*. This is somewhat surprising given that pollution perceptions are usually viewed as the main source of pro-environmental views *outside* advanced democracies where pollution levels are typically much higher. Note, for example, that for the most polluted countries, such as China and India, whose EPI values are below 50, global pollution concerns have a weaker influence on pro-environmental views than in the less polluted nations. Thus, although pollution perceptions bring about greater environmental concerns everywhere, we find – contrary to the near-consensus in the research literature – that concerns about global pollution are especially relevant in the lesser polluted nations and, conversely, are less likely to stimulate environmental concerns in the more polluted nations. Psychologically speaking, this might actually not be so surprising, because empathy for problems far beyond one's very own circumstances should grow with relief from immediate problems.

Figure 8.4 generally confirms the prevailing research consensus that as national affluence increases, so too does the impact of postmaterialism on environmental commitment. There is one new finding in the figure, namely, that postmaterialism significantly brings about environmentalism even at fairly

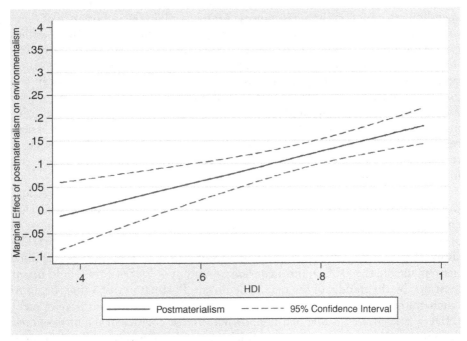

FIGURE 8.4. Relationship between postmaterialist values and environmentalism conditioned by level of development (HDI).
Note: Marginal effect based on model 4 in Table 8.4.
Source: World Values Survey 2008.

low levels of the national affluence. The 95 percent confidence interval in Figure 8.4 includes zero for levels of development (HDI) below about 0.6. This means that postmaterialism motivates a commitment to protect the environment in a host of countries not typically considered affluent. Although we do not want to exaggerate the relevance of postmaterialism in nonaffluent countries, it is remarkable that the reach of this theory now extends to nations that in the past were clearly outside its purview.

CONCLUSION

This chapter tested three theories about the formation of global environmental attitudes. Our results partially confirm the prior research literature – but also led to one surprising and unexpected result. Expectedly, we find that local pollution problems do not affect views about environmental concerns, neither in the affluent OECD countries nor in the less affluent – and more polluted – set of nations outside of the OECD. In contrast, global pollution perceptions increase individuals' willingness to pay for environmental protection nearly everywhere. Contrary to the research literature, however, these effects are especially pronounced in the least polluted nations, whereas citizens under the worst environmental conditions hardly link pollution problems to spending resources on the environment. To make plain the importance of these findings, let us emphasize that we do not just find that citizens in wealthier nations are more willing to pay for environmental protection. This is clearly not the case, as our study shows. Rather, our study reveals that the *relationship* between pollution perceptions and environmental resources is stronger in less polluted countries. This is an important and unexpected result, as most analysts have assumed that pollution perceptions are the main driving force of environmental concerns in those nations that experience severe pollution issues. These results resonate with recent findings by Welzel (2013, 376–92), who shows that the same level of environmental concern triggers more environmental activism in developed than in developing nations.

Another overall pattern is more in line with the research literature, and the theme of this book is that postmaterialist values exert a strong effect on environmental attitudes. Equally important, these relationships are stronger in affluent nations than in lesser affluent countries. Even here, however, our results show that a simplistic assumption in the literature – pollution perceptions matter outside the OECD, postmaterialism within – does not fully hold up, at least not by the middle of the new millennium. Postmaterialist values begin to reach statistical significance roughly at a modest level of human development (HDI = 0.6). If we assume that the postmaterialist coefficient ought to exceed 0.10 to be substantively relevant, it includes such countries as Brazil, Russia, and Malaysia. Thus, postmaterialism together with pollution problems drives the formation of environmental attitudes, not just one or the other.

There is one final issue we would like to address: Why are the relationships stronger in affluent countries? That is, why is it that citizens connect problem perceptions and postmaterialist values to environmental concerns in some nations but not others? A simple explanation can be removed from the agenda right off the bat: It is not because citizens in affluent nations can afford to spend more. This is (no longer) the case, as Figure 8.2 clearly indicates, which suggests that citizens in lesser affluent countries are indeed willing to commit resources to protect the environment.[8] If it is not affordability, or financial capacity, what then explains the stronger relationship?

A tentative explanation would point to the importance of political elites and social movement actors, along with the mass media, to explain why individuals connect various environmental perceptions and values to environmental spending views. The presumption in the environmental literature appears to be that citizens have to figure out these complex relationships all by themselves. But clearly their beliefs and the linkages among different components of environmental beliefs hinge to a degree on how active environmental elites are – in short, how mass publics and political elites communicate. Here, we think, lies an important explanation for why publics in affluent democracies

---

[8] From a different angle, this simple "explanation" would also assume a direct impact of affluence on environmental spending.

have it easier to figure out "what goes with what": Elites help citizens to connect various environmental concerns to the appropriate policy consequences. Green parties provide policy alternatives, and so do environmental groups. And both are much more active in advanced democracies than outside of it, in part because the societal infrastructures – freedoms, mass media, technological equipment – facilitate the formation of these elites and their communication with mass publics. There is, then, a dynamic relationship between what policies and preferences mass publics hold and the activism of elites: The former have to be in place so that green parties can succeed in elections and environmental groups can recruit members. Once they are in place, they in turn affect the way citizens view the environment and how they connect environmental belief system components. This dynamic may go some way to explain why publics in nations with a well-developed infrastructure exhibit stronger relationships among environmental belief components, even though publics in other nations also hold environmentally sympathetic views when each component is viewed in isolation as an average.

All in all, our study goes some way toward sorting out which arguments in the literature about global environmental attitudes are valid and which ones appear less relevant. In the end, our study raises a set of new questions – in particular, regarding the interplay of citizen orientations and contextual factors – which, while not being answered in this chapter, point to new avenues for future research.

APPENDIX: MEASUREMENT

National-Level Predictors

Environmental Performance Index (EPI)
This index measures the environmental performance of 168 countries by combining 25 indicators of the reduction of environmental stresses to human life and protect ecosystems and natural resources. Higher values indicate lower pollution levels. More information is available at http://epi.yale.edu/.

Human Development Index (HDI)
This index combines health, education, and living standards measures to indicate the degree of overall human development within a country. This broader measure of societal development is used to indicate the overall living conditions and affluence level of a country.

Individual Level (2000 World Values Survey)

Postmaterialism
This is measured using Inglehart's twelve-item index for each respondent in the World Values Survey.

Local Pollution Perceptions

I am going to read out a list of environmental problems facing many communities. Please, tell me how serious you consider each one to be here in your own community. Is it very serious, somewhat serious, not very serious, or not serious at all?

1. Poor water quality
2. Poor air quality
3. Poor sewage and sanitation

Global Pollution Perceptions

Now let's consider environmental problems in the world as a whole. Please, tell me how serious you consider each of the following to be for the world as a whole. Is it very serious, somewhat serious, not very serious, or not serious at all?

1. Global warming or the greenhouse effect
2. Loss of plant or animal species or biodiversity
3. Pollution of rivers, lakes, and oceans

Economic Equality

Now I'd like you to tell me your views on various issues. How would you place your views on this scale? 1 means you agree completely with the statement on the left; 10 means you agree completely with the statement on the right; and if your views fall somewhere in between, you can choose any number in between:

1 – Incomes should be made more equal.

10 – We need larger income differences as incentives for individual effort.

1 – The government should take more responsibility to ensure that everyone is provided for.

10 – People should take more responsibility to provide for themselves.

Competition

This is measured by an index of responses to questions about the degree to which an individual feels that competition and hard work are good or bad. Higher scores on this indicate opposition to competition and market principles.

Age

Year of birth.

Education

Coded in nine categories from lowest to highest.

9

Social Change and the Politics of Protest[1]

Tor Georg Jakobsen and Ola Listhaug

This chapter pursues several research questions that attempt to understand the development of nonviolent protest activity since the 1970s. Considering the behavioral repertoire of citizens, the continuing florescence of nonviolent protests is a major manifestation of the rising assertive culture on which this volume focuses. Indeed, the continuation and expansion of nonviolent protest activity in mature postindustrial democracies can be seen as a key indication of the cultural transformation from allegiant to assertive citizenship. Frequent and widespread nonviolent protest by ordinary people is an inherently "elite-challenging" activity that testifies to the rise of an assertive model of democratic citizenship. Postindustrial democracies supposedly experienced a participatory revolution over the last four decades, in which the forms and levels of non-violent protest activity expanded. This development seems to be linked to progressing social modernization and the development of new values with an overall emancipatory impetus. Thus, like others in this volume, we are interested in the process of value change in contemporary societies and view protest as an exemplary manifestation of the hypothesized impact of the changing values of the people.

In their now classic book *Political Action*, Samuel Barnes, Max Kaase, and their colleagues (1979) reported on a study of political behavior and political values in five Western democracies in the mid-1970s. In addition, they initiated a research program designed to distinguish between major types of political

[1] This is a revised version of a paper presented at the Conference on Mapping and Tracing Global Cultural Change, March 3–5, 2011, Center for the Study of Democracy, Leuphana University, Lüneburg, and at the Norwegian Political Science Meeting, NTNU, Trondheim, January 4–6, 2012. We thank the participants at the meetings and especially Chris Welzel for valuable comments.

action and to explain the variation in these actions, including new forms of political protest, and to predict future developments.

This chapter analyzes aggregate trends and national patterns in nonviolent protest activity over time. This aggregated approach has some limitations; for example, in some countries, we have a long time series, whereas for other countries, we have shorter survey evidence. Nevertheless, we are analyzing the largest existing database that can be used to study protest activities. Using these data, we observe partial support for a trend hypothesis as proposed by the authors of *Political Action* (Barnes, Kaase et al. 1979). In addition to the hypothesis about the continuing increase of protest, the *Political Action* study implied that richer countries should have higher levels of political protest than poorer countries. We find strong support for the wealth hypothesis: Economically advanced countries have significantly higher levels of protest participation than poorer countries. However, we observe a takeoff effect so that national wealth needs to rise above a certain magnitude before levels of protest increase considerably. In addition, we find empirical support for the link between political action and well-known individual-level motivators of protest participation, especially postmaterialist values and leftist orientations.

We begin by reviewing the research literature with an emphasis on recent studies that analyze generalizable patterns of protest activity. Next, we move into data analysis in country-level and multivariate models. We primarily investigate aggregate-level hypotheses of the link between modernization and political action. Our approach is relevant for the main theme of this volume because spreading nonviolent protest is a key indicator of the change from an allegiant to an assertive political culture and the increasing prominence of emancipatory orientations, such as postmaterialist values, that inspire this cultural transformation.

Before we move on right into the literature review, three clarifying remarks about our object of study are due. First, our analyses focus exclusively on *nonviolent* protest – not on violent forms of collective action, like urban riots, which are driven by a completely different set of reasons.[2] Second, at the country level, we are not interested in ups and downs of mobilization cycles as they are driven by specific events; instead, we analyze a country's *chronic* level of nonviolent protest activity that endures throughout cyclical fluctuations. Third, at the individual level, we are not interested in why someone participated in a particular protest event at a particular time; instead, we focus on whether forms of nonviolent protest have become part of a person's behavioral repertoire. The repertoire perspective is essential because repertoires can be mobilized for *variable* occasions – an empowering feature that is key to an assertive culture.

---

[2] For instance, the phenomenon of "relative deprivation" whose explanatory power over *nonviolent* protests has been cast in doubt (Dalton, van Sickle, and Weldon 2010; Welzel 2013, 215–46) still provides a major explanation of *violent* forms of collective action.

THE EVOLUTION OF RESEARCH ON PROTEST

Inspired by the student revolts at the end of the 1960s in Western democracies, the *Political Action* study became famous for the idea that political protest is a natural element of democracy, a driver of further democratization, and an emblem of the general process of modernization and human development. Indeed, Kaase and Barnes wrote in the conclusion of *Political Action*, "*We interpret this increase in potential for protest to be a lasting characteristic of democratic mass publics and not just a sudden surge in political involvement bound to fade away as time goes by*" (524; italics original). The authors saw several factors as contributing to the rise of contentious political action: cohort replacement, increasing education and cognitive skills, the emergence of new values with an emancipatory impetus, and other variables associated with the process of social modernization and human development. The study also makes an important distinction between a potential for action and action itself: The former is a general predisposition, but the latter needs events and organization, like the loosely knit networks of social movements (Kaase and Barnes 1979).

Another aspect of their social modernization approach was a change in citizen values and the impact of value change on participation. Inglehart found that postmaterialist values were strongly related to protest activity across the *Political Action* nations (Inglehart 1979). The evidence of a link between value change and protest was strengthened in his analyses of the first wave of the World Values Survey (WVS) (Inglehart 1990, Chapter 10). Then Inglehart and Welzel (2005) broadened the analysis to show how the development of self-expression values was tied to the expanding use of protest activities. More recently, Welzel (2013, 215–46) reconceptualized nonviolent protest as a key manifestation of what he calls the "human empowerment process" and showed that a broad set of "emancipative values" is the strongest motivator of these activities, even in the face of a high risk of repression.

The focus on economic development and social modernization as explanations for the "participatory revolution" of the late 1960s parallels the "civic voluntarism model" of political participation in the early studies by Verba and his colleagues (Verba, Nie, and Kim 1978; Verba, Schlozman, and Brady 1995). While these studies were primarily directed at electoral participation, political action is not limited to citizen activities in elections but covers all instances where people try to influence the political process.

The *Political Action* project also studied protest and direct citizen action that, in the extreme case, might be illegal and violent. When protest turns violent, one could think that increasing protest endangers democracy. With the specific historical background of the project and the tumult of the 1960s in mind, such an idea might not be so far off. However, the authors of the *Political Action* study repeatedly made the claim that direct political action is not per se a threat to liberal democracy. This argument was supported by the fact that only a very small number of people participate in violent or illegal political activities. The number is indeed so small that the percentages measured in surveys fall fully into the margin of sampling error – a reason why the most recent wave of the WVS excluded these activities from their question battery on protest.

The *Political Action* study offered a new definition for what should be counted as a legitimate part of citizen participation: Protest acts – initially labeled as "unconventional" participation – were becoming an important part of the citizens' standard democratic repertoire. The project also challenged the previous emphasis on grievances as a decisive source of protest. According to relative deprivation theory, political protest – both peaceful and violent – is triggered when individuals experience deprivations, especially in comparison with other groups or over the life course. These deprivations lead to frustrations and aggressions that stimulate protest action. Deprivation theory is linked to the study of collective violence – with *Why Men Rebel* (Gurr 1970) as the classic work – and has been a leading explanation to explain the onset of civil war.

In his recent overview of collective violence theories, Jakobsen (2011) contrasts deprivation theory to rational actor theory, which subsumes several specific theories. The two broad theories share the idea that political action will occur if the person calculates that he or she can achieve a net gain from the activity (participation has costs and there are uncertainties to handle). A well-known distinction between rational actor theory and deprivation theory is the dichotomy between greed and grievance as popularized by Collier and Hoeffler (2004). As economists study politics, it is not unexpected that greed or desire has become popular as an explanation of political protest.

Grievance and greed are secondary factors for a political action theory that sees activism as arising from a person's skills and capacity to understand and manage the environment. The *Political Action* study is not unique in emphasizing resources as the key explanation of political participation. This is also the core argument of Verba and Nie (1972), when they see modernization, associated economic growth, and a rise in education as sources of increasing political participation. Such resource considerations are central to Verba et al.'s "civic voluntarism model" of participation (Verba et al. 1995).

Continuing this lineage of theories, Inglehart (1990) as well as Inglehart and Welzel (2005) consider the florescence of nonviolent protest activities as an indication of "human development" writ large. In *Freedom Rising*, Welzel (2013, 215–46) goes even further and interprets the continuation of nonviolent protests as the chief manifestation of a broad process of progressing "human empowerment." This lineage of theories provides an optimistic scenario for political involvement among the masses. It is assumed that political protest is consistent with democratic norms and enhances the political influence of citizens.

However, some critics have voiced their doubts. Early on, Samuel Huntington (1974) asked rhetorically, "Postindustrial Politics: How Benign Will It Be?," and recently Marien, Hooghe, and Quintelier (2010) have shown that noninstitutionalized forms of participation have contributed to an increase in political inequality by education. But these authors also show that this is counterbalanced by a reduction, or reversal, of participation differences by gender and age. How different forms of political participation relate to equality ideals constitutes an important line of research that should be extended (see Dalton et al. 2010, 51).

The *Political Action* study was based on survey data from five countries, Austria, Britain, Germany (West), the Netherlands, and the United States, from one point in time. This was, of course, a narrow database to test a general theory. Even with the next stage of the project – *Continuities in Political Action* (Jennings, van Deth et al. 1990) – with data collected in 1979–81, partly as panels, in Germany (West), the Netherlands, and the United States, the mismatch between theoretical ambitions and empirical evidence remained. Still, Jennings et al. (1990) conclude that there was much continuity in political action within a changing economic and political context. The findings from the 1970s were not a fluke (Kaase 1990).

With the inclusion of relevant protest questions in large-scale cross-national surveys in the early 1980s and later, the study of political protest could expand in space and time. Analyzing data from the 1999–2002 wave of the WVS, Dalton et al. (2010, 51) found that protest is increasing "not because of increasing dissatisfaction with government, but because economic and political development provide the resources for those who have political demands." This study constituted an important step forward in comparison to the first generation of political action studies, analyzing data from sixty-seven countries (fifty countries in the most detailed models) and employing a multilevel model of protest activity. Besides finding significant relationships between protest activity and economic and political development at macro and micro levels, the study also observes an interesting interaction between education and political openness. Moving from the least to the most open systems, the positive impact of education on protest participation more than doubles (Dalton et al. 2010, 70).

Welzel and Deutsch (2011) build on this research and make two important contributions. First, they demonstrate that value orientations do not only matter as individual-level motivators of protest but that the *aggregate* configuration of value orientations in a whole country creates a general "psychological climate" with an impact of its very own – independent of how strongly the individuals themselves support the value orientations in question. Thus, Welzel and Deutsch use the broad set of orientations they call "emancipative values" as an individual-level measure of value preferences and also measure the prevalence of these values in each society and treat this as a country-level indicator of how strong the "emancipative climate" is in a given society. The authors assume that this emancipative climate has indeed an impact of its own in two ways: "we expect the emancipative climate to show two ecological effects: (1) an elevation effect that lifts people's protest activity above the level that their own emancipative values suggest; (2) and an amplifier effect that enhances the effect of people's own emancipative values on their protest activity" (Welzel and Deutsch 2011, 15). Using WVS data, the authors confirm both the elevator effect and the amplifier effect. This is a striking confirmation of the idea that culture is a factor at both the micro level and the macro level and that the two can be mutually reinforcing. As these analyses suggest, modernization is not only an empowerment process in the sense that it equips people with more resources to express demands, as Dalton et al. argue; modernization is an empowerment process also in the sense that it raises people's eagerness to voice demands (Welzel 2013, 215–46).

The second contribution of Welzel and Deutsch is that they move the analysis into the time dimension. They analyze changes in protest in what they label as a long-term shift model and a short-term shift model (Welzel and Deutsch 2011, 20–23). In the long-term shift model, they study forty-seven countries that have been surveyed at least twice at a minimal temporal distance of ten years between surveys. In the short-term shift model, all countries that have been surveyed at least twice are included in the study. The findings are quite similar in the two models and show that a positive change in the emancipate climate is related to a rise in protest activities. This stands in contrast to the effect of change in opportunities (negative effect) and change in economic resources (not significant).

While the *Political Action* approach is a general model, we do not expect that empirical trends are linear or parallel in all countries. Inglehart and Catterberg (2002) highlighted an important discontinuity in the development of political protest – the democratic revolution that put an end to communism and other dictatorships. In most countries this event mobilized large groups of the public in demonstrations and other contentious forms of political action. After this burst of activity, Inglehart and Catterberg (2002) observed a decline in elite challenging activities in twelve of the fifteen new democracies in Latin America and Eastern and Central Europe. The three exceptions were Hungary, Poland, and Slovenia – countries which were relatively successful in economic terms and later became European Union members. They interpreted this decline in protest activity as a "posthoneymoon" decline, which was especially strong in the Soviet successor states.

Inglehart and Catterberg (2002) found that political protest is increasing in established democracies. In line with this finding, they predicted that the posthoneymoon decline will eventually be reversed when the new democracies get on a track of economic growth and progress: "Assuming that these societies [the new democracies] reestablish economic growth, we anticipate that in the long run they will experience the gradually rising levels of elite-challenging political action linked with economic development" (314).

Many years have passed since the high point of the third wave of democracy, and this prediction can be tested. The relevant questions have been asked not only in the WVS but also in the European Social Survey (ESS), which started in 2002. Riksem (2010) analyzed the trends for the ESS in 2002, 2004, 2006, and 2008. Not every country was surveyed in all years, but seven postcommunist countries were included with at least two measurements. Essentially, she observed a flat line for all new European democracies. This was also the case for established democracies, but at a higher level (Riksem 2010, 19). Although economic growth was higher in the new democracies than in old democracies, she could not find a positive posthoneymoon effect.

As data have accumulated through a period of more than thirty years since the *Political Action* survey, or about twenty-five years in terms of the WVS studies, and surveys have expanded to include countries in all world regions, we are well positioned to judge the merits of the original predictions. The studies by Inglehart and Catterberg (2002), Inglehart and Welzel (2005), Dalton et al. (2010), Welzel and Deutsch (2011), and Welzel (2013, 215–46) emphasize developmental explanations in line with the original ideas in *Political Action*, and they find much support for the model and hypotheses of the founders.

In contrast to several of the large *N* cross-national studies, we start at a lower level of aggregation when we pursue two of the key questions in the *Political Action* study: (1) How does protest evolve over time? and (2) What is the relationship between economic development and participation in protest activities? We study the trends for each of the indicators of nonviolent protest for single countries where we have a considerable time series. This provides us with the first test of the developmental aspects of the model. Building on previous research, we expect to find an increase in protest participation over time as well as a positive correlation between protest action and national affluence – arguably still the best single indicator of development/modernization writ large.

In further extensions of the empirical analysis, we develop a multilevel model to capture the interplay between micro and macro variables that influence protest activities. The multilevel model is an important additional step to avoid ecological fallacies when inferring individual-level determinants of protest from aggregate-level findings.

DATA SOURCE

Like others in this volume, our analyses are based on the unparalleled resources of the WVS.[3] We first examine the percentage of respondents who have participated in protest behavior in different countries (we have done this for countries where we have at least four data points from the WVS). Second,

---

[3] These data were acquired from the World Values Survey website: http://www.worldvaluessurvey .org. We are responsible for the analyses and interpretation of these data.

we use scatterplots to illustrate the link between economic development and protest activity. We then sum up our analysis by testing our proposed link in a three-level logistic model employing a dichotomized variable denoting whether the respondent has participated in at least one of the three types of protest activities.[4]

We use data from all five waves of the WVS covering the period from 1981 to 2007 (specific years vary somewhat within the waves). We group the countries into four regions: Nordic and Anglo-Saxon countries (Canada, Finland, Norway, Sweden, United Kingdom, United States), Continental and Southern Europe (France, Germany, Italy, Netherlands, Spain), Eastern Europe (Bulgaria, Poland, Russia, Slovenia, Turkey), and the rest of the world (Argentina, Chile, India, Japan, Korea, Mexico, South Africa). From the viewpoint of a sound theory of culture zones, this crude categorization might not be entirely satisfactory. But for pragmatic reasons, there are no better alternatives because the countries covered by sufficient time series do not evenly represent world culture zones. The wording of the variables employed in our model is presented in the appendix.

PREDICTING PROTEST ACTIVITY

A developmental model of democracy expects that protest activities will increase over time and constitute an underlying positive trend in most countries. This is based on the assumption of economic growth and social progress expanding political participation, including protest activity. The WVS includes three types of contentious action: signing petitions, boycotts, and peaceful demonstrations (see the appendix for wording of questions). Figure 9.A1 (in the appendix) presents the results for signing petitions. The trend lines in the Nordic and Anglo-Saxon countries are mostly positive; Norway and Finland show quite linear and increasing trends, although petition signing is lowest (within the group) in Finland. The trend lines are also generally moving upward in Continental and Southern Europe, while the patterns are more irregular in Eastern Europe and the rest of the world.

The trend for joining in boycotts (Figure 9.A2 in the appendix) is positive for the Nordic and Anglo-Saxon countries and also weakly positive in Continental and Southern Europe, whereas trends in Eastern Europe and the rest of the world are again quite irregular. For participation in peaceful demonstrations, the long-term trends are again positive for the first two groups of countries but irregular in the remaining groups (Figure 9.A3 in the appendix).

---

[4] We collapse the "might do" and "would never do" response options. The reason is that we are interested in whether a given activity is part of the behavioral repertoire of a person. For this to be the case, the person must have exercised the activity in question. Only considering it is not sufficient in our eyes. Thus, we follow the standard practice set by Dalton et al. (2010). For a different approach, see Welzel (2013, 222–25).

In summary, despite frequent claims by political analysts that the era of protest politics has passed, the newest wave of the WVS describes a continuing growth in protest activity in mature postindustrial democracies. The upward trend is most apparent for Nordic and Anglo-Saxon countries but applies to other mature democracies as well. We have also run a series of regressions for each country with survey year as an independent variable to see if protest increases over time. The results are presented in Table 9.A1 in the appendix. When we combine the three protest items into a single index of protest activity, we find that the sign of the coefficient for the protest index is positive for thirty-five countries and negative for twenty-four countries, giving some support to the hypothesis of increasing protest action.

In addition, we can test the Inglehart-Catterberg prediction of a reversal of a posthoneymoon decline in political action in postcommunist countries when they experience economic growth. We have four postcommunist countries with at least four time points: Bulgaria, Poland, Russia, and Slovenia. Slovenia and Poland have had more success in developing the economy and democratic institutions than Bulgaria and Russia, so we could expect more of a development-driven process in the first pair than in the second pair of countries. In comparison to Inglehart and Catterberg (2002), we have one more wave of data: The period now extends to at least 2005. The signing of petitions increases in Slovenia but remains quite the same in Poland, Bulgaria, and Russia. For joining in boycotts, all countries show a development that is either flat or declining. Peaceful demonstrations show a strong long-term decline in Russia, a weak decline in Bulgaria, and not much of a change in Slovenia and Poland. Table 9.A1 in the appendix finds little systematic evidence of change in the summary protest index across these four nations.

Overall, there is still not much support for the hypothesis that political action has recovered from the posthoneymoon decline following the fall of communism. Needless to say, the evidence for this conclusion is still limited, and problems of over-time measurements of the political action questions also need to be taken into account. The hypothesis itself is also flexible – it is not easy to predict when the posthoneymoon period will end.

To assess the impact of economic modernization on political action, we constructed an index for protest (a count of participation in any of the three activities) for each nation and correlated this with national affluence (gross domestic product [GDP] per capita measured in purchasing power parity [PPP]) for the five WVS waves.[5] The relation between these two measures is shown in Figure 9.1 separately for each WVS wave. National affluence and protest

---

[5] The protest index is a count of the number of protest activities across the three survey questions. Respondents with missing data on an item are included as not being active. The original variables in the data set included three categories when asked whether they have participated in a certain political action: "Have done," "Might do," and "Would never do." We have chosen to collapse the two latter categories.

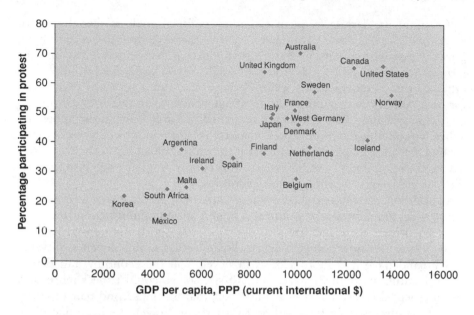

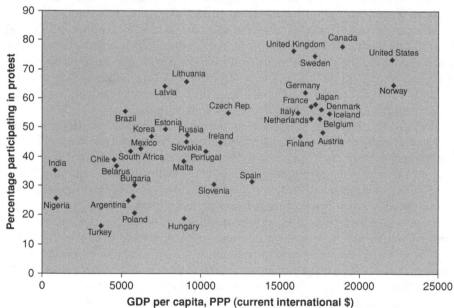

FIGURE 9.1. Protest participation by economic development and survey wave.
Note: Figures plot percentage doing at least one protest activity (petitions, boycotts, or peaceful demonstrations). Fifty-four nations, Pearson's $r = 0.789$ in wave V.
Source: World Values Survey and World Bank for GDP per capita, PPP.

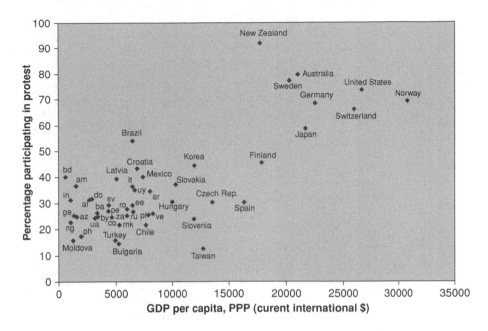

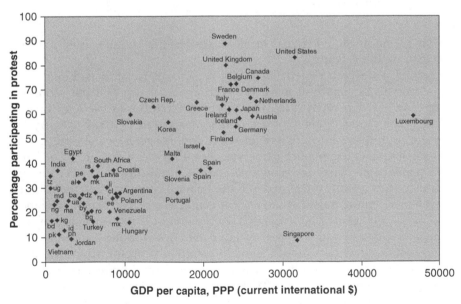

FIGURE 9.1 *(continued)*

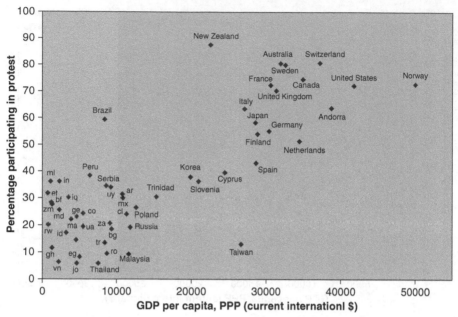

FIGURE 9.1 (*continued*)

action are positively correlated in all waves (coefficients are listed for each survey wave in the figure).

Beyond the overall pattern, there are some outliers, most strikingly Luxembourg and Singapore in wave IV; both countries are rich but score low (Singapore) or moderately (Luxembourg) on protest. It is possible to come up with ad hoc explanations for these outliers: Singapore is a rich country but dominated by an authoritarian regime that does not tolerate political protest. It is possible that Luxembourg attracts citizens from across the European Union who prefer to live there for economic reasons (i.e., a low taxation rate) and that they are not easily integrated into the political community of the country. However, we must stress that Luxembourg and, to a certain extent, Singapore have artificially inflated per capita GDPs because of the unusual size of their financial sectors. In addition, part of Luxembourg's working population lives in neighboring countries, which leads to a further overestimation of the per capita GDP. Thus, the position of Singapore and Luxembourg on the GDP scale gives an inflated picture of the true living standard of these countries' people (even though both countries are very well-off). Also, the low tax rate of such financial sector economies might discourage political mobilization in a kind of conversion of the "no taxation without representation" logic: Because government does not extract resources from people, there is less of an urge to participate in politics – no mobilization without taxation.

The overall form and distribution of protest action by economic wealth is consistent with a modernization hypothesis of increasing participation with

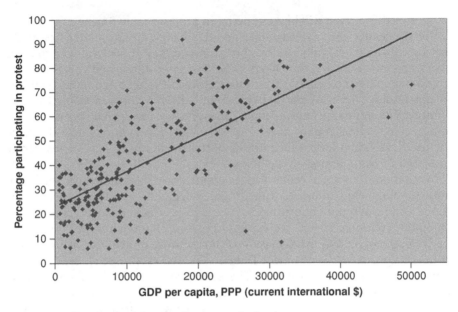

FIGURE 9.2. Protest participation by economic development.
Note: Figures plot percentage doing at least one protest activity (petitions, boycotts, or peaceful demonstrations). All five waves, GDP per capita, PPP (current international $) N = 229, Pearson's r = 0.68.
Source: World Values Survey and World Bank for GDP per capita, PPP.

economic development. To summarize this pattern, Figure 9.2 shows the distribution of protest activity for all countries in all years.[6] For this pooled analysis, there is a strong positive relationship (r − 0.68). The form of the relationship appears to be linear, but it is also possible that a nonlinear function fits the data better (i.e., only a flat increase in poorer countries and a steeper increase in affluent countries). The pattern for low-income countries may be consistent with a take-off effect – countries need to achieve a minimum level of development before protest levels start to increase. We return to this issue in the multivariate model.

A MULTIVARIATE MODEL OF PROTEST

In the next step we present a multivariate model of protest activity that includes both micro and macro variables. We include some of the most relevant individual variables from previous studies, although analyzing all five WVS waves somewhat limits the set of available variables. This might be seen as a disadvantage. However, the inclusion of data from all waves gives us a larger number of cases – and a better basis for generalization in models that include most of the relevant variables – compared to examining only one wave (e.g., Dalton et al. 2010).

[6] We use the average for each survey in each country. We use a standardized GDP measure.

We expect that men will be more active in protest than women, although the size of the gender gap may have declined (Listhaug and Grønflaten 2007). As previous research generally demonstrates, protest may appeal more to younger citizens because they are more likely to hold issue positions and values that are not accommodated by established routine politics. Political action is dependent on the resource level of the individual and the developmental level of the country. The model includes income for individuals and GDP per capita for countries as well as the mean level of education for each country. We have not used individual-level education as a control because it is inconsistently measured across countries in the first survey.

In addition to national economic development, we add a measure on democratic development. Countries with advanced democracy make it easier for citizens to find ways and opportunities to engage in political activities, especially contentious actions. Hence, we expect a positive relationship between democratic development and political action. Our measure of democracy is gathered from the Quality of Government Dataset (Teorell et al. 2011), created from Polity 2 and Freedom House data. These are two recognized and comparable measures of democracy and are well suited for quantitative analysis.[7]

In addition, political action is often associated with leftist beliefs as many of the causes that have stimulated activism have been associated with the Left (i.e., environment and gender issues). Although we see ideological commitments on both sides as potential sources of activism, we expect that leftist ideology will have a stronger impact on protest activity. Left-Right ideology covers many strands of political issues and values (Fuchs and Klingemann 1990) and works as a summation measure of the relevant dimensions for all countries.

Inglehart (1977, 1990) sees postmaterialism as an emerging value dimension with a potential to replace the Left-Right divide as countries move from an industrial to a postindustrial society. Postmaterialism provides a motivational foundation for political action, and we expect postmaterialists to score higher on political action than materialists. In contrast to Welzel and Deutsch (2011), who perform an analysis of both aggregate and individual effects of values, we study the effects of values at the micro level only (Left-Right opinions and postmaterialist values). The reason is *not* that an aggregate-level measure of postmaterialism had no meaning beyond its individual-level presence – quite the contrary. However, the aggregate level of postmaterialism correlates highly with both economic development and institutional democracy, so adding it increases multicollinearity without adding much explanatory variance. Hence, we include postmaterialism only at the individual level, using the original four-item postmaterialism index.[8]

---

[7] Both Freedom House and Polity have been transformed into 0–10 scales and averaged into one scale.

[8] This is in line with Dalton et al. (2010), but we note that Welzel and Deutsch (2011) and Welzel (2013, 215–46) prefer a broader cultural measure of emancipative values. We cannot use the broader measure for our analysis because one of its components – an emphasis on gender equality – has not been asked in round 1 of the WVS.

With these expectations in hand, we now turn to the analysis of the multivariate model (Table 9.1). There are three levels in the data: (1) individuals, (2) country-survey-years, and (3) countries. The dependent variable is dichotomous: A score of 1 denotes that the respondent has participated in peaceful protest activity (i.e., has taken part in one or more of the three contentious actions); a score of 0 indicates that a respondent has taken part in none of these actions. The basic model includes three level 2 variables: degree of democracy (0–10), mean length of education in the nation, and per capita GDP.[9] The latter variable is log-transformed to reduce the undue influence of outliers. On level 3, we include dummies for whether the county is socialist/former socialist and if it belongs to the developing world. At level 1, we include gender, age, income, Left-Right orientation (four dummies), and postmaterialism. In the second model, we add cross-level interaction terms to test whether the effect of development (per capita GDP) differs depending on geographic region.

Because we assume that variables observed at the country level have an influence on individual-level relationships, the use of multilevel analysis (hierarchical models) is beneficial. Multilevel models also can address the statistical problems that occur in mixing variables at different levels of aggregation. These models employ a one-year lag on the country-level explanatory variables.

The findings for the individual level variables in Table 9.1 generally confirm our expectations. Protest levels are higher for men, younger people, and those with higher income. Participation rates are higher on the Left and Right compared to the center, but the effect is stronger on the Left than on the Right. While protest among the Right is somewhat unexpected, it resonates with observations of political action in many countries over extended periods of time. For example, issues of race, language, and other traditional concerns have triggered demonstrations and petitions. Ideologically, this action has been aligned with political parties on the Right, even the far Right.

Affirming previous research on the relevance of values for changing patterns of political participation, protest is highest among those who hold postmaterialist values. Indeed, protest reflects the type of assertive citizenship that is a central theme in this book and contrasts most clearly with the allegiant model of the earlier political culture literature.[10]

In the basic model on the left of Table 9.1, we find the expected positive effect for two of three development indicators (education and GDP per capita) but no effect for the level of democracy. The lack of an effect of political opportunities is in line with the findings of Welzel and Deutsch (2011) and

---

[9] Data on per capita GDP are originally from the World Bank and OECD. Education is from the Institute for Health Metrics and Evaluation; the level of democracy is based on Freedom House and the Polity index. These variables are from the Quality of Government Dataset (Teorell et al. 2011)

[10] Because there is a positive correlation between postmaterialism and leftist orientations, the effect of postmaterialism is even stronger when we drop Left-Right orientations from our predictors. However, the correlation between postmaterialism and leftist orientation is not strong enough to justify eliminating the latter for reasons of multicollinearity.

228 Social Change and the Politics of Protest

TABLE 9.1. *Three-Level Models of Protest Activity, 1981–2007*

	Basic Model			Including Interaction		
	b	SE	z	b	SE	z
Constant	−2.887***	0.001	3.29	−11.772***	2.759	−4.27
Level 1 Variables						
Woman	−0.232***	0.010	−24.10	−0.232***	0.010	24.10
Age	−0.004***	0.000	−11.72	−0.004***	0.000	−11.73
Income (0–10)	0.100***	0.002	46.72	0.100***	0.002	46.74
Extreme Left[a]	0.577***	0.019	30.87	0.577***	0.019	30.87
Left[a]	0.585***	0.015	39.41	0.585***	0.015	39.41
Right[a]	0.239***	0.014	16.65	0.239***	0.014	16.65
Extreme Right[a]	0.213***	0.018	11.89	0.213***	0.018	11.90
Postmaterialism[b]	0.206***	0.006	35.97	0.206***	0.006	35.93
Level 2 Variables						
Democracy[c]	0.006	0.025	0.24	0.020	0.025	0.79
Mean education	0.072**	0.034	2.10	0.022	0.037	0.60
GDPpc	0.167*	0.099	1.69	1.082***	0.289	3.75
Level 3 Variables						
Socialist[d]	−0.874***	0.235	−3.71	7.800**	3.111	2.75
Developing[e]	−0.779***	0.248	−3.15	9.218***	2.805	3.29
Interaction						
Socialist*GDPpc				−0.845***	0.314	−2.69
Developing.*GDPpc				−1.029***	0.286	−3.60
Variance						
Level 2 variance	0.233***	0.031		0.227***	0.031	
Level 3 variance	0.298***	0.071		0.255***	0.066	
Level 1 N	229,960			229,960		
Level 2 N	205			205		
Level 3 N	83			83		
Log likelihood	−129,820.78			−129,814.47		

Note: The table presents unstandardized coefficients from multilevel logistic analysis. Variance of dependence on level 1 = 83.10%; level 2 = 3.43%; level 3 = 13.47%. The probability values are calculated using a two-tailed test. Democracy, mean education, and GDP/pc are lagged one year. GDP/pc is log-transformed. *Developed*: Australia, Austria, Belgium, Canada, Cyprus, Denmark, Finland, France, Germany, Great Britain, Greece, Ireland, Italy, Japan, Korea, Luxembourg, Netherlands, New Zealand, Norway, Portugal, Singapore, Spain, Sweden, Switzerland, Turkey, and United States. *Developing*: Algeria, Argentina, Bangladesh, Brazil, Burkina Faso, Chile, Colombia, Dominican Republic, Egypt, Ethiopia, Ghana, Guatemala, India, Indonesia, Jordan, Malaysia, Mali, Mexico, Morocco, Nigeria, Pakistan, Peru, Philippines, Rwanda, South Africa, Thailand, Trinidad & Tobago, Uganda Uruguay, Venezuela, Zambia, Zimbabwe. *Socialist/previously socialist*: Albania, Bosnia and Herzegovina, Armenia, Azerbaijan, Belarus, Bulgaria, China, Croatia, Czech Republic, Estonia, Georgia, Hungary, Kyrgyzstan, Latvia, Lithuania, Macedonia, Poland, Romania, Russia, Serbia, Slovakia, Slovenia, Tanzania, Ukraine, Vietnam.
[a] Center is reference category; original variable ranged from 1 to 10, where 1–2 = extreme Left; 3–4 = Left; 5–6 = center; 7–8 = Right; 9–10 = extreme Right.
[b] 1 = materialist values; 2 = mixed; 3 = postmaterialist.
[c] Democracy ranges from 0 to 10, where large values indicate a high degree of democracy.
[d] A dummy variable for former second world countries.
[e] Represents third world countries; first world countries are the reference category.
*Significant at 10 percent. **Significant at 5 percent. ***Significant at 1%.

Welzel (2013, 232) and suggests that the politics of protest is not limited to countries that already have a relatively advanced democracy. Protest activity may indicate an ongoing process of democratization and occurs across a wide range of levels of democratic development, from absent to deficient to mature democracy. In many cases, protest has led to democratization, so the causal arrow might point from protest to democracy rather than the other way round (cf. Welzel 2013, 245).

In the basic model, protest activity is lower in socialist/postsocialist countries and in developing countries. This may partially be due to their socioeconomic conditions, and so the second model adds interaction effects. We also added a second polynomial to the per capita GDP variable (table not included). The second model confirms the acceleration effect of GDP per capita on the likelihood of protest behavior. The model shows that there is a strong positive effect of per capita income in the developed world. That is, the richer a developed country is, the more likely it is that its inhabitants will have participated in a protest activity. There is no effect for belonging to the developing countries itself and a very small effect for belonging to the former or present socialist countries. The effect of wealth does not kick in until it reaches a certain threshold (e.g., above $10,000). People living in developed societies are more likely to have participated in protest activity than people from the developing or former or present socialist world. This finding is largely driven by per capita income.

Another way of illustrating the acceleration effect of per capita income is by including dummy variables for whether a country is industrialized. Using the coefficients from the interaction model presented in Table 9.1, where we interacted GDP per capita with the dummy variables, we estimated four lines showing the effect of per capita income for four different types of countries: nonsocialist industrialized countries (such as West Europe or North America), former socialist industrialized countries (East European nations), former socialist developing countries (China, Vietnam, etc.), and nonsocialist developing countries (such as Latin American nations). Each comparison is based on three economic levels, whether a country is poor, affluent, or in between. Of course, some of the predictions are unrealistic, as developing countries cannot have a high score on GDP per capita.

Figure 9.3 tests the acceleration effect of income within each of the four sets of nations. There is a strong effect of income on the likelihood of protest in nonsocialist industrialized countries, which are also the richest countries. For example, among the lowest income group, there is virtually no protest, and this increases to an 0.8 likelihood of protest in the most affluent industrialized democracies. These countries are above the acceleration threshold that we can see in Figure 9.2. The effect is also positive but less pronounced for countries that are industrialized but also former or present socialist. For both types of developing countries, the flat lines indicate that there is literally no effect of

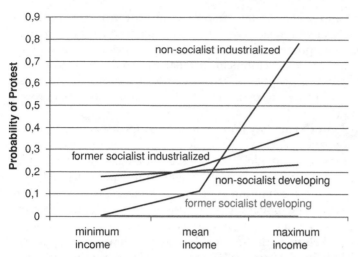

FIGURE 9.3. Effect of income in different societies on the likelihood of protest.
Source: World Values Survey and World Bank for GDP per capita, PPP.

per capita income. Former/present socialist developing countries are in general
poorer than their nonsocialist counterparts.[11]

CONCLUSION

The *Political Action* study by Barnes and Kaase et al. (1979) launched
a developmental model of protest behavior and predicted that citizens'
elite-challenging actions will increase as societies become richer. Using data
from all five waves of the World Values Survey (1981–2007), we find support –
although not without modifications – for these expectations. The positive
impact of economic development is very striking when we compare poor and
rich countries. As we move up the economic ladder, contentious political action
tends to increase, but only after a country has passed a threshold. It is difficult
to find a wealth effect among developing countries. To some extent, this finding
confirms the conventional view that *regular* political protest is found primarily
in postindustrial societies. As we recently have gone through a wave of political
protest, peaceful, but also violent, as in the Arab Spring, we need to extend the
focus beyond the study of advanced democracies.

We have also investigated the effects of the transitions to democracy in
previously communist and socialist countries. We find that if a country has
been socialist (or communist), the effect of economic growth has not moved
the country into a higher level of contentious participation following the
decline of action after the transition period. This finding suggests that the

[11] This figure, despite having some hypothetical categories, is included as an easy-to-grasp illustration.

Inglehart-Catterberg thesis about a temporary posthoneymoon decline in post-communist countries might be incorrect. But it could also be the case that their thesis sets too high a standard for what is considered a normal level of political action in these countries. The political revolutions that swept away the communist dictatorships were unique events that were accompanied with a massive popular mobilization, mostly of a nonviolent form, and it is unlikely that such exceptional political action levels will be reached again in normal times, in the absence of antiregime mobilization. Civic society groups in these nations are still developing. The outburst of mass political action contributed to the fall of communism in many countries, but the posthoneymoon decline that followed may be more difficult to reverse than expected based on the effects of an economic growth model.

The role that mass political action played in communist countries as well as recently in the Color Revolutions and the Arab Spring suggests that political protest behavior as conceptualized in the tradition of political action theory is not a simple function of the democratic level in a society. We find that political action is not related to the level of democracy in society and thus not determined by institutional opportunities for participation. The idea that political protest should be positively related to the opportunities that democracy creates has some plausibility, on one hand. On the other hand, we might also see a weak democracy, or lack of a democratic system, as a factor that creates demand for democratization and in turn leads to increasing political protest among the mass publics.

Our findings point strongly to the economic interpretation. Protest activity grows as societies get richer. But they have to reach a takeoff level before the wealth of society leads to an increase in political protest. There is also a tendency for protest to level off as societies get very rich: Among the most affluent countries, further increases in GDP have a decreasing marginal effect on protest. This is a good example of floor and ceiling effects: At the floor and the ceiling of GDP, increases in GDP have little effect on protest, whereas in the wide mid-range area, the effect is large.

Our results also confirm research from the *Political Action* project and subsequent studies that citizen values are important for protest activity. Citizens on the Left and postmaterialists are the most likely groups to protest. We also observe higher protest on the Right (when compared with centrist citizens), making protest a relatively broad access route to political influence. Protest is especially common among younger generations.

Contrasting with the allegiant passive publics of the past, contemporary publics are adopting more elite-challenging forms of nonviolent action. This trend has not receded in mature postindustrial democracies as the turbulent 1960s–70s have passed but have actually continued to increase in these societies. Moreover, protest has become an extension of conventional politics by other means, used by a wide spectrum of society. This expansion of protest is a key manifestation of the rise of assertive mass publics.

APPENDIX

Variable	Question Wording	Coding
Protest activity	*I'm going to read out some different forms of political action that people can take, and I'd like you to tell me, for each one, whether you have actually done any of these things, whether you might do it or would never, under any circumstances, do it.*	1 = "have done" 2 = "might do" 3 = "would never do"
Self-positioning on Left-Right scale	*In political matters, people talk of "the left" and "the right." How would you place your views on this scale, generally speaking?*	1 = "Left" 10 = "Right"
Postmaterialist values index	*Four-item question on societal priorities. See* Chapter 2.	1 = materialist values; 2 = mixed; 3 = postmaterialist

TABLE 9.A1. *Change in Protest over Time*

Nation	Per Annum Change	Time Period (N)
Albania	−0.012	1998–2002 (2)
Argentina	−0.000	1984–2006 (5)
Australia	0.013	1981–2005 (3)
Bangladesh	−0.072	1996–2002 (2)
Belarus	−0.022	1990–2000 (3)
Belgium	0.047	1981–1999 (3)
Brazil	0.001	1991–2006 (3)
Bulgaria	−0.006	1990–2006 (4)
Canada	0.007	1982–2006 (4)
Chile	−0.012	1990–2005 (4)
Colombia	−0.007	1997–2005 (3)
Croatia	0.005	1996–1999 (2)
Czech Republic	−0.014	1990–1999 (4)
Denmark	0.022	1981–1999 (3)
Egypt	−0.063	2000–2008 (2)
Estonia	−0.041	1990–1999 (3)
Finland	0.011	1981–2005 (5)
France	0.015	1981–2006 (4)
Georgia	−0.052	1996–2008 (2)
Germany	0.002	1981–2006 (5)

Nation	Per Annum Change	Time Period (N)
Hungary	0.006	1982–1999 (4)
Iceland	0.020	1984–1999 (3)
India	0.003	1990–2006 (4)
Indonesia	0.010	2001–2006 (2)
Ireland	0.023	1981–1999 (3)
Italy	0.013	1981–2005 (5)
Japan	0.009	1981–2005 (5)
Jordan	−0.005	2001–2007 (2)
Latvia	−0.053	1990–1999 (3)
Lithuania	−0.075	1996–1999 (3)
Malta	0.014	1983–1999 (3)
Mexico	0.004	1981–2005 (5)
Moldova	0.016	1996–2006 (3)
Morocco	0.003	2001–2007 (2)
Netherlands	0.015	1981–2006 (4)
New Zealand	−0.012	1998–2004 (2)
Nigeria	−0.008	1990–2000 (3)
Norway	0.017	1982–2007 (4)
Peru	0.019	2001–2006 (2)
Poland	0.000	1989–2005 (5)
Portugal	−0.006	1990–1999 (2)
Romania	−0.033	1993–2005 (4)
Russia	−0.021	1990–2006 (4)
Serbia	0.035	1996–2006 (3)
Slovakia	0.003	1990–1999 (4)
Slovenia	0.008	1992–2005 (4)
South Africa	−0.002	1982–2007 (5)
South Korea	0.008	1982–2005 (5)
Spain	0.002	1981–2007 (6)
Sweden	0.029	1982–2006 (5)
Switzerland	0.030	1989–2007 (3)
Taiwan	0.004	1994–2006 (2)
Turkey	−0.004	1990–2007 (4)
Ukraine	−0.008	1996–2006 (3)
United Kingdom	0.009	1981–2006 (5)
United States	0.010	1982–2006 (5)
Uruguay	0.007	1996–2006 (2)
Venezuela	−0.022	2000–2006 (2)
Vietnam	−0.002	2001–2006 (2)

Note: The table presents the per annum rate of change for the three-item protest index using a simple OLS relationship.

Source: World Values Survey waves.

Nordic and Anglo-Saxon Countries

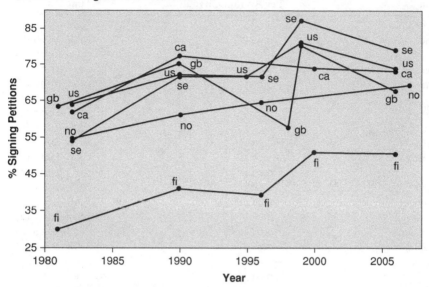

Note: ca = Canada, fi = Finland, gb = United Kingdom, no = Norway, se = Sweden, us = United States

Continental and Southern Europe

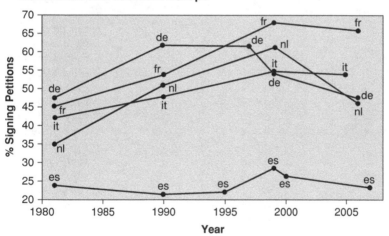

Note: es = Spain, fr = France, de = Germany, it = Italy, nl = Netherlands

FIGURE 9.A1. Signing a petition by country and year.

Eastern Europe

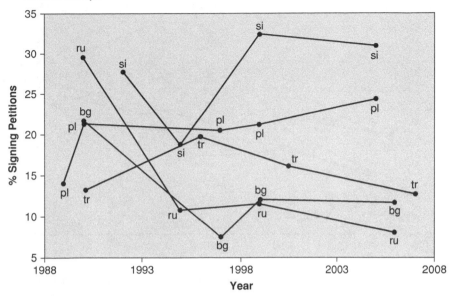

Note: bg = Bulgaria, pl = Poland, ru = Romania, si = Slovenia, tr = Turkey

Rest of the World

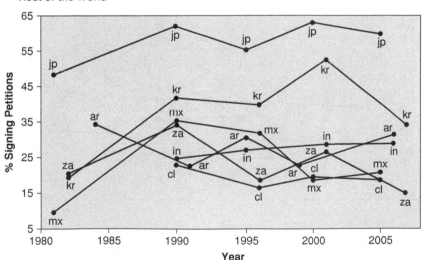

Note: ar = Argentina, cl = Chile, jp = Japan, kr = Korea, mx = Mexico, in = India, za = South Africa

FIGURE 9.A1 (*continued*)

Nordic and Anglo-Saxon Countries

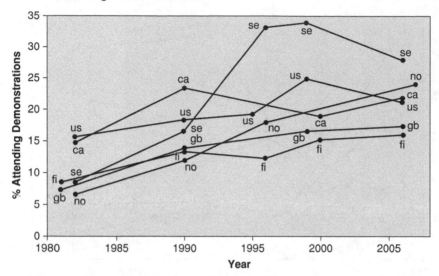

Note: ca = Canada, fi = Finland, gb = United Kingdom, no = Norway, se = Sweden, us = United States

Continental and Southern Europe

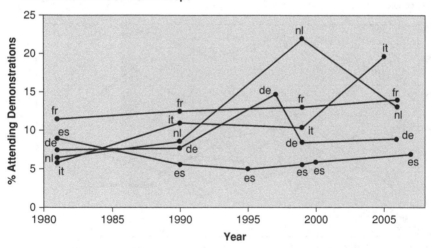

Note: es = Spain, fr = France, de = Germany, it = Italy, nl = Netherlands

FIGURE 9.A2. Joining in boycotts by country and year.

Eastern Europe

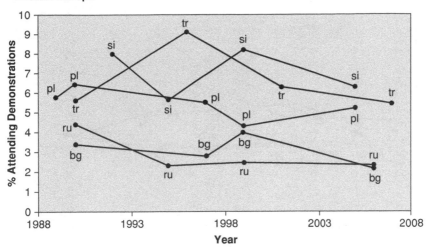

Note: bg = Bulgaria, pl = Poland, ru = Romania, si = Slovenia, tr = Turkey

Rest of World

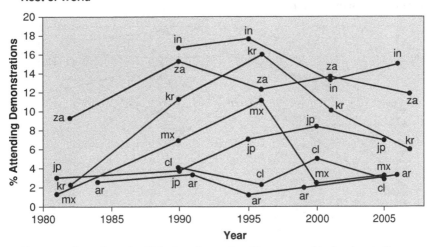

Note: ar = Argentina, cl = Chile, jp = Japan, kr = Korea, mx = Mexico, in = India, za = South Africa

FIGURE 9.A2 (*continued*)

Nordic and Anglo-Saxon Countries

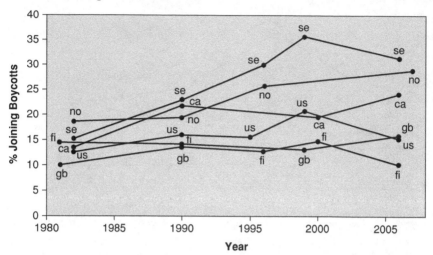

Note: ca = Canada, fi = Finland, gb = United Kingdom, no = Norway, se = Sweden, us = United States

Continental and Southern Europe

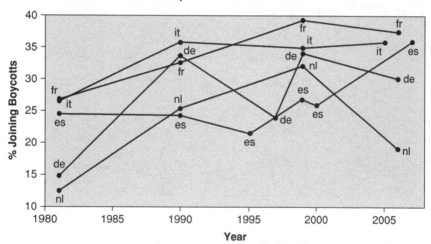

Note: es = Spain, fr = France, de = Germany, it = Italy, nl = Netherlands

FIGURE 9.A3. Attending peaceful demonstrations by country and year.

Eastern Europe

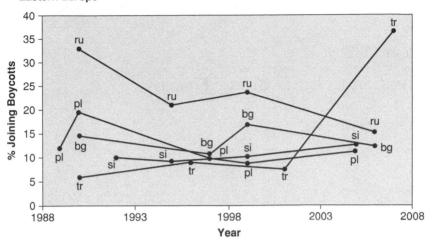

Note: bg = Bulgaria, pl = Poland, ru = Romania, si = Slovenia, tr = Turkey

Rest of the World

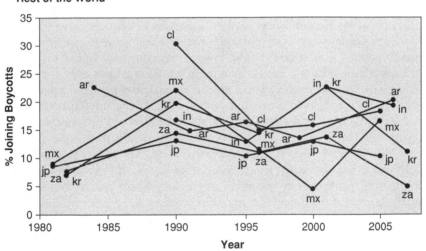

Note: ar = Argentina, cl = Chile, jp = Japan, kr = Korea, mx = Mexico, in = India, za = South Africa

FIGURE 9.A3 (*continued*)

10

Mecca or Oil?

Why Arab States Lag in Gender Equality

Pippa Norris

Achieving gender equality is a challenge for all states – but particularly for those in the Middle East and North Africa (MENA). The *Arab Human Development Report* (UNDP 2006) highlights the multiple ways that gender equality in the region continues to lag behind the rest of the world. One of the most difficult challenges concerns elected office; women members are roughly one in six of Arab parliamentarians (17.8 percent), below the world average (21.8 percent) (Interparliamentary Union 2013). The lower houses of parliament in Yemen and Oman both include only one woman member, whereas none are appointed to the Qatar national assembly. These extreme disparities persist despite some significant breakthroughs in particular states, notably the implementation of reserved seats in the lower house of parliament in Morocco (21 percent women) and gender quotas in Algeria (31.6 percent women) and Iraq (25.2 percent women) (Norris 2007). Even ultraconservative Saudi Arabia has responded to global norms; in January 2013, King Abdullah of Saudi Arabia issued a historic decree allowing women to be members of the kingdom's previously all-male parliament for the first time. The mandate creates a 20 percent quota for women in the 150-member Shura Council, the formal advisory board of Saudi Arabia, and the king immediately appointed thirty women to the assembly (20 percent).

Yet, at the same time, some Arab countries have also gone backward. In Egypt, sixty-four women (12.6 percent of the Assembly's elected membership) were elected in 2010, the highest proportion in the nation's history. Victory proved short-lived, however. Less than two months after the elections concluded, the ouster of President Mubarak prompted the dissolution of parliament by the Supreme Council of the Armed Forces (SCAF) and the abolition of reserved seats for women.

Problems of gender equality are also not simply confined to the lack of women's voices in the highest echelons of power. Most governments in the

Middle East have now formally endorsed, with reservations, the Convention on the Elimination of All Forms of Discrimination against Women (CEDAW), pledging to establish women's rights.[1] Yet the *Arab Human Development Report* documents that the region has some of the highest rates of female illiteracy and the lowest rate of female labor force participation compared with the rest of the world. Women in the region encounter serious problems with basic health care, educational access, sexual harassment, and income poverty, as well as suffering from exposure to violence, limited legal rights, and lack of access to justice. These conditions are compounded by general problems of social exclusion, the curtailment of fundamental freedoms, and lack of democracy. The uprisings toppling autocracies in the Arab region have provided some new opportunities for women's representation so that women are now 27 percent of parliamentarians in Tunisia. Nevertheless, the final outcome of regime transitions in the region remains to be determined in the months and years ahead.

Why do Arab states continue to lag behind the rest of the world in gender equality? Cultural values and structural resources offer two alternative perspectives. Drawing on modernization theory, cultural accounts emphasize that gender disparities are reinforced by the predominance of traditional attitudes toward the roles of women and men in developing societies, combined with the strength of religiosity in the Middle East and North Africa (Inglehart and Norris 2003; Norris and Inglehart 2004; Alexander and Welzel 2011a, 2011b). In fact, changing gender norms are one of the prime examples of the process of global change described in other chapters of this book (e.g., see Chapter 1, 8, and 9; Welzel 2013). An alternative structural view is presented by the "petroleum patriarchy" thesis; Michael Ross (2008) claims that oil-rich economies directly limit the role of women in the paid workforce and thus also (indirectly) restrict women's representation in parliament.

To consider these issues, the first section outlines these theoretical arguments. The next section discusses the most appropriate research design used to analyze the evidence. The following section presents multilevel models using the World Values Survey (WVS) in a large number of societies, demonstrating that religious traditions have a greater influence on attitudes toward gender equality and sexual liberalization than either labor force participation or oil rents. We then demonstrate the impact of cultural attitudes on the proportion of women in legislative and ministerial office. The conclusion summarizes the main findings and considers their implications.

THE "RESOURCE CURSE" MATTERS?

Why do contemporary Arab states lag behind the rest of the world in gender equality in elected office? One obvious historical cause concerns the legal

---

[1] The exceptions to Arab state endorsement of CEDAW are Oman, Qatar, Somalia, Sudan, and the Occupied Palestinian Territories.

barriers to women's suffrage and limited rights to stand for office in the region, but these formal restrictions have been gradually dismantled, most recently in Qatar (1999), Bahrain (2002), Oman (2003), Kuwait (2005), the United Arab Emirates (2006), and the Kingdom of Saudi Arabia (2013). Women and men now enjoy equal legal and constitutional rights to be candidates for political office in all states in the region.[2] Setting the formal legal barriers aside, therefore, alternative explanations for why so few women continue to be represented in national parliaments in the MENA region are offered by social structural and cultural accounts. These can each be regarded as rival theories (Bergh 2006), or else, more realistically, as complementary parts of the same puzzle, for a more holistic understanding.

The traditional sociological perspective, reflecting the mainstream view during the 1960s and 1970s, emphasizes that women's mass mobilization in politics and their recruitment into leadership positions in the public sphere have been hindered by the social structure, notably the traditional roles of men and women within the workforce, home, and family. Reflecting this view, an early classic study of engagement in American election campaigns by Kristi Andersen (1975) emphasized that the entry of more women into the U.S. workforce during the postwar decades gradually narrowed the gender gap in mass political participation. The structural viewpoint has become less common today, although it has not died away. Some contemporary studies continue to emphasize the impact of residual gender gaps in literacy, educational qualifications, family responsibilities, or work-based professional networks on women's entry into political elites. All of these factors are regarded as limiting the resources, experience, and capacities women bring both to civic engagement at a mass level (Schlozman 1999) and to the pursuit of elected and appointed office for legislative, executive, and judicial elites (Iversen and Rosenbluth 2008). In terms of Arab states, the structural thesis suggests that where the residual formal legal barriers to candidacy are removed, gender equality in elected office will follow if more Arab women gradually gain higher education and then move into the paid labor force, gaining entry into relevant occupations with high status, relevant skills, and organizational networks in management and the professions.

The structural perspective garnered plausibility in advanced industrialized economies during the 1960s and 1970s, an era when many more women were surging into higher education and the paid workforce in these societies, entering higher-status positions, and organizing to demand equality in the public sphere. The argument has come under increasing challenge in subsequent decades,

---

[2] In Saudi Arabia, women gained voting suffrage and the right to stand for election for the Shura Council only in September 2011. In Lebanon, elementary education is required for the female but not the male suffrage. In Kuwait, women could only run for election in 2009. In Qatar, the expansion of the franchise has not yet been implemented in national contests.

however, not least by the simple observation that millions of women in postin-dustrial economies have now entered higher education and the paid workforce, gradually rising in management and the professions. For example, a legal career is a common pathway into elected office in the United States, and the American Bar Association (2006) reports that women represent about half of the entrants to American law schools. Women now also constitute the majority of the American college population. Despite these developments, countries such as the United States and Japan continue to lag far behind the world average in the proportion of women in elected office, with the U.S. Congress currently ranked 81st and the Japan Diet 124th worldwide (Interparliamentary Union 2013). By contrast, far more women are members of parliament in some poorer developing societies and emerging economies, notably the well-known cases of Rwanda, where women are two-thirds of the lower house of parliament (ranked first), and Cuba (third), Senegal (sixth), and South Africa (eighth). Moreover, structural arguments have also gradually lost support because of their conservative policy implications. The idea of incremental social evolution in men's and women's lives over successive generations has proved less attractive politically than "fast-track" institutional solutions, including gender quotas, which can transform women's representation over just a few successive elections (Dahlerup 2006; Krook 2009).

The traditional idea that women's labor force participation will eventually lead directly to political power in the Arab region has been revived, however, by Michael Ross (2008), who has claimed that the well-known "resource curse," particularly the extraction and production of oil and gas, plays an important role in economic and political dimensions of gender equality. The notion of a resource curse has been most commonly applied to explaining why many countries apparently blessed with abundant reserves of nonrenewable mineral resources – such as Nigerian oil, the Democratic Republic of Congo's gold, or Sierra Leone diamonds – are commonly vulnerable to civil war and political instability (Auty 1993; Ross 2001; Boix 2003; Jensen and Wantchekon 2004; Dunning 2008; Collier and Sambanis 2005; Humphreys 2005; Snyder 2006; Ross 2004, 2006).

In "Oil, Islam and Women," Ross (2008) extends the resource curse thesis by suggesting that petroleum also damages equality between men and women, both directly and indirectly. Ross's argument makes two core claims, illustrated schematically in Figure 10.1a. First, he suggests that the structure of economies heavily dependent on oil and gas resources is *directly* responsible for the inequality of men's and women's participation in the paid labor force. Manual jobs in the mining, extraction, refining, and production of mineral resources are heavily male dominated, in contrast to service-sector white-collar economies. Second, lower female labor force participation in resource-based economies, he reasons, indirectly limits female opportunities to run for elected office in these states. The resource curse is thereby seen to *indirectly* reinforce patriarchal states.

a. Ross's structural model

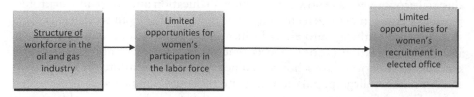

b. Norris and Inglehart's cultural model

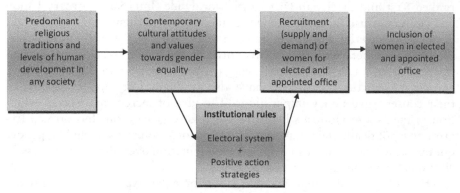

FIGURE 10.1. Structural and cultural models of women's representation.
Note: (a) Ross's structural model. (b) Norris and Inglehart's cultural model.

To support these twin claims, Ross employs econometric evidence drawn from macro-level cross-national and time series data. The key independent variable – the value of oil and gas production – is operationalized as oil and gas rents per capita. This represents the total annual value of a country's oil and gas production, minus the extraction costs in each country, divided by its population to normalize the value of the rents, measured from 1960 to 2002 in constant 2000 U.S. dollars. The dependent variables for the econometric models are aggregate-level indicators of women's status, including the proportion of women in the paid labor force and the fraction of parliamentary seats and ministerial positions held by women in 2002. Controls include levels of democracy and economic development and the Muslim fraction of each country's population. The study also contrasts illustrative case studies of women's status in North African states with poor mineral resources, including Tunisia and Morocco, compared with their position in oil-rich Algeria. Ross concludes, "The extraction of oil and gas tends to reduce the role of women in the work force, and the likelihood that they will accumulate political influence . . . In short, petroleum perpetuates patriarchy" (120). From a policy perspective, the argument implies that as long as the oil reserves hold, no matter how many women candidates challenge the status quo of male elites in Bahrain, Libya, Iran, and Jordan, few are likely to succeed.

OR TRADITIONAL CULTURAL ATTITUDES?

In fact, as can be demonstrated later, cultural explanations trump structural ones. Enduring religious traditions and the strength of religious values, in particular, have a strong impact on attitudes toward gender equality, and these cultural attitudes, in turn, influence the supply and demand for women in pursuing elected office. This is one example of the broad effects of global cultural change that are the theme of this volume.

Why might culture be expected to play an important role in determining gender equality in Arab states? A leitmotif in Ronald Inglehart's theory of societal modernization is the argument that human development has transformed gender ideologies, including societally constructed beliefs, attitudes, and values toward the roles of women and men in many postindustrial societies worldwide, whereas traditional cultural values and more rigid sex roles continue to prevail among both men *and* women in many developing nations. These core themes were first developed by Inglehart in a series of publications (Inglehart 1990, 1997) before being unpacked fully in *Rising Tide* (Inglehart and Norris 2003). Inglehart theorizes that human development fuels more egalitarian attitudes toward gendered roles in virtually any society, although the exact pace of change in each is mediated by the enduring impact of religious legacies, historical traditions, and institutional structures within each country. This development is seen as a core component of a broader process of cultural change toward "self-expression" values (Inglehart 1997; Inglehart and Baker 2000; Welzel, Inglehart, and Klingemann 2003; Inglehart and Welzel 2005). Parallel patterns of cultural transformation have been observed concerning the closely related syndrome of attitudes toward sexual morality, marriage, and the family, including greater tolerance of liberal sexual mores, homosexuality, and divorce within postindustrial societies. Theories of value change emphasize that fixed identities determined from birth (see Chapter 2), including those based on the biological characteristics of sex, give way increasingly to more flexible identities of choice, including less conformity to the strict demarcation of gendered roles for women *and* men. Moreover, within societies, Inglehart has long predicted that the most affluent and secure sectors of the population, and the process of generational replacement, will also encourage more egalitarian gender ideologies. These cultural shifts are intrinsically important for understanding the values and beliefs underpinning human behavior. But they are also expected to have significant consequences as one of the key drivers for political change.

Figure 10.1b illustrates the analytical model developed in a series of studies of cultural change (Inglehart and Norris 2003; Norris and Inglehart 2003, 2004). This suggests that long-standing religious traditions and levels of human development in each society have a deep and enduring impact on contemporary social values and moral attitudes, including support for gender equality in politics, as well as shaping broader attitudes toward sexual liberalization. In turn, Inglehart and Norris (2003) suggest that the diffusion of more egalitarian attitudes in society facilitates the recruitment of more women to elected and appointed office, both by encouraging more women to come forward to pursue political careers (on the supply side) and by shaping the attitudes of gatekeeping elites and, ultimately, the broader electorate (on the demand side) (Norris and Lovenduski 1995; Alexander and Welzel 2011a, 2011b). In highly traditional cultures, women will not be regarded as suitable candidates by party leaders and elites, and even if selected, women candidates will face a hostile climate. In the most severe cases, they may even encounter intimidation, threats, and outright violence restricting the rights of women candidates and their supporters to campaign freely.[3] Culture does not act alone; the process of pursuing elected office is also conditioned by the institutional context, set by the electoral system and the use of positive action strategies (Norris 2004). In particular, to explain the lack of female representation in the Arab states, the model suggests that any explanation needs to take account of a substantial gulf separating the more conservative and traditional attitudes toward the role of women in the public sphere that are commonly found in many Muslim-majority societies and the more egalitarian values that are far more pervasive among Western nations (Norris and Inglehart 2004).

MULTILEVEL MODELS TESTING THE ROLE OF CULTURAL VALUES AND STRUCTURAL RESOURCES

So does women's labor force participation and petroleum production matter for women in elected office in the MENA region – or are enduring religious cultural traditions at the heart of any gender gap in oil-rich states? To compare these alternative factors, and to reexamine and update the evidence, this chapter examines data drawn from the WVS (see Chapter 1). In the first step, following the logic of the Norris and Inglehart (2003) thesis, this study first compares the relative impact of religious traditions and oil rents on attitudes toward gender equality. In the second step, it then examines the relative influence of egalitarian cultures and oil rents on the election of women to office.

Before proceeding, however, the empirical evidence to examine the structural argument needs to be considered. Several concerns about the evidence Ross used can be highlighted, including problems surrounding the selection of cases, problems of poorly specified econometric models with missing controls, and the lack of any analysis of direct evidence concerning cultural values.

Case Selection

First, a number of doubts arise from the case study evidence Ross used. As Charrad (2009) points out, the choice of illustrative case studies is inevitably

---

[3] See, e.g., Human Rights Watch, "Afghanistan: Unchecked Violence Threatens Election," September 8, 2010, http://www.hrw.org/en/news/2010/09/09/afghanistan-unchecked-violence-threatens-election.

somewhat selective, and the comparison of different paired countries, such as contrasts between Morocco and Tunisia, could generate alternative interpretations. If the resource curse is defined more broadly than oil and gas production – as it should be – then the comparison would have to account for cases such as South Africa, an economy founded on gold and diamonds – and yet one where women have always made their voices felt effectively, through engagement in the antiapartheid struggles as well as through currently representing more 43.5 percent of all members of parliament. Alternatively, it might have been more persuasive to select cases from non-Muslim petroleum and gas-rich states outside of the Middle East, such as Venezuela or Russia, although both these societies fail to provide a good fit for the thesis, and energy-rich Norway and Canada (and Scotland?) are obviously even more extreme outliers. Moreover, the descriptive data presented by Ross suggest that any statistical relationship between oil rents and the economic and political status of women in the Middle East may be due primarily to a few outliers, namely, Qatar, Kuwait, and the United Arab Emirates (and, to a lesser extent, Saudi Arabia). Once these countries are excluded, there appears to be almost no linear relationship between oil rents per capita and any of the dependent variables in the descriptive scatterplots, including female participation in the nonagricultural labor force, the year of female suffrage, the proportion of parliamentary seats held by women, and gender rights.

Econometric Models

Moreover, there are also questions about the econometric models Ross used. From an institutional perspective, the controls that Ross incorporates into his models may be misspecified in one important regard. Ross controls for the impact of proportional representation electoral systems with closed lists, but he does not examine the role of different types of affirmative action used for women in elected office. Reserved seats have long been used in Muslim-majority countries, including in Pakistan and Bangladesh (Norris 2007). Research also needs to consider voluntary and legal gender quotas for parliamentary candidates as well as the interaction between the type of electoral system and the quota system (Norris 2004; Dahlerup 2006; International IDEA 2008; Krook 2009). Kang (2009) shows that where quotas are introduced in mineral-rich nations, the effects on women's representation are indeterminate.

Ross theorizes that oil rents per capita should have (1) a direct role in shaping female labor force participation and (2) an additional indirect effect on women's representation in parliament. This suggests that properly specified cross-national regression models should include an interaction effect to monitor the impact of oil rents combined with female labor force participation on women's representation. It is also unclear theoretically why the value of oil production is expected to have any *direct* impact on women's parliamentary representation. Some plausible reasons can be constructed, for example, if the resource curse depresses the process of democratization, and this may thereby limit the expansion of human rights, including women's equality. Similarly, Iversen and Rosenbluth (2008) argue that low levels of female labor force participation contribute to female underrepresentation in democratic states by reinforcing traditional voter attitudes toward women (a demand-side feature) and by constraining the supply of women with professional experience and resources who are capable of mounting credible electoral campaigns. Whatever the precise underlying reason, the linkages in the structural argument remain underdeveloped.

In terms of measures, the use of oil rents per capita as an indicator of the resource curse is also open to challenge. Ideally, a broader measure of nonrenewable natural resources would capture the underlying logic of the core argument more precisely; if the oil and gas extraction industries are overwhelmingly male dominated, then so too is the workforce mining gold, diamonds, and copper. Because the extraction and distribution of natural commodities forms a critical part of the economy in many diverse regions of the world, a measure that reflects a more comprehensive basket of resources would help to disentangle the complex effects of Muslim religious faith and oil. Moreover, the theoretical link between the value of oil rents per capita and the structure of the labor market may also prove tenuous. In some cases, such as Trinidad and Tobago, energy production generates about 40 percent of gross domestic product (GDP) and 80 percent of exports but only 5 percent of employment. It is also worth noting that even in economies heavily dependent on oil production for revenue, this does not mean that manual work directly in this industry engages the largest sector of the workforce by any means. For example, the petroleum industry in Saudi Arabia accounts for roughly 80 percent of budget revenues, 45 percent of GDP, and 90 percent of export earnings, but nevertheless almost three-quarters of the Saudi workforce is employed in the service sector. Rather than oil revenues per capita, a stricter test of the structural claim would therefore be to examine the relationship between the proportion of the labor force employed by this sector of the economy and the representation of women in elected office. Ross's measure of oil rents per capita also generates some counterintuitive patterns compared with our popular image of oil-rich states. In 2006, for example, oil rents per capita are twice as high in Trinidad and Tobago as in Saudi Arabia. The socially egalitarian welfare states of Norway and Canada also have particularly high oil rents per capita, by this measure, more so than Venezuela, Russia, Iraq, Iran, and Nigeria. This clearly suggests the need for considerable caution in generalizing about patterns of gender equality worldwide from our cultural stereotypes about oil-rich states.

Direct Evidence for Cultural Values

Leaving aside the measurement controversies for the moment, there is still one major lacuna to the resource curse thesis. Although the structural argument is explicitly framed to reject cultural explanations, Ross does not actually examine any direct survey evidence concerning attitudes and values. Thus, he is unable to test successive rival models that monitor how the public feels about women's and men's roles in the workforce, family, and public life, moral values toward sexuality, or any other direct measures of religiosity or religious identities and beliefs. As a proxy or indirect measure of culture, Ross controls for the proportion of Muslim adherents in each society. This measure (usually based on fairly crude estimates) does not take into account the important variations among Muslim societies in the type of regime, levels of human development, the official role of religion in the state, and important contrasts among types of Muslim faith, such as between Sunni, Shi'a, and Sufi traditions. The comparison of *all* Islamic societies may overlook important variations among them (Moaddel 2007; Rizzo, Abdel-Latif, and Meyer 2007; Steel and Kabashima 2008).

To replicate Ross's study, this chapter includes a measure of oil rents per capita, which Ross argues is the most appropriate indicator of oil and gas production. Paid workforce participation (either full time or part time) is also included. The analysis then adds measures of cultural attitudes toward gender equality, drawing on the WVS and European Values Survey (EVS), pooled across the three waves conducted from 1995 to 2007. The third wave was carried out in fifty-five nations in 1995–1996, the fourth wave was conducted in fifty-nine countries in 1999–2001, and the fifth wave covered fifty-five countries in 2005–2007.[4] The sixth wave (2010–2014) covers more MENA countries than ever before, but it was not available at the time of writing and thus not included in this analysis. Most important, the survey includes systematic data on public opinion in twenty diverse Islamic states containing Muslim-plurality populations, providing the broadest global comparison available from any existing representative social survey. Societies in the WVS are classified by their predominant religion, based on estimates of the religious population contained in the CIA's *World Factbook*. *Islamic* nations are defined as those where the Muslim population is the plurality (although societies may, and often do, also contain substantial minorities of other faiths). The WVS/EVS includes Arab states, both majority Sunni (such as Jordan, Algeria, Morocco, and Egypt) and majority Shi'a (such as Iran and Iraq), as well as Asian countries (Azerbaijan, Kyrgyzstan, Pakistan, Bangladesh, Malaysia), Central European countries (Bosnia Herzegovina, Albania), and countries in sub-Saharan Africa (Mali, Nigeria, Burkina Faso). The WVS also surveyed states that have adopted Islam as the foundation of political institutions (such as Saudi Arabia and Pakistan), societies where Islam is the official or established state religion (including Egypt, Bangladesh, and Malaysia), and secular states where the constitution is neutral toward religion (such as Turkey, Azerbaijan, and Indonesia). The WVS surveys contain eight of the ten most populous Muslim nations around the globe,

---

[4] Full methodological details about the World Values Survey are at http://www.worldvalues.org. Also see discussion in Chapter 1.

including the top three in size, Indonesia, Pakistan, and Bangladesh, and societies with all levels of economic and human development. For instance, income levels range from middle-level Muslim countries such as Malaysia, Turkey, and Saudi Arabia to poorer Muslim societies such as Bangladesh, Mali, and Burkina Faso, with per capita annual incomes of $500 or less. In terms of regimes, Saudi Arabia is an absolute monarchy, which Freedom House classifies as one of the world's most restrictive states in respect for civil liberties and political rights, but the WVS also monitored public opinion in the democratic states of Mali, Indonesia, and Turkey.[5]

Several items in the WVS/EVS survey monitor cultural values toward gender and sexuality, and their dimensions were examined using principal component factor analysis with varimax rotation. The results suggest that the three items monitoring tolerance of homosexuality, abortion, and divorce formed one consistent dimension, representing positive orientations toward issues of sexual liberalization. The other three items concerning gender equality tapped into approval of traditional or egalitarian roles for men and women in the workforce, elected office and university education, forming another consistent scale (Inglehart and Norris 2003; also see Alexander and Welzel 2011a). For ease of comparison, these two dimensions were each summed and standardized into 100-point scales with the full details listed in the chapter's appendix. Survey data pooled across the third to fifth waves of the WVS from 1995 to 2005 maximized cross-national coverage and the diversity of societies under comparison. Using this process, the gender equality scale was available for eighty-five societies and the liberal sexual morality scale for ninety-five societies worldwide.

WHAT EXPLAINS CULTURAL VALUES TOWARD GENDER
EQUALITY: RELIGION OR OIL?

The first step in the analysis tests the relative importance of religious traditions or oil rents on support for either traditional or liberal values toward gender equality and sexual liberalization. On the basis of cultural theories (Norris and Inglehart 2004), this study predicts that religious traditions will play a central role in shaping attitudes at two levels. In particular, this study predicts that (Hypothesis 1) *individual Muslim religious identities will strengthen traditional values toward gender equality and sexual liberalization.* For the same reasons, it is expected that (Hypothesis 2) *the strength of individual religiosity will also bolster traditional values.* The strength of religiosity is measured by the importance of religion, a question closely associated with religious practices and behavior (Norris and Inglehart 2004). It is also predicted that there will be

---

[5] These regimes are classified according to the Freedom House assessments of political rights and civil liberties, *Freedom in the World*, http://www.freedomhouse.org.

a more diffuse cultural effect, so that (Hypothesis 3) *living in Islamic societies will also strengthen traditional values*. In this regard, individuals who do not subscribe to the Muslim religious identity or faith, such as Christians in Iraq or Hindus living in Pakistan, may still be influenced by the predominant norms and moral attitudes within their communities. To compare cultural explanations against the resource curse thesis, this study also tests the rival prediction (Hypothesis 4) that *societies with high oil rents will display more traditional values*. The use of the two alternative indicators of cultural attitudes – toward gender equality and sexual liberalization – provides an important cross-check on the robustness and reliability of the results.

The key models involve measurement at two distinct levels. A representative sample of individual respondents (level 1) is nested within national-level contexts (level 2). Hierarchical linear models, in particular multilevel regression analysis, is the most appropriate technique for comparing the impact of societal-level and individual-level factors simultaneously. The models use restricted maximum likelihood techniques (REML) to estimate direct and cross-level effects for hierarchical data. Individual respondents are thus grouped into countries. Each country has a different set of parameters for the random factors, allowing intercepts and slopes to vary by nation (Raudenbush and Bryk 2002; Gelman and Hill 2007; Bickel 2007).[6]

Level 1 in the core models includes *individual-level* Muslim religious identities, the strength of religiosity, and several other standard controls, described in the appendix, including male gender (0/1), household income using a 10-point scale, age (in years), an education scale, marital status, and labor force participation. Level 2 includes *national-level* variables, including the classification of Islamic or non-Islamic societies, based on the plurality faith in each country's population. In addition, we control for the regional location, classified as in the Middle East or elsewhere in the world, to test whether global areas differ.

---

[6] As is customary in hierarchical linear models, all independent variables were centered by subtracting the grand mean (which becomes zero). The standardized independent variables all have a standard deviation of 1.0. This process also helps to guard against problems of collinearity in the independent variables in the ordinary least squares (OLS) models. The independent variables were treated as fixed components, reflecting the weighted average for the slope across all groups, whereas nation was treated as a random component, capturing the country variability in the slope. The strengths of the beta coefficients (slopes) can be interpreted intuitively as how much change in the dependent variable is generated by a 1 percent change in each independent variable. The multilevel regression models used in this study usually generate small differences in the size of the slope coefficient (b) compared with the results of OLS models, but the average standard errors for level 2 variables tend to be slightly larger. The process is thus more rigorous and conservative than OLS, avoiding Type I errors (false positives, concluding that a statistically significant difference exists when, in truth, there is no statistical difference). In the REML model, by contrast, Schwarz's Bayesian criterion (BIC) is used, where the model with the lower value is the best fitting.

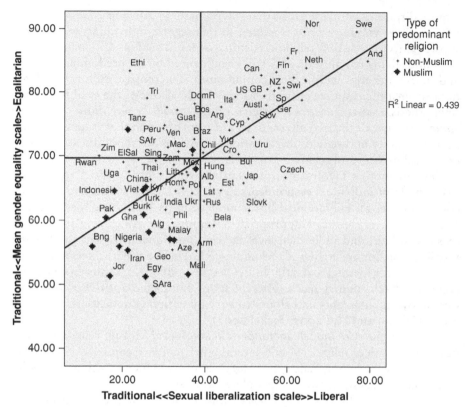

FIGURE 10.2. Sexual liberalization and gender equality values by type of society.
Note: For the two 100-point value scales, see the appendix.
Source: Pooled World Values Survey 1995–2007.

This study also models the effects of oil rents per capita to test the alternative resource curse thesis.

If we first examine the descriptive statistics, Figure 10.2 illustrates the mean opinions of Islamic and Western societies on the gender equality and the sexual liberalization scales, without any controls. The scatterplot shows the strong clustering of societies on these two dimensions, with the Islamic societies concentrated in the bottom left quadrant, displaying the most traditional attitudes. Saudi Arabia, Jordan, and Egypt prove the most conservative on these items, but other predominately Muslim states from Asia and Africa are closely located. By contrast, the affluent postindustrial Western societies are all clustered in the top right quadrant, led by Sweden, representing the most egalitarian and liberal values.

Attitudes among oil-rich and oil-poor economies can also be seen by dichotomizing oil rents per capita as above/below the mean as well as by comparing countries with predominant Islamic or non-Islamic religious traditions. The mean support for gender equality and the sexual liberalization scales can be compared across societies without any controls. The results confirm that the most traditional attitudes toward gender equality values are found in the oil-rich Islamic states. But does an oil economy or religious culture matter most in this regard? Mean support for gender equality varied sharply among the Muslim and non-Muslim oil-rich states, generating a 25-point gap between these groups; this suggests that without any controls, the type of faith is more important than natural resources per se. A smaller 10-point gap in support for gender equality can be observed among Muslim and non-Muslim societies without substantial oil rents, and this gap pointed in the expected direction. To check whether these patterns are due to the selection of the particular questions used in constructing the gender equality scale or whether the results are robust, similar comparisons can examine the sexual liberalization scale. The results provide even stronger indications that the type of oil-rich or -poor society makes no difference to these moral attitudes; by contrast, people living in Muslim and non-Muslim religious cultures expressed sharply contrasting sexual values.

Obviously many other factors could be driving these differences beyond religious culture, such as levels of economic development. Table 10.1 presents the results of the multilevel regression models predicting cultural values, including individual and societal-level predictors and control variables. The models explaining attitudes toward both gender equality and liberal sexual morality show strikingly consistent relationships across nearly all variables, lending confidence to the robustness of the results. The most important findings are the relative strength of the key predictor variables: individual Muslim identities, living in an Islamic society, and the strength of religiosity were all significantly associated with more traditional gender attitudes. The coefficient for oil rents per capita is also significant across both models, *but in a positive, not negative, direction*, contrary to the oil resource thesis. Labor force participation is significantly associated with more liberal attitudes, however. Most importantly, among all the predictor variables, the coefficients demonstrate that living in a predominately Muslim society is the strongest factor of support for traditional gender equality attitudes. The diffuse impact of a society's religious traditions on attitudes toward women thus appears more important for gender ideologies than individual religious identities and the strength of religiosity. In other words, what seems to matter is where you live more than your type of faith or your adherence to religious practices. By contrast, sexual liberalization attitudes are influenced more by the strength of adhering to religious values, irrespective of the particular type of faith-based society.

Although oil is not driving the key relationships, the other structural variables associated with human development do matter, as expected by theories of how culture responds to societal modernization. The remaining controls mostly behaved as expected, with support for gender equality and sexual liberalization stronger among the younger generation, women, the more affluent,

TABLE 10.1. *Multilevel Model Predicting Cultural Values*

Predictor Variables	Gender Equality	Liberal Sexual Morality
Muslim religious identity	−0.45***	−0.67***
	(0.064)	(0.083)
Islamic society	−5.51**	−2.79*
	(2.51)	(2.89)
Strength of religiosity	−0.86***	−5.70***
	(0.090)	(0.060)
Oil rents per capita	0.620***	1.80***
	(1.13)	(0.098)
Individual-Level Controls		
Age (years)	−0.95***	−2.17***
	(0.041)	(0.084)
Gender (male = 1)	−3.47***	−1.52***
	(0.067)	(0.047)
Household income 10-point scale	1.03***	1.21***
	(0.044)	(0.050)
Education 9-point scale	2.79***	2.65***
	(0.046)	(0.054)
Labor force participation	0.53***	0.98***
	(0.043)	(0.050)
Marital status	−0.58**	−1.03***
	(0.042)	(0.048)
National-Level Controls		
Middle East	−3.10**	0.155
	(1.13)	(1.33)
Logged GDP per capita	2.74***	7.01***
	(0.828)	(0.920)
Constant (intercept)	70.5	40.2
Schwartz BIC	139,093	170,834
No. respondents	165,322	192,999
No. nations	75	83

Note: All independent variables were standardized using mean centering (z-scores). Models present the results of the REML multilevel regression models including the unstandardized beta coefficient (standard error in parentheses) and the significance. The dependent variables are constructed from the items listed in the appendix.
***$p > 0.000$. **$p = 0.01$. *$p > 0.05$.
Source: Pooled World Values Survey 1995–2007.

the better educated, those in paid employment, and the unmarried. More affluent nations are also more liberal, as expected by modernization theories. Once all these factors were entered into the models, the MENA region is a significant negative predictor of attitudes toward gender equality but not sexual liberalization. Overall, the models indicate that the predominant or diffuse religious traditions in Muslim societies, Muslim identities, and the strength of religiosity provide strong predictors of traditional attitudes toward gender roles – as well as shaping lower tolerance of homosexuality, divorce, and abortion. Other general structural indicators of human development therefore also affect gender equality attitudes, as expected. By contrast, there appears to be no support for the thesis that oil-dependent economies are associated directly with more traditional cultural attitudes toward women and sexual morality.

WHAT EXPLAINS WOMEN'S REPRESENTATION IN PARLIAMENT: CULTURAL VALUES OR OIL?

A second step in this study compares the societal-level impact of religious cultures, egalitarian cultural values, human development, and oil rents on women's representation in national parliaments and in ministerial offices. For each WVS/EVS nation, we measured the percentage of women in the national parliament and in the cabinet of the national government (see the appendix).

We can start by comparing how particular countries are distributed using the scattergrams presented in Figure 10.3. The top graph displays the cross-national relationship between the mean support for egalitarian cultural attitudes and the proportion of women members in the lower house of parliament. Societies are also classified as either in the Islamic or non-Islamic religious tradition. The results further confirm the significant positive correlation between egalitarian attitudes and women's election, as noted in 2000 (Inglehart and Norris 2003). This pattern is stronger in the non-Islamic societies ($R^2 = 0.177$) but also exists to differentiate more or less traditional Islamic cultures ($R^2 = 0.108$). The correlation is not particularly strong, not surprisingly, as many other institutional conditions also influence men's and women's access to elected office, not least the type of electoral system and any affirmative action measures used in the recruitment process (Norris 2004; Krook 2009). In some cases, such as Rwanda, the proportion of women in office is ahead of public opinion (which can be explained institutionally by the implementation of top-down measures such as gender quotas). In a few other cases, such as the United States and France, this pattern is reversed, suggesting that public opinion is less of a potential barrier to women seeking elected office than practical obstacles such as the need to gain party endorsements or to raise sufficient campaign resources. Nevertheless, this evidence suggests that the predominant religious tradition in any society also matters by influencing the supply and demand for female recruitment.

To consider again the rival structural account, the bottom graph in Figure 10.3 compares women in elected office against the logged distribution of natural resources (oil rents per capita). There appears to be no significant correlation, and countries are widely scattered across the graph. Women are elected

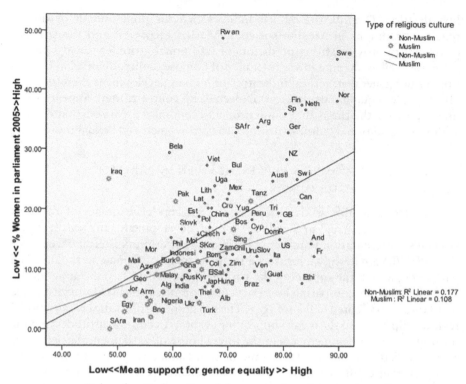

FIGURE 10.3. Cultural attitudes, oil, and the proportion of women in parliament, 2005. *Note:* The proportion of women in the lower house of parliament (2005) is derived from the Inter-Parliamentary Union, http://www.IPU.org. See the appendix for the other measures.

in relatively substantial numbers in societies as diverse as Iraq, Canada, and Trinidad and Tobago (as well as Norway), despite relatively high oil rents per capita. Among the oil-poor nations, few women enter elected office in Jordan and Armenia, while they perform remarkably well in Sweden and Finland. Indeed, the overall story is summarized by the tight clustering of Scandinavian countries in the top graph in Figure 10.3 (with a shared egalitarian culture that favors equal opportunities for women), compared with the wide dispersion of oil-poor Sweden and oil-rich Norway on the bottom graph.

To examine the more comprehensive multivariate evidence, Table 10.2 examines seventy-five societies using regression models predicting the proportion of women in the lower house of parliament by cultural values (the gender equality scale). The models control for several structural conditions commonly thought to influence gender equality in elected office, namely, natural resources (logged oil rents per capita, the Ross thesis) and the level of liberal democracy (the Freedom House scale), economic development (logged

TABLE 10.2. *Regression Model Predicting Women's Representation in Elected Office*

Cultural Attitudes	% Women in the Lower House		
	B	SE	β
Gender equality index	0.426***	(0.094)	0.644
Structural Conditions			
Islamic society	−1.26	(2.99)	−0.053
Oil rents per capita	0.000	(0.002)	−0.018
Middle East	−1.58	(4.29)	−0.044
Economic development	0.000	(0.000)	0.022
Institutional Context			
PR electoral system	−0.751	1.85	−0.039
Any legal gender quotas	0.001	(0.000)	0.002
Constant (intercept)	−5.67		
Adjusted R^2	0.423		
No. nations	75		

Note: Models present the results of the ordinary least squares regression models at a national level, including the beta coefficient, the standard error, the standardized beta, and the significance. For details of all variables, see the appendix.

***$p > 0.000$. **$p = 0.01$. *$p > 0.05$.

per capita GDP), and the type of religious tradition (whether the nation was classified as Muslim-predominant). Models also control for the institutional context set by proportional representation electoral systems and the use of constitutional or legal gender quotas for elected office.

The analysis shows that out of all these factors, gender equality attitudes are strongly and significantly related to the proportion of women in the lower house of parliament. By contrast, the coefficients for the other variables usually point in the expected direction but none prove statistically significant. Overall, the model explains 42 percent of the variance in women's representation in elected office around the globe.

CONCLUSIONS

Does petroleum perpetuate patriarchy? Any observers looking at the limited rights that women face in some of the major oil-rich states, such as Saudi Arabia, Qatar, and the United Arab Emirates, might be tempted to believe that there could be a strong linkage. Yet general oil-based accounts of gender inequality suffer from several major flaws, and the petroleum patriarchy thesis, in particular, does not stand up to scrutiny against the evidence presented here.

Like others in this volume, this chapter considered the impact of cultural factors on gender issues. On the basis of our findings, it seems more plausible to conclude that long-standing religious traditions and broader processes of human development generate an enduring mark on the gendered norms and beliefs, the attitudes and values, that characterize different societies. These cultural values leave a deep imprint on the way that men *and* women see the most appropriate division of labor for men and women in the home, family, and public sphere – including the contemporary role of women in elected office. Thus Buddhist and Confucian, Catholic and Protestant, Hindu and Muslim societies each display certain distinctive ideas about gender and sexuality – and these values continue to leave an imprint on the lives of women and men, even when postindustrial societies become more secular in orientation (Norris and Inglehart 2004). For example, active engagement in Protestantism has gradually dwindled and died out in Scandinavian countries, including involvement in religious services and church organizations as well as adherence to the importance of religion in people's lives. Nevertheless, the legacy of Protestant traditions continues to be evident in the DNA of contemporary Scandinavian values.

The imprint of predominant religious traditions thus influences many cultural values, including attitudes about whether women should play a leadership role in public life. In turn, as illustrated in Figure 10.1, these attitudes can facilitate or hinder the recruitment of women into elected and appointed office. Cultural barriers are not fixed in stone; there is a wealth of evidence that values toward gender equality can and do gradually change on a generational basis (Brooks and Bolzendahl 2003), reflecting long-term processes of societal modernization and human development. In the short term, as well, cultural barriers to women's equality can be overcome by the effective implementation of well-designed institutional reforms, as exemplified most dramatically by the election of women through the use of reserved seats in Afghanistan and of candidate gender quotas in Algeria and Iraq. Through these fast-track mechanisms, where parliaments are effective, women can have a voice in the future of their countries. Therefore the extensive body of research literature presents a wealth of evidence that the resource curse can probably be blamed for a multitude of ills, from conflict and civil war to anemic economic growth, corruption, state capture, and autocracy. But the resource curse – at least petroleum – does not appear to be a major factor at the heart of the problems facing the continuing gender disparities in elected office among Arab states.

APPENDIX: CONCEPTS AND MEASURES

Variable	Definitions, Coding, and Sources
Per capita GDP	Measured in constant international $ in PPP. Various years. *Source:* The World Bank World Development Indicators
Type of religion	V184: *"Do you belong to a religious denomination? [IF YES] Which one?"* Coded: No, not a member; Roman Catholic; Protestant; Orthodox (Russian/Greek/etc.); Jewish; Muslim; Hindu; Buddhist; Other. *Source:* World Values Survey
Type of predominant religion in each society	The classification of the major religion (adhered to by the plurality groups in the population) in all 193 states around the world is based on the CIA's *World Factbook, 2009.* *Source:* http://www.cia.gov/cia/publications/factbook
Islamic societies	Based on the societies with Muslim plurality populations, based on the above source, as listed in Table 10.1. It should be noted that throughout the chapter, the term *Islamic* is used to refer to Muslim-plurality societies, and it is not used to describe the official religion or policies of the state, or the relation between religious and political authorities. *Muslim* refers to individuals who identify with the Muslim faith.
Gender equality scale	The combined 100-point gender equality scale is based on the following three items: MENPOL Q118: *"On the whole, men make better political leaders than women do."* (Agree coded low); MENJOBS Q78: *"When jobs are scarce, men should have more right to a job than women."* (Agree coded low); BOYEDUC Q.119: *"A university education is more important for a boy than a girl."* (Agree coded low). These items were added and standardized to create a 100-point scale. *Source:* World Values Survey 1995–2007
Sexual liberalization value scale	*"Please tell me for each of the following statements whether you think it can always be justified (10), never justified (1), or somewhere in-between, using this card ... Abortion, Homosexuality, Divorce."* These items were added and standardized to create a 100-point scale. *Source:* World Values Survey
Occupational class	Coded for the respondent's occupation. *"In which profession/occupation do you, or did you, work?"* The scale is coded into four categories: Professional/manager (1); Other nonmanual (2); Skilled nonmanual (3); Unskilled manual worker (4). *Source:* World Values Survey
Paid work status	V220. *"Are you employed now or not?"* Coded full-time, part-time, or self-employed (1), other (0). *Source:* World Values Survey
Education	V217. *"What is the highest educational level that you have ever attained?"* Coded on a 9-point scale from no formal education (1) to university level with degree (9). *Source:* World Values Survey

(continued)

Variable	Definitions, Coding, and Sources
Age	Age coded in continuous years derived from date of birth. *Source:* World Values Survey Age groups: Younger (18–29), middle (30–49), and older (50+)
Religiosity	V192. *"How important is God in your life?"* 10-point scale
Household income	V253. *"On this card is a scale of incomes on which 1 indicates the 'lowest income decile' and 10 the 'highest income decile' in your country. We would like to know in what group your household is. Please, specify the appropriate number, counting all wages, salaries, pensions, and other incomes that come in."* (Code one number). *Source:* World Values Survey
Education scale	V238. *"What is the highest educational level that you have attained?"* [NOTE: *if respondent indicates to be a student, code highest level he or she expects to complete*]: (1) No formal education; (2) Incomplete primary school; (3) Complete primary school; (4) Incomplete secondary school: technical/vocational type; (5) Complete secondary school: technical/vocational type; (6) Incomplete secondary: university-preparatory type; (7) Complete secondary: university-preparatory type; (8) Some university-level education, without degree; (9)University-level education, with degree. *Source:* World Values Survey
% Women in parliament	Proportion of women in the lower house of the national parliament, latest election 2005. *Source:* Inter-Parliamentary Union
% Women ministers	Proportion of women ministers in the national cabinet, 2005. *Source:* Inter-Parliamentary Union
Proportional electoral system	PR electoral system (1) or not (0); *Source:* Norris *Electoral Engineering*
Legal gender quota	Any type of legal gender quota employed for elected office, at whatever target level. *Source:* http://www.quotasproject.org
Oil rents per capita	Oil and gas rents per capita, measured by the total value of production minus the extraction costs, normalized by the country's population. The data relate to the year closest to the WVS survey wave. *Source:* Ross (2008)
Oil rent categories	"Low" and "high" oil rent societies are classified for the countries contained in the WVS by dichotomizing the value of oil rents per capita (see earlier) around the mean.

Note: Full details of the World Values Survey codebooks and questionnaires can be found at http://www.worldvaluessurvey.com.

11

Allegiance Eroding

People's Dwindling Willingness to Fight in Wars[1]

Bi Puranen

Among the conditions that allow political authorities to demand people's allegiance, existential insecurity is crucial. Under existential insecurity, authorities can appeal to threat perceptions and nurture a protective mentality that is easily turned against out-groups, legitimizing discrimination and even prompting genocide in the most extreme case (Gat 2013). Protective mentalities tend to breed national, ethnic, religious, and other divisive identities that make the in-group exclusive. Under existential pressures, divisive identities can absorb people so entirely that they are willing to sacrifice almost everything for their own group's sake, including their freedoms and even their lives. The stronger an exclusionary group identity grows, the more self-sacrifice the authorities can demand from the individuals. All these patterns are well known from "group-threat theory" (Coenders, Lubbers, and Scheepers 2008).

Against this background, we argue that an obvious – yet understudied – indication of self-sacrificial dispositions in a society is the percentage of people who say that they are willing to risk their lives for their own country in the case of war (Díez-Nicolás 2009; Puranen 2008c, 2009a, 2009b). We also argue that these self-sacrificial dispositions are a core ingredient of an allegiant political culture. Vice versa, a decline in people's willingness to sacrifice their lives for their country indicates the erosion of allegiance. More than that, we suggest that diminishing willingness to sacrifice human lives in war is a consequence of the rising emancipatory spirit of an assertive political culture.

[1] The analyses in this chapter have been conducted in cooperation with Christian Welzel. This chapter refers extensively to my joint article with him and Ronald Inglehart on the same topic (Inglehart, Puranen, and Welzel 2014). I am very grateful to Juan Díez valuable contributions to earlier versions of this chapter. I also acknowledge Ronald Inglehart's restless efforts on developing the theme of this chapter.

These propositions are informed by a lineage of theories on the changing nature of human lives, originating in the theory of postmaterialism in Inglehart's (1977) *Silent Revolution* and culminating in the general theory of emancipation in Welzel's (2013) *Freedom Rising*. According to these theories, various existential improvements – from better material conditions to longer life expectancies to broader education and information – turn the lives of increasing population segments from a source of threats to suffer into a source of opportunities to thrive. Envisioning longer and more promising lives, people become less willing to sacrifice life. Instead, they increasingly insist on actually living it, and living it the way that they *themselves* prefer and agree. This tectonic cultural shift is visible in rising "emancipative values": an emerging emphasis on universal freedoms – freedoms people need to be able to take advantage of the multiple opportunities offered by a more promising life. Hence, we suggest that rising emancipative values bring a dwindling willingness to risk lives in war among publics around the world. Possibly, this cultural shift pinpoints some of the deeper reasons underlying the general decline of interhuman violence that Pinker (2012) documents in *The Better Angels of Our Nature*.

To demonstrate this proposition, this chapter proceeds in four sections. The first section reviews the theories informing our proposition. The second section introduces our data, methods, and measurements. The third section reports the findings of the analyses, beginning with an explanation of country-level differences in willingness to fight. This is followed by an explanation of the temporal decline in this willingness and ends with a multilevel model to illuminate the micro-foundation of the aggregate-level patterns. We finish with a conclusion.

THEORY AND HYPOTHESES

"When are people willing to risk their lives for their own country in the case of war?" Or alternatively, "What are the conditions that erode this willingness and make people insist on retaining their freedoms and actually living their lives instead of risking them?" Inglehart's (1977, 1990) theory of postmaterialism and its further development into Welzel's (2013) general theory of emancipation provides plausible and testable answers to these questions.

The basic line of thought in this theoretical tradition assumes a *utility ladder of freedoms* on which societies climb as life improves. Indeed, fundamental improvements – from better material conditions to longer life expectancies to broader education and information – transform the lives of increasing population segments from a source of threats to suffer into a source of opportunities to thrive. Where this happens, universal freedoms gain utility because practicing and tolerating freedoms becomes instrumental to taking advantage of the opportunities that a safer, longer, and more promising life offers. Thus, as societies transit from pressing to permissive existential conditions, they ascend the utility ladder of freedoms. Because evolution has shaped humans as perceptive beings who communicate their life perceptions, collective awareness emerges that universal freedoms are indeed mutually beneficial. Consequently, people begin to share an emphasis on universal freedoms, which is evident in the rise of postmaterialism and emancipative values (the latter encompass the former, as we see in the data and methods section).

Accompanying this value change, people's readiness to sacrifice their lives gives way to an increasing insistence on actually living it. This, too, is a utility-driven preference change: Sacrificing lives that people have more and more reason to consider worth living becomes an intolerable waste of promise. Consequently, the willingness to fight for one's country in the case of war dwindles on a mass scale. In line with this proposition, Inglehart (1990, 413–14) was the first author to show that postmaterialists are less willing to fight than materialists.

Rising emancipative values and the parallel erosion of willingness to fight are self-reinforcing processes. They are driven by what Welzel (2013, 108–11) calls "social cross-fertilization." The reason is that the universal freedoms on which emancipative values focus are a *reciprocal* good: Universal freedoms always also include the freedoms of the *other*, which you are more likely to recognize if you can expect that the other reciprocates the favor and recognizes your freedoms too. Thus, emancipative values flourish through mutual recognition, making it increasingly easy to embrace them the more other people have already done so. By the same token, the supposed consequences of emancipative values – including the dwindling willingness of people to risk human lives in war – become ever more powerfully evident the more widespread emancipative values have grown.

These general propositions can be boiled down to three concrete and testable hypotheses, as outlined by Inglehart, Puranen and Welzel (2014):

1. In a *cross section*, people's willingness to fight in war is lower in countries with stronger emancipative values.
2. *Longitudinally*, countries in which emancipative values grew more experienced a larger decline in people's willingness to fight in war.
3. In a *multilevel perspective*, individuals are less willing to fight in war when emancipative values are widely shared in their society; whether the individuals emphasize these values more than others in their society is less relevant.

METHODS, DATA, AND MEASUREMENTS

To demonstrate that these hypotheses are accurate, we refer to our own findings and those reported in Inglehart, Puranen and Welzel (2014). Both sets of findings are based on data from the WVS/EVS, which have been conducted in five rounds (a sixth currently under completion), covering random national samples of an average size of twelve hundred respondents in almost a hundred

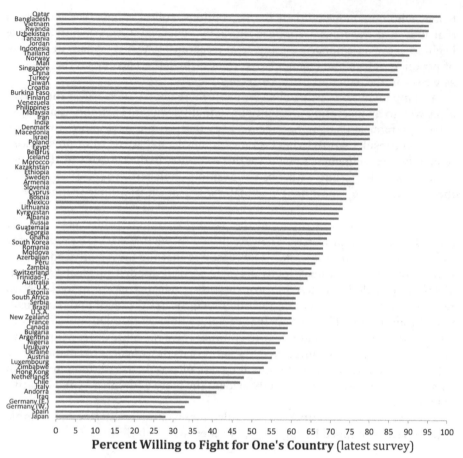

Percent Willing to Fight for One's Country (latest survey)

FIGURE 11.1. Percentage of national publics willing to fight for their countries (latest available survey).
Source: World Values Survey and European Values Study.

societies around the globe.[2] These societies include the countries with the largest populations and biggest economies from each world region, representing almost 90 percent of the world population (see Figure 11.1 for a list of nations).[3]

We report findings in three steps from three different angles in the order of the previously mentioned hypotheses. In the first step, we apply a cross-sectional country-level perspective: We examine the fraction of people willing

---

[2] For descriptive statistics, we include evidence from the incomplete sixth round of the WVS. The analytical results, however, are only based on pre–sixth wave rounds because only these have sufficient statistical leverage for multivariate analyses.

[3] Information about the questionnaires, fieldwork, and data files is available from the WVS website at http://www.worldvaluessurvey.org.

to fight in war per society. We explain these fractions in multivariate regressions, testing the supposed impact of a society's mean emphasis on emancipative values against explanations looming prominent in the peace and conflict literature (for an overview, see Gat 2013). The control variables include enduring democracy, technological advancement, international cooperation, and a measure of encompassing peace.

In the second step, we report longitudinal findings from Inglehart, Puranen and Welzel (2014), tracking changes over time in people's willingness to fight in war, from the earliest to the latest available survey in each society. The findings explain change in people's willingness to fight in war by change in potential predictors over the same period – selecting those variables that proved important in the cross-sectional analysis. To ensure that the change measures capture a long-term trend, Inglehart, Puranen, and Welzel only examine changes that cover at least fifteen years. This reduces the country sample from some ninety to some forty societies. Despite this limitation in size, this sample is free from a selection bias because it covers the societies with the largest populations and biggest economies in each world region and shows the full range of variation in all involved variables.

Third, we use multilevel models to study the interaction between an individual's emancipative values and the prevalence of these values in the society as a whole.

Our key dependent variable is willingness to fight in war, which the WVS asks in the following way: "Of course, we all hope that there will not be another war, but if it were to come to that, would you be willing to fight for your country?" The response options are "yes" and "no." Respondents who did not answer this question (i.e., 29.7 percent of all respondents who have been asked) are treated as "missing."[4] At the country level, we analyze the fraction of respondents per society who answer that they are willing to fight. At the individual level, we analyze each person's binary response.

Figure 11.1 presents the distribution of willingness to fight across the ninety nations for which we have data from at least one time point. There is dramatic cross-national variation, from less than one-third expressing a willingness to fight in Japan, Spain, and Germany to nearly unanimous support in Qatar, Bangladesh, Vietnam, and Rwanda. These simple distributions already suggest that modernization, democracy, and enduring peace all contribute to lower

---

[4] One might assume that social desirability in most societies operates in favor of the "pro-fight" answer and respondents who do not want to fight feel embarassed to admit it but also do not want to lie, which leads them to refuse a response. This would justify treating all missing responses as a "no fight" answer. Even though there is no way to be certain that this is a correct treatment, we reran all analyses under this assumption. Another alternative is to use multiple imputations to replace missing values with multiple estimated values, which we also did. Because neither of these alternatives produces different results, we report the findings obtained under the simple assumption that nonresponse is adequately treated as a missing value. Interestingly, nonresponse among women is only two percentage points higher than among men.

levels of willingness to fight. It is our goal to see what rising emancipative values contribute to this same end relative to the other factors.

In the cross-sectional analyses, the country-level variables are measured to tap permissive societal conditions at the beginning of the period over which willingness to fight in war is measured. Taking the latest available measure of willingness to fight in war from each society, the observation period in the cross-sectional analyses spans the years 1995 to 2005. Thus, the societal variables are measured in about 1995.

Data on the societies' structural characteristics are taken from the Quality of Governance Dataset (Quality of Governance Institute 2010). The appendix provides further information on measurement.

A key permissive condition is democracy, and especially enduring democracy, because enduring democracy grants people lasting entitlements. To measure the endurance of democracy, we use Gerring et al.'s (2005) "democracy stock" index. The index measures a society's historically accumulated experience with democracy.[5]

For the longitudinal analysis, it does not make sense to use this indicator because the dramatic improvements that some postauthoritarian societies experienced in their levels of democracy do not show up in a measure of long-term historic experience with democracy. For this reason, the longitudinal analyses documented in Inglehart, Puranen and Welzel (2014) use change in levels of democracy from the earliest to latest point in time, based on Welzel's (2013, 249–77) "citizen rights index." The index combines Freedom House's political rights and civil liberties ratings while downgrading these ratings for uncovered rights violations tapped by data from the Cingranelli/Richards Human Rights Data Project (Freedom House 2012; Cingranelli and Richards 2010).

We suppose that international cooperation facilitates information flows and thus makes it easier for the people of a society to develop a sense of an interconnected world in which other countries have a legitimate place and are not necessarily threatening. Logically, this should reduce willingness to fight other countries in war. To measure international cooperation, we use Dreher, Gaston, and Martens's (2008) index of "political globalization" from the year of the survey. This multipoint index summarizes the number of international treaties a country has signed, the number of peacekeeping operations it has joined, and the number of international organizations of which it is a member.

Technological advancement widens people's opportunities in life in manifold ways – proliferating technologies that make people's lives easier and more entertaining, providing incomes that grant consumer power and increase education, access to information, and life expectancies. To measure

---

[5] The index adds up the scores on the Polity autocracy-democracy index from a given reference year all the way back to the time of the national independence or the first year when the time series starts. As the reference year, we use the year of the survey, as we do with all explanatory variables.

technological advancement, we choose the World Bank's (2005) "Knowledge Index," which uses indicators of a population's mean level of education, access to information technology, and per capita scientific output. These indicators are standardized and summarized into a multipoint index of knowledge development, yielding a multipoint scale with minimum 0 and maximum 10. This is an appropriate indicator of the rise of modern knowledge economies.

The technological advancement index is not available in sufficient time series for the longitudinal analyses. For this reason, Inglehart, Puranen and Welzel (2014) use an alternative multicomponent indicator of development, including per capita gross domestic product (GDP), the mean number of schooling years, tertiary enrollment ratios, life expectancies, the inverse of the fertility rate, and the inverse Gini index. As Welzel (2013) shows, these measures are very strongly correlated, reflecting a single dimension of cross-country variation, which is socioeconomic development. The reliability of the summary index of these six measures is high, showing a Cronbach's alpha of 0.83. Thus, we average these six measures into an encompassing index of socioeconomic development, after having standardized each measure into the same scale range from minimum 0 to maximum 1.0.[6]

An alternative argument attributes the pacifying effects of socioeconomic development to its tendency to increase trade openness. The interdependencies created by trade openness are supposed to increase the costs of war above its benefits. To test this hypothesis, we use Dreher et al.'s (2008) index of economic exchange. It turns out that socioeconomic development is the stronger predictor of people's willingness to fight in war. Because the two measures are collinear, the article only reports results with socioeconomic development instead of economic exchange.

Another indication of secure and permissive societal conditions is encompassing peace. We take the inverse of the "global peace index" from the Vision of Humanity (2008), which uses more than twenty indicators of the incidence of both internal and external violence and conflict in a society.

The independent variable of main interest is emancipative values – an extension of Inglehart's postmaterialist values. Welzel (2013, 66–69) measures these values over twelve items, which group into four distinct components: (1) autonomy orientations measure an emphasis on personal autonomy, (2) equality orientations measure an emphasis on gender equality, (3) voice orientations measure an emphasis on people's voice, and (4) choice orientations measure an emphasis on reproductive freedoms. All four components of emancipative

---

[6] We calculate a weighted average so that each measure flows in with a weight reflecting its representativeness of the common dimension: First, we multiply each measure by its factor loading on the common underlying dimension (0.91 for schooling years, 0.87 for life expectancy, 0.79 for the inversed fertility rate, 0.78 for the tertiary enrollment ratio, 0.73 for the per capita GDP, 0.61 for inversed Gini index), then we add up these weighted scores and, finally, divide the sum by the sum of factor weights (4.69).

values negatively affect people's willingness to fight, but voice orientations and, above all, choice orientations have an even stronger negative effect. For this reason, we focus on these two components of emancipative values rather than the overall measure, paying special attention to choice orientations. As Inglehart, Puranen and Welzel (2014) show, the rise of emancipative values has turned most vigorous particularly with respect to choice orientations.

Choice orientations are based on an item battery that asks whether "homosexuality," "abortion," and "divorce" are justifiable on a scale from 1 (never justifiable) to 10 (always justifiable). The three indicators are one-dimensional on the aggregate level as well as on the individual level. The Cronbach's alpha of the three items is 0.87 at the individual level and more than 0.90 at the aggregate level. We average the respondent scores over the three items and standardize the resulting 30-point index of choice orientations into a range from minimum 0 to maximum 1.0. At the aggregate level, we use the population mean in choice orientations to capture a society's overall emancipatory climate.

Voice orientations are most closely linked to Inglehart's postmaterialist values, focusing on those three postmaterialist items of the original 12-item battery that emphasize the voice of the people. Thus, voice orientations measure people's combined priority for "protecting freedom of speech," "giving people more say in important government decisions," and "giving people more say in how things are done in their jobs and their communities." These priorities are summarized into a 6-point index.

Many of these societal characteristics are strongly interrelated. For example, voice and choice orientations correlate both with each other and with better living conditions: Across eighty countries, voice and choice orientations correlate at $r = 0.60$ with each other. At the same time, voice orientations correlate with material prosperity[7] at $r = 0.58$ and with technological advancement at $r = 0.55$, whereas choice orientations correlate with material prosperity at $r = 0.77$ and with technological advancement at $r = 0.85$ (all significant at $p < 0.001$). Figure 11.2 visualizes the exceptionally strong relationship between technological advancement and choice orientations.

The utility ladder of freedoms suggests a two-step sequence. First, improving living conditions such as those evident in technological advancement reorient cultures toward an emphasis on universal freedoms, which is visible in stronger voice and choice orientations. Second, these orientations then lower people's willingness to sacrifice lives in war. If these assumptions are accurate, any direct effect of technological advancement and other objectively favorable conditions on people's willingness to fight is mediated by these conditions' tendency to strengthen voice and choice orientations. In a multivariate regression, then,

---

[7] Material prosperity is measured as the per capita gross domestic product at the year of the survey in purchasing power parities. Data are taken from the World Bank Development Indicators series (2008).

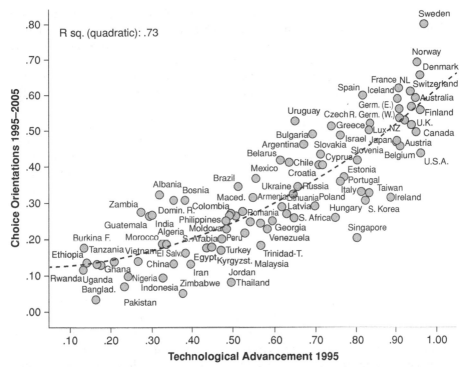

FIGURE 11.2. Relationship between technological advancement and choice orientations. *Source:* World Values Survey and European Values Study (latest survey from each society) and World Bank (Knowledge Index).

the impact of objectively favorable conditions on people's willingness to fight should turn insignificant once we control for voice or choice orientations. The multivariate section will show that this is indeed the case.

Sacrificial dispositions, such as the willingness to fight for one's country in the case of war, require a strong identification with the respective group, in this case, the nation. Thus, Díez-Nicolás (2009) and Puranen (2009a, 2009b) showed that stronger national pride correlates at both the individual and country levels with a stronger willingness to fight. National pride is measured by the question "How proud are you to be [Interviewer: name nationality]? Very proud, quite proud, not very proud, not at all proud?" At the country level, we measure the fraction of people indicating to be very proud of their nationality.

Willingness to fight in war is arguably a protective orientation, which often associates with confidence in the armed forces and preferences for authoritarian leadership (Díez-Nicolás 2009; Puranen 2009a, 2009b). Thus, our multilevel model also tests the impact of confidence in the armed forces and preferences for authoritarian leadership on people's willingness to fight. Confidence in the armed forces is measured on a 4-point index from weaker to stronger confidence. Preferences for authoritarian leadership are measured as the inverse of Klingemann's (1999) 7-point index, which measures the prevalence of democratic over authoritarian regime preferences. Inverted, the index measures the exact opposite: preferences for authoritarian leadership.

As routine demographic controls at the individual level, we include a dummy variable for gender, an indexed version of birth year, and a 9-point index for the level of education.

Most of our measures are multipoint indices, and we have rescaled all of them into a range from minimum 0 to maximum 1.0, with fractions for intermediate positions. This makes unstandardized regression coefficients between different variables directly comparable and easily interpretable, showing how much a shift in the theoretical range of an independent variable contributes to the shift in the theoretical range of the dependent variable.

FINDINGS

Country-Level Patterns

At both the individual level and the country level, all components of emancipative values associate negatively with people's willingness to fight, but this negative link is most pronounced for voice and even more so for choice orientations. For this reason, the subsequent analyses focus on choice orientations.

Inglehart, Puranen and Welzel (2014, Figure 3) show the relationship between choice orientations and willingness to fight across all countries for which these variables are available (using the latest survey from each country). The overall correlation between choice orientations and willingness to fight in war is reasonably strong and points in the predicted direction: In countries with more prevalent choice orientations, people's willingness to fight in wars tends to be lower. As expected, the combination of strong choice orientations with weak willingness to fight is typical of societies with permissive existential conditions: All these societies are materially affluent, technologically advanced, and politically democratic. Conversely, the combination of weak choice orientations with strong willingness to fight in war is typical of societies that are materially less prosperous, technologically less advanced, and politically less, if not entirely, undemocratic. Exceptions from this pattern, with a strong willingness to fight in war despite strong choice orientations, include Israel and Taiwan – two societies whose legitimate existence is questioned by powerful neighbors.

Apart from these country-specific singularities, there are two systematic groups of outlier countries. These two groups represent shared historic experiences that are unique among the countries belonging to them. For this reason, these experiences cannot be measured by a general variable. The only way to capture them is to use dummy variables to represent these two country groups – dummies on which all other countries are coded 0. The first group includes East and West Germany, Italy, and Japan: People in these countries show a much lower willingness to fight in war than even their high level of choice orientations predicts. Most plausibly, this is to be interpreted as the historic lesson from World War II. Compatible with this interpretation, these societies are also known to exhibit some of the lowest national pride levels in the world (Díez-Nicolás 2009).

The second and more unexpected group of outliers are the Nordic countries. Even though the residents of these societies exhibit some of the highest levels of choice orientations, their willingness to fight is not low, as strong choice orientations would otherwise predict. Instead, the Nordic societies' willingness to fight is much higher than one would expect. Perhaps the Nordic populations have traversed a profound transformation in the meaning of fighting for one's country along with a changing role of the military over recent decades. Sweden is the most obvious case in point. In 2000, the Swedish parliament passed a resolution that brought important changes in the role of the Swedish Armed Forces (SAF). The new policy held that "defending a nation has historically been equivalent to protecting its borders. Today, defending a nation can take place far away, through creating peace, stability and prosperity in turbulent parts of the world. In this manner, defending a nation has come to include defending its values, and protecting democracy or human rights" (Puranen 2008a, 2008c, 2009a, 2009b). Accordingly, SAF personnel are now involved in international peacekeeping operations. The other Nordic countries have moved in the same direction, and military service is now considered as a commitment to international aid, democracy promotion, and peacekeeping. Whether this development becomes a model for other countries remains to be seen. For now, it is largely a Nordic phenomenon. In the world as a whole, willingness to fight for one's country still associates with protective mentalities rather than emancipative values.

The outlier groups have many things in common, especially in our main explanatory variables: They are all technologically advanced, have mature democracies, and exhibit relatively high levels of choice orientations – all of which suggests a weak willingness to fight. However, because of unique historic experiences, these two groups pull away from this suggestion, and they do so in opposite directions. Hence, the otherwise clearly inverse link between choice orientations and willingness to fight is partly obscured if we do not recognize these two country groups' historic peculiarities.

If, however, we use dummy variables to control for these two groups' unusually low and high willingness to fight, the determination of this willingness by choice orientations becomes clearer. As Inglehart, Puranen and Welzel (2014, Figure 3) illustrate, when we take into account whether a country is a war loser or a Nordic society, choice orientations account for 53 percent of the cross-national variance in willingness to fight.

Do these results hold after including additional control variables? The multivariate regressions in Table 11.1 test the impact of choice orientations on

TABLE 11.1. *Explaining Willingness to Fight for One's Country (National-Level Regression Analyses)*

Predictors	Dependent Variable: Willingness to Fight				
	Model 1	Model 2	Model 3	Model 4	Model 5
National pride	0.40 (2.06)*	0.12 (0.73)	0.02 (0.11)		
Technological advancement	−0.12 (−1.07)	−0.17 (−1.91)*	−0.04 (−0.40)		
Enduring democracy	−.13 (−1.55)	−0.15 (−2.03)**	−0.08 (−1.12)		
World War II Axis power dummy		−0.29 (−4.30)***	−0.30 (−4.59)***	−0.29 (−5.04)***	−0.30 (−6.07)***
Nordic country dummy		0.23 (3.73)***	0.28 (4.49)***	0.36 (5.87)***	0.30 (6.18)***
Choice orientations			−0.38 (−2.67)**	−0.52 (−6.13)***	−0.64 (−9.02)***
International cooperation				−0.01 (−1.52)	
Encompassing peace				−0.26 (−1.72)*	
Constant	0.53 (2.85)**	0.80 (5.01)***	0.90 (5.70)***	0.99 (14.61)***	0.95 (7.44)***
outliers included?	Yes	Yes	Yes	No	No
Adjusted R^2	0.22	0.47	0.52	0.67	0.66
Number of societies (N)	79	79	78	66	77

Notes: Entries are unstandardized regression coefficients with their *T*-values in parentheses. All variables normalized into a scale range from a theoretical minimum of 0 to a theoretical maximum of 1.0. Outliers beyond 3 standard deviations are Iraq and Zimbabwe. Test statistics for heteroskedasticity (White test) and multicollinearity reveal no violation of ordinary least squares assumptions. Variables are measured at the time of the latest survey for each country (1995–2005). ***$p < 0.001$. **$p < 0.01$. *$p < 0.05$.

a society's mean willingness to fight while controlling for societal levels of national pride, technological advancement, enduring democracy, international cooperation, encompassing peace, and the Nordic country and Axis power dummies.

The first regression model introduces national pride, technological advancement, and enduring democracy as predictors. Only national pride shows a significant effect, and it operates in the direction that Puranen (2009a) and Díez-Nicholás (2009) expected: In societies with more widespread national pride, willingness to fight is more widespread too. But as we already know, the exceptional experience of the Nordic countries and the former Axis powers obscures the pacifying effect of permissive existential conditions. Accordingly, as model 2 shows, when we include these two country dummies, the pacifying effects of technological advancement and enduring democracy become significant. Although the two country dummies contain only four countries and five countries, respectively, they are remarkably powerful predictors of the willingness to fight. Including them increases the explained variance from 22 to 47 percent.

Moreover, model 3 demonstrates that the pacifying effect of permissive existential conditions is fully absorbed by choice orientations when we include them in the model – confirming the expectation that permissive conditions operate mostly through their tendency to produce an emancipative culture. When we introduce peace and cooperation as additional permissive conditions, instead of technological advancement and enduring democracy (model 4), neither cooperation nor peace has a strong effect on willingness to fight. Nor does either of them diminish the effect of choice orientations. In fact, choice orientations now show a stronger effect than before. Thus, the most efficient model with the largest explanatory power relative to the number of included variables is model 5. With only the two country groups and choice orientations (and excluding outliers), it explains 66 percent of the cross-national variance in willingness to fight across the seventy-seven societies in the analyses. As the partial regression plot in Inglehart, Puranen, and Welzel's analyses shows, 53 percent of the variance is accounted for by choice orientations alone.

Longitudinal Evidence

The evidence so far indicates that broader choice orientations are linked to less widespread willingness to fight. This holds true even while controlling for other plausible causes. However, these results are purely cross-sectional; thus they cannot be interpreted as causal evidence. To come closer to a causal interpretation, we must establish that a dynamic relationship between choice orientations and willingness to fight exists even while controlling for alternative influences.

During the past thirty years, the world as a whole has become substantially more prosperous, educated, and connected, and people's lives have become longer. At the same time, there has been a pervasive rise in emancipative values, especially in the domain of reproductive freedoms on which choice orientations focus (Inglehart and Welzel 2005; Welzel 2013). If this development has the supposed pacifying effect, over the same period, there should be a sizeable shrinkage of people's willingness to fight.

Figure 4 in Inglehart, Puranen, and Welzel's analysis includes all forty-eight societies for which we have data covering a time span of at least fifteen years. Fortunately, this smaller sample does not embody an obvious selection bias. It includes the societies with the biggest populations and largest economies from each world region. And there is no selection on the dependent or independent variables: The full spectrum of variation among the key variables is covered.

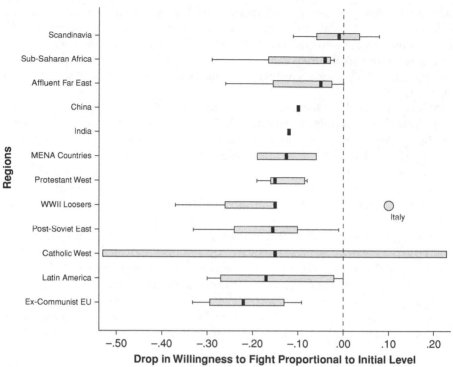

FIGURE 11.3. Proportional drop in willingness to fight by global region.
Note: Figure shows regional averages on a drop index calculated by dividing the percentage point decline in willingness to fight by the percentage level in willingness to fight before the decline. Calculations are made from the earliest to the latest available survey, provided that they are at least ten years apart (which leaves us a total of forty-eight countries). The most common time distance covered is from 1990 to 2008. Regional averages are calculated by weighting each national sample in a region equally. Countries are arranged into regions as follows: *Ex-Communist East,* Bulgaria, Estonia, Hungary, Lithuania, Poland, Romania, Slovenia; *Latin America,* Argentina, Brazil, Chile, Mexico, Peru, Uruguay; *Catholic West,* France, Spain; *Post-Soviet East,* Armenia, Azerbaijan, Belarus, Georgia, Kyrgyzstan, Moldova, Russia, Ukraine; *World War II Losers,* Austria, Germany, Italy, Japan; *Protestant West,* Australia, Canada, Netherlands, New Zealand, Switzerland, United Kingdom, United States; *MENA Countries,* Morocco, Turkey; *Affluent Far East,* South Korea, Taiwan; *Sub-Saharan Africa,* Nigeria, South Africa, Zimbabwe; *Scandinavia,* Finland, Norway, Sweden. For a country-wise listing of percentage declines, see Inglehart, Puranen, and Welzel (2014, Figure 4).

Among this set of forty-eight nations, the public's willingness to fight decreased almost everywhere and did so significantly in by far most of the countries. Figure 11.3 shows the decline in proportion to the level from where it started for twelve different country groups around the globe. It is evident from this figure that declines prevail in each region and that standard deviations around the regional averages are relatively small, except for the Catholic West, where we find a large discrepancy between Spain's decline and France's increase in willingness to fight (the latter is entirely against regional trends and the global trend, as is true for the increase in Italy). It is not far-fetched to assume that the general worldwide decline in people's willingness to fight in war pinpoints the deeper reason underlying the decline of interhuman violence that Pinker (2011) documents in *Our Better Angels*.

Can we explain the decrease in people's willingness to fight in war by the concurrent rise of choice orientations? To answer this question, Inglehart, Puranen and Welzel (2014) regress willingness to fight at the time of the latest survey for each society (T_2) on (1) the willingness at the time of the earliest survey (T_1) and (2) on change from T_1 to T_2 in the supposed predictor variables. Obviously, this is a lagged-dependent variable model: Other predictors in the model explain willingness to fight at the later point in time *insofar* as it remains unexplained by willingness to fight at the earlier time point. This is equivalent to explaining change in willingness to fight. In addition, the model is dynamic because the presumed predictors themselves measure change. Hence, the regressions show to what extent change from T_1 to T_2 in a given predictor helps to shift away willingness to fight at T_2 from its level at T_1.

What are the results of Inglehart, Puranen, and Welzel's temporal analyses? Surprisingly from the viewpoint of the democratic peace thesis, change in democracy from time T_1 to time T_2 (which turns out to be mostly increases for the covered societies and observation period) does not significantly shift willingness to fight at time T_2 below its level at time T_1. Neither does further technological advancement have an effect. An increase in international cooperation has only a slightly significant effect. The strongest effect, and the only one that is highly significant, is due to an increase in choice orientations: A one unit increase in choice orientations from time T_1 to time T_2 shifts willingness to fight at time T_2 a little more than half a unit below its level at time T_1.

Of course, with longitudinal data available for only a subset of countries, these results should be taken with a strong note of caution. Yet, the fact that Inglehart, Puranen, and Welzel's longitudinal evidence unequivocally supports the second hypothesis is noteworthy.

Multilevel Evidence

Do choice orientations diminish one's willingness to fight mainly as a *personality* trait? Or do they diminish willingness to fight through a *culture* of choice? In other words, are people less willing to fight in a war mainly because their own choice orientations are stronger than those of most people in their society? Or are they less willing to fight mainly because the overall choice climate in their society is more pronounced? Hypothesis 3 states that the latter is the case

because the emphasis of choice orientations on *universal* freedoms characterizes them as a reciprocal orientation whose effects surface through their social
commonness rather than their unique presence among given individuals.

To answer this question, we must introduce choice orientations into a multilevel model simultaneously as a country- and as an individual-level variable.
Choice orientations measure two different things at these two levels: At the
country level, they measure how prevalent choice orientations are in the individual's society – which is an indication of a choice-oriented *culture*. At the
individual level, these orientations measure how much more (or less) choice
oriented an individual is than others in the society – which is an indication of
a choice-oriented *personality*. To fully separate the two measures, we center
each individual's choice orientations on the country mean. Doing so removes
any overlap between the country- and individual-level measures. Similarly,
we mean-center the other attitudes used in the multilevel model. As standard
demographic controls, we introduce female gender, an indexed version of birth
year, and formal education.

Table 11.2 shows the results of the multilevel analysis using a linear probability model to explain the willingness to fight in war.[8] The country-level regressions in Table 11.1 found that national pride has no significant independent
effect on willingness to fight. The country-level component of the multilevel
model confirms this finding. However, at the individual level, national pride
shows by far the strongest effect on willingness to fight – confirming previous
research by Puranen (2008a, 2008b) and Díez-Nicolás (2009). Hence, it is the
personality component much more than the culture component of national
pride that enhances people's willingness to fight.

In contrast, we find a strong country-level effect for choice orientations but
no significant individual-level effect on willingness to fight (even though the
sign of the individual-level effect points in the expected direction). In this case,
it is a choice-oriented *culture* rather than a choice-oriented *personality* that
diminishes people's willingness to fight.

We suggest this pattern indicates that choice orientations, like other components of emancipative values, are a distinctively *reciprocal good*. For national
pride, this is less the case. An individual can have a strong sense of national
pride regardless of whether other people feel the same way. But emphasizing
universal freedoms is different: It is difficult to respect the freedoms of others
when others do not reciprocate the same respect. Because of their inherent

---

[8] The dependent variable is a dummy indicating whether an individual is willing to fight in war
(coded 1) or unwilling to do so (coded 0). For decades, the standard choice of functional form
for such models has been logistic probability models. Since Mood's (2010) study, this has
changed, because she shows that odds ratios and log odds are incomparable across groups and
samples – which is a blowing criticism in the context of a multilevel framework with many
different national samples. At the same time, Mood's study proves that the standard criticisms
held against linear probability models (i.e., linear regressions with binary dependent variables)
are unjustified in most cases of application.

TABLE 11.2. *Multilevel Model of Willingness to Fight for One's Country*

Predictors	b	T-Value
Individual-Level Effects (IL)		
Female sex	−0.11	(−13.30)***
Birth year (indexed)	0.09	(3.63)***
Formal education	0.00	(0.08)
Confidence in army	0.18	(10.87)***
National pride	0.30	(19.38)***
Authoritarian preferences	−0.03	(−2.54)**
Voice orientations	−0.01	(−1.17)
Choice orientations	−0.02	(−1.26)
Country-Level Effects (CL)		
National pride	0.03	(0.26)
Enduring democracy	−0.09	(−1.07)*
War loser dummy	−0.28	(−7.46)***
Nordic country dummy	0.33	(7.14)***
Choice orientations	−0.48	(−4.28)***
Cross-Level Interactions (IL * CL)		
Birth Year (IL) * Enduring Democracy (CL)	−0.43	(−3.21)***
Birth Year (IL) * Choice Orientations (CL)	0.18	(0.90)
National Pride (IL) * Nordic Country (CL)	−0.21	(−2.49)**
National Pride (IL) * Choice Orientat.s (CL)	0.27	(2.50)**
Constant	0.80	(80.78)***
Number of observations (N)	69,338 individuals in 69 countries	
Error Reduction		
Within-country variation of DV	05.2% (04.5% of total)	
Between-country variation of DV	48.1% (06.9% of total)	

Notes: Entries are unstandardized regression coefficients with their T-values in parentheses. Models calculated with HLM based on robust standard errors. Latest survey used from each country, weighting country samples to equal size without changing the overall N. Individual-level variables are country-mean centered; country-level variables are global-mean centered. Percentage error reduction calculated from random variance in empty model. Variance in the DV is 14.3% between, 86.7% within countries.
Source: World Values Survey.

reciprocity, the effects of choice orientations operate more through a socially shared emphasis than through individually unique emphases on them.

How do the personality aspect of national pride and the culture aspect of choice orientations interact? Table 11.2 shows that there is a positive cross-product term. This means that when a culture of choice flourishes, the generally positive effect of a person's national pride is further enhanced. This is logical: A culture of choice reduces the mean level of willingness to fight in war, making more people *un*-willing to fight. Under this condition, national pride is needed more to sustain a person's willingness to fight.

The Nordic country dummy interacts with national pride in the opposite direction, which also is logical: Living in a Nordic country means living in an environment with a widespread willingness to fight. Under this condition, national pride is needed less to sustain a person's willingness to fight. Consequently, we find a negative interaction between the Nordic country dummy and an individual's level of national pride.

CONCLUSION

Willingness to fight in the case of war is a key indicator of an allegiant political culture in which citizens are willing to risk their lives for their country. Thus, understanding the forces that erode the willingness to fight helps us to understand how the transition from an allegiant to an assertive culture proceeds. A growing body of theory, going back to the theory of postmaterialism and culminating in the general theory of emancipation, suggests that broadening existential opportunities elevate societies on the utility ladder of freedoms (Inglehart 1990; Inglehart and Welzel 2005; Welzel 2013; Inglehart et al. 2014). This ascension encourages an emancipatory culture of voice and choice, which grows at the expense of protective mentalities and their components, including sacrificial attitudes such as willingness to fight for one's country in wars.

These predictions turn out to be largely accurate, with two systematic deviations related to the historic experiences of two distinct country groups. Nations defeated in World War II are until today scarred by this collective trauma and exhibit an even much lower willingness to fight than their high level of emancipative values suggests. Conversely, the Nordic countries show a stronger willingness to fight than their high level of emancipative values suggests. This seems to indicate a cultural transformation in the meaning of fighting for one's country, in which the Nordic countries are potentially a vanguard: The meaning has dramatically shifted from defending one's nation to providing international aid and promoting values, such as democratic values, and human rights.

Interestingly, the pacifying effects of emancipative values do not derive from the *personality* aspects of these orientations. It is the *culture* of emancipation from which the pacifying effects emanate: People are less willing to fight not because they are more emancipatory in their orientations than others in their society but, instead, because they share highly emancipatory orientations with many others in their society. Emancipative values are a reciprocal good whose benign effects begin to flourish when these orientations are widely shared.

Equally interesting, when an emancipatory culture flourishes, national pride becomes a more important personality attribute to sustain a strong willingness to fight: When an emancipatory culture diminishes most people's willingness to fight, a strong sense of national pride is more necessary than before to sustain a willingness to fight against the mainstream.

Under existential pressures, people will fight to survive, as had been demonstrated throughout history. This is a part of our evolutionary heritage. Even today, the dominant pattern remains one in which fighting for one's country is largely motivated by the perception that it is necessary to protect one's national territory in an insecure world. But the data also suggest that this can change when life concerns shift from worrying about threats to suffer and become centered on opportunities to thrive. If so, even the meaning of fighting for one's country itself can take on a more pacifist and benign connotation, as the Nordic experience demonstrates. It remains to be seen if this experience can become a role model for other countries.

To conclude, let us emphasize that the findings of this chapter and the article by Inglehart, Puranen, and Welzel correspond neatly with the general decline of interhuman violence documented in Pinker's (2012) *Our Better Angels*. In fact, our evidence might identify the key cultural force behind the pacifying trend.

APPENDIX

Concept	Question	Codes
Willingness to fight	"In case of war, are you willing to fight for your country?"	We code the answers "yes" 1, and "no" 0
Choice orientations (subcomponent of emancipative values)	Measures the combined acceptance of "homosexuality," "abortion," and "divorce." Each of these is measured on a 10-point scale from 1 (never justified) to 10 (always justified).	We recoded each item to a 0–9 scale. An additive combination yields a 28-point scale, which we normalize into a range from minimum 0 to maximum 1.0.
Voice orientations (subcomponent of emancipative values)	The combined priority for "protecting freedom of speech," "giving people more say in important government decisions," and "giving people more say in how things are done in their jobs and their communities."	Measurement is on a 6-point index from minimum 0 to maximum 1.0.
National pride	How proud are you to be [Interviewer: name nationality]?" Very proud, quite proud, not very proud, not at all proud?	Recoded so "not at all proud" 0, "not very proud" 0.33, "quite proud" 0.66, and "very proud" 1.0.

(continued)

(continued)

Concept	Question	Codes
Confidence in army	"How much confidence do you have in the army." A great deal, quite a lot, not very much, or no [confidence] at all? of confidence and 1.0 for "a great deal" of confidence.	We recoded to 0 for "no confidence," 0.33 for "not very much," 0.66 for "quite a lot," and 1.0 for "a great deal."
Authoritarian preferences		The 12-point index is 0 when people fully support "having democracy" while fully rejecting "having the army rule" and "having a strong leader." The index is at minimum 1.0 in the opposite conditions.
Gender		0 is male and 1 is female
Age	"In what year were you born?"	We created an indexed version of birth year, 0 for 1900, 1.0 for 1990, and respective fractions for years in between.
Education		Education is measured on a 9-point scale from no or incomplete primary education to completed tertiary-level education. We normalize into a scale from minimum 0 to maximum 1.0.
Aggregate Variables		
Enduring democracy	We transform this multipoint measure into a normalized index from minimum 0 for no endurance of democracy to maximum 1.0 for the longest endurance (the United States).	
Technological advancement	Technological advancement is measured from minimum 0 to maximum 1.0 at the year of the survey.	

Concept	Question	Codes
Encompassing peace	We reverse this multipoint index so that larger numbers indicate more encompassing peace and normalize the scale between minimum 0 and maximum 1.0. Data are taken for the year of the respective survey.	
Nordic country	1 for Denmark, Finland, Iceland, Norway, Sweden; all other countries 0.	
World War II Axis power	1 for East and West Germany, Italy, Japan; all other countries 0.	

12

From Allegiant to Assertive Citizens

Christian Welzel and Russell J. Dalton

Still today, *The Civic Culture* by Gabriel Almond and Sidney Verba counts as one of the most influential studies in comparative politics. The opus was pathbreaking because it formalized a model to describe the political culture of a nation and applied this model cross-nationally in five countries. As Sidney Verba (2011) has recently suggested, *The Civic Culture*'s most important legacy has been planting the seed of political culture research for the following half-century.

The evolving literature on political culture has shown how citizen values can change over time, as Almond and Verba (1980) demonstrated in *The Civic Culture Revisited*. Indeed, their second study provided some of the first insights into the social dynamics that affect postindustrial democracies and transform their political cultures.

More recently, public opinion research has expanded beyond a small number of established democracies to a true global scale. Before that expansion, attempts to identify the political culture in the developing world were based on the impressionistic insights of expert observers. Although rich in their descriptions of local traditions, these experts could only observe what was observable; they could not provide voice to what people were thinking in autocratic states. Congruence theory suggested that autocracies were supported by a noncivic political culture in which the populace accepted or even embraced rule by monarchs, dictators, or military governments. But to what extent this assumption was true could not be tested in the absence of systematic evidence. Today, this situation has changed significantly: The World Values Survey (WVS), the Global Barometer Surveys and other cross-national survey projects provide plenty of public opinion data that can help answering the question of regime legitimacy in different parts of the world.

Current research, including the chapters of this volume, presents a nuanced view of the relationship between a nation's political culture and its political regime. On one hand, mass publics in most countries around the world express strong support for democracy – in democratic and nondemocratic states alike. On the other hand, widespread popular support for democracy often coexists with the lack or even the absence of democracy. And where this is the case, people's notion of democracy is often twisted in that it incorporates authoritarian elements (Chapter 4; also Welzel 2013, 307–32). The WVS, developed by Ronald Inglehart and others, has enabled us to study how political cultures differ and how they have evolved before and after the democratic transitions that reshaped the globe's political map. Rather than refuting the findings of *The Civic Culture*, we prefer to see this book as reaping the harvest that grew from the first seeds of political culture research sown by Almond and Verba.

This chapter first reviews the findings presented in this volume. Then we broaden the perspective from the single chapters to paint a larger picture of the culture-institution nexus that characterizes the political systems of given countries. We use WVS data to examine how two distinct manifestations of political culture – an *allegiant* and an *assertive* orientation – are linked with two equally distinct aspects of institutional performance: *accountable* and *effective* governance. Finally, we consider what the sum of the evidence says to the role of political culture in supporting a democratic political system and the expansion of democracies in the future.

AN OVERVIEW OF OUR FINDINGS

We began our study with an examination of the core tenets of Inglehart's early research on value change – the claim that the basic value priorities of Western publics were changing, with generations as the carrier of change. Paul R. Abramson's chapter in this volume (Chapter 2) is an extension of Inglehart's early research on postmaterialist value change. He shows that European publics have become steadily more postmaterialist in their value orientations. Moreover, the generational patterns that Inglehart initially described for Europeans in the mid-1970s have endured to the present (Inglehart 1971, 1977). Younger generations progressively became more postmaterialist, and these value orientations persisted – contrary to expectations that people would become more materialistic as they moved through the life cycle and accumulated economic and social responsibilities. Thus, the early life socialization of values largely endures, so that the balance of value priorities shifts in a postmaterialist direction as younger cohorts replace the older ones.

Neil Nevitte complements the examination of value change by focusing more closely on shifts in the citizens' authority beliefs (Chapter 3). He tracks orientations toward authority in family relations, the workplace, and the polity over time. Updating his earlier study, *The Decline of Deference* (Nevitte 1996), he finds a continuing shift away from obedience to authority toward more individual autonomy in shaping family, work, and social relations. He concludes that the shift toward postmaterialist, self-expressive, or emancipative values described by Inglehart and others reflects these rising individual autonomies in how people connect to each other in the family, the workplace, and politics.

Christian Welzel and Alejandro Moreno Alvarez focus on support for democracy across the globe and how emancipative values shape this support. They examine a paradox from the viewpoint of congruence theory: the fact that widespread popular support for democracy often coexists with severe deficiencies and even the absence of democracy. Their analyses reveal that wherever this apparent paradox occurs, people's democratic aspirations are decoupled from emancipative values – lacking the critical-liberal impetus that these values infuse into people's democratic preferences. Hence, in disjunction from emancipative values, democratic mass preferences provide no source of pressure to democratize. This is precisely the condition under which severe democratic deficiencies endure despite the apparent spread of democratic preferences.

The second section of this volume examines the link between political culture and political development in contemporary societies. Almond and Verba and their colleagues provided a framework for this connection. They maintained that democracies were built on allegiant participants as the ideal type of citizen, albeit in a mixed political culture. In contrast, less developed nations were supposedly characterized by a "subject" or "parochial" political culture in which people were disengaged from politics, deferential to elites, and acceptant of whatever policies the authorities impose on them.

Russell Dalton and Doh Chull Shin, in Chapter 5, demonstrate that this classification is no longer accurate. First, these authors show that citizens' political interest differs only slightly across nations with varied levels of socioeconomic development. Specifically, people in less developed nations are not substantially less interested than those in postindustrial democracies. Second, contemporary democracy does not create a supportive, allegiant culture; instead, there is strong evidence that the introduction and endurance of democracy tend to make citizens more critical of political elites and the political process. Thus, the simple contrast in political cultures between developing and developed nations no longer is so apparent, and the model of the allegiant citizens seems inconsistent with contemporary democratic politics. In part this may be a reflection of changes in communication patterns and political awareness wrought by globalization and increasing access to information in societies today. But there also appears a link to the changing values of contemporary publics – from the allegiant political norms of the past to a new, assertive citizenship in both developed and developing nations. The theoretical model that Almond and Verba described no longer fits contemporary political cultures.

The next two chapters focus on regions that provide critical test cases to examine some of the key theoretical expectations of the political culture paradigm. Hans-Dieter Klingemann, in Chapter 6, examines the level and correlates of "dissatisfied democrats" in old and new European democracies. He finds broad support for the democratic ideal among Europeans in both regions. However, about one-third of the public expresses dissatisfaction with how the democratic system performs while simultaneously endorsing the democratic ideal. These dissatisfied democrats have increased slightly among Western Europeans and decreased slightly among Eastern Europeans from the late 1990s to the late 2000s. After exploring multiple correlates of being a dissatisfied democrat, Klingemann concludes that these individuals are inspired by the participatory, self-expressive, and emancipatory beliefs typical of postmaterialists. This new "species" of citizens infuses today's political cultures with an assertive orientation – consistent with the theoretical framework of this book.

In Chapter 7, Christian W. Haerpfer and Kseniya Kizilova examine patterns of political culture and trajectories of change in the postcommunist Europe and post-Soviet Eurasia, which have made contrasting experiences with the surge of democracy. They pay special attention to where democratic institutions stand most resilient against reviving authoritarian temptations. Haerpfer and Kizilova find that those states are the most resilient in which strong support for democracy as a regime associates with a critical distance to concrete political institutions and incumbents. This pattern applies most strongly to the more Western-oriented postcommunist societies, such as the Baltic countries. Conversely, those states with strong trust in the specific institutions and incumbents – Russia, Belarus, and the post-Soviet Eurasian societies – usually display the lowest support for democracy as a regime form and experience the strongest authoritarian resilience or revival. In contrast to the Western-oriented postcommunist societies, leaders in the societies of post-Soviet Eurasia describe themselves as representatives of a distinct culture that refuses Western values. These results echo an important point in Welzel and Moreno Alvarez's as well as Klingemann's findings: The combination of commitments to democracy in principle and critical evaluations of its practice characterizes assertive cultural orientations, which are grounded in postmaterialist and emancipative values.

The third section of the book explicitly considers how changes in the political culture of contemporary publics affect political behavior. For instance, scholars have linked the emergence of the environmental movement and a green political agenda with the process of value change in postindustrial democracies (Inglehart 1981; Dalton 1994), whereas others have questioned this link (Dunlap and Mertig 1997; Dunlap 2008). Robert Rohrschneider, Matthew Miles, and Mark Peffley (Chapter 8) study the sources of environmental concerns across global regions. They find that postmaterialist values stimulate environmental concerns in postindustrial societies. But direct exposure to environmental degradation in developing societies – in which postmaterialism has not yet grown strong – also raises environmental concerns. In other words, two distinct causes feed concern about environmental problems: postmaterialist value change and direct problem exposure. Interestingly, the varied causes of environmental concerns also produce different consequences. Where postmaterialism is the cause, it is more likely that new social movements form to mobilize public support for environmental protection. This finding provides yet another indication of the increasingly assertive orientation of postindustrial political cultures. Environmental issues are a chief manifestation of people's increasing inclination to join forces and act together on behalf of a shared concern.

Tor Georg Jacobsen and Ola Listhaug, in Chapter 9, examine the rise of nonviolent protest activity. The initial studies found that the self-expressive, elite-challenging impulse of postmaterialist values strongly encourages protest behavior (Barnes and Kaase et al. 1979; Jennings and van Deth et al. 1989). Contrasting with the allegiant but passive publics of the past, Jacobsen and Listhaug find that the trend toward contentious forms of nonviolent mass action has continued in postindustrial democracies. Outside this set of highly developed societies, however, the trend patterns are more mixed. This finding underlines that the rising assertive culture is a consequence of economic development and social modernization.

Pippa Norris (Chapter 10) examines another emancipatory aspect of the emerging assertive culture: gender equality and sexual liberalization. The author focuses on those types of societies that have shown the strongest resistance against emancipatory gains: Muslim-majority nations. Paralleling an earlier study by Alexander and Welzel (2011b), Norris tests two rival explanations of the Muslim societies' patriarchal stance on matters of gender equality and sexual liberalization: a cultural explanation based on the persistence of strong religiosity versus a structural explanation based on low female labor force participation and strong dependence on oil rents. In line with previous evidence, Norris finds that religiosity explains patriarchal orientations better than does a low female labor force participation or a strong dependence on oil rents. In summary, this chapter provides an important view on the theme of a rising assertive culture, showing where and why the emancipatory impulses of this culture meet the strongest resistance.

Another reverse perspective on the rising assertive culture opens up when one analyzes the erosion of the allegiant culture. Thus, Bi Puranen, in Chapter 11, examines the forces that erode a key indicator of the allegiant culture: willingness to fight for one's country in case of war. The author suggests that broadening existential opportunities – from longer life expectancies to better education to wider social connections – change people's life approach from a sacrificial orientation to a fulfillment orientation: Faced with longer lives that harbor more opportunities for fulfillment than threats of suffering, people's priorities make a tectonic shift, away from the readiness to sacrifice life to an emphasis on actually living it. This sea change in collective mentalities should dramatically diminish people's willingness to fight for their country in the case of war. These predictions turn out to be largely accurate, with one systematic deviation. The Nordic countries show a much stronger willingness to fight than their strong fulfillment orientations suggest. Puranen speculates that this reflects a Nordic cultural transformation in the meaning of fighting for one's country: The meaning has shifted from defending one's own country toward improving the lives of people in other countries – through peacekeeping missions, development aid, and the promotion of human rights. Whether other countries will follow this example remains to be seen.

In summary, the chapters in this volume strongly confirm the theories of postmaterialist and emancipatory cultural change in their characterization of contemporary social transformations as a process of human empowerment (Inglehart 1990, 1997; Inglehart and Welzel 2005; Welzel 2013). This is evident from three recurrent patterns in this volume. First, where social modernization improves living conditions on a mass scale, the emphasis of traditional values on order, discipline, and security erodes and gives way to an increasing emphasis on freedom of choice, equality of opportunities, and the assertion of human dignity. These newly emerging orientations might be known as "postmaterialist values," "self-expressive values," "engaged citizenship," "emancipative values," or a host of other terms – but the content is similar: There is an assertive spirit encouraging people to claim control over their lives.

Our second finding is that changing social values carry over to political orientations. In contrast to the allegiant citizen of the past, contemporary publics more often combine a deep normative commitment to democratic ideals with dissatisfaction on how governments fulfill these ideals. These dissatisfied democrats epitomize the new style of assertive citizenship described in this book. Social modernization also increases a more liberal understanding of the meaning of democracy, which contributes to critical assessments of democratic performance. These patterns are most evident in mature postindustrial democracies but are also emerging in the political cultures of those developing nations in which living conditions are rapidly improving.

Third, postmaterialist, self-expressive, or emancipative values are strongly linked to environmental concerns and support for gender equality – two domains of social movement activity that expanded as these values spread among younger generations. Similarly, a growing number of people are adopting more expressive and contentious, yet nonviolent, forms of political action that challenge elites rather than displaying deferential respect. Thus, the shift from allegiant to assertive cultures reshapes contemporary publics in ways that have a deep impact on the content and style of democratic governance. The following section provides a broad picture of this impact.

CULTURE AND INSTITUTIONS

The numerous findings in the chapters of this volume all suggest that how a society's political culture is shaped has far-reaching consequences for how this society is governed. If this is indeed true, one of the most fundamental premises of the political culture paradigm – congruence theory – would be confirmed (Eckstein 1966, 1998). Congruence theory was one of the strongest inspirational ideas of the *Civic Culture* study: The basic assumption is that for a state to find a sustainable order, its institutions must match the culture of the society. In other words, the way in which institutions are designed needs to be in accordance with people's legitimacy beliefs (Almond and Verba 1963, 498).

For democracies, this seems obvious. Unless democratic institutions are widely believed to be the only acceptable way to organize power relations, political parties that campaign against democracy can become popular and voted into office – especially during times of social stress. Once in power, such parties can hollow out democratic procedures, and this might not even hurt their popularity.

For autocracies the situation might look fundamentally different, at first glance. Unlike democracies, autocracies can use repression to silence opposition, without betraying their own principles. It is thus tempting to conclude that unpopularity does not matter for regime survival in autocracies. However, no power can rule perpetually merely by brute force against large dissenting majorities. Gaining legitimacy is the only way to eliminate mass resistance as a possible cause of regime termination – even for autocracies. Time and again, this becomes obvious when what Kuran (1991) calls the "element of surprise" kicks in: Apparently "out of nowhere," a seemingly stable autocratic regime is swept away by suddenly swelling mass opposition (Karatnycki and Ackerman 2005; Schock 2005; Carter 2012).

Acknowledging the importance of mass regime support, some scholars suggest that, for short or for long, a public's democratic aspirations are met by corresponding democratic entitlements: Elites tend to supply democracy inasmuch as the masses demand it (Inglehart and Welzel 2005). This matching hypothesis implies a strong correlation between the spread of democratic aspirations in given societies and the scope of democratic entitlements of the respective regime. Surprisingly, however, the spread of support for democracy in a society only weakly predicts the respective regime's scope of democratic entitlements (Inglehart 2003). The prediction becomes actually entirely insignificant when one controls for the dependence of democratic mass support on prior democratic entitlements (Fails and Pierce 2010). Hence, the presumed institution-culture match may be entirely a myth.

This conclusion resonates with elite theories of democracy whose proponents reason since long that mass attitudes do not matter for democracy; what counts is whether elites find a consensus to concede democracy (Burton and Higley 2006). Such views are in accordance with another prominent perspective according to which the masses always anyways want democracy; so again it is an elite-level calculus that decides whether they get it (Acemoglu and Robinson 2006).

Against these views, Welzel and Klingemann (2008, 2011) maintain that the hypothesized culture-institution congruence does not surface in previous research because scholars are not looking close enough. Overt support for democracy might indeed be ubiquitous and variation might be too small to provide any meaningful explanation of the vast regime variation in democratic entitlements. Yet, the values for the sake of which people support democracy differ dramatically from one society to the next – and it is these values that make democratic mass aspirations consequential. The spirit of democracy resides in the inherently emancipatory idea that the people themselves should be the masters of their lives and have a legitimate right for this reason to make their preferences heard and count in collective decisions that affect everyone (Sen 1999; Diamond 2008). Thus, when we qualify democratic aspirations for how strongly they are grounded in emancipative values, the previously missing congruence suddenly surfaces with striking evidence: Aspirations for democracy that are motivated by emancipative values very strongly explain the scope of democratic entitlements in a society (Welzel 2013, 276).

As mentioned earlier, this finding dissolves the coexistence paradox: Wherever democratic mass aspirations seem to coexist with lack of democratic entitlements, these aspirations lack the grounding in emancipative values that otherwise would mobilize people in pursuit of democratic achievements.

Of course, correlation is not causation. Thus, it might as well be that the strong congruence between democratic entitlements and democratic aspirations (properly understood) exists because democratic entitlements generate democratic aspirations. Yet, this assumption is at odds with how democratic aspirations emerged in history: Democratic aspirations emerged under the very denial of democratic entitlements (Grayling 2007). Thus, granting democratic entitlements was a response to swelling democratic aspirations but did not create these. Supporting this interpretation, Welzel (2013, 278–306) examines the causal direction in the coevolution of democratic aspirations and democratic entitlements and finds that the causal arrow points more strongly from democratic aspirations to democratic entitlements than the other way round. In light of this evidence, we take it as a proven assumption that a culture-institution congruence with respect to democracy does indeed exist.[1]

THE CIVIC CULTURE AND GOOD GOVERNANCE

The idea of a culture-institution congruence suggests that how a society is governed reflects key features of its culture. Ever since Lipset (1981) hypothesized an inherent trade-off between "legitimate" and "effective" governance, scholars have developed quite strong ideas about the cultural features that are conducive to these two performance dimensions of governance. Interestingly, the cultural features in question pretty closely match our distinction between allegiant and assertive cultures.

---

[1] Two scholarly contributions attempt to invalidate the argument of a causal impact of democratic aspirations on democratic entitlements (Hadenius and Teorell 2005; Dahlum and Knutsen 2012). In both cases, these attempts have been rebutted persuasively (Welzel and Inglehart 2006; Welzel 2007; Inglehart, Kruse, and Welzel forthcoming). For reasons of space restriction, we refrain from rephrasing these critiques' rather technical arguments against the impact of democratic aspirations.

For instance, when the student revolt of the late 1960s showed the signs of an emerging assertive culture, prominent scholars were deeply concerned (Crozier, Huntington, and Watanuki 1975). Even today, scholars have reservations to interpret nonviolent citizen protest in the same positive way as they do when outlining the manifold civic benefits of activity in voluntary associations (Deutsch, Inglehart, and Welzel 2005). These divergent views on nonviolent protest and association membership are a legacy of an influential article by Huntington (1968), in which he contrasted the dangers of noninstitutionalized mass participation with the benefits of institutionalized citizen action: While the latter is regulated, the former easily runs out of control, potentially ending up in disorder.

In light of the reservations against self-coordinated citizen action, the expansion of protest politics was seen as a disruptive force. Lipset's (1981) idea of an inherent trade-off between legitimate and effective governance played an important role in framing the problem. Thus, Crozier et al. (1975) claimed that rising protest politics increases the response pressure on governments, which might initially seem like a push toward more legitimate governance. Yet, responding to public pressures distracts time and energy from solving problems and effective governance suffers. Eroding government effectiveness then backfires to government legitimacy, which will also suffer. To Huntington and his colleagues, the inevitable result is a governance crisis.

The negative view on assertive citizens is influential until this day. It is obvious in Putnam's (1993, 2000) work on social capital and his views of how a civic culture needs to look if it is to make democracy flourish. In *Bowling Alone*, he discussed several countertrends to his thesis of declining social capital, among them the rise of social movement activity and citizen protest. But he dismissed these and other countertrends, arguing that they provide no surrogate for the social capital that goes lost with declining activity in formal associations. Putnam's implicit distaste for the rising assertive culture is also evident in the way he measures social capital. Literally any indicator he uses, from trust to membership to voting and church attendance, falls into the allegiant category of civic activism. But there is nothing inherent in the definition of social capital that limits it to allegiant activism. The exclusion of assertive civic activity has no justification on the basis of the definition of social capital as networks of reciprocity. On the contrary, because social movement activity cannot emerge without extensive citizen networks, its presence is testimony to social capital in action.

In summary, we face a widespread skeptical view of assertive orientations and activities, in stark contrast with an overly positive view of allegiant orientations and activities. The dominant expectation is that allegiant citizens are good for both legitimate and effective governance. By contrast, the impact of assertive citizenship is widely believed to be unclear at best, if not outright negative. However, no one has tested on a broadly comparative basis how the mixture of allegiant and assertive features in a country's political culture relates to legitimate and effective governance. Given that assumptions about this relationship shape so strongly our thinking about the positive and negative externalities of political culture, this is a profound gap in the literature. The following analysis attempts to close this gap. We consider how the culture-institution nexus functions when relating legitimate and effective governance to the allegiant and assertive elements of political culture.

MEASURING ALLEGIANT AND ASSERTIVE ORIENTATIONS

In the sense of what Almond and Verba had in mind, an allegiant political culture consists of orientations that tie citizens loyally to their society and its institutional order. Using data from the WVS, one can distinguish three manifestations of such allegiant orientations:

- *Institutional confidence*: people have confidence in the institutions that constitute the pillars of state order, including the courts, the police, and the army.
- *Philanthropic faith*: people trust in others, believe in democracy, and are interested in politics.
- *Norm compliance*: people abide by the laws and dismiss violations of cooperative norms, such as taking bribes, avoiding tax payments, and cheating on state benefits.

In juxtaposition to allegiant orientations, we define assertive orientations as a posture that encourages people to be critical and to voice shared concerns. Following Welzel (2013), we believe that such orientations coincide with what he calls emancipative values. These values combine libertarian, egalitarian, and expressive views, involving an emphasis on "individual liberties," "equal opportunities" and "people's voice." These priorities make people sensitive of their rights and those of others, make them upset about rights violations, and create an urge to voice their indignations through collective action. WVS data allow us to measure these three elements of assertive orientations in the following way:[2]

- *Individual liberties*: the belief that people should be free in deciding how to live their lives, which includes the freedom to divorce an unloved partner, to abort an unintended pregnancy, and to follow a homosexual orientation.
- *Equal opportunities*: the belief that group differences, including most notably gender differences, do not justify unequal opportunities in access to education, jobs, and politics.

---

[2] Our measure summarizes three of the four components of Welzel's (2013, 66–73) emancipative values in *Freedom Rising*. We leave out the fourth component (i.e., an emphasis on personal autonomy as a desired child quality) because it is more remote from politics. Thus, it is less relevant than the other three components from a *political* culture point of view. Otherwise, we follow exactly Welzel's measurement procedure, as outlined in all detail in the Online Appendix to *Freedom Rising* at http://www.cambridge.org/welzel (see 20–28).

- *People's voice*: the belief that people should have a voice in collective decisions on various levels, so that these decisions reflect what most people want.

Screening the WVS for items that fit our concepts of allegiant and assertive orientations, we identify a total of eighteen items, with nine items for each of these two overarching groups of orientations. The items are shown in Table 12.1, together with their dimensional structure.

The dimensional structure shown in Table 12.1 closely mirrors the stepwise way in which we conceptualize political cultures. In the first step, the eighteen items group into six subdimensions; these subdimensions reflect precisely the components by which we define the two overarching cultures. In the second step, then, the six subdimensions merge into two overarching dimensions exactly in the way in which we define the allegiant culture and the assertive culture. In light of this analysis, the overall dimensional structure of the eighteen items is largely in accordance with the conceptual definition of allegiant and assertive cultures.[3]

To calculate an overall score of allegiant and assertive orientations for each respondent, we standardized the scores for each item between a minimum of o and a maximum of 1.0. Then we average the respondent scores over the nine items on both of the two cultural orientations, yielding very fine-grained multipoint indexes for both allegiant and assertive orientations.[4]

However, "culture" is not an individual attribute. Instead, it is a collective property that represents the *aggregate* configuration of all individual

---

[3] The displayed loadings are from a hierarchical, two-stage factor analysis conducted with the country-pooled individual-level data, taking the latest survey from each society (after weighting national samples to equal size). In the first stage, the eighteen items group into six factors, each consisting of three items, representing the domains of (1) institutional confidence, (2) philanthropic faith, and (3) norm compliance as well as (4) individual liberties, (5) equal opportunities, and (6) people's voice – as previously defined. We extract these six factors and assign each respondent a score on each of them. This is done under an oblique rotation ("direct oblimin" with delta = o) that allows the six factors to be correlated. In the second stage, we subject these six factors to another factor analysis (under nonoblique, varimax rotation). This stage of the analysis shows that the six factors group into two meta-factors, which represent, respectively, allegiant orientations (factors 1–3) and assertive orientations (factors 4–6). In summary, the two overarching cultural configurations of our interest – allegiance and assertion – would not show up in a one-step factor analysis because they represent second-order cultural dimensions. An alternative way to make them visible is to give up the Kaiser criterion right away and enforce the extraction of only two factors in the first analytical step.

[4] Using this measurement approach, we treat all constituent orientations of allegiant and assertive cultures as equally important, complementary components of their overarching constructs – in the way our theoretical concepts define them. Calculating factor scores instead to measure the respondents' position with respect to allegiance and assertion would mean to treat the constituent orientations as differently relevant representatives of their underlying latent dimension. However, if a concept has a clear theoretical definition, it should indeed be measured in the way it is defined in theory, irrespective of the empirical variance overlaps among its components. For this reason, we prefer our "compository" measurement approach. For a more in-depth discussion of the two measurement alternatives, see Welzel (2013, Box 2.1, 60–62).

TABLE 12.1. *Measuring Allegiant Culture and Assertive Culture with WVS Data*

Items	L1 Loadings	Subconstructs	L2 Loadings	Overall Constructs
Confidence in the courts	0.81			
Confidence in the police	0.80	Institutional confidence	0.71	
Confidence in the army	0.75			
Belief in democracy	0.68			
Trust in people	0.61	Philanthropic faith	0.64	ALLEGIANT CULTURE
Interest in politics	0.60			
Dismissing bribe taking	0.83			
Dismissing benefit cheating	0.82	Norm compliance	0.55	
Dismissing tax evasion	0.80			
Acceptance of abortion	0.87			
Acceptance of divorce	0.85	Individual liberties	0.73	
Acceptance of homosexuality	0.75			
Women's equality: Politics	0.78			
Women's equality: Education	0.77	Equal opportunities	0.72	ASSERTIVE CULTURE
Women's equality: Jobs	0.67			
Priority more say: Local	0.80			
Priority more say: National	0.80	People's voice	0.65	
Freedom of speech	0.76			

Note: Results are from a two-stage, hierarchical factor analysis conducted with the country-pooled individual-level data set of WVS waves III–V, taking the latest survey from each society and weighting national samples to equal size ($N = 1,000$ per sample). Factors are oblimin-rotated at the first stage. Number of extracted factors due to the Kaiser criterion. Number of respondents is about 95,000 in 92 countries. Factor loadings below 0.40 are not shown.

orientations. Thus, to measure the strength of allegiant and assertive "cultures," we need aggregate measures showing how *prevalent* allegiant and assertive orientations are in each society. Likewise, institutions only exist at the aggregate level, for which reason individual orientations can affect them only by their aggregate configuration. Thus, the supposed culture-institution nexus needs to be analyzed at the aggregate level. The key question is how the *prevalence* of allegiant and assertive orientations in a society's political culture relates to its governance performance.[5]

---

[5] It should be clear that this research question cannot be analyzed in a multilevel framework because it is asking for an aggregate-level relationship.

We use national mean scores on both allegiant and assertive orientations as our aggregate measures of each nation's political culture. The national mean scores provide valid estimates of a population's central tendency because in each national sample, the individuals' allegiant and assertive orientations cluster in a single-peaked and bell-shaped curve around the mean. Accordingly, national mean scores account for almost 30 percent of the variation in assertive and allegiant orientations among all individual respondents. The clustering power of national mean scores over the individuals' allegiant and assertive orientations proves that these mean scores are no artificial aggregations but real: They represent truly existing cultural gravities.

Despite the fact that the two culture measures are calculated in a way that allows them to be closely correlated, they are very weakly correlated. At the individual level, the two culture measures correlate at $r = -0.08$; at the aggregate level, the correlation is $r = -0.06$ across ninety nations. Although these correlations are negative, the key point is that they are statistically insignificant at the aggregate level. This shows that allegiant and assertive orientations are not necessarily antipodes; they can be considered independent of each other. Only because of this dimensional independence is it even possible that these two manifestations of political culture affect governance performance in distinct ways. If the two cultures were simply antipodes on the same dimension, a positive impact of the assertive culture would automatically mean a negative impact of the allegiant culture, and vice versa. Because this is apparently not the case, the two cultures can affect the two types of governance in various ways.

The dimensional independence between the allegiant and assertive cultures only describes the *cross-sectional* linkage between these two cultures. For this reason, it does by no means contradict our thesis that the assertive culture grows as the allegiant culture shrinks – because this is a *longitudinal* thesis. The longitudinal thesis certainly implies a negative *temporal* link but not necessarily a negative *cross-sectional* link between the two cultures. As we see later, cohort patterns suggest that this negative temporal link indeed exists.

Figure 12.1 plots the strength of the assertive culture in a society against the strength of its allegiant culture for more than ninety nations, using the latest available WVS survey from each society. All quadrants of the figure are beset with real observations. For instance, a combination of strongly allegiant with weakly assertive cultures in the lower right quadrant characterizes China, India, and other developing nations, especially in South Asia. The combination of weakly allegiant with weakly assertive cultures in the lower left quadrant is most typical of the post-Soviet world. The weakness of both cultures in this part of the world might indicate a moral vacuum – so to speak, the absence of a normative compass after the breakdown of the communist belief system. In the upper left quadrant, combining weakly allegiant with strongly assertive cultures, we find France, Argentina, Slovenia, and other traditionally Catholic societies that have relatively high levels of economic development. Finally, the

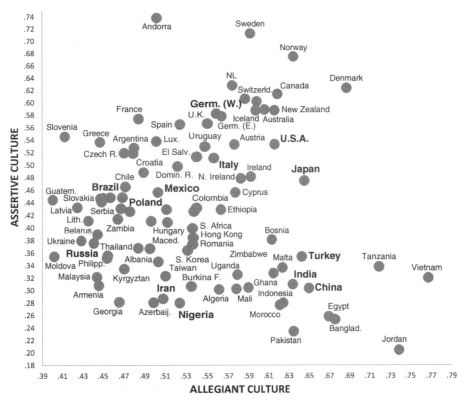

FIGURE 12.1. Allegiant and assertive cultures (societies).
Source: World Values Survey, most recent survey of each society.

combination of strongly allegiant with strongly assertive cultures in the upper right quadrant characterizes the Scandinavian countries and other postindustrial democracies that are historically Protestant. The close correspondence of the allegiance-assertion configuration with country families underlines the fact that these are measures of culture.

We gain more insight into the basic pattern when we group countries into culture zones and plot the mean positions of these zones on the map. This exercise comes with relatively little loss of information because the ten culture zones depicted in Figure 12.2 account for more than 70 percent of the cross-national variation in both allegiant and assertive orientations across our more than ninety countries.[6] As is evident from this figure, the weakly allegiant cultures of the ex-communist West and East and Latin America do not differ

---

[6] Countries are grouped into culture zones as shown in the Online Appendix to Welzel's (2013, 23–24) *Freedom Rising* at http://www.cambridge.org/welzel (see 28, footnote to Appendix-Table 2.1).

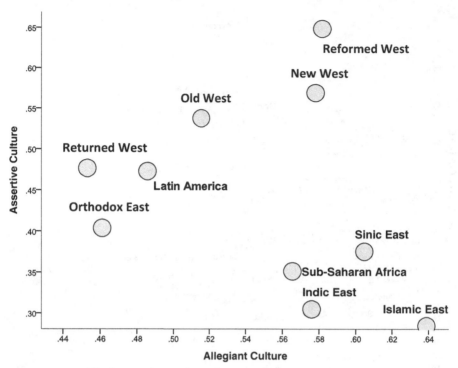

FIGURE 12.2. Allegiant and assertive cultures (culture zones).
Source: World Values Survey, latest survey from each society, surveys weighted to equal sample size.

in assertiveness: All three are on a medium level in the assertive dimension.[7] Among strongly allegiant cultures, the pattern bifurcates. Within Western culture zones, higher allegiance comes with stronger assertion: The nations in the European Union and North America cluster in this area. In contrast, in the Eastern culture zones and sub-Saharan Africa, the opposite is the case: More allegiance associates with less assertion.

The evidence of longitudinal patterns is uneven for the different culture zones because of the WVS's limited time span and the changing set of nations in each wave. Consequently, comparisons of allegiant and assertive cultures over time are problematic. As a surrogate, we break the cultural zones down into eight birth cohorts, with each cohort spanning a ten-year interval.[8] Assuming that cultural change is driven to a large extent by cohort replacement, tracing the mix of allegiant and assertive values from the oldest to the youngest cohort in each cultural zone gives us a sense of changes over time.

[7] A look at Figure 12.1 shows that the Czech Republic and Slovenia in the ex-communist West and Argentina and Uruguay in Latin America deviate from this pattern: They have strongly assertive cultures.

[8] National samples are divided here into cohorts as shown in the Online Appendix to Welzel (2013) at http://www.cambridge.org/welzel (see p. 33).

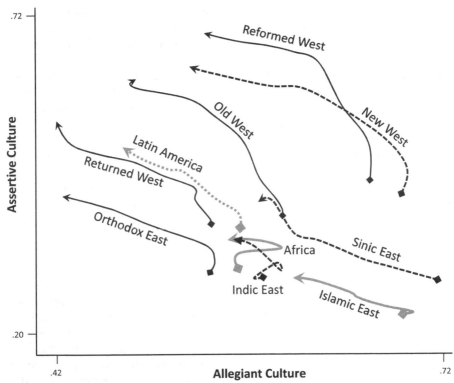

FIGURE 12.3. Allegiant and assertive cultures (culture zone cohort trajectories).
Source: World Values Survey, latest survey from each society, surveys weighted to equal sample size and broken down into eight successive birth cohorts: people born before 1921, between 1920 and 1930, between 1930 and 1940, between 1940 and 1950, between 1950 and 1960, between 1960 and 1970, between 1970 and 1980, and after 1980. Arrows follow the trace from the oldest cohort at the arrow tail to the youngest one at the arrow head.

If the cohorts in Figure 12.3 reflect the historical pattern of cultural change, this book's theme obtains striking confirmation: There seems to be a pronounced and worldwide transition from allegiant cultures to assertive cultures. This is evident from the fact that in most culture zones (except sub-Saharan Africa), the cohort sequence points toward weaker allegiant cultures and stronger assertive cultures.

For example, the oldest generation in Sinic Asia scores among the highest on allegiant orientations and among the lowest in assertive orientations. The process of cultural change moves successive Sinic cohorts steadily toward a more assertive and less allegiant position. The youngest cohort in Sinic Asia displays the mix of values that typifies the oldest generation in Catholic Europe. In a sense, the young in Sinic Asia caught up to the values of older citizens in Catholic Europe. In the meantime, subsequent generations in Catholic Europe have also moved, toward an even more assertive and less allegiant position. In fact, generations from most culture zones around the world have moved in that direction. Yet, the world did not become more similar as a result of this rather uniform cultural change. Even if all societies moved with the same pace into the same direction, the fact that they start from different positions means that they end up in positions as distant as before. Thus, people from the Protestant West have been and still are the most assertive, whereas people from the Islamic East have been and still are the least assertive in their cultural orientations.

Interestingly, although allegiant and assertive orientations are independent from each other in the *cross section*, the cohort pattern suggests a trade-off in the *temporal* dimension: The emergence of assertive orientations is concomitant with an erosion of allegiant orientations. This is not contradictory because cross-sectional and longitudinal evidence offers different perspectives that do not need to be identical.

PREDICTING GOVERNANCE PERFORMANCE

If cultural change has been as pronounced as the cohort pattern suggests, this raises the question of what such change means for the quality of governance. Some people might indeed see the erosion of allegiance and the parallel rise of assertion as worrisome. In fact, from the Huntingtonian "organization over mobilization" point of view, one would expect that a stronger allegiant culture is a force of order that favors both legitimate and effective governance. In contrast, a stronger assertive culture would be seen as a disruptive force that harms both legitimate and effective governance.

We follow Lipset's (1981) lead in identifying legitimacy and effectiveness as the two key dimensions of the quality of institutions and governance performance. This is a well-established approach. For instance, Tilly (2007), Rose (2009), and Alexander and Welzel (2011a) distinguish between political regimes on two accounts: democratic accountability and regulatory capacity. Democratic accountability represents the legitimacy dimension and regulatory capacity the effectiveness dimension in Lipset's original concept.

Our measures of governance performance are drawn from the World Bank's Governance Indicators Project (GIP). The GIP assumes that a limited number of factors characterize the institutional quality of governance, among them democratic accountability and regulatory capacity.[9] Hence, by bundling several dozen indicators into a smaller number of overarching dimensions, the

---

[9] This contrasts with a situation in which a bewildering number of organizations produce their own indices to measure aspects of governance quality. For instance, democracy is measured by Freedom House, the Polity Project, the Bertelsmann Foundation, and *The Economist*. This leaves researchers with the difficult decision of which indicator to choose or how to combine them. The latter question is particularly prevalent because it is reasonable to assume that the many single measures all provide in their own way an imperfect representation of an unobserved latent dimension.

measurement biases of the single indicators average each other out, providing more reliable and more fine-grained measures of the few key performance aspects of governance (Kaufman, Kraay, and Mastruzzi 2010).[10]

First, the "Voice and Accountability" index is a formidable indicator of democratically legitimate governance, summarizing information from various democracy indices into one compact and fine-grained measure. The index includes the civil liberties and political rights ratings from Freedom House as well as the "autocracy-democracy" scores from the Polity project, along with many more indicators to extract a common dimension of *accountable governance.*

Second, "Control of Corruption" and "Rule of Law" measure regulatory state capacity and are derived from an equally broad set of indicators. Obviously, if a state is able to prevent its officeholders from abusing their power for private benefit, and if this state is able to enforce its laws, then it has strong regulatory capacity. Hence, we use the average score of "Control of Corruption" and "Rule of Law" as our measure for *effective governance.* This approach covers Lipset's two dimensions of institutional quality.[11]

To analyze the culture-institution link, we use the ninety societies covered by the WVS for which we have measures of the two key cultural orientations, allegiance and assertion, as well as the institutional qualities of accountability and effectiveness. Table 12.2 shows two sets of regression models, one set for each of the two aspects of institutional quality. Allegiant and assertive cultures are measured before the governance indicators (i.e., over 1995–2005). The governance indicators are for the year 2009 – the latest measure available at the time of this writing. The first two models in both sets of regressions (models 1.1 and 2.1) control the effects of the two cultural orientations against each other.

Looking at model 1.1, the strength of the assertive culture has a highly significant and strongly positive effect on accountable governance. The strength of the allegiant culture, by contrast, is irrelevant for accountable governance,

[10] Some of these indicators are taken from survey data. But first, this is the much smaller set of indicators; second, it is used for a minority of countries in the world; and third, these survey items do not overlap with the ones we use to measure culture. Thus, there can be no tautological correlation between institutions and culture when we relate our culture measures to the governance indicators. At any rate, the GPI provide the most information-rich data on government performance that are available. For the most part, they represent mutually triangulated expert judgments of the objective state of governance in a country.

[11] The measures of accountable and effective governance are originally given in factor scores. As we do with every other variable in our analyses, we normalize these scores into a scale from minimum 0 for the worst ever observed scores in accountable and effective governance to 1.0 for the best ever observed scores. Intermediate positions are fractions of 1. Mathematically, the normalization is done by subtracting from the observed score of a given country in a given year the worst ever observed score and then dividing this difference by the difference between the best and worst ever observed scores. The advantages of using scales normalized between minimum 0 and maximum 1.0 are outlined in Welzel (2013, 64, Box 2.2).

TABLE I2.2. *Country-Level Regressions Examining the Effects of Allegiant Culture and Assertive Culture on Accountable Governance and Effective Governance*

	Dependent Variable							
	Accountable Governance 2009				*Effective Governance 2009*			
Predictors	M1-1	M1-2	M1-3	M1-4	M2-1	M2-2	M2-3	M2-4
Constant	0.13 (1.7)*	0.32 (4.5)***	0.16 (4.1)***	0.03 (0.7)†	−0.17 (−2.2)**	−0.01 (−0.2)	0.15 (3.7)***	−0.06 (−1.0)†
Allegiant Culture	0.05 (0.4)†	−0.14 (−1.2)†		0.00 (0.1)†	0.49 (4.0)***	0.36 (3.5)***		0.15 (1.6)†
Assertive Culture	0.91 (11.0)***		0.49 (3.6)***	0.20 (2.6)**	0.99 (12.1)***		0.20 (1.5)†	0.45 (4.8)***
Knowledge Economy		0.18 (2.5)**	0.14 (1.8)*			0.29 (4.6)***	0.16 (2.2)**	
Democratic Tradition		0.16 (3.3)***	0.12 (2.5)**			0.12 (2.9)**	0.14 (3.0)***	
Global Linkage		0.01 (1.8)*	0.00 (0.6)			0.01 (2.4)**	0.01 (2.6)**	
Lagged DV 1995				0.79 (11.9)***				0.61 (9.2)***
Adj. R^2	0.58	0.68	0.70	0.84	0.64	0.81	0.76	0.82
N (countries)	89	82	85	88	89	82	85	87

Note: Entries are unstandardized regression coefficients with their T-values in parentheses. Test statistics for heteroskedasticity (White test), multicollinearity (variance inflation factors), and outliers/leverage cases (DFFITs) reveal no violation of ordinary least squares assumptions. Allegiant and assertive culture are measured over 1995–2005, all control variables at the start of the observation period, in 1995.
†$p > 0.10$. *$p < 0.100$. **$p < 0.050$. ***$p < 0.005$.

showing no significant effect at all. This pattern was already visible in Figure 12.1. Some of the strongest allegiant cultures exist in nondemocratic countries, including China, Jordan, Pakistan, Tanzania, and Vietnam. Conversely, all countries scoring higher than 0.50 scale points in the assertive culture are democratic.

The two partial regression plots in Figure 12.4 visualize this finding. Controlling for the allegiant culture, the assertive culture explains 59 percent of the cross-national variance in accountable governance (right-hand diagram). In contrast, controlling for the assertive culture, the allegiant culture explains none of the variation in accountable governance (left-hand diagram).

Let us look at some illustrative cases. As the left-hand diagram in Figure 12.4 shows, people in Bangladesh, Jordan, Tanzania, and Vietnam score much higher in allegiant orientations than other societies at the same level of assertive orientations. Yet, this comparatively strong allegiance in Bangladesh, Jordan, Tanzania, and Vietnam does not make accountable governance better than it is in other societies at the same level of assertive orientations. By the same token, the diagram shows that many ex-communist countries (including Latvia, Slovakia, and Moldova) have much weaker allegiant orientations than other societies at the same level of assertive orientations. But comparatively weak allegiance in the ex-communist societies does not make accountable governance worse than it is in other societies at the same assertiveness. Thus, at the same level of assertiveness, more or less allegiance does not make governance more or less accountable. Allegiance has simply no effect on accountable governance, holding assertiveness constant.

In contrast, the right-hand diagram in Figure 12.4 shows that, when countries have stronger assertive orientations than other societies at the same level of allegiant orientations, this makes accountable governance better. This pattern is most clearly represented by the Scandinavian countries as well as Australia, Canada, New Zealand, and the Netherlands. At the opposite end of the distribution, we see that, when a society's assertive orientations are weaker than their allegiant orientations suggest, their accountable governance is worse. This pattern is typical for many Islamic countries (like Egypt, Iran, and Pakistan) as well as Belarus, China, and Russia.

With effective governance, the allegiant culture seems to fare better (model 2.1). The assertive culture still exerts the stronger effect, but the allegiant culture also shows a positive and significant effect on governance. As the two diagrams in Figure 12.5 show, although the assertive culture explains 63 percent of the cross-national variation in effective governance, the allegiant culture still accounts for another 16 percent.

The next two sets of models separately include each of the two culture measures with additional – and very plausible – controls. These controls include the development of the knowledge economy in a society, the length of its democratic tradition and the strength of its "global linkage" (all controls measured at

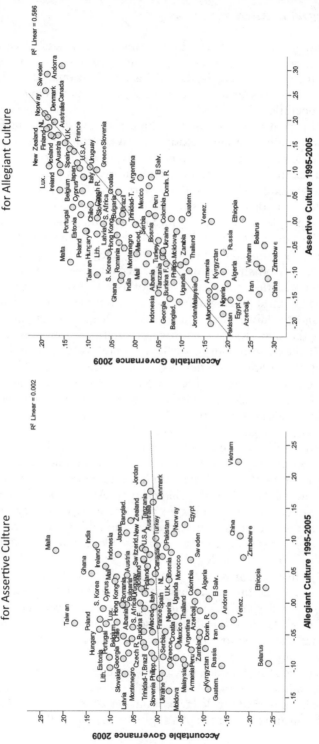

FIGURE 12.4. Visualization of model 1.1 of Table 12.2.

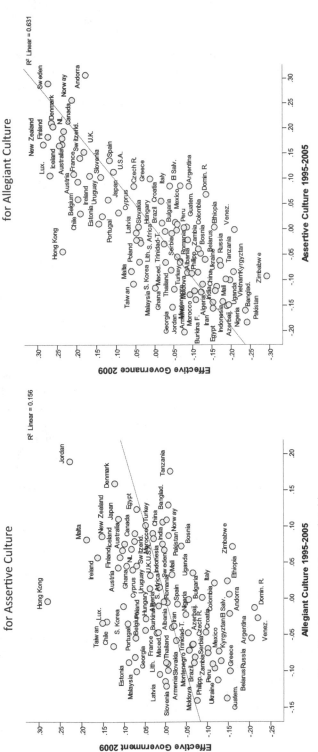

FIGURE 12.5. Visualization of model 2.1 of Table 12.2.

the beginning of the observation period, in 1995).[12] The strength of the knowledge economy is a plausible predictor of governance because "good" governance involves organizational know-how and societies advanced in knowledge should have large stocks of know-how, including organizational know-how (Glaeser et al. 2004). A long democratic tradition is another plausible predictor of "good" governance because it means a richer experience with best practice standards in governance (Gerring et al. 2005). Finally, global linkage is a plausible predictor of "good" governance because internationally more deeply integrated countries have more exposure to best practice standards in governance in other countries (Levitsky and Way 2010).

As the models with controls illustrate, the development of a society's knowledge economy and the length of its democratic tradition both show significant and positive effects on accountable as well as effective governance. The strength of a society's global linkage usually has a less significant and weaker effect on both forms of governance (the other two controls absorb much of this effect).

If we look at which cultural variable survives the controls, we see that the assertive culture still has a significant and positive effect on accountable governance, whereas the allegiant culture retains a significant and positive effect on effective governance.

This might lead us to a mixed conclusion: The assertive culture is beneficial for accountable governance, whereas the allegiant culture is conducive to effective governance. Hence, the erosion of one and rise of the other is a mixed blessing. It is best when both the allegiant and the assertive culture are strong because then we are likely to get both accountable and effective governance. The striking governance performance of the Scandinavian societies, which combine strongly assertive cultures with strongly allegiant cultures, seems to confirm this point. The allegiance-assertion combination, then, would be the best of all worlds and could be seen as the "healthy mixture" that shapes Almond and Verba's civic culture.

However, this conclusion is premature. The last pair of models (models 1.4 and 2.4) makes this evident. These two models use Granger causality methods to test if the two cultures shift the subsequent governance performance

---

[12] The strength of the knowledge economy is measured by the World Bank's "Knowledge Index," which summarizes information on overall availability of information technology in a society, years of schooling, and scientific output per capita (see http://info.worldbank.org/etools/kam2/KAM_page5.asp). The democratic tradition is measured by the "Democracy Stock" index (Gerring et al. 2005), which indicates the temporal accumulation of Polity democracy scores from 1900 until 1995 with a 1 percent deflation for each additional year back into the past. We measure "global linkages" by Dreher, Gaston, and Marten's (2008) combined economic, social, and political globalization index. All three measures are standardized into a scale range from minimum 0 to maximum 1.0. Further measurement details can be found in the Online Appendix to Welzel (2013) at http://www.cambridge.org/welzel (see "OA 1: Technological Progress Index" at 2 for the measurement of knowledge economy development, 29 for the "democratic tradition," and 77 for "global linkages").

above the level of the prior governance performance. The two models also test if the two cultures do this bare of their own dependence on the prior governance performance. Thus, we include a lagged version of the dependent variable among our predictors. Doing so takes care of two issues. First, we solve the problem of omitted variable bias because the lagged dependent variable embodies every prior influence on governance, including influences of which we are not even aware. Second, insofar as culture is endogenous to governance, we remove this endogeneity by isolating the variation in culture that exists independent of prior governance. For instance, if the assertive culture depends strongly on prior accountable governance, introducing the latter as a control will largely absorb the effect of the assertive culture. In this case, the latter will show no more effect of its own on subsequent accountable governance.

This is not what we find, however. To the contrary, the fourth models in both regression panels demonstrate that the assertive culture survives the Granger causality test in the case of both accountable and effective governance. The allegiant culture, by contrast, does not have a significant effect on either aspect of governance. This shows us that the allegiant culture is strongly shaped by effective governance prior to it. Therefore, as long as we do not control for this, it seems as if the allegiant culture strongly affects subsequent effective governance. Controlling for the allegiant culture's dependence on prior effective governance, the illusiveness of its contribution to subsequent effective governance becomes obvious.

Hence, the overall conclusion is more straightforward. The erosion of allegiant cultures and the parallel emergence of assertive cultures should not be worrisome developments as regards the societies' governance performance. Instead, in terms of both accountable and effective governance, the cultural change has positive consequences.

CONCLUSION

The transition from allegiant to assertive cultures is real. In the mid-twentieth century, democracies expected their citizens to be supportive and largely quiescent – and there was general conformance to this model. Such a pattern was considered essential for democratic government to function properly. It is also likely that many individuals in less developed nations were unaware of or at least untouched by politics. But these patterns have changed. People in mature postindustrial democracies have become skeptical of state authority and institutions and are now more willing to assert their own views. People in developing societies have also become more connected to politics because of the forces of social modernization and global communication. The modal citizen today is more likely to be the assertive citizen we described in this volume.

This development is not worrisome for the quality and prospects of democracy. Almond and Verba and other political culture scholars maintained that democracy depends on an allegiant and relatively passive public and worried about the cultural changes that became evident as societies experienced the student revolts of the late 1960s. Quite to the contrary of these presumptions, our evidence suggests that accountable and effective governance both thrive in the course of this glacial cultural change.

Inglehart's (1977) *theory of postmaterialism* has anticipated the glacial cultural change of recent decades. This cultural change does not erode social capital but is a process that Welzel's (2013) *general theory of emancipation* aptly describes as "human empowerment": improving living conditions – from increasing life expectancies to longer education to wider connectivity – transform the lives of increasing population segments from a source of threats into a source of opportunities. As this happens, societies ascend the "utility ladder of freedoms": Practicing and tolerating universal freedoms becomes increasingly vital to taking advantage of the opportunities that a more promising life offers. Because evolution has shaped humans as perceptive beings, such fundamental changes in objective utilities do not escape people's attention. Thus, in recognition of the grown utilities of universal freedoms, people adopt emancipative values that emphasize these freedoms. Eventually, this micro-level value change accumulates to a mass-scale collective trend, visible in a shift from allegiant to assertive political cultures.

Certainly, rising assertive cultures present new challenges for democracies. A more assertive public places new demands on the political process. A more assertive public also produces more contention and conflict. And it may question existing democratic institutions and require reforms to update them to meet contemporary needs.[13] Eventually, however, rising assertive cultures bring us closer to realizing democracy's key inspirational promise: empowering people to make their own decisions and to make their preferences heard and counted in politics.

---

[13] See the discussion of institutional changes that have already occurred in Cain, Dalton, and Scarrow (2004) and Smith (2009).

References

Abramson, Paul. 1983. *Political Attitudes in America: Formation and Change.* San Francisco: W. H. Freeman.

Abramson, Paul. 2010. "Postmaterialism and Social Values in the United States, Britain, France, West Germany, and East Germany." Unpublished manuscript, Michigan State University.

Abramson, Paul. 2011. "Critiques and Counter-Critiques of the Postmaterialism Thesis: Thirty-Four Years of Debate." Research paper series, Center for the Study of Democracy, University of California, Irvine. http://escholarship.org/uc/item/3f72v9q4.

Abramson, Paul. 2012. *Politics in the Bible.* New Brunswick, NJ: Transaction Publishers.

Abramson, Paul, Susan Ellis, and Ronald Inglehart. 1997. "Research in Context: Measuring Value Change." *Political Behavior* 19 (March): 41–59.

Abramson, Paul, and Ronald Inglehart. 1986. "Generational Replacement and Value Change in Six West European Societies." *American Journal of Political Science* 30: 1–25.

Abramson, Paul, and Ronald Inglehart. 1987. "Generational Replacement and the Future of Post-Materialist Values." *Journal of Politics* 49: 231–41.

Abramson, Paul, and Ronald Inglehart. 1992. "Generational Replacement and Value Change in Eight West European Societies." *British Journal of Political Science* 22: 183–228.

Abramson, Paul, and Ronald Inglehart. 1994. "Education, Security, and Postmaterialism: A Comment on Duch and Taylor's 'Postmaterialism and the Economic Condition.'" *American Journal of Political Science* 38: 797–814.

Abramson, Paul, and Ronald Inglehart. 1995. *Value Change in Global Perspective.* Ann Arbor: University of Michigan Press.

Abramson, Paul, and Ronald Inglehart. 2007. "Generational Replacement and Value Change in the United States and Eight West European Societies: 1970 to 2006." Unpublished manuscript.

Abu-Lughod, Lila, ed. 1998. *Remaking Women: Feminism and Modernity in the Middle East.* Princeton, NJ: Princeton University Press.

Acemoglu, Daren, and John Robinson. 2006. *Economic Origins of Democracy and Dictatorship.* New York: Cambridge University Press.

Adeola, F. O. 1998. "Cross-National Environmentalism Differentials: Empirical Evidence from Core and Noncore Nations." *Society and National Resources* 11: 339–65.

Alexander, Amy, Ronald Inglehart, and Christian Welzel. 2012. "Measuring Effective Democracy: A Defense." *International Political Science Review* 33: 41–62.

Alexander, Amy, and Christian Welzel. 2011a. "Measuring Effective Democracy: The Human Empowerment Approach." *Comparative Politics* 43: 271–89.

Alexander, Amy, and Christian Welzel. 2011b. "How Robust Is Muslim Support for Patriarchal Values? A Cross National, Multilevel Study." *International Review of Sociology* 21: 249–76.

Alexander, Amy, and Christian Welzel. 2011c. "Explaining Women's Empowerment: The Role of Emancipative Beliefs." *European Sociological Review* 27: 364–84.

Almond, Gabriel. 1990. Cover synopsis from *Culture Shift in Advanced Industrial Societies.* Princeton, NJ: Princeton University Press.

Almond, Gabriel. 1998. "The Civic Culture: Prehistory, History and Retrospect." Research paper series, Center for the Study of Democracy. http://www.democracy.uci.edu.

Almond, Gabriel, and James Coleman, eds. 1960. *The Politics of Developing Areas.* Princeton, NJ: Princeton University Press.

Almond, Gabriel, and G. Bingham Powell. 1978. *Comparative Politics: Systems, Process and Policy.* Boston, MA: Little, Brown.

Almond, Gabriel, and G. Bingham Powell, eds. 1984. *Comparative Politics Today: A World View.* Boston: Little, Brown.

Almond, Gabriel, and Sidney Verba. 1963. *The Civic Culture: Political Attitudes in Five Western Democracies.* Princeton, NJ: Princeton University Press.

Almond, Gabriel, and Sidney Verba, eds. 1980. *The Civic Culture Revisited.* Boston, MA: Little, Brown.

Alter, Robert. 2004. *The Five Books of Moses: A Translation with Commentary.* New York: W. W. Norton.

American Bar Association. 2006. *Charting Our Progress: The Status of Women in the Profession Today.* Chicago: ABA/Commission on Women in the Profession. http://www.abanet.org/women/reports.html.

Andersen, Kristi. 1975. "Working Women and Political Participation, 1952–1972." *American Political Science Review* 19: 439–53.

Arendt, Hannah. 1970. *On Violence.* San Francisco: Harcourt Brace.

Auty, Richard. 1993. *Sustaining Development in Mineral Economies: The Resource Curse Thesis.* London: Routledge.

Baker, Kendall, Russell Dalton, and Kai Hildebrandt. 1981. *Germany Transformed: Political Culture and the New Politics.* Cambridge, MA: Harvard University Press.

Banfield, Edward. 1963. *Moral Basis of a Backward Society.* New York: Free Press.

Barnes, Samuel, Max Kaase, et al. 1979. *Political Action: Mass Participation in Five Western Democracies.* Beverly Hills, CA: Sage.

Bentler, P. 1990. "Comparative Fit Indexes in Structural Models." *Psychological Bulletin* 107(2): 238–52.

Bergh, Johannes. 2006. "Gender Attitudes and Modernization Processes." *International Journal of Public Opinion* 19: 5–23.

Bermeo, Nancy. 2003. *Ordinary People in Extraordinary Times: The Citizenry and the Breakdown of Democracy.* Princeton, NJ: Princeton University Press.

Bickel, Robert. 2007. *Multilevel Analysis for Applied Research: It's Just Regression!* New York: Guilford Press.

Binder, Leonard. 1965. *The Ideological Revolution in the Middle East.* New York: John Wiley.

Blalock, Herbert. 1966. "The Identification Problem and Theory Building." *American Sociological Review* 31: 52–61.

Boix, Carles. 2003. *Democracy and Redistribution.* Cambridge: Cambridge University Press.

Booth, John, and Mitchell Seligson. 2008. *The Legitimacy Puzzle in Latin America: Political Support and Democracy in Eight Latin American Countries.* New York: Cambridge University Press.

Boulding, Elise. 2000. *Cultures of Peace: The Hidden Side of History.* Syracuse, NY: Syracuse University Press.

Bratton, Michael, and Robert Mattes. 2001. "Support for Democracy in Africa." *British Journal of Political Science* 31: 447–74.

Bratton, Michael, et al. 2004. *Public Opinion, Democracy, and Market Reform in Africa.* New York: Cambridge University Press.

Brettschneider, Corey. 2007. *Democratic Rights.* Princeton, NJ: Princeton University Press.

Brooks, Clem, and Catherine Bolzendahl. 2004. "The Transformation of US Gender Role Attitudes: Cohort Replacement, Social Structural Chance, and Ideological Learning." *Social Science Research* 33: 106–33.

Burnel, P., and P. Calvert. 2004. *Civil Society in Democratization.* London: Frank Cass.

Burns, Nancy, Kay Lehman Schlozman, and Sidney Verba. 2001. *The Private Roots of Public Action: Gender, Equality, and Political Participation.* Cambridge, MA: Harvard University Press.

Burton, Michael, and John Higley. 2006. *Elite Foundations of Liberal Democracy.* Lanham, MD: Rowman and Littlefield.

Cain, Bruce, Russell Dalton, and Susan Scarrow. eds. 2004. *Democracy Transformed? Expanding Citizen Access in Advanced Industrial Democracies.* Oxford: Oxford University Press.

Campbell, David. 2006. *Why We Vote: How Schools and Communities Shape Our Civic Life.* Princeton, NJ: Princeton University Press.

Carena, Neil, Raj Andrew Ghoshalb, and Vanesa Ribasa. 2011. "A Social Movement Generation Cohort and Period Trends in Protest Attendance and Petition Signing." *American Sociological Review* 76: 125–51.

Carter, A. 2012. *People Power and Political Change.* London: Routledge.

Catterberg, Gabriela. 2003. "Evaluations, Referents of Support, and Political Action in New Democracies." *International Journal of Comparative Sociology* 44: 173–98.

Chanley, V., T. Rudolph, and W. Rahn. 2000. "The Origins and Consequences of Public Trust in Government: A Time Series Analysis." *Public Opinion Quarterly* 64: 239–56.

Cheung, G., and R. Rensvold. 2002. "Evaluating Goodness-of-Fit Indexes for Testing Measurement Invariance." *Structural Equation Modeling: A Multidisciplinary Journal* 9: 233–55.

Chirot, Daniel. 1989. *The Origins of Backwardness in Eastern Europe.* Berkeley: University of California Press.

Christie, D., R. Wagner, and D. Winter, eds. 2001. *Peace, Conflict, and Violence: Peace Psychology for the 21st Century*. Upper Saddle River, NJ: Prentice Hall.

Chu, Yun-han, Larry Diamond, Andrew Nathan, and Doh Chull Shin, eds. 2008. *How East Asians View Democracy*. New York: Columbia University Press.

Cialdini, R. B. 1993. *Influence: Science and Practice*. New York: HarperCollins.

Cingranelli, David L., and David L. Richards. 2010. *CIRI Dataset 2008*. http://ciri .binghamton.edu/index.asp.

Clarke, Harold. 2000. "Refutations Affirmed: Conversations Concerning the Euro-Barometer Values Battery." *Political Research Quarterly* 53: 477–94.

Clarke, Harold, and Nitish Dutt. 1991. "Measuring Value Change in Western Industrialized Societies: The Impact of Unemployment." *American Political Science Review* 85: 905–20.

Clarke, Harold, Nitish Dutt, and Jonathan Rapkin. 1997a. "Conversations in Context: The (Mis)Measurement of Value Change in Advanced Industrial Societies." *Political Behavior* 19: 19–39.

Clarke, Harold, Nitish Dutt, and Jonathan Rapkin. 1997b. "(Mis)Measuring Value Change: A Brief Postscript." *Political Behavior* 19: 61–63.

Clarke, Harold, Allan Kornberg, Chris McIntyre, Petra Bauer-Kaase, and Max Kaase. 1999. "The Effect of Economic Priorities on the Measurement of Value Change: New Experimental Evidence." *American Political Science Review* 93: 637–47.

Coenders, Marcel, Marcel Lubbers, and Peer Scheepers. 2008. "Support for Repatriation Policies of Migrants." *International Journal of Comparative Sociology* 49: 175–94.

Collier, David, and Steven Levitsky. 1997. "Democracies with Adjectives." *World Politics* 49: 430–51.

Collier, Paul, and Anke Hoeffler. 2004. "Greed and Grievance in Civil War." *Oxford Economic Papers* 56: 563–95.

Collier, Paul, and Nicholas Sambanis, eds. 2005. *Understanding Civil War*. Washington, DC: World Bank.

Cook, Thomas. 1985. "The Bear Market in Political Socialization and the Cost of Misunderstood Psychological Theories." *American Political Science Review* 79: 1079–93.

Converse, Philip. 1964. "The Nature of Belief Systems in Mass Publics." In *Ideology and Discontent*, ed. David Apter, 206–61. New York: Free Press.

Converse, Philipp E. 1969. "Of Time and Partisan Stability." *Comparative Political Studies* 2: 139–71.

Cotgrove, Stephen. 1982. *Catastrophe and Cornucopia*. New York: John Wiley.

Crozier, Michel, Samuel Huntington, and Joji Watanuki, eds. 1975. *The Crisis of Democracy*. New York: New York University Press.

Dahl, Robert. 1973. *Polyarchy*. New Haven, CT: Yale University Press.

Dahl, Robert. 2000. *On Democracy*. New Haven, CT: Yale University Press.

Dahlerup, Drude, ed. 2006. *Women, Quotas and Politics*. London: Routledge.

Dahlum, Sirianne, and Carl Henrik Knutsen. 2012. "Democracy by Demand? Reinvestigating the Effect of Liberal Values on Regime Type." EPSA 2013 Annual General Conference Paper 631. http://ssrn.com/abstract=2224988.

Dahrendorf, Ralf. 1991. *Reflections on the Revolutions in Europe*. London: Chatto and Windus.

Dalton, Russell. 1977. "Was There a Revolution? A Note on Generational Versus Life Cycle Explanations of Value Differences." *Comparative Political Studies* 9: 459–73.

Dalton, Russell. 1982. "The Pathways of Parental Socialization." *American Politics Quarterly* 10: 139–57.

Dalton, Russell. 1994. *The Green Rainbow: Environmental Groups in Western Europe.* New Haven, CT: Yale University Press.

Dalton, Russell. 1999. "Political Support in Advanced Industrial Democracies." In *Critical Citizens: Global Support for Democratic Governance*, ed. Pippa Norris, 57–77. Oxford: Oxford University Press.

Dalton, Russell. 2004. *Democratic Challenges, Democratic Choices.* Oxford: Oxford University Press.

Dalton, Russell J. 2006. *Citizen Politics: Public Opinion and Political Parties in Advanced Industrial Democracies.* Washington, DC: CQ Press.

Dalton, Russell. 2009. *The Good Citizen: How a Younger Generation Is Transforming American Politics.* Rev. ed. Washington, DC: CQ Press.

Dalton, Russell. 2014. *Citizen Politics: Public Opinion and Political Parties in Advanced Industrial Democracies.* 6th ed. Washington, DC: CQ Press.

Dalton, Russell, Scott Flanagan, and Paul Beck, eds. 1984. *Electoral Change in Advanced Industrial Democracies: Realignment or Dealignment?* Princeton, NJ: Princeton University Press.

Dalton, Russell, and Nhu-Ngoc Ong. 2006. "Authority Orientations and Democratic Attitudes: A Test of the 'Asian Values' Hypothesis." In *Citizens, Democracy, and Markets around the Pacific Rim: Congruence Theory and Political Culture*, ed. Russell Dalton and Doh Chull Shin, 97–112. Oxford: Oxford University Press.

Dalton, Russell, and Doh Chull Shin, eds. 2006. *Citizens, Democracy and Markets around the Pacific Rim.* Oxford: Oxford University Press.

Dalton, Russell, and Doh Chull Shin. Forthcoming. "Growing Up Democratic: Generational Change in East Asian Democracies." *Japanese Journal of Political Science.*

Dalton, Russell, Doh Chull Shin, and Willy Jou. 2007. "Understanding Democracy: Data from Unlikely Places." *Journal of Democracy* 18: 142–54.

Dalton, Russell, and Martin Wattenberg, eds. 2000a. *Parties without Partisans.* Oxford: Oxford University Press.

Dalton, Russell, and Martin Wattenberg. 2000b. "Unthinkable Democracy: Political Change in Advanced Industrial Democracies." In *Parties without Partisans: Political Change in Advanced Industrial Democracies*, ed. Russell Dalton and Martin Wattenberg, 3–16. Oxford: Oxford University Press.

Dalton, Russell, Alix van Sickle, and Steve Weldon. 2010. "The Individual-Institutional Nexus of Protest Behavior." *British Journal of Political Science* 40: 51–73.

Dawson, Richard, and Kenneth Prewitt. 1969. *Political Socialization.* Boston: Little, Brown.

Dawson, Richard, Kenneth Prewitt, and Karen S. Dawson. 1977. *Political Socialization.* 2nd ed. Boston: Little, Brown.

De Tocqueville, Alexis. 1835. *Democracy in America.* Ed. J. P. Mayer. New York: Harper Perennial.

Deutsch, Franziska, Ronald Inglehart, and Christian Welzel. 2005. "Social Capital, Voluntary Associations, and Collective Action." *Journal of Civil Society* 1: 121–46.

Deutsch, Franziska, and Christian Welzel. 2011. "Emancipative Values and Nonviolent Protest: The Importance of 'Ecological' Effects." *British Journal of Political Science* 42: 465–479.

Diamond, Larry. 1999. *Developing Democracy: Toward Consolidation*. Baltimore, MD: Johns Hopkins University Press.

Diamond, Larry. 2008. *The Spirit of Democracy*. New York: Henry Holt.

Díez-Nicolás, Juan. 1999. *Identidad Nacional y Cultura de Defensa*. Madrid: Editorial Síntesis.

Díez-Nicolás, Juan. 2006. *La Opinión Pública Española y la Política Exterior y de Seguridad. Informe INCIPE 2006*. Madrid: Instituto de Cuestiones Internacionales y Política Exterior (INCIPE).

Díez-Nicolás, Juan. 2009. "Cultural Differences on Values about Conflict, War and Peace." In *Religion, Democratic Values and Political Conflict*, ed. Y. Esmer, H. D. Klingemann, and Bi Puranen, 257–76. Uppsala: Uppsala University.

Díez-Nicolás, Juan. 2011a. "¿Regreso a los valores materialistas? El dilema entre seguridad y libertad en los países desarrollados" (Returning to material values? The dilemma between security and freedom in developed countries). *Revista Española de Sociología* 15: 9–46.

Díez-Nicolás, Juan. 2011b. *La Seguridad Subjetiva en España: Construcción de un Índice Sintético de Seguridad Subjetiva (ISSS)*. Madrid: Ministerio de Defensa.

Dreher, Axel, N. Gaston, and W. J. M. Martens. 2008. *Measuring Globalization*. New York: Springer.

Duch, Raymond, and Michaell Taylor. 1993. "Postmaterialism and the Economic Condition." *American Journal of Political Science* 37: 747–79.

Duch, Raymond, and Michaell Taylor. 1994. "A Reply to Abramson and Inglehart's 'Education, Security, and Postmaterialism.'" *American Journal of Political Science* 38: 815–24.

Dunlap, Riley. 2008. "The Globalization of Environmental Concern and the Limits of the Postmaterialist Values Explanation: Evidence from Four Multinational Surveys." *The Sociological Quarterly* 49: 529–63.

Dunlap, Riley, and Ann Mertig. 1997. "Global Environmental Concern: An Anomaly for Postmaterialism." *Social Science Quarterly* 78: 24–29.

Dunlap, Riley, and R. Yolk. 2008. "The Globalization of Environmental Concern and the Limits of the Postmaterialist Values Explanation: Evidence from Four Multinational Surveys." *The Sociological Quarterly* 49: 529–63.

Dunning, Thad. 2008. *Crude Democracy: Natural Resource Wealth and Political Regimes*. New York: Cambridge University Press.

Easton, David. 1965. *A System's Analysis of Political Life*. New York: John Wiley.

Easton, David. 1975. "A Re-Assessment of the Concept of Political Support." *British Journal of Political Science* 5: 435–57.

Easton, David, and Jack Dennis. 1970. "The Child's Image of Government." *The Annals of the American Academy of Political and Social Science* 361: 40–57.

Eckstein, Harry. 1966. *Division and Cohesion: A Study of Democracy in Norway*. Princeton, NJ: Princeton University Press.

Eckstein, Harry. 1969. "Authority Relations and Democratic Performance." *Comparative Political Studies* 2: 269–325.

Eckstein, Harry. 1988. "A Culturalist Theory of Political Change." *American Political Science Review* 82: 789–804.

Eckstein, Harry. 1992. *Regarding Politics: Essays on Political Theory, Politics and Change*. Berkeley: University of California Press.

Eckstein, Harry. 1998. "Congruence Theory Explained." In *Can Democracy Take Root in Post-Soviet Russia: Explorations in State-Society Relations*, ed. Harry Eckstein, F. Fleron, E. Hoffmann, and William Reisinger, 3–34. Lanham, MD: Rowman and Littlefield.

Eckstein, Harry, and Ted Gurr. 1975. *Patterns of Authority: A Structural Basis for Political Inquiry*. New York: John Wiley.

Fails, M., and H. Pierce. 2010. "Changing Mass Attitudes and Democratic Deepening." *Political Research Quarterly* 63: 174–87.

Firebaugh, Glenn. 1989. "Methods for Estimating Cohort Replacement Effects." *Sociological Methodology* 19: 243–62.

Flanagan, Scott. 1987. "Value Change in Industrial Society." *American Political Science Review* 81: 1303–19.

Flanagan, Scott, and Aie-Rie Lee. 2001. "Value Change and Democratic Reform in Japan and Korea." *Comparative Political Studies* 33: 626–59.

Flanagan, Scott, and Aie-Rie Lee. 2003. "The New Politics, Culture Wars, and the Authoritarian-Libertarian Value Change in Advanced Industrial Societies." *Comparative Political Studies* 36: 235–70.

Foweraker, John, and Todd Landman. 1997. *Citizenship Rights and Social Movements*. Oxford: Oxford University Press.

Franzen, Axel, and Dominikus Vogl. 2013. "Two Decades of Measuring Environmental Attitudes: A Comparative Analysis of 33 Countries." *Global Environmental Change*.

Freedom House. 2012. *Freedom in the World*. New York: Freedom House. http://www .freedomhouse.org.

Freymeyer, R., and B. Johnson. 2010. "A Cross-Cultural Investigation of Factors Influencing Environmental Actions." *Sociological Spectrum* 30: 185–95.

Fuchs, Dieter. 2007. "The Political Culture Paradigm." In *The Oxford Handbook of Political Behavior*, ed. Russell Dalton and Hans-Dieter Klingemann, 161–84. Oxford: Oxford University Press.

Fuchs, Dieter, G. Guidorossi, and Palle Svensson. 1995. "Support for the Democratic System." In *Citizens and the State*, ed. Hans-Dieter Klingemann and Dieter Fuchs, 323–53. Oxford: Oxford University Press.

Fuchs, Dieter, and Hans-Dieter Klingemann. 1990. "The Left-Right Schema." In *Continuities in Political Action*, ed. M. Kent Jennings and Jan van Deth, 203–34. Berlin: Walter de Gruyter.

Fuchs, Dieter, and Hans-Dieter Klingemann. 1995. "Citizens and the State: A Relationship Transformed." In *Citizens and the State*, ed. Hans-Dieter Klingemann and Dieter Fuchs, 419–43. Oxford: Oxford University Press.

Fukuyama, Francis. 1992. *The End of History and the Last Man*. New York: Free Press.

Gallup International Associates. 2005. *Voice of the People: Trends in Democracy*. http:// www.voice-of-the-people.net.

Galston, William. 2001. "Political Knowledge, Political Engagement, and Civic Education." *Annual Review of Political Science* 4: 217–34.

Galtung, Johan. 1975–1980. *Essays in Peace Research*. 5 vols. Copenhagen: Christian Ejlers.

Gartzke, E., and Li Quan. 2003. "War, Peace and the Invisible Hand: Positive Political Externalities of Economic Globalization." *International Studies Quarterly* 47: 561–80.

Gartzke, E. 2000. "Preferences and Democratic Peace." *International Studies Quarterly* 44: 191–212.

Gat, A., with A. Yakobson. 2013. *Nations: The Long History and Deep Roots of Political Ethnicity and Nationalism.* New York: Cambridge University Press.

Geissel, Bettina. 2008. "Do Critical Citizens Foster Better Governance? A Comparative Study." *West European Politics* 31: 855–73.

Gelman, Andrew, and Jennifer Hill. 2007. *Data Analysis Using Regression and Multi-level/Hierarchical Models.* New York: Cambridge University Press.

Gerring, J., P. Bond, W. T. Barndt, and C. Moreno. 2005. "Democracy and Economic Growth." *World Politics* 57: 323–64.

Gilley, Bruce. 2009. *The Right to Rule: How States Win and Lose Legitimacy.* New York: Columbia University Press.

Glaeser, E., R. LaPorta, F. Lopez-de-Silanes, and A. Shleifer. 2004. "Do Institutions Cause Growth?" *Journal of Economic Growth* 9: 271–303.

Glenn, Norval. 2005. *Cohort Analysis.* 2nd ed. Thousand Oaks, CA: Sage.

Goertz, Gary. 2006. *Social Science Concepts.* Princeton, NJ: Princeton University Press.

Gouldner, A. W. 1979. *The Future of Intellectuals and the Rise of the New Class.* London: Macmillan.

Grayling, A. C. 2007. *Toward the Light of Liberty.* New York: Walker.

Greenstein, Fred. 1960. "The Benevolent Leader: Children's Images of Political Authority." *American Political Science Review* 54: 934–43.

Gurr, Ted. 1970. *Why Men Rebel.* Princeton, NJ: Princeton University Press.

Habermas, Jurgen. 1973. *Legitimationsprobleme im Spaetkapitalismus.* Frankfurt: Suhrkamp. In English as *Legitimation Crisis* (Boston: Beacon Press, 1975).

Hadenius, A., and J. Teorell. 2005. "Cultural and Economic Prerequisites of Democracy: Reassessing Recent Evidence." *Studies in Comparative International Development* 39: 87–106.

Haerpfer, Christian W. 2002. *Democracy and Enlargement in Post-Communist Europe. The Democratisation of the General Public in Fifteen Central and Eastern European Countries.* London: Routledge.

Haerpfer, Christian W. 2008. "Support for Democracy and Autocracy in Russia and the Commonwealth of Independent States, 1992–2002." *International Political Science Review* 29: 411–32.

Haerpfer, Christian, Ronald Inglehart, P. Bernhagen, and Christian Welzel, eds. 2009. *Democratization.* Oxford: Oxford University Press.

Hagenaars, J., L. Halman, and G. Moors. 2003. "Exploring Europe's Basic Values Map." In *The Cultural Diversity of the European Union,* ed. W. Arts, J. Hagenaars, and L. Halman, 23–66. Leiden, Netherlands: Brill.

Held, David. 1987. *Models of Democracy.* Cambridge: Polity Press.

Hess, Robert, and David Easton. 1960. "The Child's Changing Image of the President." *Public Opinion Quarterly* 24: 632–44.

Humphreys, M. 2005. "Natural Resources, Conflict, and Conflict Resolution – Uncovering the Mechanisms." *Journal of Conflict Resolution* 49: 508–37.

Huntington, Samuel P. 1968. *Political Order in Changing Societies.* New Haven, CT: Yale University Press.

Huntington, Samuel. 1974. "Postindustrial Politics: How Benign Will It Be?" *Comparative Politics* 6: 163–91.

Huntington, Samuel. 1984. "Will More Countries Become Democratic?" *Political Science Quarterly* 99: 193–218.

Huntington, Samuel. 1991. *The Third Wave*. Norman: University of Oklahoma Press.

Huntington, Samuel. 1996. *The Clash of Civilizations and the Remaking of the World Order*. New York: Simon and Schuster.

Ignazi, P. 2003. *Extreme Right Parties in Western Europe*. Oxford: Oxford University Press.

Inglehart, Ronald. 1970. "Cognitive Mobilization and European Identity." *Comparative Politics* 3: 45–70.

Inglehart, Ronald. 1971. "The Silent Revolution in Europe: Intergenerational Change in Post-Industrial Societies." *American Political Science Review* 65: 991–1017.

Inglehart, Ronald. 1977. *The Silent Revolution: Changing Values and Political Styles among Western Publics*. Princeton, NJ: Princeton University Press.

Inglehart, Ronald. 1979. "Political Action: The Impact of Values, Cognitive Level, and Social Background." In *Political Action*, ed. Samuel Barnes, Max Kaase et al., 343–80. Beverly Hills, CA: Sage.

Inglehart, Ronald. 1981. "Post-Materialism in an Environment of Insecurity." *American Political Science Review* 75: 880–900.

Inglehart, Ronald. 1990. *Culture Shift in Advanced Industrial Society*. Princeton, NJ: Princeton University Press.

Inglehart, Ronald. 1995. "Public Support for Environmental Protection: Objective Problems and Subjective Values in 43 Societies." *PS: Political Science and Politics* 28: 57–72.

Inglehart, Ronald. 1997. *Modernization and Postmodernization: Cultural, Economic, and Political Change in 43 Societies*. Princeton, NJ: Princeton University Press.

Inglehart, Ronald. 2003 "How Solid Is Mass Support for Democracy – and How Do We Measure It?" *PS: Political Science and Politics* 36: 51–57.

Inglehart, Ronald. 2008. "Changing Values among Western Publics from 1970 to 2006." *West European Politics* 31: 130–46.

Inglehart, Ronald, and Paul Abramson. 1994. "Economic Security and Value Change." *American Political Science Review* 88: 336–54.

Inglehart, Ronald, and Paul Abramson. 1999. "Measuring Postmaterialism." *American Political Science Review* 93: 665–77.

Inglehart, Ronald, and Wayne Baker. 2000. "Modernization, Globalization and the Persistence of Tradition: Empirical Evidence from 65 Societies." *American Sociological Review* 65: 19–55.

Inglehart, Ronald, and Gabriela Catterberg. 2002. "Trends in Political Action: The Developmental Trend and the Post-Honeymoon Decline." *International Journal of Comparative Sociology* 43: 300–16.

Inglehart, Ronald, and Pippa Norris. 2000. "The Developmental Theory of the Gender Gap: Women's and Men's Voting Behavior in Global Perspective." *International Political Science Review* 21: 441–62.

Inglehart, Ronald, and Pippa Norris. 2003. *Rising Tide: Gender Equality and Cultural Change Around the World*. New York: Cambridge University Press.

Inglehart, Ronald, and Pippa Norris. 2009. *Cosmopolitan Communications: Cultural Diversity in a Globalized World*. New York: Cambridge University Press.

Inglehart, Ronald, and Pippa Norris. 2011. "The Four Horsemen of the Apocalypse: Understanding Human Security." Paper presented at the Johan Skytte Award Ceremony, Uppsala University, September 23–24.

Inglehart, Ronald, and Christian Welzel. 2005. *Modernization, Cultural Change, and Democracy*. New York: Cambridge University Press.

Inglehart, Ronald, and Christian Welzel. 2009. "How Development Leads to Democracy: What Do We Know about Modernization Today?" *Foreign Affairs* 88: 33–48.

Inglehart, Ronald, Bi Puranen, and Christian Welzel. 2014. "Re-Inventing the Kantean Peace: The Emerging Mass Basis of Global Security." Higher School of Economics Research Paper WP BRP 28?SOC/2013. doi:10.2139/ssrn.2373154.

Inglehart, Ronald, Stefan Kruse, and Christian Welzel. 2015. "Demand-Driven Democracy: Theory and Evidence." *World Values Research* 8: forthcoming.

Inkeles, Alex. 1969. "Participant Citizenship in Six Developing Countries." *American Political Science Review* 63: 112–41.

Inkeles, Alex. 1975. "Becoming Modern: Individual Change in Six Developing Countries." *Ethos* 3: 323–42.

Inkeles, Alex. 1983. *Exploring Individual Modernity*. New York: Columbia University Press.

Inkeles, Alex, and David Smith. 1974. *Becoming Modern*. Cambridge, MA: Harvard University Press.

International IDEA. 2008. *The Arab Quota Report: Selected Case Studies*. Stockholm: International IDEA.

Interparliamentary Union. 2013. *Women in Parliaments Worldwide*. http://www.ipu .org.

Iversen, Torben, and Frances Rosenbluth. 2008. "Work and Power: The Connection between Female Labor Force Participation and Female Political Representation." *Annual Review of Political Science* 11: 479–95.

Jackman, Robert W., and Ross A. Miller. 1998. "Social Capital and Politics." *Annual Review of Political Science* 1: 47–73.

Jakobsen, Tor. 2011. "Theories of Collective Violence." In *War: An Introduction to Theories and Research on Collective Violence*, ed. Tor Jakobsen, 1–35. New York: Nova Science.

Jennings, M. Kent. 2002. "Generation Units and the Student Protest Movement in the United States: An Intra- and Intergenerational Analysis." *Political Psychology* 23: 303–24.

Jennings, M. Kent. 2007. "Political Socialization." In *The Oxford Handbook of Political Behaviour*, ed. Russell Dalton and Hans-Dieter Klingemann, 29–44. Oxford: Oxford University Press.

Jennings, M. Kent, Laura Stoker, and J. Bowers. 2009. "Politics across Generations: Family Transmission Reexamined." *Journal of Politics* 71: 782–99.

Jennings, M. Kent, Jan van Deth et al. 1990. *Continuities in Political Action*. Berlin: Walter de Gruyter.

Jensen, N., and L. Wantchekon. 2004. "Resource Wealth and Political Regimes in Africa." *Comparative Political Studies* 37: 816–41.

Jost, J., J. Glaser et al. 2003. "Political Conservatism as Motivated Social Cognition." *Psychological Bulletin* 129: 339–75.

Kaase, Max. 1990. "Mass Participation." In *Continuities in Political Action*, ed. M. Kent Jennings and Jan van Deth, 23–66. Berlin: Walter de Gruyter.

Kaase, Max. 1999. "Interpersonal Trust, Political Trust and Non-Institutionalized Political Participation in Western Europe." *West European Politics* 22: 1–23.

Kaase, Max, and Samuel Barnes. 1979. "In Conclusion: The Future of Political Protest in Western Democracies." In *Political Action*, ed. Samuel H. Barnes, Max Kaase et al., 523–36. Beverly Hills, CA: Sage.

Kaase, Max, and Kenneth Newton. 1995. *Beliefs in Government: Vol. 5. Beliefs in Government.* New York: Oxford University Press.

Kang, Alice. 2009. "Studying Oil, Islam, and Women as if Political Institutions Mattered." *Politics and Gender* 9: 560–68.

Karatnycky, A., and P. Ackerman. 2005. "How Freedom Is Won: From Civic Resistance to Durable Democracy." http://www.freedomhouse.org.

Kaufmann, Daniel, Art Kraay, and Massimo Mastruzzi. 2010. *Governance Matters VI.* World Bank Policy Research Department Working Paper 2195. Washington, DC: World Bank.

Kelman, Herbert. 1996. "The Interactive Problem-Solving Approach." In *Managing Global Chaos: Sources and Responses to International Conflict*, ed. Chester Crocker, Fen Osler Hampson, and Pamela Aall, 501–20. Washington, DC: United States Institute of Peace Press.

Kitschelt, Herbert. 1989. *The Logics of Party Formation.* Ithaca, NY: Cornell University Press.

Klandermans, Bert. 1984. "Mobilization and Participation." *American Sociological Review* 49: 583–600.

Klingemann, Hans-Dieter. 1999 "Mapping Political Support in the 1990s: A Global Analysis." In *Critical Citizens: Global Support for Democratic Governance*, ed. Pippa Norris, 31–56. New York: Oxford University Press.

Klingemann, Hans-Dieter, and Dieter Fuchs, eds. 1995. *Citizens and the State.* Oxford: Oxford University Press.

Klingemann, Hans-Dieter, Dieter Fuchs, S. Fuchs, and Jan Zielonka. 2006. "Support for Democracy and Autocracy in Central and Eastern Europe." In *Democracy and Political Culture in Eastern Europe*, ed. Hans-Dieter Klingemann, Dieter Fuchs, and Jan Zielonka, 1–22. London: Routledge.

Klingemann, Hans-Dieter, Dieter Fuchs, and Jan Zielonka, eds. 2006. *Democracy and Political Culture in Eastern Europe.* London: Routledge.

Klingemann, Hans-Dieter, and Christian Welzel. 2010. "Democratic Congruence Re-Established: The Perspective of 'Substantive' Democracy." In *How Democracy Works: Political Representation and Policy Congruence in Modern Societies*, ed. M. Rosema, B. Denters, and Kees Aarts, 89–114. Amsterdam: Amsterdam University Press.

Kohn, Melvin. 1959. "Social Class and Parental Values." *American Journal of Sociology* 64: 337–51.

Kohn, Melvin, and Carmi Schooler. 1969. "Class, Occupation, and Orientation." *American Sociological Review* 34: 659–78.

Knutsen, Oddbjorn. 2013. "Party Choice." In *Society and Democracy in Europe*, ed. K. Silke and O. Gabriel, 244–69. New York: Routledge.

Kuran, Timur. 1991. "Now Out of Never: The Element of Surprise in the East European Revolution of 1989." *World Politics* 44: 7–48.

Kurtz, Lester, ed. 2008. *Encyclopedia of Violence, Peace, and Conflict.* 2nd ed. San Diego, CA: Academic Press.

Krook, Mona Lena. 2009. *Quotas for Women in Politics: Gender and Candidate Selection Reform Worldwide*. Oxford: Oxford University Press.

Lasswell, Harold. 1951. *Psychopathology and Politics; Politics: Who Get What, When, and How; Democratic Character*. Glencoe, IL: Free Press.

LeDuc, Larry, Richard Niemi, and Pippa Norris, eds. 1996. *Comparing Democracies*. Thousand Oaks, CA: Sage.

LeDuc, Larry, Richard Niemi, and Pippa Norris, eds. 2010. *Comparing Democracies 3*. Thousand Oaks, CA: Sage.

Lerner, Daniel. 1958. *The Passing of Traditional Society*. Glencoe, IL: Free Press.

Levitsky, Steven, and Lucian Way. 2010. *Competitive Authoritarianism*. New York: Cambridge University Press.

Linde, J. 2004. *Doubting Democrats? A Comparative Analysis of Support for Democracy in Central and Eastern Europe*. Oerebro, Sweden: Oerebro universitet.

Linz, Juan, and Alfred Stepan. 1978. *The Breakdown of Democratic Regimes: Crisis, Breakdown and Reequilibration*. Baltimore: Johns Hopkins University Press.

Linz, Juan, and Alfred Stepan. 1996. *Problems of Democratic Transition and Consolidation: Southern Europe, South America, and Post-Communist Europe*. Baltimore: Johns Hopkins University Press.

Lipset, Seymour Martin. 1959 "Some Social Requisites of Democracy." *American Political Science Review* 53: 69–105.

Lipset, Seymour Martin. 1981. *Political Man: The Social Bases of Politics*. Expanded ed. Baltimore: Johns Hopkins University Press.

Lipset, Seymour Martin. 1994. "The Social Requisites of Democracy Revisited." *American Sociological Review* 59: 1–22.

Listhaug, Ola. 1986. "War and Defence Attitudes: A First Look at Survey Data from 14 Countries." *Journal of Peace Research* 23: 69–76.

Listhaug, Ola, and Lars Grønflaten. 2007. "Civic Decline? Trends in Political Involvement and Participation in Norway, 1965–2001." *Scandinavian Political Studies* 30: 272–99.

Longworth, Philio. 1992. *The Making of Eastern Europe*. New York: St. Martin's Press.

Lowe, Philip, and Jane Goyder. 1983. *Environmental Groups in Politics*. New York: Allen and Unwin.

Marien, Sofie, Marc Hooghe, and Ellen Quintelier. 2010. "Inequalities in Non-Institutionalised Forms of Political Participation: A Multi-level Analysis of 25 Countries." *Political Studies* 58: 187–213.

Markoff, John. 1996. *Waves of Democracy*. Thousand Oaks, CA: Pine Forge Press.

Markoff, John, and Amy White. 2009. "Waves of Democratization." In *Democratization*, ed. P. Bernhagen et al., 55–73. Oxford: Oxford University Press.

Marsh, David. 1971. "Political Socialization: The Implicit Assumptions Questioned." *British Journal of Political Science* 1: 453–65.

Marshall, T. H. 1950. *Citizenship and Social Class and Other Essays*. Cambridge: Cambridge University Press.

Martin, Aaron, and Juliet Pietsch. 2013. "Future Shock or Future Stability? Generational Change and the Australian Party System." *Australian Journal of Politics and History* 59: 212–21.

Mattes, Robert, and Michael Bratton. 2007. "Learning about Democracy in Africa: Awareness, Performance, and Experience." *American Journal of Political Science* 51: 192–217.

Mazower, Mark. 2008. *Hitler's Empire: How the Nazis Ruled Europe.* New York: Penguin.

McAdam, Doug, Sidney Tarrow, and Charles Tilly. 2003. *Dynamics of Contentious Action.* New York: Cambridge University Press.

McDonough, Peter, et al. 1998. *The Cultural Dynamics of Democratization in Spain.* Ithaca, NY: Cornell University Press.

McFaul, Michael. 2002. "The Fourth Wave of Democracy and Dictatorship: Noncooperative Transitions in the Postcommunist World." *World Politics* 54: 212–44.

Meade, A., E. Johnson et al. 2008. "Power and Sensitivity of Alternative Fit Indices in Tests of Measurement Invariance." *Journal of Applied Psychology* 93: 568–92.

Meriwether, Margaret, and Judith Tucker, eds. 2000. *Social History of Women and Gender in the Modern Middle East.* Boulder, CO: Westview Press.

Merritt, Anna, and Richard Merritt. 1970. *Public Opinion in Occupied Germany: The OMGUS Surveys, 1945–1949.* Urbana: University of Illinois Press.

Mertig, Ann, and Riley Dunlap. 2001. "Environmentalism, New Social Movements, and the New Class: A Cross-National Investigation." *Rural Sociology* 66: 113–36.

Milbrath, Lester. 1984. *Environmentalists.* Buffalo: SUNY Press.

Miller, Stephen, and David Sears. 1986. "Stability and Change in Social Tolerance: A Test of the Persistence Hypothesis." *American Journal of Political Science* 30: 215–35.

Mishler, William, and Richard Rose. 2001. "Political Support for Incomplete Democracies: Realist vs. Idealist Theories and Measures." *International Political Science Review* 22: 303–20.

Mishler, William, and Richard Rose. 2007. "Generation, Age and Time: The Dynamics of Learning during Russia's Transformation." *American Journal of Political Science* 51: 822–34.

Moaddel, Mansoor, ed. 2007. *Values and Perceptions of the Islamic and Middle Eastern Publics.* New York: Palgrave Macmillan.

Moghadam, Valentine. 1993. *Modernizing Women: Gender and Social Change in the Middle East.* Boulder, CO: Lynne Reiner.

Mood, Carina. 2010. "Logistic Regression: Why Cannot Do What We Think We Can Do, and What We Can Do About It." *European Sociological Review* 26: 67–82.

Mueller-Rommel, Ferdinand. 1985. "New Social Movements and Smaller Parties: A Comparative Perspective." *West European Politics* 8: 41–54.

Muller, Edward, and Mitchell Seligson. 1994. "Civic Culture and Democracy: The Question of Causal Relationships." *American Political Science Review* 88: 635–52.

Niemi, Richard, and Mary Hepburn. 1995. "The Rebirth of Political Socialization." *Perspectives on Political Science* 24: 7–16.

Nevitte, Neil. 1996. *The Decline of Deference.* Ontario: Broadview Press.

Nevitte, Neil, and Mebs Kanji. 2001. "The Decline of Deference Revisited: Some Preliminary Findings from the 2000 Survey Data." Paper presented to the WVS Conference, Stellenbosch, South Africa, November 17–21.

Newton, Kenneth. 2001. "Trust, Social Capital, Civil Society, and Democracy." *International Political Science Review* 22: 201–14.

Newton, Kenneth. 2007. "Social and Political Trust." In *The Oxford Handbook on Political Behavior,* ed. Russell Dalton and Hans-Dieter Klingemann, 342–61. Oxford: Oxford University Press.

Norris, Pippa. 1999. *Critical Citizens: Global Support for Democratic Governance.* Oxford: Oxford University Press.

Norris, Pippa. 2002. *Democratic Phoenix: Political Activism Worldwide.* Cambridge: Cambridge University Press.

Norris, Pippa. 2004. *Electoral Engineering.* New York: Cambridge University Press.

Norris, Pippa. 2007. "Opening the Door: Women Leaders and Constitution-Building in Iraq and Afghanistan." In *Women Who Lead,* ed. Barbara Kellerman, 195–226. New York: Jossey Bass.

Norris, Pippa. 2011. *Democratic Deficit: Critical Citizens Revisited.* Cambridge: Cambridge University Press.

Norris, Pippa, and Ronald Inglehart. 2003. "Muslims and the West: Testing the 'Clash of Civilizations' Thesis." *Comparative Sociology* 1: 235–65.

Norris, Pippa, and Ronald Inglehart. 2004. *Sacred and Secular: Politics and Religion Worldwide.* New York: Cambridge University Press.

Norris, Pippa, and Joni Lovenduski. 1995. *Political Recruitment: Gender, Race and Class in the British Parliament.* Cambridge: Cambridge University Press.

Nye, Joseph, Philip Zelikow, and D. King, eds. 1997. *Why People Don't Trust Government.* Cambridge, MA: Harvard University Press.

O'Donnell, Guillermo, Philippe Schmitter, and Lawrence Whitehead, eds. 1986. *Transitions from Authoritarian Rule.* Baltimore: Johns Hopkins University Press.

Omar, Samira. 1995. "Constraints That Hinder Women's Participation in Development: The Case of Kuwait." *Pakistan Journal of Women's Studies* 2: 17–26.

Opp, Karl. 1990. "Postmaterialism, Collective Action, and Political Protest." *American Journal of Political Science* 34: 212–35.

Ostrom, Charles, Jr. 1990. *Time Series Analysis: Regression Techniques.* 2nd ed. Newbury Park, CA: Sage.

Paris, R. 2001. "Human Security: Paradigm Shift or Hot Air?" *International Security* 26: 87–102.

Pateman, Carole. 1970. *Participation and Democratic Theory.* Cambridge: Cambridge University Press.

Pettersson, Thorleif. 2007. "Muslim Immigrants in Western Europe: Persisting Value Differences or Value Adaptation?" In *Values and Perceptions of the Islamic and Middle Eastern Publics,* ed. Mansoor Moaddel, 71–104. New York: Palgrave Macmillan.

Pew Center. 2002. *What the World Thinks in 2002: The Pew Global Attitudes Project.* Washington, DC: Pew Center for People and the Press.

Pharr, Susan, and Robert Putnam, eds. 2002. *Disaffected Democracies: What's Troubling the Trilateral Countries?* Princeton, NJ: Princeton University Press.

Piirainen, Timo. 1997. *Towards a New Social Order in Russia: Transforming Structures and Everyday Life.* Aldershot, UK: Dartmouth.

Pinker, Steven. 2011. *The Better Angels of Our Nature.* London: Allen Lane.

Puranen, Bi. 2005. *The Core Values of the Swedish Armed Forces.* Stockholm: Swedish Armed Forces.

Puranen, Bi, et al. 2006. *Values as a Driving Force: The Culture Gap between Military Culture and Civilian Reality.* Stockholm: Swedish Armed Forces.

Puranen, Bi. 2008a. *Values as a Driving Force: The Headquarter – To Build Trust in the Swedish Armed Forces.* Stockholm: Swedish Armed Forces.

Puranen, Bi. 2008b. "The Importance of Shared Values for a European Security Strategy." Paper for EU-ISS (Institute for Security Strategies), Paris.

Puranen, Bi. 2008c. *How Values Transform Military Culture – The Swedish Example.* Stockholm, Sweden: Values Research Institute.

Puranen, Bi. 2009a. "European Values on Security and Defense: An Exploration of the Correlates of Willingness to Fight for One's Country." In *Religion, Democratic Values and Political Conflict*, ed. Y. Esmer, H. D. Klingemann, and Bi Puranen, 277–304. Uppsala: Uppsala University.

Puranen, Bi. 2009b. *Willingness to Fight for One's Country and the Importance of Democracy: European Values on Security and Defence.* Stockholm: Swedish Armed Forces and Values Research Institute.

Putnam, Robert. 1993. *Making Democracy Work.* Princeton, NJ: Princeton University Press.

Putnam, Robert. 2000. *Bowling Alone.* New York: Simon and Schuster.

Pye, Lucian. 2006 "Culture as Destiny." In *Political Culture in Post-Communist Europe*, ed. D. Pollack, Joerg Jacobs, Olaf Mueller, and Gert Pickel, 3–16. Surrey, UK: Ashgate.

Pyc, Lucian. 1985. *Asian Power and Politics: The Cultural Dimension of Authority.* Cambridge, MA: Belknap Press.

Pye, Lucian, and Sidney Verba, eds. 1965. *Political Culture and Political Development.* Princeton, NJ: Princeton University Press.

Rawls, John. 1971. *A Theory of Justice.* Boston: Harvard University Press.

Rasinski, K. A., Tom Smith, and Juan Díez-Nicolás. 2005. "When the Trains Exploded in Madrid: Fear, Anger, Public Opinion, and Government Change." *Public Opinion Pros.* http://www.publicopinionpros.norc.org.

Raudenbush, Stephen, and Anthony Bryk. 2002. *Hierarchical Linear Models.* 2nd ed. Thousand Oaks, CA: Sage.

Ray, James. 1998. "Does Democracy Cause Peace?" *Annual Review of Political Science* 1: 27–46.

Riksem, Brita. 2010. "Direkte politisk deltaking på tvers av Europa" (Direct Political Participation across Europe). Research paper in political science, Norwegian University of Science and Technology, Trondheim.

Rizzo, H., A. Abdel-Latif, and K. Meyer. 2007. "The Relationship between Gender Equality and Democracy: A Comparison of Arab versus non-Arab Muslim Societies." *Sociology* 41: 1151–70.

Rohrschneider, Robert. 1990. "The Roots of Public Opinion toward New Social Movements: An Empirical Test of Competing Explanations." *American Journal of Political Science* 34: 1–30.

Rohrschneider, Robert. 1993. "New Party versus Old Left Realignments." *Journal of Poltiics* 55: 682–701.

Rohrschneider, Robert. 1996. "Institutional Learning versus Value Diffusion." *Journal of Politics* 58: 422–46.

Rohrschneider, Robert. 1999. *Learning Democracy: Democratic and Economic Values in Unified Germany.* Oxford: Oxford University Press.

Rokeach, Milton. 1968. *Beliefs, Attitudes and Values.* San Francisco: Jossey-Bass.

Rokeach, Milton. 1973. *The Nature of Human Values.* New York: Free Press.

Rose, Richard. 2009. "Democratic and Undemocratic States." In *Democratization*, ed. P. Bernhagen et al., 10–23. Oxford: Oxford University Press.

Rose, Richard, Christian Haerpfer, and William Mishler. 1998. *Democracy and Its Alternatives: Understanding Post-Communist Societies.* Baltimore: Johns Hopkins University Press.

Rose, Richard, and Doh Chull Shin. 2001. "Democratization Backwards: The Problem of Third-Wave Democracies." *British Journal of Political Science* 31: 331–75.

Ross, Michael. 2001. "Does Oil Hinder Democracy?" *World Politics* 53: 325–61.

Ross, Michael. 2004. "How Do Natural Resources Influence Civil War? Evidence from Thirteen Cases." *International Organization* 58: 35–67.

Ross, Michael. 2006. "A Closer Look at Oil, Diamonds, and Civil War." *Annual Review of Political Science* 9: 265–300.

Ross, Michael. 2008. "Oil, Islam and Women." *American Political Science Review* 102: 107–23.

Rustow, Dankwart. 1970. "Transitions to Democracy." *Comparative Politics* 2: 337–63.

Sandholtz, Wayne, and K. Stiles. 2009. *International Norms and Cycles of Change.* Oxford: Oxford University Press.

Sartori, Giovanni. 1984. "Guidelines for Concept Analysis." In *Social Science Concepts*, ed. Giovanni Sartori, 15–85. Beverly Hills, CA: Sage.

Sartori, Giovanni. 1987. *The Theory of Democracy Revisited.* Chatham, NJ: Chatham House.

Scarbrough, Elinor. 1995. "Materialist-Postmaterialist Value Orientations." In *The Impact of Values*, ed. Jan W. Van Deth and Elinor Scarbrough, 123–59. New York: Oxford University Press.

Schedler, A., and R. Sarsfield. 2006. "Democrats with Adjectives." *European Journal of Political Research* 46: 637–59.

Schlozman, Kay. 1999. "What Happened at Work Today? A Multistage Model of Gender, Employment, and Political Participation." *Journal of Politics* 61: 29–53.

Schock, Kurt. 2005. *Unarmed Insurrections.* Minneapolis: University of Minnesota Press.

Schwartz, Shalom. 1992. "Universals in the Content and Structure of Values." In *Advances in Social Psychology*, ed. M. P. Zanna, 1–65. New York: Academic Press.

Schwartz, Shalom. 2006. "Value Orientations: Measurement, Antecedents and Consequences across Nations." In *Measuring Attitudes Cross-Nationally – Lessons from the European Social Survey*, ed. Roger Jowell, C. Roberts, R. Fitzerald, and G. Eva, 161–93. London: Sage.

Schwartz, Shalom, G. Melech, A. Lehmann, S. Burgess, and M. Haris. 2001. "Extending the Cross-Cultural Validity of the Theory of Basic Human Values with a Different Method of Measurement." *Journal of Cross Cultural Psychology* 32: 519–42.

Sen, Amatra. 1999. *Development as Freedom.* New York: Knopf.

Shin, Doh Chull. 2012. *Confucianism and Democratization in East Asia.* Cambridge: Cambridge University Press.

Shin, Doh Chull, and L. Qi. 2011. "How Mass Political Attitudes Affect Democratization." *International Political Science Review* 32: 245–62.

Shin, Doh Chull, and Roland Tusalem. 2007. "The Cultural and Institutional Dynamics of Global Democratization." *Taiwan Journal of Democracy* 3: 1–28.

Shin, Doh Chull, and J. Wells. 2005. "Is Democracy the Only Game in Town?" *Journal of Democracy* 16: 88–101.

Shively, W. Phillips. 1991. Feature Review of *Culture Shift in Advanced Industrial Society. Journal of Politics* 53: 235–38.

Smith, Graham. 2009. *Democratic Innovations: Designing Institutions for Citizen Participation.* Cambridge: Cambridge University Press.

Sniderman, Paul. 1975. *Personality and Democratic Politics*. Berkeley: University of California Press.

Sniderman, Paul, Richard Brody, and Philip Tetlock. 1991. *Reasoning and Choice: Explorations in Political Psychology*. New York: Cambridge University Press.

Sniderman, Paul, and Thomas Piazza. 1993. *The Scar of Race*. Cambridge, MA: Harvard University Press.

Snijders, T., and R. Bosker. 1999. *Multilevel Analysis: An Introduction to Basic and Advanced Multilevel Modeling*. Thousand Oaks, CA: Sage.

Snyder, Richard. 2006. "Does Lootable Wealth Breed Disorder? A Political Economy of Extraction Framework." *Comparative Political Studies* 39: 943–68.

Snyder, Timothy. 2010. *Bloodlands: Europe between Hitler and Stalin*. New York: Basic Books.

Spierings, Niels, Jeroen Smits, and Mieke Verloo. 2009. "On the Compatibility of Islam and Gender Equality: Effects of Modernization, State Islamization, and Democracy on Women's Labor Market Participation in 45 Muslim Countries." *Social Indicators Research* 90: 503–22.

Steel, Gill, and Ikuo Kabashima. 2008. "Cross-Regional Support for Gender Equality." *International Political Science Review* 29: 133–56.

Steiger, J. 1990. "Structural Model Evaluation and Modification: An Interval Estimation Approach." *Multivariate Behavioral Research* 25: 173–80.

Suad, Joseph, and Susan Slyomovics. 2001. *Women and Power in the Middle East*. Philadelphia: University of Pennsylvania Press.

Teorell, Jan, Marcus Samanni, Sören Holmberg, and Bo Rothstein. 2011. "The Quality of Government Dataset, version 6," April 2011. http://www.qog.pol.gu.se.

Tilly, Charles. 2007. *Democracy*. New York: Cambridge University Press.

Todd, Emmanuel. 1976. *La chute final: Essai sur la décomposition de la sphère soviet*. Paris: Èditions Robert Lafont.

Ulfelder, Jay. 2005. "Contentious Collective Action and the Breakdown of Authoritarian Regimes." *International Political Science Review* 26: 311–34.

UNDP. 2006. *Arab Human Development Report: Towards the Rise of Women in the Arab World*. Washington, DC: United Nations Development Programme.

Uslaner, Eric. 2002. *The Moral Foundations of Trust*. Cambridge: Cambridge University Press.

Vecernik, Jiri. 1996. *Markets and People: The Czech Reform Experience in a Comparative Perspective*. Aldershot, UK: Avebury.

Verba, Sidney. 1965. "Conclusion: Comparative Political Culture." In *Political Culture and Political Development*, ed. Lucian Pye and Sidney Verba, 512–60. Princeton, NJ: Princeton University Press.

Verba, Sidney. 2011. "A Life in Political Science." *Annual Review of Political Science* 14: i–xv.

Verba, Sidney, and Norman Nie. 1972. *Participation in America: Political Democracy and Social Equality*. New York: Harper and Row.

Verba, Sidney, Norman Nie, and Jae-on Kim. 1978. *Participation and Political Equality: A Seven Nation Comparison*. Cambridge: Cambridge University Press.

Verba, Sidney, Kay Schlozman, and Henry Brady. 1995. *Voice and Equality*. Cambridge, MA: Harvard University Press.

Webb, Paul, David Farrell, and Ian Holliday, eds. 2002. *Political Parties in Advanced Industrial Democracies*. Oxford: Oxford University Press.

Welzel, Christian. 2006. "Democratization as an Emancipative Process." *European Journal of Political Research* 45: 871–96.

Welzel, Christian. 2007. "Are Levels of Democracy Affected by Mass Attitudes? Testing Attainment and Sustainment Effects on Democracy." *International Political Science Review* 28: 397–424.

Welzel, Christian. 2013. *Freedom Rising: Human Empowerment and the Quest for Emancipation.* New York: Cambridge University Press.

Welzel, Christian, and Franziska Deutsch. 2011. "Emancipative Values and Non-Violent Protest: The Importance of 'Ecological' Effects." *British Journal of Political Science* 42: 465–79.

Welzel, Christian, and Ronald Inglehart. 2006. "Emancipative Values and Democracy." *Studies in Comparative International Development* 41: 74–94.

Welzel, Christian, and Ronald Inglehart. 2009. "Political Culture, Mass Beliefs, and Value Change." In *Democratization,* ed. Christian Haerpfer, P. Bernhagen, Ronald Inglehart, and Christian Welzel, 126–44. Oxford: Oxford University Press.

Welzel, Christian, and Ronald Inglehart. 2010. "Values, Agency, and Well-Being: An Evolutionary Model of Life Strategy Change." *Social Indicators Research* 97: 43–63.

Welzel, Christian, Ronald Inglehart, and Franziska Deutsch. 2005. "Social Capital, Voluntary Associations, and Collective Action: Which Aspects of Social Capital Have the Greatest 'Civic' Payoff?" *Journal of Civil Society* 1: 121–46.

Welzel, Christian, Ronald Inglehart, and Hans-Dieter Klingemann. 2003. "The Theory of Human Development: A Cross-Cultural Analysis." *European Journal of Political Research* 42: 341–80.

Welzel, Christian, and Hans-Dieter Klingemann. 2008. "Evidencing and Explaining Democratic Congruence." *World Values Research* 1: 57–94.

Welzel, Christian, and Hans-Dieter Klingemann. 2011. "Democratic Congruence Re-Established: The Perspective of 'Substantive' Democracy." In *How Democracy Works: Political Representation and Policy Congruence in Modern Societies,* ed. M. Rosema, B. Denters, and Kees Aarts, 89–114. Amsterdam: Amsterdam University Press.

Wood, Gordon. 1991. *The Radicalism of the American Revolution.* New York: Vintage Books.

World Bank Data Catalog. http://data.worldbank.org/data-catalog.

World Bank. 2005. *World Development Indicators.* Washington, DC: World Bank. http://.info.worldbank.org/etools/kam2/ KAM_page5.asp.

Zmerli, Sonja, and Kenneth Newton. 2008. "Social Trust and Attitudes towards Democracy." *Public Opinion Quarterly* 72: 706–24.

Index